Titles include:

Xymena Kurowska and Fabian Breuer (*editors*)
EXPLAINING THE EU's COMMON SECURITY AND DEFENCE POLICY
Theory in Action

Finn Laursen (*editor*)
DESIGNING THE EUROPEAN UNION
From Paris to Lisbon

Karl-Oskar Lindgren and Thomas Persson
PARTICIPATORY GOVERNANCE IN THE EU
Enhancing or Endangering Democracy and Efficiency?

Daniel Naurin and Helen Wallace (*editors*)
UNVEILING THE COUNCIL OF THE EUROPEAN UNION
Games Governments Play in Brussels

Dimitris Papadimitriou and Paul Copeland (*editors*)
THE EU's LISBON STRATEGY
Evaluating Success, Understanding Failure

Emmanuelle Schon-Quinlivan
REFORMING THE EUROPEAN COMMISSION

Roger Scully and Richard Wyn Jones (*editors*)
EUROPE, REGIONS AND EUROPEAN REGIONALISM

Mitchell P. Smith (*editor*)
EUROPE AND NATIONAL ECONOMIC TRANSFORMATION
The EU After the Lisbon Decade

Asle Toje
AFTER THE POST-COLD WAR
The European Union as a Small Power

Liubomir K. Topaloff
POLITICAL PARTIES AND EUROSCEPTICISM

Richard G. Whitman and Stefan Wolff (*editors*)
THE EUROPEAN NEIGHBOURHOOD POLICY IN PERSPECTIVE
Context, Implementation and Impact

Richard G. Whitman (*editor*)
NORMATIVE POWER EUROPE
Empirical and Theoretical Perspectives

Sarah Wolff
THE MEDITERRANEAN DIMENSION OF THE EUROPEAN UNION'S INTERNAL SECURITY

Jan Wouters, Hans Bruyninckx, Sudeshna Basu and Simon Schunz (*editors*)
THE EUROPEAN UNION AND MULTILATERAL GOVERNANCE
Assessing EU Participation in United Nations Human Rights and Environmental Fora

---

Palgrave Studies in European Union Politics
Series Standing Order ISBN 978–1–4039–9511–7 (hardback) and
ISBN 978–1–4039–9512–4 (paperback)
(*outside North America only*)

You can receive future titles in this series as they are published by placing a standing order.
Please contact your bookseller or, in case of difficulty, write to us at the address below with
your name and address, the title of the series and one of the ISBNs quoted above.

Customer Services Department, Macmillan Distribution Ltd, Houndmills, Basingstoke,
Hampshire RG21 6XS,UK.

Designing the European Union

From Paris to Lisbon

Edited by

Finn Laursen
Professor of Political Science and Canada Research Chair in European Union Studies, Director of the EU Centre of Excellence (EUCE), Dalhousie University, Halifax, Canada

First published 2012 by
PALGRAVE MACMILLAN

Palgrave Macmillan in the UK is an imprint of Macmillan Publishers Limited,
registered in England, company number 785998, of Houndmills, Basingstoke,
Hampshire RG21 6XS.

Palgrave Macmillan in the US is a division of St Martin's Press LLC,
175 Fifth Avenue, New York, NY 10010.

Palgrave Macmillan is the global academic imprint of the above companies
and has companies and representatives throughout the world.

Palgrave® and Macmillan® are registered trademarks in the United States,
the United Kingdom, Europe and other countries.

ISBN 978–0–230–36776–0

This book is printed on paper suitable for recycling and made from fully
managed and sustained forest sources. Logging, pulping and manufacturing
processes are expected to conform to the environmental regulations of the
country of origin.

A catalogue record for this book is available from the British Library.

A catalog record for this book is available from the Library of Congress.

10   9   8   7   6   5   4   3   2   1
21 20 19 18 17 16 15 14 13 12

Printed and bound in Great Britain by
CPI Antony Rowe, Chippenham and Eastbourne

Contents

List of Tables and Boxes

Tables

Boxes

Preface

After taking up the position of Professor of International Politics at the University of Southern Denmark, Odense, in 1999, I started offering a course on EU Treaty Reforms. I discovered that there was no good textbook for such a course, but, of course, a syllabus could be put together with selected book chapters and articles, especially for the more recent reforms. When I moved to Canada in 2006 to take up a position as Canada Research Chair in European Union Studies (Tier I) at Dalhousie University in Halifax, Nova Scotia, I kept offering this course. It had to be adapted due to developments in Europe, including the French and Dutch rejection of the Constitutional Treaty in 2005 and subsequent efforts to adopt the so-called Reform Treaty, which eventually became the Treaty of Lisbon. I kept feeling the need for a book that would have a chapter on each of the 'constitutive' treaties of the EU, starting with the Treaty of Paris, which established the European Coal and Steel Community (ECSC) in 1951, and including all the subsequent treaties. Financial support from the EU's Jean Monnet Programme became the vehicle that allowed me to get the project going.

A number of scholars have studied the various treaties over the years, at the beginning especially historians and lawyers. Eventually political scientists became interested, especially after the Single European Act (SEA) of 1986, which institutionalised the Intergovernmental Conference (IGC) as the main negotiation forum for a treaty reform. When, subsequently, the Treaty of Maastricht established the EU in 1993 and this treaty was reformed several times in the following years, treaty reform consolidated its place on the research and teaching agendas of political scientists.

In the spirit of the Jean Monnet Programme, the team put together for this project was interdisciplinary. Ann-Christina Knudsen and Desmond Dinan are historians, Jacques Ziller a lawyer and the remaining authors are political scientists. But even political scientists offer different perspectives on treaty reforms, including the questions of who are the main actors, what kind of interests they have and how they go about influencing the outcomes, including the choice of institutions.

This will leave food for thought for the readers, including teachers and students, who can hopefully continue these debates.

Finn Laursen
Halifax, March 2012

Acknowledgements

This book started as a Jean Monnet Information and Research Activity (IRA) co-funded by the European Union's Education and Cultural Executive Agency (EACEA) in 2009. I am grateful to EACEA for the financial support. A gathering took place at Dalhousie University on 22–3 March 2010, where most of the contributors to this book met and presented drafts and discussed how to move forward. I want to thank all the authors who agreed to contribute to the project. I was happy to be able to put a team of distinguished scholars together.

I also want to thank Acting Dean of Dalhousie's Faculty of Arts and Social Sciences, Dr. Jure Gantar, for his encouragement and support, as well as the secretary of the EU Centre of Excellence (EUCE) at Dalhousie, Tatiana Neklioudova, who helped with the logistics in connection with the meeting. My assistants Karen Snaterse and Sarah Hucsko (now Sarah Dunphy) helped putting the application together and during the conference. I thank them both for their help. Finally I want to thank my students who turned up at the gathering and contributed to the discussion.

Finn Laursen

Notes on Contributors

Derek Beach is an associate professor of Political Science at the University of Aarhus, Denmark, where he teaches integration theory, international relations and methodology. He is the author of numerous articles, chapters and books on case-study methods, international negotiations, European integration, including co-authoring the book *Process Tracing Methods: Foundations and Guidelines* (University of Michigan Press, 2012). He has been a visiting fellow at American University, Georgetown University and the Johns Hopkins School of Advanced International Studies.

Desmond Dinan is professor of Public Policy at George Mason University, Virginia, USA, and holds an *ad personam* Jean Monnet Chair. He has written extensively on EU history, institutions and governance. His publications include *Ever Closer Union: An Introduction to European Integration*, fourth edition (Palgrave Macmillan, 2010) and *Europe Recast: A History of European Union* (Palgrave Macmillan, 2006).

Iris Glockner is a lecturer at the Chair of Political Science and Contemporary History as well as scientific manager at the Economics Department at the University of Mannheim. Her research focus and teaching experience lie in the field of national and European identities, European integration theory and history, the institutional and legal developments within the EC and EU as well as in the field of Political Psychology. Her publications include 'Cultural versus Multiple Identities? Applying Political and Cultural Identity Approaches to the Question of Multiple Identification in the European Union' in M. Beers and J. Raflik (eds) *National Cultures and Common Identity: A Challenge for Europe?* (Brussels: Peter Lang, 2010).

Ann-Christina L. Knudsen received her PhD from the European University Institute in Florence, Italy, in 2001. She is now an associate professor of European Studies at the University of Aarhus, Denmark, and has taught at the University of California at Los Angeles. A historian by training, her research has focused on a variety of themes in European integration and transnational history. Among others, she is the author of the monograph *Farmers on Welfare: The Making of Europe's Common Agricultural Policy* published with Cornell University Press in 2009. She currently directs a research project funded by the Danish Research Council titled *Institutions of Democracy in Transition. Transnational Fields in Politics, Bureaucracy and Law after 1945*, and researches the socio-cultural and transnational history of the European Parliament and other parliamentary assemblies.

Finn Laursen received his PhD from the University of Pennsylvania in 1980. He now holds a Canada Research Chair (Tier 1) of EU Studies at Dalhousie University, Halifax. In 2008 he also received an *ad personam* Jean Monnet Chair. He directs the EU Centre of Excellence at Dalhousie. Previously he has been professor at the European Institute of Public Administration, Maastricht (1988–95), and professor of International Politics at the University of Southern Denmark, Odense (1999–2006). Recent edited books include *Comparative Regional Integration* (Ashgate, 2010), *The EU and Federalism* (Ashgate, 2011), *The Making of the Lisbon Treaty: The Role of Member States* (P.I.E Peter Lang, 2012), *The EU's Lisbon Treaty: Institutional Choices and Implementation* (Ashgate 2012), *The EU, Security and Transatlantic Relations* (P.I.E. Peter Lang, 2012). The following books are forthcoming: *The EU and the Political Economy of Transatlantic Relations* (P.I.E. Peter Lang), *The EU and the Eurozone Crisis: Policy Challenges and Strategic Choices* (Ashgate), and *EU Enlargement: Current Challenges and Strategic Choices* (P.I.E. Peter Lang).

Colette Mazzucelli (MALD, Tufts/Fletcher; EdM, Teachers College/Columbia; PhD, Graduate School/Georgetown) teaches graduate courses in the Center for Global Affairs, New York University, including international relations in the post-Cold War era, ethnic conflicts, Europe in the 21st Century, India's Democracy and its Discontents as well as Global Civil Society. A participant in the Robert Bosch Foundation Fellowship Program for Future American Leaders in the Federal Republic of Germany (1992–3), Professor Mazzucelli assisted with the ratification of the Treaty on EU (Maastricht) in the Foreign Office (*Auswärtiges Amt*), which led to the creation of the Euro. She is the author and co-editor of several books and numerous chapters in edited volumes Analysing the EU and transatlantic security. Professor Mazzucelli is presently co-authoring a volume with Dr. Oya Dursun-Ozkanca analysing evolving security relations between the EU (CDSP) and NATO for Routledge.

Berthold Rittberger is professor and chair of International Relations at the Ludwig-Maximilians-University of Munich and an External Fellow at the Mannheim Centre of European Social Research (MZES).

After obtaining his DPhil in Oxford, he held positions at Nuffield College (Oxford), Kaiserslautern and Mannheim. His recent publications include B. Rittberger and A. Wonka (eds) (2012), *Agency Governance in the European Union* (London: Routledge) and B. Rittberger (2012), 'Institutionalizing Representative Democracy in the European Union: The Case of the European Parliament', *Journal of Common Market Studies*, 50th Anniversary Special Issue, 50, 18–37.

Joaquín Roy (Lic. Law, University of Barcelona, 1966; PhD, Georgetown University, 1973) is Jean Monnet Professor and director of University for the Miami European Union Center of Excellence. He has published over 200 academic articles and reviews and has authored or edited 35 books, including *Cuba, the US and the Helms-Burton Doctrine: International Reactions* (University of Florida Press, 2000), *Las relaciones exteriores de la Unión Europea* (UNAM, 2001), *The European Union and Regional Integration* (EU Center, 2005), *La Unión Europea y la integración regional* (CARI/ U. Tres de Febrero, 2005), *Towards the Completion of Europe* (EU Center, 2006), *A Historical Dictionary of the European Union* (Scarecrow Press / Rowman & Littlefield, 2006) and *The Dollar and the Euro* (Ashgate, 2007). He has also published over 1400 columns and essays. He was awarded the *Encomienda* of the Order of Merit by King Juan Carlos of Spain.

Sophie Vanhoonacker is Jean Monnet Professor and has a chair in Administrative Governance at the Faculty of Arts and Social Sciences, Maastricht University, where she is head of the Politics Department. Since September 2011, she is also co-director of the new Maastricht Centre for European Governance (MCEG), an EU-funded 'Jean Monnet Centre of Excellence'. Her main field of research is in the area of the Common Foreign and Security Policy. Recent publications have dealt with the emerging system of an EU-level system of diplomacy and its processes of institutionalisation, including S. Vanhoonacker, K. Pomorska and P. Petrov (eds) (2012), 'The Emerging EU Diplomatic System', *The Hague Journal of Diplomacy*, 7 (1) (special issue); H. Dijkstra and S. Vanhoonacker (2011), 'The Changing Politics of Information in European Foreign Policy', *Journal of European Integration*, 33 (5), 541–58; and S. Vanhoonacker, H. Dijkstra and H. Maurer (eds) (2010), 'Understanding the Role of Bureaucracy in the European Security and Defence Policy', *European Integration online Papers*, Special Issue 1, 14.

Jacques Ziller is professor of European Union Law, University of Pavia. He was formerly at the European University Institute, Florence, and at

Paris-I Panthéon-Sorbonne. His recently published work include *Il nuovo Trattato europeo* (Il Mulino, 2007), translated into French as *Les nouveaux traités européens: Lisbonne et apres* (Lexis Nexis, 2008), and into Portuguese as *O tratado de Lisboa; The LisbonTreaty – EU Constitutionalism without a Constitutional Treaty?* (edited by Stefan Griller and Jacques Ziller) (Springer, 2008); 'La Naturaleza del Derecho de la Unión europea', in *Tratado de Derecho y Politicas de la Union Europea*, Tomo IV (edited by José Maria Beneyto Pérez) (Aranzadi-Thomson Reuters, 2011).

1
Introduction: On the Study of EU Treaties and Treaty Reforms

Finn Laursen

This book deals with the study of EU treaty making and treaty reforms, which have constituted important elements in the history of European integration. Whether the original treaties, which formed the first European Communities in the 1950s, or later reform treaties, they have mostly been negotiated by states in what has become known as inter-governmental conferences (IGCs). The founding treaties formalised the use of IGCs in treaty reforms, and they started becoming more important and formalised from the negotiation of the Single European Act (SEA) in the mid-1980s.

The focus will be on the formal treaty making or reform process. But arguably the treaties have also changed over time due to interpretations by the decision-making institutions set up by the treaties. Some changes in the scope of common policies have taken place through normal decision-making mechanisms, involving the Commission, the Council and increasingly also the European Parliament, for example, on the basis of Article 235 of the original European Economic Community (EEC) Treaty and later versions of the article, now Article 352 TFEU after the entry into force of the Lisbon Treaty.[1] The development of a common environmental policy from the early 1970s is an example of how flexibility in the founding treaties could be used. The founding treaties did not explicitly mention the environment. Only in the SEA in 1987 did the environment get a formal treaty chapter. Also some institutional reforms have taken place without the use of IGCs, like the decision in the 1970s to have the European Parliament elected directly (see for instance Herman and Hagger 1980). Some of the decisions by the European Court of Justice (ECJ) have also had profound effects on the institutional structure and policy scope of the EU, especially the early decisions about supremacy of community law and its direct effect (see for instance Hix 2005).

1

In many treaty reforms linkages were created between scope of policy-making and institutional capacity, the main exceptions being the Merger Treaty in 1965 and the Treaty of Nice in 2001, both of which nearly exclusively dealt with institutional changes. It is also worth mentioning that many treaty reforms were linked with proposed accession of new member states. Some formal treaty amendments have taken place through accession treaties, like the change of voting weights in the Council in connection with the first enlargement, which brought the UK, Denmark and Ireland into the European Communities (EC) in 1973.

Delimiting the subject matter

The reforms we are interested in concern the European Coal and Steel Community (ECSC), the European Economic Community (EEC) and the European Atomic Energy Community (EAEC or EURATOM) from the 1950s as well as the European Union (EU) from 1993. How and why were these treaties negotiated? And, how and why did they go through so many reforms?

The original European communities, which were based on three treaties, are listed in Table 1.1.

The Treaty of Paris creating the ECSC expired in 2002 after 50 years. The two communities created by the Treaties of Rome, the EEC and

Table 1.1   The founding treaties of the European communities

	Name	Signed	In force	Published
1	Treaty establishing the European Coal and Steel Community (*Treaty of Paris*)	18 April 1951	24 July 1952. It expired on 23 July 2002, after 50 years	Not published in *Official Journal*
2	Treaty establishing the European Economic Community (*Treaty of Rome*)	25 March 1957	1 January 1958	Not published in *Official Journal*
3	Treaty establishing the European Atomic Energy Community (A second *Treaty of Rome* also known as the *Euratom Treaty*)	25 March 1957	1 January 1958	Not published in *Official Journal*

Source: http://europa.eu/scadplus/treaties/eec_en.htm. Treaty texts can be found at http://www.ena.lu/. French versions are available in Roussellier 2007.

EAEC, were concluded for an unlimited period and survived various amendments including the Treaty of Maastricht in 1992, where the EEC became part of the European Union's first pillar. Apart from the first community pillar the Maastricht Treaty added Common Foreign and Security Policy (CFSP) in a second pillar and Justice and Home Affairs (JHA) cooperation in a third pillar as intergovernmental cooperation. The Lisbon Treaty has now abolished the pillar structure, but CFSP retains separate decision-making procedures.

The founding treaties were negotiated in diplomatic conferences later referred to as Intergovernmental Conferences (IGCs). Early treaty making also included negotiation of a European Defence Community (EDC) as well as a European Political Community in 1951–2. This project was rejected by the French National Assembly in 1954. The Fouchet Plan negotiations (1961–2), a Gaullist plan for political union, followed later. This plan failed because of disagreements among the then six EC member states (Bodenheimer 1967).

The founding treaties had articles foreseeing reforms. In the EEC Treaty this was Article 236. In the ECSC Treaty it was Article 96, and in the EURATOM Treaty it was Article 204. These articles were replaced by Article N in the Maastricht Treaty, later changed to Article 48 TEU in the Consolidated Treaty worked out after the negotiation of the Amsterdam Treaty in 1997. The Lisbon Treaty now includes an ordinary revision procedure, which involves both a convention and an IGC, as well as a simplified revision procedure, which allows the European Council (the meeting of heads of state or government) to amend a certain part of the treaty on the Functioning of the European Union without a convention or IGC, namely the part dealing with policies (Article 48 TEU).

The language used in the treaties has been 'a conference of representatives of the Governments of the Member States'. This conference, according to Article 236 EEC, would determine 'by common accord the amendments to be made' to the treaty. Amendments would 'enter into force after being ratified by all the Member States in accordance with their respective constitutional requirements' (*Treaties establishing the European Communities* 1987, p. 413). In the following such a conference has become known as an IGC. An IGC can be called by a majority of the member states but a new treaty requires unanimity to be adopted (the meaning of 'common accord'). The current Article 48 TEU also requires the consultation of the European Parliament to convene a Convention and 'where appropriate, the Commission' as well as the European Central Bank 'in the case of institutional changes in the monetary area'.

The treaty also foresees the possibility of not convening a convention, in which case the European Parliament must give its consent.

Legally speaking any meeting of government representatives based on art. 236 of the EEC Treaty, now Article 48 TEU, can be called an IGC. But it seems fair also to include the conferences that negotiated the founding treaties as IGCs. An IGC is a forum for inter-state negotiation. Consensus is required for a new treaty to be adopted. This has implications for the dynamics of such a forum.

The three founding EC treaties went through a number of reforms based on Article 236 EEC or later versions of the article. Leaving out treaties dealing with the Dutch West Indies, the European Investment Bank and Greenland we get the list in Table 1.2 as the most important treaty reforms.

The latest reform, the Reform Treaty or Lisbon Treaty, which was signed in December 2007, has replaced the Constitutional Treaty, which was prepared through a so-called European Convention (2002–3) and finalised by an IGC (2003–4) (Laursen 2008a). Because of 'no' votes in referendums in France and the Netherlands in 2005 the Constitutional Treaty was not fully ratified, and in June 2007 it was decided to replace it by a simplified treaty, a Reform Treaty, which would not be called a Constitutional Treaty. This Reform Treaty was negotiated by an IGC during the Portuguese Presidency in the second part of 2007 but much preparatory work was carried out during the German Presidency in the first half of 2007. It became known as the Lisbon Treaty. It was in turn rejected by the Irish voters on 12 June 2008. But after a second Irish referendum on 2 October 2009 it could enter into force from 1 December 2009 (Laursen 2012a and 2012b).

The treaties amending the founding treaties, negotiated through or adopted by IGCs, are of course not equally important. The earlier reforms, prior to the SEA in 1986, have attracted less scholarly interest than the later reforms from the SEA to the Constitutional Treaty and Lisbon Treaty.[2] Further, the early reforms of the EC treaties, like the Merger Treaty in 1965 and the budgetary treaties in 1960 and 1965 were largely negotiated through normal legislative procedures, through Council and Committee of Permanent Representatives (COREPER) negotiations. The IGC formally required was a short meeting at the end of the process. It is only from the SEA in the 1980s that the IGC becomes the decisive negotiating forum (Smith 2002). It is also from this moment that the IGC becomes 'institutionalised' and starts attracting scholarly interest.

The first IGCs were not referred to by that name. The very first one in 1950–1 was called the Schuman Plan conference. The officials

Table 1.2 Important treaty reforms applying intergovernmental conferences (IGCs)

No	Name	Signed	In force	Published
1	Treaty establishing a single council and a single commission of the European Communities (*Merger Treaty*)	8 April 1965	1 July 1967	OJ L 152, 13.07.67
2	Treaty amending certain budgetary provisions (*Treaty of Luxembourg*, also known as the *First Budget Treaty*)	22 April 1970	1 January 1971	OJ L 2, 02.01.71
3	Treaty amending certain financial provisions (*Treaty of Brussels*, also known as the *Second Budget Treaty*)	10 July 1975	1 June 1977	OJ L 91, 06.04.78
4	The *Single European Act*	28 February 1986	1 July 1987	OJ L 169, 29.06.87
5	Treaty of European Union (*Maastricht Treaty*)	7 February 1992	1 November 1993	OJ L 224, 31.08.92
6	*The Amsterdam Treaty*	2 October 1997	1 May 1999	OJ C 340, 10.11.97
7	*The Treaty of Nice*	26 February 2001	1 February 2003	OJ C 80, 10.03.01
8	*The Treaty of Lisbon*	13 December 2007	1 December 2009	OJ C 306, 17.12.07

Source: Compiled by the author. See also Gray (2000), note 6. The official treaty website of the EU is http://eur-lex.europa.eu/en/treaties/index.htm

negotiating the first community treaty actually considered themselves 'experts' and some delegations included not only government representatives but also representatives from the coal and steel industries. However, the delegations sought instructions from the governments and the foreign and prime ministers were called upon to settle the more difficult issues, and in the end all participating states had to accept the result (Diebold 1959, pp. 60–75). So we conclude that the Schuman Plan conference was an IGC as defined here.

No doubt, the IGCs negotiating the founding treaties were less formalised than later IGCs, from the SEA onwards. But they were negotiations between government representatives and they had to reach a consensus. These are the essential ingredients of an IGC.

It is probably fair to say that scholarly interest in IGCs start from the SEA in the 1980s. The IGCs from the SEA to the Nice Treaty have worked on three levels: heads of state or government, foreign ministers and personal representatives of foreign ministers. The personal representatives would normally meet fairly frequently, often weekly, the foreign ministers less often, such as once a month, and the heads of state or governments (the European Council) even less frequently, once or twice per presidency. But all recent IGCs have been concluded with meetings of the European Council, where the remaining difficult issues have had to be negotiated (Smith 2002, pp. 13–15). Interestingly enough, the IGC 2003–4 that followed the European Convention used a simplified structure. It dispensed with the personal representatives (for more, see Laursen 2008a).

Strictly speaking it should be mentioned that enlargement negotiations have also been referred to as IGCs, between the applicant country and the EU member states. Accession treaties usually include institutional stipulations, such as voting weights. The politics of enlargement, however, is different from the politics of treaty reforms as such. Accessions are based on a separate article (Art. 237 in the EEC Treaty, Art. O in Maastricht, now Art. 49 TEU). Apart from each member state being a veto player here too, accession also requires the 'assent' of the European Parliament since the entry into force of the SEA (now called 'consent' in the Lisbon Treaty). The EP has not succeeded in getting a similar power in connection with treaty reforms.

Theories and research questions

A classic political science treatise on the first community, the ECSC, was written by Ernest Haas (1958). In his book, *The Uniting of Europe*, he developed the neo-functionalist theory, which became a reference point for later theoretical developments (Pentland 1973; Rosamond 2000; Laursen 2003). There is also an important account of the early years of the EEC by another American political scientist, Leon Lindberg. Based on Haas' neo-functionalism Lindberg analysed the EEC in *The Political Dynamics of European Economic Integration* (1963). But disappointingly neither Haas nor Lindberg studied the actual negotiations of the founding treaties in detail. Recent scholarship has tended to be critical of the early theories, although contemporary historical institutionalism resembles neo-functionalism in various ways (see for instance Pierson 1996).

Scholarship dealing with treaty reforms has asked questions about agenda setting, the actual negotiations and how to explain the outcome. Who are the most important actors, what are their interests, how do they influence outcomes? How are they constrained by rules and norms? What is the role of power? Is some kind of leadership needed to produce agreements? Are agreements efficient? Are they equitable?

In IGCs the actors are governments representing formally sovereign states. The Commission has been allowed to take part in IGCs, but it cannot block decisions. The European Parliament has only had an advisory role, being loosely associated with IGCs, and it has not been allowed to play the role it would like to play (Gray 2000). In IGCs the governments thus try to stay in full control. To what extent they succeed in this is of course an interesting research question.

Many scholars use theories from comparative politics when they study the existing EU system (e.g. Hix 2005). When you study IGCs, many would argue that theories from International Relations (IR) can be applied. Another way to look at it is to say that IGCs deal with 'history-making' decisions at the super-systemic level while the EU system as such makes policy-setting decisions at the systemic level (Peterson 1995, 2001; Peterson and Bomberg 1999 p. 9). The bargaining mode is intergovernmental at the super-systemic level but inter-institutional at the systemic level. It is also suggested that the best theories at the super-systemic level are 'macro theories' such as liberal intergovernmentalism or neo-functionalism and the best theories at the systemic level are various versions of 'new institutionalism'. Some scholars argue that you need to combine different theories at the different levels to fully account for reforms.

I shall now proceed to review some theoretical approaches to the study of treaty reforms and see what kind of research questions have been asked by some leading scholars.

The liberal intergovernmentalist analytical framework

Andrew Moravcsik's liberal intergovernmentalism (Moravcsik 1993, 1998) has become an important reference point for most recent studies of treaty reforms. The framework includes three phases: national preference formation, interstate bargaining and institutional choice.

The first stage concerns national preference formation. The central question asked by Moravcsik here is whether it is economic or geopolitical interests that dominate when national preferences of member states are formed. The answer based on major decisions in the European integration process was that economic interests are the most important.

The second stage, interstate bargaining, seeks to explain the efficiency and distributional outcomes of EU negotiations. Here two possible explanations of agreements on substance are contrasted: asymmetrical interdependence or supranational entrepreneurship. Moravcsik arrives at the answer that asymmetrical interdependence has most explanatory power. Some member states have more at stake than others. They will work harder to influence outcomes and may have to give more concessions. On the other hand, the role of the community actors, first of all the European Commission, is not considered very important.

The third stage, institutional choice, explores the reasons why states choose to delegate or pool decision making in international institutions. Delegation in the EC/EU case refers to the powers given to the Commission and the European Court of Justice (ECJ). Pooling of sovereignty refers to the application of majority voting in the Council, in practice mostly qualified majority voting (QMV). To explain institutional choice Moravcsik contrasts three possible explanations: Federalist ideology, centralised technocratic management or more credible commitment. The answer he gives is that states delegate and pool sovereignty to get more credible commitment. Pooling and delegation is a rational strategy adopted by the member states to pre-commit governments to future decisions, to encourage future cooperation and to improve future implementation of agreements (ibid., p. 73).

Using theories of decision making, negotiations and international political economy in general in an elegant combination has allowed Moravcsik to construct a parsimonious framework for the study of international cooperation including 'grand bargains' like EU treaty reforms.

But liberal intergovernmentalism has been criticised by several scholars. Some find it too parsimonious. The preference formation part pays too little attention to partisan aspects of domestic politics, the political games between governments and oppositions (Milner 1997). The negotiation part does not really open the 'black box' of negotiations (Beach 2000). The role of ideas is underestimated (Parsons 2003). But at least Moravcsik's scheme can help us structure studies of 'history-making' decisions and it does suggest a number of important research questions.

When *The Choice for Europe* was published *The Journal of European Public Policy* arranged a review section symposium including Helen Wallace, James Caporaso and Fritz Scharpf, with a response from

Moravcsik. All three in their critiques talked about case selection. Scharpf was the most outspoken on this.

> [G]iven his selection of cases – most of his preferred hypotheses have such a high degree of a priori plausibility that it seems hard to take their competitors quite as seriously as he does. Since only intergovernmental negotiations are being considered, why shouldn't the preferences of national governments have shaped the outcomes? Since all case studies have issues of economic integration as their focus, why shouldn't economic concerns have shaped the negotiation positions of governments? And since only decisions requiring unanimous agreement are being analysed, why shouldn't the outcomes be affected by the relative bargaining powers of the governments involved?
>
> (Wallace et al. 1999, p. 165)

Wallace wanted more about the politics within the member states. Similarly Caporaso asked 'Do domestic institutions matter?', suggesting that 'differences in the organization of interest groups (pluralist vs. corporatist), political parties (two party vs. multiparty), and executive-legislative relations (parliamentary vs. presidential) make a difference' (ibid., p. 162). Wallace also suggested that ideology or doctrine has played a bigger role than admitted by Moravcsik (ibid., p. 159).

Rational choice institutionalists

Rational choice institutionalists assume that actors have fixed preferences and that they behave instrumentally to maximise the attainment of preferences. 'They tend to see politics as a series of collective action dilemmas.' They 'emphasize the role of strategic interaction in the determination of political outcomes'. And, they explain the existence of institutions by reference to the functions those institutions perform (Hall and Taylor 1996, pp. 944–5).

Moravcsik does not assign much importance to community institutions in history-making decisions, including IGCs and treaty reforms. At first sight it can look surprising that an approach which includes 'institutional choice' as an important part of the process should end up assigning a relatively unimportant role to institutions in major EU reforms. However, the unique institutions created by the EC/EU treaties do play an important role in day-to-day decision making in the EU at the systemic level according to Moravcsik.

Institutionalists certainly assign great importance to EC institutions in day-to-day EC/EU politics (see especially Hix 2005). The European

Commission proposes legislation. The EC institutions, including the Commission and the European Court of Justice (ECJ), get involved with surveillance and enforcement of decisions. The Commission issues reports on implementation of directives. Member states which do not implement will be shamed at first and face the prospects of an ECJ infringement case later.

But there are also institutionalists who argue that EC institutions can play an important role in treaty reforms, too. Derek Beach studied the role of EC institutions in successive reforms, from the SEA to the Constitutional Treaty (Beach 2005).[3] Based on negotiation literature Beach finds two reasons why leadership may be required in international negotiations, including IGCs:

1. The first bargaining impediment in complex, multi-party negotiations is that parties can have difficulties in finding a mutually acceptable, Pareto-efficient outcome owing to *high bargaining costs.*
2. The second bargaining impediment relates to *coordination problems* that can prevent the parties from agreeing upon an efficient agreement – even if there are low bargaining costs.

(Ibid., 18–19)

These bargaining problems can be solved if an actor with privileged information steps in and helps the parties get to the Pareto frontier. Leadership can also create a *focal point* around which agreement can converge (ibid., 19–20). Bargaining costs are 'often so high that most governments are forced to rely upon the expertise of the Council Secretariat and Commission for legal and substantive knowledge, and assistance in brokering key deals' (ibid., p. 258).

When the original European Ccmmunities were created, there were no pre-existing community institutions that could play the role of EC institutions (although the high authority of the ECSC played a certain role when the latter two communities were created). An intergovernmentalist analysis should therefore be expected to be the way to analyse the creation of the communities as distinguished from their later reforms. But doesn't the initial creation then depend on national leadership of some kind? Can we explain the creation of the ECSC without looking at the role of leadership by Jean Monnet, Robert Schuman and others? Can we explain the creation of the EEC without the leadership roles played by some Benelux leaders, including especially Paul Henri Spaak from Belgium?

Liberal intergovernmentalism finds agreement in the 'grand bargains' among states in Europe relatively easy. The states have enough information to find relatively efficient solutions without a political entrepreneur. 'Transaction costs of generating information and ideas are low relative to the benefits of interstate cooperation.' National governments have resources to generate information. They can, 'regardless of size ... serve as initiators, mediators, and mobilizers'. So EC negotiations are 'likely to be efficient' (Moravcsik 1998, p. 61).

The Moravcsik proposition has been questioned by other institutionalists than Beach. A similar critique has been formulated by Jonas Tallberg in the book *Leadership and Negotiation in the European Union* (2006).

The argument by Beach is not that community institutions always have influence in IGCs and treaty reforms. The research question is when and under what conditions community institutions have influence? His model singles out a number of variables that help explain influence, like resources, negotiation context and leadership strategies.

So the role of the EU institutions, the Commission, the Council secretariat or the EP should not be ignored. Also the role of the presidency is sometimes important (Svensson 2000; Dür and Mateo 2006). Especially the negotiation of the Constitutional Treaty raises some important new questions (Magnette and Nicolaïdis 2004; Laursen 2006c, 2008). The European Convention (2002–3), which initiated the reform, was more a process of deliberation than inter-state bargaining, even if there was an end-game in the convention with negotiations playing an important part, and where the members of the convention anticipated the reactions of the member states in the IGC, which followed (2003–4). To what extent did the deliberation frame the questions for the governments? Did the wider participation of members of parliaments (MPs) and members of the European Parliament (MEPs) in the convention give the draft from the convention a kind of legitimacy that made it difficult for the member states to reopen the issues during the IGC?

There can be no doubt that preparatory bodies can help set the agenda and sort out difficult technical issues. It is also fair to conclude that the convention framed the issues of the IGC 2003–4 in an influential way. Much of the content that had not been accepted by the Nice Treaty IGC in 2000 was now accepted by the member states – only to be rejected by the French and Dutch voters, which underscores the two-level nature of EU treaty making and reform.

Historical and sociological institutionalists

A number of institutionalists have developed explicit criticisms of liberal intergovernmentalism. Institutionalism is usually divided into three main groups: rational choice, historical and sociological (see for instance Hall and Taylor 1996; Aspinwall and Schneider 2001).

Historical institutionalists 'tend to have a view of institutional development that emphasizes path dependency and unintended consequences'. Institutions structure a nation's response to new challenges (Hall and Taylor 1996, 941–2). An important article suggesting how historical institutionalism can be used to study European integration was written by Pierson (1996). Pierson puts emphasis on the gaps that emerge in the member states' control of the process. Sociological institutionalists give a very broad definition of institutions including 'not just formal rules, procedures or norms, but the symbol systems, cognitive scripts, and moral templates that provide the "frames of meaning" guiding human action'. Institutions provide cognitive templates that affect identities and preferences. Culture is important. Sociological institutionalists are interested in 'what confers "legitimacy" or "social appropriateness" on some institutional arrangements but not others' (Hall and Taylor 1996, 947–9).

Whereas liberal intergovernmentalists see the EU member states as unitary rational actors that are in control of the process of integration, historical institutionalists see gaps emerging in the member states' control and attribute more importance to EU institutions. Sociological institutionalists pay attention to values, ideas and identities.

A special issue of the *Journal of European Public Policy* in 2002 raised a number of theoretical issues inspired by historical and sociological institutionalism. Gerda Falkner argued in the introduction that treaty-reform studies should move 'beyond formal treaty reform, and ... transcend economic interests and bargaining power' (Falkner 2002a, p. 1). This was of course a critique directed towards Moravcsik's approach. Reforms also take place through ECJ decisions as well as day-to-day interpretations by the Commission and the governments. Treaty-reform studies should be interested in 'agency by EU-level actors' and 'dynamics such as learning, socialization, and the incremental institutionalization of policy paradigms at the EU level' (ibid., p. 2). She suggested that EU treaty reforms could be studied as three-level games, with EU institutions forming a third level. 'This approach contextualizes member state power and bargaining to see how both are embedded in a dense web of structuring factors, many of which originate from EU-level institutions and procedures' (ibid., p. 4). Sociological institutionalists believe that institutions shape preferences. A rationalist approach is seen as insufficient when it comes to understanding preferences.

More recently Thomas Christiansen and Christine Reh (2009) have produced a book on constitutionalisation of the EU which fits in with the sociological institutionalist approach and arguably forms the most coherent effort in that direction so far. As suggested earlier in this introduction, to fully explain 'constitutionalisation' you have to move beyond IGCs and treaty reforms, certainly also looking at the role of the ECJ and other actors. But even with the more narrow focus on treaties and treaty reforms no one will deny the importance of the wider context.

Some of the criticisms from historical and sociological institutionalists, arguably, go in different directions. Scholars who like a clear parsimonious model will like the one developed by Berthold Rittberger in his book *Building of Europe's Parliament: Democratic Representation beyond the Nation-State* (2005).

Rittberger formulates the following sociological institutionalist hypothesis concerning the empowerment of the European Parliament:

> States will create or empower the EP as a response to a perceived lack of resonance between domestically internalized norms of democratic governance and progressive European integration which generates a mismatch between collectively held norms of democratic governance and governance at the EU level.
>
> (Rittberger 2005, p. 19)

This hypothesis has been developed to explain the increased importance of the EP in the EU institutional setup. It does not claim to explain other institutional reforms produced by IGCs. But it suggests that normative constraints play a role in IGCs.

It can be argued that rationalists have underestimated the issue of procedural or 'input' legitimacy. In the early years European integration was very much based on performance or so-called output legitimacy. Good, relevant decisions were supposed to lead to support for the process (Lindberg and Scheingold 1970). But the question of 'input' legitimacy (Scharpf 1999) has also played a role. How accountable are the decision makers? How transparent is the process? These questions have been very much on the agenda in recent years. Indeed, they got on the agenda already in the 1970s, when the empowerment of the European Parliament started.

The debate about the EU's alleged 'democratic deficit' became a central aspect of the political debate in Europe during the 1990s. How democratic is the EU and how democratic can it become? (Schmitter 2000). Does European democracy require a European *demos*? (Weiler 1999). Or can parallel improvements of the roles played by national parliaments and the European Parliament improve the EU's input legitimacy?

This kind of question were quite decisive in taking the EU through the Laeken summit in 2001, with the decision to have a convention prepare yet a treaty reform when the Nice Treaty did not live up to expectations. On the other hand, the ultimate fate of that approach, the non-acceptance of the Constitutional Treaty by voters in France and the Netherlands in 2005, and the very different way the Lisbon Treaty was subsequently negotiated, also raises questions concerning our understanding of the forces behind EU treaty reforms.

Outline of the book

This book has a chapter on each of the main EC/EU treaties. Iris Glockner and Berthold Rittberger start with the very first treaty, the Treaty of Paris which established the first community, the European Coal and Steel Community (ECSC) in 1951. They also cover the treaty which would have established a European Defence Community (EDC), had it been ratified by all member states and entered into force. They include a discussion of what they consider the main fault lines in the literature: who are the main actors (state-centric vs. transnational perspectives), what is the nature of their preferences (materialist vs. ideational explanations) and how to explain institutional design (rational design vs. constructivist explanations). Also included is a section where they analyse why Great Britain stayed out.

The next chapter by Joaquin Roy covers the Treaties of Rome which established the next two communities, the European Economic Community (EEC) and the European Atomic Energy Community (EAEC) in 1957. This is followed by a chapter by the editor which looks at the so-called Merger Treaty, which merged the executives of the three communities, especially establishing a single commission for the three, in 1965.

Ann-Christina L. Knudsen then covers the so-called Budget Treaties from 1970 and 1975. These were the treaties that started giving the Parliamentary Assembly – or European Parliament, as it started calling itself – budgetary powers. Next, Desmond Dinan covers the Single European Act (SEA), which introduced qualified majority voting (QMV) to harmonise national legislation in view of speeding up the completion of the internal market. Intergovernmental Conferences (IGCs) now start playing a major role in treaty reforms.

The following treaty, the Maastricht Treaty of 1992, which established the European Union (EU), was negotiated through two IGCs, one on Economic and Monetary Union and one on Political Union.

This major development in the history of European integration is covered by Colette Mazzucelli. The first reform that followed Maastricht was the Amsterdam Treaty in 1997. This chapter is written by Sophie Vanhoonacker. The treaty was supposed to prepare for the big eastern enlargement by adapting the institutions and making decision making more efficient. In this it largely failed, but it did start moving some of the matters that Maastricht had included in a third intergovernmental pillar, Justice and Home Affairs, to the first community pillar. It was left to the next treaty, the Treaty of Nice adopted in 2000, to solve some of the perceived institutional problems prior to the eastern enlargement that followed in 2004. The editor has written that chapter.

The inadequacy of Nice takes us into the next reform efforts, first the failed Constitutional Treaty, which is covered by Derek Beach, and then its replacement by the Treaty of Lisbon, covered by Jacques Ziller. Lisbon includes a number of institutional changes supposed to create more coherence and efficiency as well as legitimacy. It was also supposed to be the last treaty reform for many years. However, the recent financial crisis affecting especially some of the countries that have adopted the single currency, the euro, has caused a rethink and already produced a couple of treaty reforms, albeit minor, as shall be discussed in the final concluding chapter.

Notes

1. The Treaty of Lisbon has two parts: The Treaty on European Union (TEU) and the Treaty on the Functioning of the European Union (TFEU).
2. For an account of the early years by a historian, see especially Gerbet (1983). For a more recent historic overview, see Dinan (2004).
3. On leadership, see also Beach and Mazzucelli (2007).

2
The European Coal and Steel Community (ECSC) and European Defence Community (EDC) Treaties

Iris Glockner and Berthold Rittberger

Introduction

The European Coal and Steel Community (ECSC) marks a milestone in international cooperation as it represents the first supranational treaty organisation in history: The national governments of France, Germany, Italy and the Benelux countries decided to delegate domestic decision-making authority in the coal and steel sectors to a new supranational organisation, the High Authority (Thiemeyer, 1998, p. 6). The plan to pool coal and steel resources and create a High Authority was presented to the public by the French foreign minister, Robert Schuman, on 9 May 1950. Robert Schuman and Jean Monnet, the 'mastermind' behind the Schuman Plan, referred to the plan as a 'bold, constructive act' and François Duchêne, author of a much-celebrated Monnet biography, referred to the contents of the plan as a 'break with the past' in the light of its novel supranational quality (Duchêne, 1994, p. 205). One central objective of the plan was to alleviate French concerns that post-war Germany would employ its regained industrial strength as a threat to French autonomy, both in economic and security terms. These concerns arose in particular against the backdrop of imminent German economic recovery and the prospect that Germany would be 'freed' from allied oversight. In June 1950, the intergovernmental negotiations among the 'Six' to implement the Schuman Plan were launched. The Treaty establishing the European Coal and Steel Community was signed in April 1951 and, after successful ratification in France, Germany, Italy and the Benelux countries, it entered into force on 24 July 1952.

With the negotiations of the prospective ECSC Treaty barely under way, the outbreak of the Korean War in late June of 1950 provided the impetus of another initiative to spur cooperation and integration among Western European states. When the United States and Great Britain, under the effect of the outbreak of the Korean War, brought up the prospect of German rearmament, the French government saw the success of the Schuman Plan in peril (Dinan, 2004, p. 58). In the eyes of French policymakers, the risk of German rearmament under a framework of equal partners had to be rendered manageable by launching 'a broader Schuman Plan' (Pastor-Castro, 2006, p. 389), which was drawn up by Monnet, Schuman and the majority of the French cabinet, and presented by French Prime Minister René Pleven on 24 October 1950 (Lipgens, 1984, p. 650). The so-called Pleven Plan envisaged West German rearmament and hence the deployment of troop contingents within a supranational army under joint European command, while Germany itself would not have its own independent army or general staff (Ruane, 2000, p. 4). Due to its discriminatory nature through the rejection of a partnership among equals, the initial Pleven Plan met with little enthusiasm not only among German policymakers, but also among US officials, who considered the Plan an attempt to delay German rearmament and to hence be 'a stalling tactic' that could not be taken seriously (Parsons, 2003, p. 72). France subsequently revised its position and launched a new draft that was more symmetrical in nature, allowing for an increased German military contribution, supranationality and equality (Ruane, 2000, p. 15f.). In February 1951 the negotiations were launched. On 27 May 1952 the 'Six' signed the Treaty establishing the European Defence Community, one day after Britain, France, the United States and Germany had signed the Bonn-Paris Conventions, which effectively ended the allied occupation of Germany and thereby restored its sovereignty (ibid., p. 17). Whereas Germany and the Benelux states succeeded in ratifying the EDC Treaty (the Italians waited for the French to go ahead), the ratification process in France turned out to be lengthy and problematic. The French National Assembly finally rejected the EDC Treaty on a procedural motion on 30 August 1954 with 319 to 264 votes.

In this chapter, we will offer an in-depth exploration of the ECSC and EDC treaties. The first section offers an overview of the main institutional and policy-related provisions of the two treaties. In the second section, we address and seek answers to the following questions: Why did the ECSC Treaty enter into force while the EDC Treaty has not been successfully ratified? Why did Great Britain abstain from both of these integration initiatives? To explain these outcomes and the processes leading to these outcomes, we will explore and contrast several positions in the academic debate about these two Communities with regard to (a) the key actors involved in the formulation of the treaties; (b) the nature of preferences of the key political actors; and (c) the rationale behind the institutional design of the two treaty organisations.

Content of the treaties: Institutional and policy-related provisions

The treaty establishing the European Coal and Steel Community

Institutional provisions

Institutionally, the key component of the Schuman Plan was the supra-national High Authority, which was composed of independent experts and authorised by the governments of the prospective member states to regulate the market for coal and steel by issuing decisions that would be binding for the member states. The ECSC Treaty stipulated that two was the maximum number of members a state could send to the helm of the High Authority. In practice, France, Germany and Italy sent two members, while Belgium, the Netherlands and Luxembourg were assigned one High Authority member each. The term of the members was restricted to six years with the opportunity of reappointment. The 'supranational character' of the High Authority was to reveal itself in Article 9 of the Treaty, stipulating that 'members of the High Authority shall exercise their functions in complete independence, in the general interest of the Community'.

Even though the Schuman Plan made no mention of an institution to represent the member states and their governments, it was clear from the outset of the Plan negotiations that no government delega-tion was ready to accept the High Authority having far-reaching policy prerogatives and decision-making powers absent governmental control. Support for the ECSC in general and the High Authority in particular was thus dependent on the insertion of an institution representing the interests of the respective member state governments. The Council, consisting of the six member state governments, was to be consulted by the High Authority and, on a various policy issues, had to approve pro-posals by the High Authority by either majority or unanimity. Majority voting in the Council followed a system of weighted votes, which required not only the support of the majority of governments, but this majority also had to include the support of one of the member states, producing at least 20 per cent of the total value of the community's coal and steel output. The special role accorded to countries producing at least 20 per cent of the total value of coal and steel produced in the community actually implied that two countries, Germany and France, held a privileged position when it came to approve or veto decisions (Sahm, 1951, p. 7).

The supranational character of the High Authority not only raised the question about how governments could hold the High Authority at bay; it also prompted questions about its democratic accountability. In this context, the idea that a supranational parliamentary assembly should hold the High Authority to account made its entry into the Schuman Plan negotiations (see Rittberger, 2005, 2009). The Common Assembly of the ECSC consisted of 18 members from France, Germany and Italy respectively, ten from Belgium and the Netherlands each, and four from Luxembourg, amounting to a total of 78 representatives. Even though Article 21 of the Treaty envisaged the possibility of holding direct elections for the members of the Assembly, these were not realised until 1979 and the member states decided to grant national parliaments the right to designate delegates among their members. The powers conferred upon the Common Assembly by the ECSC Treaty were mainly supervisory. Members of the Assembly could ask questions to the High Authority and the High Authority had to present a report on the activities of the Community and on its administrative expenditures to the members of the Assembly on an annual basis. As a 'nuclear' control option, the Treaty conferred upon the Assembly to right to cast a motion of censure, which – if supported by a two-thirds majority of the delegates present, as well representing a majority of the total membership – could force the High Authority to resign *en bloc*.

The ECSC Treaty also contained provisions for the operation of a court with the chief purpose to ensure that the High Authority would not overstep its Treaty-based mandate (see Alter, 1998; Pollack, 2003). According to Article 32 of the ECSC Treaty, the Court consists of seven judges appointed by agreement among the member state governments. The judges were eligible for reappointment after the termination of their first six-year period in office. In order to fulfil its 'checking role' and to 'fill in incomplete contracts' (see Pollack, 2003), the Court had a variety of instruments at its disposal. The Court could issue annulment measures for acts adopted by the High Authority, the Assembly or the Council. Moreover, the Court could initiate actions when the High Authority's failure to issue a decision or recommendation was considered in breach of the Treaty.

Jean Monnet's experience in the French Economic Planning Commission gave rise to another institutional innovation attached to the High Authority, the Consultative Committee. The work of the French planning authority followed a 'corporatist style' characterised by 'involving networks of outside producer and interest groups. Specifically, it was the practice of consulting representatives of industry to work out the details of policy' (Featherstone, 1994, p. 155). The task of the Consultative Committee, which consisted of appointed representatives from producers, employees, dealers and consumers in the coal and steel sectors, was to assist the High Authority in its activities by providing information and expert advice. This is reflected in the Treaty, which stipulates that members of the committee should not be bound by mandate or instructions from their respective organisation. Yet, as the name of the institution already suggests, the Consultative Committee was not accorded real decision-making competencies, as the High Authority was merely obliged to consult the committee and keep it informed.

Policy-related provisions

The ECSC Treaty embodies an attempt to prevent military conflict by means of economic integration. This is made explicit in the Schuman Declaration of 9 May 1950: '[The French government] proposes that Franco-German production of coal and steel as a whole be placed under a common High Authority, within the framework of an organisation open to the participation of the other countries of Europe. The pooling of coal and steel production should immediately provide for the setting up of common foundations for economic development as a first step in the federation of Europe, and will change the destinies of those regions which have long been devoted to the manufacture of munitions of war, of which they have been the most constant victims.' The connection between economic integration as a means to lock-in peaceful relations and as an initial step to political integration is echoed in the preamble of the ECSC Treaty. The aim of the new community is 'to create, by establishing an economic community, the basis for a broader and deeper community among peoples long divided by bloody conflicts'.

In the following paragraphs, we offer a short overview of the substantive provisions as they are laid down in the ECSC Treaty. The High Authority was accorded not only an important role as economic planner but also as competition authority, addressing market imperfections. In its role as economic planning authority, the High Authority could offer or deny investments or support investment decisions and measures 'to increase production, lower production costs or facilitate marketing' in the coal and steel sectors (Art. 54). Moreover, if the High Authority considered the Community to be facing a period of economic crisis, it had the prerogative to establish a system of production quotas or import restrictions with the approval of the Council (Art. 58). To combat a serious shortage of products, the Council was to set consumption priorities and to decide on the allocation of coal and steel to the member states, export, and other consumption (Art. 59). The High Authority was also entitled to establish restrictions on exports to third countries (Art. 59).

The High Authority was not only accorded competencies as an economic planner; in the realm of competition, the Treaty envisaged the High Authority to prevent market distortions, such as unfair competitive and discriminatory pricing practices (Art. 60). Apart from fighting unfair pricing practices, agreements and practices by firms endangering free market competition were ruled out (Art. 65), as was the abuse of a dominant market position (Art. 66). Moreover, the establishment of mergers had to be authorised by the High Authority.

The Treaty also contained a set of social and labour policy provisions, some of which fed directly into the conditions for ensuring fair market competition. For example, the High Authority could issue recommendations if a firm imposed low wages as a means of permanent economic adjustment or to increase its competitiveness (Art. 68). Yet, the fixing of wages and provision for social benefits were domains left to the relevant actors ('social partners') in the member states. Commercial policy was also kept at the national level and remained the prerogative of national governments. However, the member states were obliged to inform the High Authority on domestic commercial policy activities insofar as these related to coal, steel or other raw materials (Art. 75). In 'external' relations with third countries, the High Authority was empowered to adopt countermeasures against dumping operations of third countries and other cases that conflicted with the Treaty or endangered its core principles (Art. 74). The Treaty also contained a provision that set its duration to fifty years. In July 2002, the ECSC Treaty expired; coal and steel related policy provisions that were still deemed applicable by the EU member states were integrated into the relevant treaty.

The European Defence Community Treaty

Institutional provisions

The institutional set-up of the EDC mirrors the institutional structure of the ECSC. Like the ECSC, the institutional system of the EDC contains supranational executive und judiciary bodies, the Commissariat as well as the Court, as well as institutions representing the interests of the member state governments, the Council, and those of the citizens, the Assembly.

The supranational counterpart of the EDC to the High Authority was the Commissariat. Like the High Authority it was composed of nine members, with no state entitled to more than two members, and the Treaty also provided for its statutory independence. While the High Authority was accorded a strong economic planning role, the Commissariat assumed the function of a military planner. It was accorded the task to draw up and implement plans for organising the armed forces. This included the management of training programmes, drafting mobilisation plans, as well as the preparation and implementation of armament programmes, and the preparation of the budget (von der Heydte and Wanke, 1952, p. 21). For this purpose, the Commissariat could issue decisions, recommendations and opinions.

As in the case of the ECSC, the institutional system of the EDC guaranteed national influence through a Council representing the governments of the member states. The EDC Council's general task was to coordinate the actions of the Commissariat with the respective national security and defence policies. Just as the ECSC Council had the right to vote on the acts of the High Authority, so had the EDC Council the right to approve or reject in advance the decisions and recommendations the Commissariat was willing to make. Like in the case of the ECSC Council, majority requirements necessary to approve, amend or reject a policy differed, depending on the nature of the policy. On the request of one of its members, a two-thirds majority in the Council could ask the Commissariat to take measures within its area of responsibility.

The EDC also contained a parliamentary organ. With three additional parliamentarians from Germany, France and Italy, the Assembly of the ECSC was equally to function as the parliamentary organ of the EDC. Some of the tasks entrusted to the expanded Assembly were equivalent to those it performed as Assembly of the ECSC, such as the right to control the respective executive institution of the community. As in the case of the ECSC Assembly and the High Authority, the Commissariat had to resign as a body if a censure motion carried a two-thirds majority of the votes cast in the EDC Assembly. As part of its supervisory function, the EDC Assembly was able to pose questions to the Commissariat and receive its annual general report. Compared to the ECSC Assembly, however, the EDC Assembly was granted more extensive rights. Among these was, first of all, the right to co-decide on the community's budget. Second, Article 38 of the EDC Treaty endowed the Assembly with the task to examine and prepare the formation of a genuine EDC Assembly through direct democratic elections. More importantly, Article 38 also called upon the Assembly to delineate a permanent organisational structure for the community, which should be either federal or confederal in character, respect the principle of the separation of powers, and contain a two-chamber legislature.

The provisions in the EDC Treaty relating to the Court and its competencies mirror those of the Court of the ECSC: one of its key tasks was to settle disputes between member states or between community actors over the application of the Treaty rules. Moreover, the Court could annul actions deemed to be in violation of the Treaty or deliver verdicts over complaints that community institutions failed to act despite a legal obligation to do so. In the context of the preliminary reference procedure, the Court was to assist national courts in the uniform application and interpretation of Treaty rules.

Policy-related provisions

The EDC Treaty is both a treaty establishing a European army as well as a defence alliance of like-minded states (von der Heydte and Wanke, 1952, p. 16). Article 2 establishes the principle of mutual assistance in the case of an attack on one of its member states. The mutual assistance provision was of particular importance for Germany, providing assurance that in case of Soviet aggression Germany would be assisted by its new allies (ibid., p. 17). The armed forces of the EDC were 'a true community army' in the sense that they were uniformly armed, equipped, dressed and paid (Fenwick, 1952, p. 699). The EDC Treaty required all member states to transfer sovereignty over their armed forces by creating a common European army subject to European command structures (Ruane, 2000, p. 15). Exceptions were made for national troop contingents overseas and existing international commitments. The Treaty fixed military integration at the division level: The total of 43 divisions was made up of 14 divisions from France, 12 from Germany and Italy, respectively, and the other five from the Benelux countries. The EDC was granted a common budget based on national contributions, which in turn reflected national economic and social conditions. Moreover, the EDC Treaty expected the member states, with the assistance of the Commissariat, to draw up a common armament program. The European army was supposed to be operational by the end of 1954 (von der Heydte and Wanke, 1952, p. 18f.).

Explaining the treaties

Why did the ECSC Treaty 'succeed' while the EDC Treaty failed to be ratified? How can the dynamics and processes leading to the adoption and rejection of the respective treaties be best captured and explained? Why did Britain decide not to join the 'Six' in both treaty projects? Before we answer these questions, we proceed by discussing the central analytical categories necessary to shed light on theses pressing questions.

Analytical framework

We identify three debates or 'fault lines' in the literature on the ECSC and EDC Treaties See Table 2.1. First, scholarly accounts of the ECSC and EDC Treaties differ in their respective assessments of who were the most relevant actors driving the European integration process in its early phase. Intergovernmentalists argue that the governments of member states are the dominant actors: they shape European integration according to nationally defined goals and interests. Most historical or political science accounts of these treaty episodes are representative of such a state-centric perspective, emphasising the dominate role of diplomats and leading figures in government in the process. While it is uncontroversial that, especially in the initial phases of integration, governments could – in the absence of supranational actors – negotiate in a more or less unconstrained fashion, some studies begin to challenge the exclusive state-centrism in most accounts of the early days of European integration. In this context, transnational actor coalitions and, at later stages, supranational actors are said to play an increasingly relevant role in influencing integration by constraining governments.

The debate about the origins and substantive quality of actors' preferences for European integration represents a second fault line in the literature: 'Materialist' accounts of preference formation are contrasted with 'ideational' accounts of preference formation. While the former focus on economic and geopolitical factors conditioning actors' preferences, the latter stress that material conditions are subject to (potentially different) interpretations based on collectively held ideas, values or norms, which are, in turn, constitutive for actors' interests and preferences. As a conceptual guide, it is again helpful to consult integration theoretic perspectives: For intergovernmentalists, preferences are 'material' in that

Table 2.1   Fault lines in the literature on the ECSC and EDC

Fault line	Contrasting perspectives and explanations
Actors	State-centric vs. transnational perspectives
Preferences	Materialist vs. ideational explanations
Institutional design	Rational design vs. constructivist explanations

they either stress security or economic conditions (see Schimmelfennig and Rittberger, 2006, pp. 78–84). 'Realist' intergovernmentalists assume that states' overall interest is to maximise autonomy, security and influence (see, for example, Hoffmann, 1966; Grieco, 1996). A state's interest in integration can, for instance, be spurred by stark power asymmetries. If states face an overwhelmingly powerful opponent and if power is symmetrically distributed between the threatened countries, the latter will opt for integration and thus engage in balancing (Rosato, 2011, p. 32). The liberal variant of intergovernmentalism sets out with the assumption that states' preferences reflect the interests of dominant (economic) interest groups, which can mostly be found among producers (Moravcsik, 1998, p. 36). Liberalisation through economic integration enables internationally competitive producers to reap the gains of international economic interdependence (ibid., pp. 35, 49). Liberal intergovernmentalism not only stresses the relevance of economic interests in general, but offers a 'liberal' explanation of governments' preferences, which are expected to reflect the interests of dominant societal interest groups in a particular sector (Moravcsik, 1993, p. 481). For example, in energy policy, governmental preferences should reflect the interests of dominant energy producers and consumers. While intergovernmentalism emphasises the material origins of state preferences – that is, economic and geopolitical conditions – constructivist accounts emphasise the ideational underpinnings of preferences: societal norms and ideas affect the ways political actors interpret the material world. As Parsons puts it: 'Ideas are autonomous factors in politics, and certain institutions arise because of the ideas actors hold' (Parsons, 2003, p. 25). He argues that variation in support for European integration can be traced back to 'three ideational groups' or cognitive models, which affect the way political actors interpret the material world around them. According to the 'traditional' model, the nation state enjoys lasting primacy and the ideas associated with this model prescribe the impossibility and undesirability of sovereignty transfers. The 'confederal' model agrees with the traditional model in that nation states are 'lasting realities' but appreciates the benefits that accrue from 'a loose continental framework of cooperation' (ibid., p. 23f.). Supporters of the 'community' model believe that the nation state could no longer guarantee security and welfare and that 'integration within a supranational community was the best path to future peace and prosperity' (ibid.).

Third, this contribution turns to a body of literature exploring the question of institutional design: What prompted policymakers to opt for a supranational organisation in the cases of the ECSC and the EDC? The fault line in this section pits proponents of functionalist and rational-ist explanations for institutional design against constructivism-inspired institutionalist accounts emphasising the legitimacy-enhancing effects of institutional choices. According to rational-functionalist accounts of institutional design, member state governments delegate powers to supranational institutions, such as the High Authority or Court, with the expectation that these institutions efficiently address a set of collective action problems arising from international cooperation: monitoring compliance, filling in incomplete contracts, or ensuring the credibility of policy commitments (Pollack, 1997, 2003). Constructivism-inspired accounts, in contrast, emphasise the legitimacy-seeking motivation behind institutional choices. Rather than maximising power or efficiency when designing institutions, actors design institutions on the basis of what they consider a desirable, appropriate or legitimate order.

Explaining the ECSC

In the following section we take recourse to our analytical framework and associated explanations to account for the successful ratification process and the ensuing coming into force of the ECSC treaty on 24 July 1952. Who were the decisive actors from the Schuman Plan up to the final decision on the ECSC? How can their preference for integration in the coal and steel sector be explained? And why did the negotiators opt for a supranational institutional design?

Identifying the key actors

The majority of important works on the ECSC have been written by historians who adopt a state-centric 'diplomatic history' perspective, emphasising the role of 'national' interests and conceptualising governments as purposeful and (more or less) cohesive actors (Kaiser and Leucht, 2008, p. 35). The works of William Hitchcock are emblematic of this approach. Not only does he stress the importance of the 'international diplomatic context' (Hitchcock, 1997, p. 604) for the formulation of foreign policy, but he particularly points to the role of French Foreign Minister Schuman 'and the upper echelons of his staff' in the Quai d'Orsay in putting Jean Monnet's ideas on a supranational ECSC 'into action' (ibid., p. 605).

The study by Creswell and Trachtenberg (2003) equally adopts a state-centric 'diplomatic history' approach in which French political leaders and high-ranking officials in the Foreign Ministry are considered to play the central role in defining France's European policy.

Alan Milward also echoes the importance of national governments and bureaucratic elites in controlling the process of European integration.

Since Milward stresses the importance of economic considerations behind integrative efforts and French European policy, the French Planning Commissariat, led by Monnet, is attributed an important role in policy formulation alongside the Foreign Ministry. Actors within both governmental institutions can claim credit for developing a new policy towards Germany, which culminated in the launch of the Schuman Plan: 'From Monnet's first proposals for an economic plan the Ministry of Foreign Affairs had sought to use the plan as a justification of French policy in Europe to the allies' (Milward, 1984, p. 396). A small circle of political leaders and high-ranking officials is thus said to have pulled the strings of policy formulation. Anglo-American pressure for a new French policy towards Germany – which came to a head at the London Conference opening in February 1948 – leads Milward to conclude that the 'first origins of the Schuman Plan were really in the Ministry of Foreign Affairs during the London conference' (ibid.). As early as June 1949, 'the Ministry of Foreign Affairs began the task of moving ministers, governments, parliament and people towards the alternative policy of a Franco-German economic association' (ibid., p. 468). Moreover, Milward's work is derogatory of those accounts, which emphasise that individual political leaders – like Schuman, Monnet, Adenauer or de Gasperi – were primarily driven by 'lofty' ideals in their pursuit of European integration policies. The acclaimed 'miraculous doings of [the] European saints' (Milward, 1992, p. 318) were not so miraculous after all: political leaders did not and could not operate in a vacuum but were constrained by socio-economic and geo-political contexts. To address these political challenges, the nation-state quite naturally 'continued to be the central point of reference of their political activities' (ibid., p. 335).

Most political scientists who have written on the early phase of European integration history can also be located inside the state-centric camp. In sync with the assumptions of a 'liberal' interpretation of inter-governmentalism, these studies focus not merely on political elites, top level officials and bureaucrats, but also on 'intermediary actors', such as domestic-level interest groups and political parties, which are considered crucial in the formation of the 'national interest' (see Moravcsik, 1998). For example, Helen Milner (1997) emphasises the relevance of domestic interest groups whose endorsement was required by governments in Germany and France for negotiating and adopting the ECSC Treaty. Craig Parsons (2002 and 2003) places particular emphasis on the role of domestic politicians in the French *Assemblée National* and political parties in France; even though he does not dispute that the plans to create a common coal and steel pool were influenced by geopolitical events, he argues that different interpretations of the geopolitical threat posed by Germany clustered in the French domestic political debate and cut across party lines, creating more or less mouldable majorities.

More recently, historians have begun to depart from the state-centrism characteristic of most research on the ECSC. As one prominent critic of state-centric approaches has argued, '[m]ost integration history has ignored the importance of supranational institutions and transactional actors [...] in EU politics' (Kaiser, 2006, p. 196). According to Wolfram Kaiser, state-centric approaches overlook that 'national actors and collective interests stand no realistic chance of influencing the policy-making process significantly unless they are well connected across borders in transnational political networks' (Kaiser, 2007, p. 1). The conceptual 'turn' proposed in these works is not entirely new, as the research on transnationally organised federalist movements amply demonstrates (see Lipgens, 1982). Criticism voiced against 'Federalists' such as Lipgens mostly takes issue with the strong normative orientation of this work and the importance attributed to the 'Federalist social movement' in influencing the course of European integration. Recent research by Wolfram Kaiser posits that the most relevant actors in post-war European integration 'were not the resistance and European movements, but [...] political parties and party leaders. Only they could use the various channels to translate transnationally deliberated and negotiated ideas and policies into national governmental policy-making and European-level decision-making' (Kaiser, 2007, pp. 8–9). More specifically, Kaiser argues that Christian democratic parties assumed a 'hegemonic' position in shaping the European integration agenda in post-war Europe (ibid.). We will return to the role of Christian Democratic parties in advancing the integration process in the first half of the 1950s in the following section.

Forming preferences[1]

Materialist accounts about the substantive character of actors' preferences are prevalent in the literature on the ECSC. Advancing a realist interpretation of preference formation, William Hitchcock (1997) has prominently argued that Germany's economic advances in the post-war era carried profound negative security externalities for France. Moreover, the Anglo-American shift of focus from promoting economic recovery in Western Europe to planning European (including German) rearmament 'gripped the Quai d'Orsay' (Hitchcock, 1997, p. 610). Hitchcock's analysis of France's European policy suggests that French foreign policy was at the time both autonomy- and influence-seeking. When, due to external events (the Prague Coup 1948 and the Berlin blockade 1948–9), the goal to maximise France's autonomy by keeping Germany's economic and political development under allied control was no longer a viable option, Robert Schuman and the French Foreign Ministry turned to influence-seeking policies. This shift in orientation, based on changes in the geopolitical (material) environment, triggered the demand for the creation of self- and other-binding supranational institutions, as expressed in the Schuman Plan.

The initial response by the German government to the Schuman Plan strongly mirrors the primacy of security- and autonomy-related preferences. Given its position in the international community after World War II, Germany possessed only limited sovereignty (the majority of political decisions had to be approved by the allied High Commission). Therefore, the prospect of international cooperation signalled an opportunity to regain domestic and foreign policymaking capacity. The Schuman Plan offered an immediate opportunity to become an equal member in the European concert of states. Given various signals by the US and Britain regarding potential rearmament, Germany could also expect its status as occupied power to cease in the short to medium run. Consequently, enthusiasm to unconditionally abide by the French proposal to engage in self-binding supranational integration was increasingly unpopular with a significant part of the German political and economic elite as soon as alternative avenues for cooperation opened. While opposition to the Schuman Plan was mainly on economic grounds, Germany's governing political elite was initially relatively autonomous from domestic economic pressures in forging ahead with Schuman's proposal (though the major opposition force in the *Bundestag*, the Social Democrats actually opposed the Schuman Plan). The supranational principle, enshrined in the institution of the High Authority, was readily accepted, as were economic concessions in order to regain sovereignty through participation in the ECSC project. On behalf of Chancellor Adenauer and his aides, it was not a very difficult decision to renounce those aspects of national sovereignty that fell into the High Authority's jurisdiction: The prospective coal and steel pool opened a path to more international influence and the regaining of national policymaking prerogatives in other fields through the weakening of the occupation status as well as a guarantee of peace between France and Germany (Küsters, 1988, p. 78; Lappenküper, 1994, pp. 411–13). Even though some commentators argue that the German government's stance on the ECSC hardened as a result of domestic economic pressure and the prospect that allied control of Germany would ease in the near future, Milward claims that 'Adenauer insisted throughout on the prime political priority for the Federal Republic on the removal of the Ruhr Authority and the weakening of the Occupation Statute' (Milward, 1984, p. 413) to bolster German sovereignty.

Turning to liberal intergovernmentalist accounts of preference formation, several authors have highlighted the economic rationale for the formation of governments' preferences in the creation of the ECSC. According to Lynch, the positive economic externalities of a common coal and steel pool were apparent in the French case since they would directly contribute to France's economic modernisation as spelled out in the Monnet Plan (Lynch, 1988, pp. 124–6). Other accounts see economic and security-related objectives to be inextricably connected: Monnet's proposed coal and steel pool has to be seen as a means to protect French security and promote economic reconstruction through the international control of Germany's heartland of heavy industry, the Ruhr (Gillingham, 1991, p. 229). With France being – at the time – the world's largest importer of coal and coke (Lynch, 1988, p. 119), a common market for coal and steel promised to ensure sufficient and cheap supply of German combustible for French industry and for the realisation of the French economic modernisation plan (ibid., p. 125). To what degree did domestic industries influence the substance of the ECSC treaty? The literature attributes a rather limited role to the French coal and steel industry: it was only after the announcement of the Schuman Plan that the steel industry launched fierce campaigns against the way the negotiations were conducted, yet they were mostly excluded from the talks which was mainly the result of the industry's lack of a concerted stance (see Milward, 1984, p. 419; Mioche, 1988). Diebold echoes this view, claiming that there was no initial 'push' by French industry to integrate these sectors of the economy (Diebold, 1959, pp. 16–17). Even though the producers demanded to be involved in the Schuman Plan negotiations, this never happened in practice (Gillingham, 1991, p. 236). The literature thus points to a reading of French policy largely unconstrained from domestic interest group pressures: the motivation of the French governing elite to tie Germany's coal and steel industry to a supranational coal and steel pool was not driven by the sector- or issue-specific demands articulated by organised interests but rather by domestic economic policy objectives that were spelled out in the Monnet Plan. However, as argued above, these economic concerns existed alongside geopolitical and security ones (Abelshauser, 1994, p. 7).

Turning to preference formation in Germany, the literature considers economic objectives to be of secondary importance (see Hitchcock,

1997). Contrary to what liberal intergovernmentalism would expect, domestic interest groups exercised little influence in the formation of the German government's preferences. For example, the German Iron and Steel Manufacturers' Association was informed by the government early in the negotiations that 'the political aim was in the foreground, and economic aims were more or less subordinate to it' (Milward, 1984, p. 413). Despite massive opposition from industrialists and labour unions, Chancellor Adenauer succeeded in imposing the crucial elements of the Schuman Plan even against considerable domestic dissent. Milward thus concludes, 'without Adenauer's autocratic imposition of his own foreign policy on the Federal government [the French] proposals would surely not have been made' (ibid., p. 390).

Contrary to the German and French cases, macroeconomic objectives and domestic interest groups played a much more important role in the formation of state preferences in the Benelux countries. The primacy of economic interests is mainly reflected in the sectoral approach towards cooperation taken by the Benelux countries. The respective governments sought cooperation in policy areas in which the expected economic gains of integration would be highest and existing domestic social and economic policies would not be prohibitively affected. For example, Dutch import-dependence on the one hand, and Belgium's and Luxembourg's export-dependence with regard to coal and steel on the other hand, led the respective governments and domestic interest groups to press for low common tariffs. The Benelux delegations thus advocated that the High Authority should not be given the opportunity to set a tariff level which, so the Benelux countries feared, would be higher than the one that the three countries had negotiated among themselves. Belgium and Luxembourg were particularly more dependent on the steel market for their exports than the other negotiating partners because steel amounted to a fifth of their total exports: 'For them the issues, economically, were more crucial than for France or Germany' (ibid., pp. 415–16). In wage policy, macro-economic policy objectives were seen to be under attack from the prospective ECSC. The prospect that the High Authority would be empowered to equalise living conditions and prevent countries that wished to catch up economically from pursuing a low-wage strategy was rejected by the Dutch government, whose low wage policy was a cornerstone to its post-war recovery policy (see Griffiths, 1990, p. 271; Gillingham, 1991, p. 244). Griffiths argues that any powers delegated to the High Authority to influence wage levels 'were inimical to the Dutch, who interpreted them as a fundamental threat to their newly enforced system of national wage bargaining'

(Griffiths, 1988, p. 40). Similar examples could be provided for the highly contested questions about investment control, price levels, cartels/restrictive practices and transitional agreements. In the Benelux cases, then, the liberal intergovernmentalist account for preference formation provides a good fit, while the preferences of the French and German governments are better explained with reference to the realist variant of intergovernmentalism.

More recently, approaches to explain governmental preferences on a 'materialist' basis have been complemented by accounts emphasising the ideational underpinnings of preferences. Some scholars argue that the existing literature has largely ignored 'the significance of ideas in early European integration as an independent variable' (Kaiser and Leucht, 2008, p. 36). Kaiser argues that the glue for transnational cooperation between Christian Democrats, whose leaders were in the key positions in government among the founding states, was a shared 'ideological predisposition' (Kaiser, 2001) that eventually helped to spur supranational integration in Europe. More specifically, post-war Christian Democrats throughout Western Europe shared a set of ideas, which sided well with the notion of delegating sovereignty to the European level: the 'quasi-supranational' authority exercised by the Pope, the discourse linking the present exigencies of integration with the experiences of the early-medieval organisation of secular authority in the Frankish Empire, as well as the principle of subsidiarity, a hallmark of Catholic social teaching. This set of ideas and ideological predispositions facilitated a convergence of preferences in favour of supranational integration: Via the informal Christian Democratic transnational party network, political leaders were in the situation not only to debate and define common objectives, but also to effectively set the policy agenda on matters of European integration (Kaiser and Leucht, 2008, pp. 39–42).

Craig Parsons (2002 and 2003) echoes Kaiser's argument that ideational variables are important to explain preferences for European integration. Parsons analyses the impact of 'cross-cutting ideas' on the formulation of European integration policy in France and juxtaposes his ideational account with material or 'objective-interest theories' (Parsons, 2002, p. 50). How can it be explained that seemingly similar economic or geopolitical conditions led to radically different foreign and security policy trajectories? Ideational approaches rest on the assumption that 'actors interpret their interests through ideas that can vary independently from their objective positions' (ibid.). The causal effect of ideas on policy preferences can be best demonstrated in instances where ideas cut across different actors placed in similar 'objective' (read 'material') conditions: 'Take two French diplomats, with similar social backgrounds and party sympathies, in the same office of the Foreign Ministry in 1950. One insists on French interests in a new 'supranational' Franco-German federation; the other sees French interests in policies based on an informal partnership with Britain. These similarly placed individuals face *all* the same objective pressures but seem to interpret them differently' (ibid., p. 51, emphasis in original). Parsons demonstrates that different sets of ideas about European institution-building – traditionalist, confederalist and community notions of cooperation – were viable in the French domestic political debate surrounding the creation of the ECSC (ibid., pp. 57–8).

Choosing institutions

The third fault line in the academic debate about the ECSC treaty addresses the choice of the particular set of institutions adopted by the member states. Two issues will be highlighted in this regard. First, the ECSC marks the first international treaty in the history of international cooperation to propose a supranational organisation, the High Authority, to which the authority to issue binding decisions was delegated. How can we account for this unprecedented form of supranational delegation? Second, the institutional order laid down in the treaty includes additional bodies, such as a parliamentary assembly, a member state Council and a court. How can the broader institutional structure of the ECSC be explained?

According to Mark Pollack, the creation of the High Authority corresponds to a functionalist logic for delegation. Following the functional rational design approach, problems of delegation and discretion 'were foremost in the minds of negotiators of the ECSC Treaty' (Pollack, 2003, p. 77). Besides monitoring compliance with ECSC policies, only an independent High Authority could 'credibly and impartially regulate the coal and steel sector' (ibid., p. 78). In the historical and political science literature, the partial delegation of sovereignty in the areas of coal and steel is most commonly interpreted as a solution to the problem of ensuring the credibility of policy commitments. Individual security and economic concerns could be best addressed by a supranational organisation to which the concerned states would delegate portions of their sovereignty. For the French government, delegated sovereignty implied that Germany could not use its economic power 'unchecked'. For the German government, delegated sovereignty implied that it would be able to act on par with the other Western states (see, for example, Eilstrup-Sangiovanni and Verdier, 2005).

But the supranational High Authority could not be left to its own devices: with a view to limit its discretion, Pollack argues that the creation of the Council, Court and Parliamentary Assembly primarily served a control or 'checking' function. Karen Alter underlines this argument with a view to the court of the ECSC: 'The ECJ was created as part of the European Coal and Steel Community in order to protect member states and firms by ensuring that the supranational high authority did not exceed its authority' (Alter, 1998, p. 124). The concern that the High Authority would overstep its mandate was pointedly made by the leader of the Dutch delegation to the Schuman Plan negotiations, Dirk Spierenburg. He posed the provoking question of whether the High Authority actually embodied a dictatorship of experts. To circumscribe its powers and limit the High Authority's discretion, the Benelux countries thus insisted on the creation of a Council in which the member state governments would be represented to protect their interests (Rittberger, 2001, pp. 695–6). Moreover, the member state Council should ensure that the independent supranational High Authority would not direct its activism to the detriment of the 'smaller' member states or establish itself as a dictatorship of experts (Küsters, 1988, p. 79).

In sync with Pollack's rational design approach, the Schuman Plan negotiations demonstrated that 'the concern for 'executive control' was unanimously shared among all participating [national] delegations, yet the delegations' *interpretation* of the norm of executive control as to *who* should control and *how* control should be exercised varied' (Rittberger, 2001, p. 696, emphasis in original). More recent empirical research based on the analysis of primary documents reveals the limitations of functional rational design explanations for the institutional design of the ECSC: While it can be argued that the creation of an intergovernmental Council provided a check on the High Authority by the 'principals', not all actors perceived of the 'control problem' in the same way. In sync with a constructivist argument, which points to the relevance of ideas in informing institutional design preference, the German delegation to the Schuman Plan negotiations interpreted the control problem in a radically different manner: internal documents reveal that the proposal for creating a Council was not primarily discussed in terms of how the High Authority's powers could be most effectively checked, but was discussed in normative terms – that is, whether it provided a 'fit' with prevailing (domestic) notions of appropriate constitutional design. German delegates to the Schuman Plan negotiations thus reasoned that if the High Authority constitutes a nascent executive of a European federal state (*Bundesstaat*), chambers representing the territorial interests of the constituent states (qua 'upper chamber') and of the peoples (qua 'lower chamber') are appropriate constitutional design feature (see Rittberger, 2005, p. 98). The federal state analogy was time and again expressed by members of the German delegation as a guide to institutional design. This became particularly apparent in the case of the creation of the parliamentary assembly of the ECSC (ibid., pp. 98–104).

Explaining the EDC

While the ECSC sailed rather smoothly through the ratification process in the six member states, the EDC failed to be ratified. In the ensuing sections we will try to explain this failure by first asking who the central actors during the entire process up to the negative vote were, how their initial preference for integration in the defence sector can be explained, and when and why preferences changed between 1950 and 1954.

Identifying the key actors

As in the case of the ECSC, the majority of research on the EDC adopts a state-centric perspective inspired by realist and liberal intergovernmentalist assumptions. Leadership by high-ranking politicians and public officials is said to have been behind the proposal for the EDC. According to Parsons, the initiative for the EDC can be traced back to few leading lights such as Monnet, Schuman and Alphand (Parsons, 2003, p. 75). When, in 1951, the Pleven Plan was transformed to the EDC Treaty, 'no political majority, bureaucratic elite, or interest group coalition had driven the transformation' (ibid., p. 75). In the Quai D'Orsay, which had not been involved in the deliberations about how to tackle the issue of German rearmament, different camps formed around the project. One group of civil servants followed Monnet and Schuman despite British non-participation in the proposed integration project, while the other group was more sceptical about the idea (Pastor-Castro, 2006, p. 394). Whereas the discreet way of launching the European Coal and Steel Community by a few members of the political elite had been successful, the same approach towards the EDC was not. Not only were members of the French government more divided on the common army project, shifts in government and party coalitions in the French National Assembly jeopardised the ratification process.

Governments were only partially bowing to the demands of transnational societal actors in the negotiations over Article 38 of the EDC Treaty, which calls upon the member states to endow the community with a permanent institutional structure. According to Lipgens, the inclusion of Article 38 reflects that the demands of transnational interest groups, most notably of the Federalist Movement, provided a decisive impetus for the negotiations among governments (Lipgens, 1984, p. 656). In sum, it can be argued that – in line with intergovernmentalism – where governments had clear and precise ideas about how prospective treaty measures would impact their deeply felt security-related preferences, the impact of transnational actors would be minimal. However, where, as in the case of Article 38, a prospective treaty measure was judged to pose no immediate challenge to governments' objectives, we can observe tightly circumscribed influence of transnational actors in the treaty negotiations.

Forming preferences

A liberal theory of preference formation, such as liberal intergovern-mentalism, not only includes producer interests, but powerful societal interests more generally. In the realm of defence, the implications of integration for the military is thus of particular interest. For example, if top-level officers of the armed forces were in favour of an integrated European army due to negative security externalities arising from the defence policies of other countries, they might have lobbied their governments to press for the EDC. Yet, there is no indication that army officials considered a joint European military superior to exist-ing multilateral (such as NATO) or even unilateral alternatives. Even though there was agreement on the necessity of a German defence contribution to keep the USSR in check, there was no advocacy of a common European army as envisaged in the EDC treaty. Both French and German military officials did not approve of the Pleven Plan (Watt, 1985, p. 83). By ignoring the military reality, the authors of the Pleven Plan, Monnet in particular, withdrew the support of an important social group from the EDC (ibid., p. 97). In addition, French military in particular quarrelled with the supranational integration of their armed forces (Parsons, 2003, p. 76).

Liberal intergovernmentalism in the stricter sense focuses on eco-nomic interdependence and integration attempts that follow the inter-ests of dominant producer groups in a certain sector. In the realm of defence policy, the armament industry can be considered a potentially powerful group. If it gained economically from the EDC, it would push its government towards integration. Pitman, for example, argues 'the politics of French industry partially accounted for both the rise and the fall of the EDC' (Pitman, 2000, p. 53). From the French economic perspective, the EDC offered the prospect of controlling German arms production within a supranational framework. In addition, the

French aircraft industry, which had been cut back in previous years to the advantage of British and American aircraft industry, hoped for an upswing from the EDC and German rearmament, as did the industries for electronics and heavy weaponry (ibid., p. 58). Whereas the French aeronautic and electronic industry supported the EDC, the French steel and textile industry, light weaponry, munitions and military transport vehicles producers were opposed because they feared German and Italian competitors would be at an advantage (ibid., p. 59). In general, French business was 'broadly opposed' to the EDC, which was perceived to be a just another step towards a supranational market within which it had to compete with prospering German business (Parsons, 2003, p. 75). That the EDC would have been *de facto* 'supervising and enforcing the cartelisation of European arms production' furthermore ran counter to the interests of liberals such as the German economics minister Ludwig Erhard (Pitman, 2000, p. 55). The influence of business interests on the failure of the EDC and the explanatory power of liberal intergovern-mentalism, however, should not be overestimated. Moravcsik argues as follows: 'in matters with little or no calculable impact on economic interests, such as [...] defence policy, [...] political economy theory generate[s] predictions similar to those of the geopolitical theory. Since issue-specific interests prevail, 'high politics' concerns will dominate the latter area' (Moravcsik, 1998, p. 50). It is this kind of geopolitical approach that we will turn to now.

Sebastian Rosato explains the initial move towards the EDC as a con-sequence of balance-of-power politics. With the onset of the Cold War, European states were facing an overwhelming competitor: the USSR. Compared to the military power of the USSR, 'the former great powers were hopelessly overmatched' (Rosato, 2011, p. 107). Acting unilaterally, France, Britain and West Germany could not stand up to the USSR. In the form of a balancing coalition, they 'would be weaker than the USSR, but not at such a disadvantage as to be unable to defend [themselves]' (ibid., p. 109). The Europeans not only had the motive and means but also the opportunity to provide for their own defence: American troops on the continent deterred the USSR from strangling attempts at build-ing a west European military force at birth, while at the same time the Americans were quite clear about their intention to reduce their mili-tary involvement in Europe – thereby providing an additional incentive for European states to join forces for a common European defence (ibid., p. 113). Believing that US commitment to defend Europe would sooner or later come to an end, Germany considered European integration in the defence sector as the only available solution to counterbalance the imminent security threat arising from the USSR. The outbreak of the Korean War confirmed Adenauer in his conviction that West Germany not only must rearm, but that it has to provide for its defence within a European coalition (ibid., pp. 114–17). For the German government, the Pleven Plan did not satisfy its demand for equal participation in the command structure, which led to a hardening of its position and domestic disapproval. When the EDC treaty finally satisfied Germany's call for equality, the ratification procedure went smoothly and in 1953 the *Bundestag* and *Bundesrat* approved of Germany's membership in the EDC (ibid., p. 124).

Realist explanations for preference formation in France trace the French government's approach towards the EDC also back to 'straight-forward power and sovereignty calculations' (ibid., p. 125). While united with Germany in the desire to deter the Soviet Union, France, unlike Germany, also worried about the balance of power within Western Europe: Acknowledging the desirability of a German contribution to a European military force effective enough to balance against the USSR, France was concerned about an immediate, unconditional, uncon-trolled and public rearmament of Germany (ibid., p. 124f.). At the time, German rearmament was expected to irritate French public opinion. According to Rosato, the French government would have preferred not to give up sovereignty in the military sector and rather rely on American troops in Europe to balance against the USSR (ibid., p. 127). Given, however, the premonition of US army withdrawal from Europe, France favoured a European defence contribution, which included the British and was suited to control German rearmament (ibid., p. 125). The out-break of the Korean War increased French fears and uncertainty of the military intentions of the Soviet Union and nourished the perception that German rearmament within the limits of a European defence sys-tem was necessary (ibid., p. 128). A realist balance-of-power argument thus seems to be in a good position to account for the preferences of the French and German governments to sign the EDC Treaty. Still, the EDC never whipped up wholehearted support in France. Even after German ratification, French politicians (and public opinion) were uncertain whether Germany might, one day, decide to secede from the EDC and confront France with a revival of German militarism (Greenwood, 1992, p. 53). In addition, France's military involvement in Indochina limited defence resources that it could muster for its European defence effort and triggered 'fears of being outnumbered by German troops in the EDC' (Ruane, 2000, p. 11). Hence, several successive French governments wanted to postpone ratification until the end of war in

Indochina and the return of French military forces (ibid., p. 38). Other geopolitically relevant events – Stalin's death in March 1953 and the end of the Korean War in July 1953 – finally offered the prospect of *détente*, easing the imminent threat emanating from the USSR. The EDC option thus lost appeal (ibid., p. 39). Moreover, integrating Germany into NATO seemed to be an increasingly viable solution, which required no autonomy loss on behalf of France. Hence, as soon as alternatives to a supranational solution leaked, these were prioritised as a way to balance the Soviet security threat (Parsons, 2003, p. 81).

A constructivist account of the EDC, that is, of the preferences for a joint army as well as of the outcome, focuses on the conditions for ideational consensus. As already outlined in the section of the ECSC, Wolfram Kaiser emphasises the communality of ideas within the Christian-Democratic party network, which was united in its attempt to push for European integration (Kaiser, 2007). Initially there was an agreement among French and German political leaders such as Schuman and Adenauer that a European defence organisation was the most promising way to counterbalance the USSR. This elite-level consensus, however, was not mirrored in broader domestic consensus on the issue. In France, different ideas about how to address the Soviet threat were widespread: 'Community advocates called for integrating German units into a supranationally run European Army. Confederalists preferred to allow German forces into a looser organisation under Franco-British direction. Traditionalists either rejected German rearmament outright or accepted it in a standard alliance framework' (Parsons, 2003, p. 67). Parsons emphasises that even though 'aggressive pro-community leadership' fuelled by geopolitical events imposed the supranational option at first, all three ideas were equally viable domestically (ibid., p. 69). When, however, the French government coalition changed due to unrelated domestic policy issues, the opportunity arose to express opposition to the EDC (ibid., p. 75). Not only were bureaucrats, business and the military rather hostile to the EDC, 'traditionalists' within the Third Force governing coalition joined the Gaullists and Communists in their opposition to the EDC. The 'confederalists' within the different Third Force parties, too, seized the opportunity to express their opposition to the supranational EDC so that in the end antagonism across all parties in France provided the deathblow to the EDC (ibid., p. 77ff.).

Turning to Germany, Chancellor Adenauer's pro-community stance on the EDC was, according to Noack, a 'necessary evil' (Noack, 1985, p. 241). Although Adenauer employed a strong pro-European discourse in his speeches on the EDC, it is argued that he was more convinced by the joint army project than driven by a European vision. He used pro-community rhetoric to domestically isolate opponents of German rearmament, such as the German Social Democrats. In the aftermath of World War II, rearmament ran counter to pacifist sentiment in West Germany; the fear of antagonising the Soviet Union and thereby thwarting German unification was another concern he had to assuage. By underlining a European vision of German forces fighting in the name of Europe, Adenauer tried to sell rearmament to the German public (Ruane, 2000, p. 18), while, at the same time, lessen French fears about German rearmament (Noack, 1985, p. 244).

Choosing institutions

According to a functional explanation of delegation, co-binding institutions enhance the credibility of policy commitments. In order to be effective and assuage concerns about defection, the balancing coalition had to go beyond more traditional forms of cooperation by renouncing sovereignty and establishing a centralised organisation that exercised joint control of the emerging European army (Rosato, 2011, p. 118ff.). The French and German governments agreed that a centralised form of integration with shared control of the decision-making structure was desirable (ibid., p. 134). France approved of this 'fairly even within-coalition distribution of power' (ibid., p. 134) because each country's military contribution to the EDC depended on the absolute military resources of the country and, therefore, France did not fear German supremacy and introduced the principle of equality in 1951 as a means of guaranteeing a within-Western Europe balance of power (ibid., p. 135). Full German autonomy in the defence sector, however, could have endangered this balance of power and therefore was inconceivable for France (ibid., p. 135).

The broad array of control, budgetary and legislative competences that the EDC's assembly was to possess, which exceeded the competences of the ECSC's assembly, is remarkable and difficult to capture by taking recourse to a functionalist institutional design logic (Rittberger, 2006, p. 1212). According to constructivists, a consensus based on federalist ideas accounts for those elements of the EDC's institutional structure that cannot be accounted for by functional design theory. In the final phase of the negotiations leading to the EDC Treaty, incremental sectoral integration and functional considerations about the institutional design trumped proposals inspired by federalist ideology (ibid.). Yet some concessions were made to the demands of the supporters of a federal institutional design. First, it was acknowledged that the EDC constituted some kind of interim phase on the way to a European federation. Second, it was conceded that the creation of the EDC, with its supranational character, raised the question of democratic legitimacy, which had to be addressed commensurately. As a consequence, a 'democratic 'self-healing' mechanism' sprang into action in order to democratically compensate a loss of national parliamentary influence because of the surrender of sovereignty to supranational institutions (ibid.).

Why did Great Britain stay out?

A history and explanation of the ECSC and EDC treaties would be incomplete without highlighting a final pressing question: why did Britain stay away from both the ECSC and the EDC despite widespread demand on behalf of the founding member states for British participation? As we will show, the attitude of the British political elite was quite nuanced and did not favour outright rejection of European integration. Rather, it was decided to remain closely associated with its continental partners in matters of both coal and steel as well as military cooperation.

In the post-World War II era, maintaining good relations with a united Europe, of which Britain is not part, constituted the third priority in Winston Churchill's three spheres of influence (George, 1990, p. 14) or what Foreign Secretary Anthony Eden called 'three unities' on which British foreign policy rested. British interests primarily focused on the unity and consolidation of the Commonwealth and, second, on the Anglo-American partnership (Ruane, 2000, p. 21; Watt, 1985, p. 86; George, 1990, p. 14). This preference order was underpinned by, first, a sense of distinctiveness from Europe gained during the war as well as, second, by a 'deeply pessimistic view of the condition of the mainland European states' (Gowland, Turner and Wright, 2010, p. 26).

Britain and the ECSC

Not being informed about the Schuman Plan in advance, the British government felt passed over and many within it were suspicious of being booted out (Greenwood, 1992, p. 35). In spite of being ignored and being presented with a *fait accompli*, Britain carefully considered the implications of the Plan. But when the French government set a 24-hour ultimatum for Britain to decide whether to accept the supranational elements of the Schuman Plan and to join negotiations, the British bowed out because the proposal did not contain clear limits to supranationalism (ibid., p. 36). For the British government, to 'talk in terms of principles', such as supranationalism, 'without knowing their actual effect' was impossible (Young, 1993, p. 34) and was 'comparable to signing a blank cheque' (Gowland, Turner and Wright, 2010, p. 30). Parliamentary debates in June 1950 displayed no difference in opinion on this matter between Labour and Conservatives (Greenwood, 1992, p. 39). Even though the door was still open to join the ECSC negotiations, Britain decided to look for ways of association without taking part in the ECSC (ibid., p. 40). After the High Authority's hands were tied by the inclusion of a Council of ministers to placate the Benelux countries, Britain either had the option to wait for a further watering down of supranationalism during the negotiations or it could start to play a more active role (ibid., p. 58). Eden decided in favour of the latter option, proposing to the Cabinet a non-supranational common market in steel with the 'Six': first, because the ECSC was expected to be economically influential; second, 'British steel, being more competitive than coal, could pioneer the economic association' (ibid., p. 58). Moreover, European competition was expected to have positive effects on the development of the British steel industry (Young, 1993, p. 40). This proposal, however, encountered resistance from the British steel industry as well as from the Board of Trade (Greenwood, 1992, p. 58). The Anglo-ECSC Treaty of Association that was finally signed in December 1954 was far less uninspiring than Eden's initial proposal, for the institutional link established to the 'Six', the Council of Association, only formally established what had been consultative practice already before (ibid., p. 58).

From the perspective of realist intergovernmentalism, Franco-German reconciliation suited Britain's geopolitical interests well. The Ministry of Defence, the Foreign Office, and the Treasury all welcomed this aspect of the Schuman Plan (Young, 1993, p. 31; Greenwood, 1992, p. 37). In contrast to French elite and public opinion, Britain considered Germany to be less threatening and instead focused on 'a greater perceived threat further to the east' (Greenwood, 1992, p. 33). Accordingly, Britain's policy supported German recovery and backed its coal and steel production instead of curtailing its economic freedoms by means of the ECSC (ibid., p. 33). At the same time, the Foreign Office suspected the Schuman Plan to create a 'third force federated Europe between the two super-powers' which might endanger the Atlantic alliance and which in turn was not compatible with Britain's focus on the Anglo-American relationship (Gowland, Turner and Wright, 2010, p. 28; Young, 1993, p. 31). The Western alliance system, instead, was judged 'the best way to supervise the recovery of West Germany' (Gowland, Turner and Wright, 2010, p. 31).

Apart from geopolitical considerations, Britain scrutinised the economic implications of the Schuman Plan carefully. Britain's post-war economic growth was quite remarkable. Its coal and steel sectors were 'the largest in Europe' (Young, 1993, p. 33). 'Surrendering control over this asset, therefore, held no obvious appeal' especially because European exports amounted to only five per cent of total steel exports (Greenwood, 1992, p. 34). Trade with the Commonwealth was more important than with continental Europe, making up about 50 per cent of Britain's total imports and exports (ibid., p. 59f.) and in particular about 60 per cent of British steel exports (Gowland, Turner and Wright, 2010, p. 33). The economic ministry therefore feared that membership in the ECSC would be damaging for the British steel industry, not least by prohibiting the special steel export conditions for the Commonwealth (George, 1990, p. 21). The Labour government, being more preoccupied with domestic day-to-day fiscal crisis management (Gowland, Turner and Wright, 2010, p. 29), had no interest in surrendering influence over these two recently nationalised industries (see Young, 1993, p. 33; Gowland, Turner and Wright, 2010, p. 33; George, 1990, p. 20). Opposition to the ECSC on economic grounds was thus also supported by the British steel industry as well as the Board of Trade (Greenwood, 1992, p. 58).

Despite these economic considerations, the supranational elements in the Schuman Plan were Britain's true 'sticking point' (ibid., p. 34) and 'ultimately the formal major obstacle to British membership' (Gowland, Turner and Wright, 2010, p. 28; also Greenwood, 1992, p. 34). Dinan considers British reservations in this regard 'excessive', because the government of the Netherlands, harbouring a similar aversion to supranationalism, was quite successful in watering down supranational provisions (Dinan, 2004, p. 47). This points to the relevance of ideational or identity concerns, which – if not decisive for Britain not joining the ECSC – added to the British opposition based on 'material' considerations.

Britain and the EDC

When Winston Churchill, who had called for the creation of a European army in August 1950 (Ruane, 2000, p. 20), became British prime minister in October 1951, hopes were raised in some Western European circles that British hostility towards European integration would be attenuated (Watt, 1985, p. 81). However, the alliance of national forces envisaged by Churchill was quite different from the EDC and it did not take long until Foreign Secretary Anthony Eden devastated these hopes (ibid., p. 81). The prime minister's and foreign minister's opposition to the EDC was not only backed by their colleagues in the Cabinet, but also by parliamentary and public opinion (Ruane, 2000, p. 21). British policy towards Europe continued to follow an intergovernmental approach by encouraging and assisting further integration without taking part in it (ibid., p. 28). When the US government began to back the EDC, the initiative also became a matter of Anglo-American relations (ibid., p. 25). As a consequence, the British government supported a successful completion of the negotiations of the EDC between the 'Six'. Until August 1954, the British government tried to promote ratification of the EDC Treaty and the implementation of the associated Bonn Conventions.

To assuage French concerns about German rearmament, the so-called Eden Plan proposed to 'mesh organs of the existing Council of Europe with those of the emerging ECSC and EDC' (Greenwood, 1992, p. 57; for details, see Watt, 1985, p. 89). This plan was not well received and instead an Anglo-EDC Treaty was agreed upon in 1952 to provide assurance for France that British forces would be maintained in Western Europe (Ruane, 2000, p. 34). The French government considered these concessions insufficient (Watt, 1985, p. 90) and successive French governments in the 1952 and 1953 decided to postpone ratification because there was no majority in favour of the EDC. Instead, subsequent French governments pressed for further British commitment through the guarantee of keeping a certain number of troops on West German soil (Ruane, 2000, p. 35).

For its part, the US government exercised pressure on France as well as Britain to get the EDC off the ground. At one point, the US administration even issued a threat of an 'agonizing reappraisal' that might lead to military withdrawal from Europe if the EDC failed (ibid., p. 63). This was grist for the mills of French EDC-opposition who deeply disapproved of American coercive diplomacy (ibid., p. 67). Finally the British succumbed to American pressure and on 13 April 1954 formally agreed not only to maintain present fighting capacity, but also offered the French to put a British armoured division under EDC command (ibid., p. 71). This agreement on British association with the EDC included provisions on a permanent British representation in the Commissariat, the participation of a British minister in Council meetings, and the promise not to withdraw British forces from the continent as long as the security of Western Europe and the EDC were in danger. Furthermore, the armed forces on the continent were kept in numbers necessary to defend the NATO area and detailed military provisions were made on the integration of British forces into the EDC (Watt, 1985, p. 98; Ruane, 2000, p. 75). These measures were received favourably by the US government, which declared its willingness to keep armed forces in Western Europe 'in terms that were almost identical to those of Britain' but of course without putting forces under the command of the EDC (Ruane, 2000, p. 75). British diplomacy and the concessions made in 1952 and 1954, however, were not sufficient to avert French rejection of the Treaty (ibid., p. 31).

How can the British policy of assistance and support of the EDC without formally taking part in the EDC be explained? Notwithstanding its foreign policy focus, Britain supported French-German reconciliation, and it was well aware of the importance of close British association with Europe to assuage French concerns that Germany might soon dominate France economically and militarily (Watt, 1985, p. 86). For the British government, the EDC was not only considered a means of tying Germany to the West, Germany's defence contribution would also strengthen NATO's defence capability (Ruane, 2000, p. 24). To skim off the security advantages of a supranational European defence organisation, British participation did not seem necessary, for joining a supranational community did not appear to provide extra benefits. And the benefits of the EDC were trumped by the importance of Britain's relationship with the Commonwealth, which would enable Britain 'to speak with a louder voice in international affairs than could other European states' (George, 1990, p. 15). The special relationship with the US finally also prevented British involvement in Europe, as Britain feared to become to the US 'simply another European power' (Ruane, 2000, p. 23). From a realist intergovernmentalist perspective, one could thus argue that British security concerns pointed in the direction of the EDC; participation, however, was not necessary to reap the gains. Autonomy-seeking behaviour thus dominated over influence-seeking behaviour *vis-à-vis* the continent, pointing away from Europe towards both the United States and the Commonwealth. But it was also this focus on the US and the fear of the US withdrawing their forces from Europe (in the case of a failure of the EDC) that prevented Britain from sitting back and abandoning the EDC to her own fate. The diplomatic efforts and military concessions the British made to support French ratification were mainly to avoid becoming the scapegoat of the US in case the EDC ratification process would not be successful. The explanatory potential of realist intergovernmentalism as compared to a liberal approach might be a matter of the policy sector (defence). There is no conclusive evidence that domestic actors, such as the British armed forces, were decisively influencing the government's stance on the EDC (Watt, 1985, p. 88). From an ideational point of view, the British government's aversion to supranationalism was congruent with the motivation to stay out for 'material' (that is, geopolitical) reasons and hence strengthened the government's stance and resolve not to subscribe to supranational integration.

Summary and the legacy of the ECSC and EDC

The failure of the EDC and the high 'federalist' hopes that were associated with it and the related project of a European Political Community, which was buried with the EDC in August 1954, led political leaders to adopt a more 'pragmatic' approach to European integration in the years to come. With the security threats emanating from the USSR and West Germany being attenuated as a consequence of geopolitical events, and Germany's integration in the West European Union and NATO, political leaders turned to the economy as a field where gains from integration could be more easily reaped, while – at the same time – avoiding 'federalist' discourse. It should take almost half a century for defence policy to re-appear on the agenda of the EU. Against the backdrop of EU member states' inability (and US reluctance) to address security problems and challenges in its immediate neighbourhood, the EU began to define a joint security and defence policy with the ultimate objective to develop its own operational capacities. Far from the aspirations of political leaders in the 1950s, the common security and defence policy remains intergovernmental in its decision-making mode and accords only a very limited consultative role to supranational institutions such as the Commission and European Parliament.

The ECSC Treaty expired in July 2002, 50 years after it entered into force. Its legacy for the politics and theory of European integration is disputed. John Gillingham points at the political importance of the ECSC claiming laconically that the ECSC 'made good only one promise, the most important one: It advanced the process of integration' (Gillingham, 1991, p. 299) against the background of a still war-torn Europe, in which successive French governments sought security reassurances from Germany. Yet, the ECSC also provided an institutional precedent and context, serving as blueprint for future attempts at integration. As far as the substantive mission of the ECSC was concerned, the story is all but a grand success: 'The economic impact of the community was slight. Few of its policies had demonstrable effect; the overall increase in the coal and steel trade during the early years of its operation stemmed from the general growth of the European economy' (ibid., p. 300). Alter and Steinberg (2007) echo the assessment that the political implications of the ECSC – mirrored in the rapprochement between France and Germany – were way more important than its economic effects: 'it is hard to say that the ECSC has left a stamp on the face of the European steel industry that would not exist otherwise' (ibid., p. 103). Instead, the ECSC 'did become a venue in which policies toward steel were discussed and sometimes implemented. But the ECSC remained throughout its entire history a framework of convenience, to be used when there was a coalition of support for collective responses and ignored when the support faded' (ibid., p. 103). Moreover, the expectations that Ernst Haas's (1958) neofunctionalist theory associated with ECSC, that the operation of the ECSC would engender 'spillover' processes were hardly met: not only did the (economic) situations for which the ECSC was created fail to materialise, functional and political 'spillovers' equally failed to ensue. The ECSC neither 'produced a new relationship between public authority and private power, nor [did the ECSC] shift [...] the locus of economic policy [...] from national state to supranational agency' (Gillingham, 1991, p. 300). The supranationalist story for a lack of further integration is quickly told: given that firms 'were quite happy to segment European markets to avoid competition, and European governments were happy to protect and subsidise national production' (Alter and Steinberg, 2007, p. 104), there was no demand for supranational rules from affected transnational (industrial) interests that supranational institutions, such as the High Authority or the Court, could act upon.

Note

1. This section draws on Rittberger (2005, Chapter 3).

3

All Roads Lead to Rome: Background, Content and Legacy of the Treaties on the European Economic and European Atomic Energy Communities

Joaquín Roy

The rebirth of the European integration and the making of the EEC

The rejection by the French National Assembly of the ill-fated European Defence Community (EDC) treaty on 30 August 1954, together with the automatic shelving of the equally problematic European Political Community (EPC) proposal, put an end, at least for that time being, to any form of political and military union of Western Europe on a supranational level. It was a difficult time in Europe, and the international atmosphere was cloudy. The end of the Korean War coincided with the insistence of the Soviets to stick to a policy of *détente*, leading to the suppression of the Hungarian rebellion in 1956. France was facing opposition to its colonial presence in Indochina, as well as in North Africa. But the Suez crisis prompted the French government to distance itself from the United States. The defeat of the EDC and EPC was not going to be the end of the process started by Monnet and Schuman in 1950. It was not long before plans in favour of a European re-launch were taking shape.[1]

The main force this time came from the three Benelux countries. The economic and nuclear energy sectors were seen as the most promising by some, including Jean Monnet, but the six members of the European Coal and Steel Community (ECSC) had not arrived at an agreement regarding the pursuit of sectoral integration or of establishing a general common market based on a customs union. Things then moved very fast, given the need to take advantage of what was seen as a propitious political juncture and international situation. Only 21 months were to pass between June 1955 and March 1957, when the treaties establishing the European Economic Community (EEC) and the European Atomic Energy Community (EAEC, or Euratom) were signed in Rome. This rather brief period, however, was a time of busy activity and the sometimes exhausting quest for a compromise among the six original members of the ECSC. The establishment of the EEC and Euratom marked a decisive step towards the building of a Europe that was still confined to the six original members but allowed scope for expansion and might pave the way for political union. This was a new, even more ambitious 'bold step' of the process of European integration inaugurated by the Schuman Declaration and the foundation of the ECSC.

The Benelux Memorandum

To trace the process from the defeat of the EDC in 1954 to the entry into force of the Treaties of Rome we have to start with the Benelux Memorandum of May 1955 (Grosbois 2009).

The idea of more general economic integration instead of sector integration was spearheaded by Dutch politician Johan Willem Beyen from 1952 in connection with the ad hoc Assembly considering the creation of the EPC. He first presented his ideas of a customs union to the Dutch cabinet in November 1952. The Economics Minister Jelle Zijlstra suggested that a customs union would be insufficient. There should also be removal of barriers on payments and migration to be accompanied with policy harmonisation in economic and social fields. In the end the Dutch proposal to the ad hoc Assembly was for a customs union with a common external tariff, leaving implementation to the institutions of the EPC. A second Dutch memorandum in February 1953 involved automatic steps towards a customs union (Griffiths 2000: 96–101).

None of the five ECSC partners jumped to accept the Beyen Plan in 1953. But after the defeat of the EDC – and thus also EPC – in 1954 Beyen revived his idea. It was clearly in the Dutch interest to get freer trade in Europe and beyond, but the Dutch found progress on these issues in the General Agreement on Tariffs and Trade (GATT) and the Organisation for European Economic Cooperation (OEEC) insufficient.

Beyen tells in his memoirs that the atmosphere was ripe for a 'relance européenne' in the spring of 1955. He contacted his Benelux colleagues Paul-Henri Spaak and Joseph Bech. The three had worked together in London when Benelux was formed at the end of World War II. All had practical experience with international cooperation. And they agreed that a plan was needed. They were aware of support for energy integration, but felt that more general integration was needed (Beyen 1968: 237–8). Spaak actually favoured atomic energy integration at the outset but under pressure from Beyen he agreed to include both in what became the Benelux Memorandum (Dinan 2004: 66).

The memorandum was published on 18 May 1955. In the preamble the three governments stated:

> The Governments of Belgium, Luxembourg and the Netherlands believe that the time has come to take a new step on the road towards European integration.
>
> They are of the opinion that such integration must be achieved in the first place in the economic field.
>
> They consider that the establishment of a united Europe must be sought through the development of common institutions, the progressive fusion of national economies, the creation of a large common market and the progressive harmonization of social policies.
>
> Such a policy seems to them indispensable for maintaining Europe's position in the world, for restoring its influence and prestige and for securing a constantly rising standard of living for its people.
>
> (Text in Patijn 1979: 93)

Later on in the memorandum the importance of 'transport, energy and the peaceful uses of atomic energy' are singled out. There is a call for 'a joint study of development plans'.

Concerning general economic integration the goal was an economic community. It should be based on 'a common market to be achieved by progressive elimination of quantitative restrictions and customs duties'. The establishment of such economic community 'presupposes, to the mind of the Benelux States, the creation of a common authority with such powers of its own as are necessary for the achievement of the objectives decided on'. There should be harmonisation of financial, economic and social policies, a system of safeguard clauses and a so-called re-adaptation fund should be created (ibid.: 97).

The Messina Conference

The next step was the conference held in the Italian city of Messina, Sicily, on 1–3 June 1955. It was composed of the ministers of foreign affairs and other delegates from the member states of the ECSC. The participating foreign ministers were a truly outstanding group: Johan Willem Beyen (the Netherlands), Gaetano Martino (Italy), Joseph Bech (Luxembourg), Antoine Pinay (France), Walter Hallstein (Germany), and Paul-Henri Spaak (Belgium). The meeting was chaired by Joseph Bech (Procès-verbal de la conference de Messine 1955).

The meeting was first of all called to elect a successor to Jean Monnet as president of the ECSC High Authority. On the first day the ministers selected former French Prime Minister René Meyer for that job, and then turned to a discussion of further economic integration. The Benelux Memorandum, released a couple of weeks earlier became the focus of the discussion. The governments of Germany and Italy had also produced memorandums, which were distributed at the beginning of the meeting (Gerbet 1987: 81–2). France was the country having the greatest difficulties with the idea of a general common market. There were very few advocates of market liberalisation in France at the time. French business leaders were still very protectionist. The other countries were more open to the idea of a common market and not very supportive of atomic energy integrations. Hallstein representing Germany was personally in favour of the customs union, but back home Economics Minister Ludwig Erhard favoured a multilateral approach through GATT. Chancellor Adenauer was in favour of the common market but was careful not to upset Erhard for political reasons (Dinan 2004).

In the end the meeting agreed on a declaration which included much of the text from the Benelux Memorandum. In his memoirs Spaak singles out the following passage as particularly important: 'The six governments agree that the establishment of a European common market free from tariff barriers and all quantitative restrictions on trade must be the aim in the economic sphere. They consider that this objective should be attained in stages' (Spaak 1971: 228–9). Spaak then goes on to give credit to Beyen: 'This passage was a triumph for Beyen. His colleagues had agreed that this should be our goal, but it was he who had put forward the idea' (ibid. 229).

The main decision at Messina was to establish a committee to study the issues:

1. Conferences will be called to work out treaties or other arrangements concerning the questions under consideration.
2. The preparatory work will be the responsibility of a Committee of Governmental representatives, assisted by experts, under the chairmanship of a political personality responsible for co-ordinating the work in different fields.
3. The Committee will invite the High Authority of the ECSC and the Secretariats of OEEC, the Council of Europe and the European Conference of Ministers of Transport, to give the necessary assistance.

4. The report of the Committee, covering the whole field, will be submitted to the Ministers of Foreign Affairs by not later than the 1 October 1955.

(Text in Patijn 1970: 107)

Spaak was eventually asked to chair the preparatory committee established in Messina (Küsters 1987: 84).

The preparatory committee and the Spaak Report

The committee held its constituent meeting on 9 July 1955 in Brussels (Dumoulin 1989; Küsters 1989; Snoy 1989). The team of delegates was quite impressive: Carl Friedrich Ophüls, minister plenipotentiary of the Federal Republic of Germany; Baron Jean-Charles Snoy et d'Oppuers, secretary-general of the Ministry for Economic Affairs of Belgium; Félix Gaillard, member of the National Assembly and former government minister of France; Lodovico Benvenuti, former under-secretary of state at the Ministry for Foreign Affairs of Italy; Lambert Schaus, Luxembourg's ambassador in Brussels; and Professor Gerard Marius Verrijn Stuart of the University of Amsterdam of the Netherlands.

The representatives of the ECSC in the Spaak Committee were Dirk Spierenburg, Dutch member of the High Authority and two French officials Pierre Uri and Paul Delouvrier. Uri had already played an important role in connection with the negotiation of the Paris Treaty establishing the ECSC, working closely with Jean Monnet. Other 'experts' who were to play important roles at this stage included Hans von der Groeben from the German Ministry of Finance and the Belgian diplomat Albert Hupperts. Louis Armand (France) played an important role in drafting the section concerning atomic energy (Gerbet 2007: 142–3).

A steering committee, chaired by Spaak, was formed to coordinate the work of a number of specialised sub-committees. They were dedicated, on the one hand, to the central issue of the common market (a central piece of the project), and, on the other hand, to sectoral fields. The most important were investments and social problems; energy sources; nuclear energy; and transport and public works. In the course of the meetings proposals to develop the decisions agreed upon at the Messina conference were examined. Institutional matters were intentionally left for later discussions, while efforts and attention were concentrated on a primary objective, considering the notion of a 'common market' as a hypothesis.

The United Kingdom had already received special treatment in the course of previous experiments of European integration through the association agreement with the ECSC. The country was invited to participate in the discussions of the project of the EEC as a special observer, though it was clear that the UK was not really interested in the ambitious formation of a customs union. London, pressed by business sectors, wanted to protect its industries and to maintain its preferential relations with the Commonwealth partners. The British had already possessed the atomic bomb since 1952 and had an advanced nuclear programme in cooperation with the United States and Canada. Membership in a new organisation (Euratom) dedicated to nuclear energy was seen as a disadvantage.

Moreover, the prospect of the common market was then interpreted as a sure path towards some sort of federation, something beyond the British concept of international cooperation. It was bluntly seen as a violation of national sovereignty. In any event, when the EEC was set in motion, Britain prioritised links with the OEEC and prepared the way for the foundation of the European Free Trade Area (EFTA), an organisation designed in principle to unite the efforts of the western European countries and in turn compete with the EC (Young 1993; Camps 1964).

In contrast to this negative British attitude, Franco-German relations became even more important in the setting of the new stage of European integration. The sticky issue of the status of the Saarland was treated very effectively through an agreement made in October 1954. In October 1956, the French Prime Minister, Guy Mollet, and the German chancellor, Konrad Adenauer, met in Paris to complete an overall settlement, on the way to being full partners in the projects of the common market and Euratom. The Saar territory was finally restored to Germany in January 1957.

Negotiations and further discussion in the Spaak Committee continued in Noordwijk, near The Hague, on 6 September 1955, and then in the Brussels conference of 11–12 February 1956. Spaak, backed by an array of experts' reports, now pushed for a customs union. On the complex institutional dimensions, Spaak explained that their important role would be highly dependent on how flexible the treaty itself was. It was decided that basically four institutions were needed: a council of ministers, a body resembling the High Authority, a parliamentary Assembly and a court of justice. Spaak considered at the time that the Council should take its decisions unanimously wherever possible. However, it was also felt that a less rigorous procedure for decision-making should be established in the future, with an option for a qualified majority once the common market was in place and its policies were well in the realm of community control. The supranational nature of the community was to become pivotal to avoid the threat of a veto.

On 20 April 1956 the heads of delegation of the six member states of the ECSC approved the *Report by the Heads of Delegations to the Foreign Ministers*, which became known as the Spaak Report. After reaffirming that the common market was the central issue to be resolved, other sensitive topics were also addressed: agriculture, transport and conventional energy.

The Spaak Report was a major achievement. In 135 pages it outlined first how to create a Common Market and in a second part how to create the Atomic Energy Community (EURATOM). (Comité Intergouvernemental creé par la Conférence de Messine 1956.)

In the foreword, there was the clear notion that Western Europe was in an inferior status, competing with the United States. The separate European markets could not be effective. The remedy for this was to address the issue of bringing nuclear research under one authority and to set a general common market. Consequently, the report was divided into three parts: the common market, Euratom, and the third dedicated to urgent areas.

The concept of the common market implied the creation of a large area with a common economic policy, fostering production, continuous expansion, increased stability, an accelerated increase in the standard of living, and the development of harmonious relations between the member states. The merging of the separate markets into a common one would serve to eliminate unnecessary waste of resources and also open up new outlets. The market should be based on a customs union and pursued by means of a three-pronged strategy: elimination of all protective measures obstructing trade; rules and procedures designed to cancel out the effects of state intervention or of monopoly situations; and new resources for the purpose of boosting underdeveloped regions and taking advantage of unused labour forces. All this should be accomplished through a period of transition divided in stages.

Regarding the institutions, before getting into the details, basic principles were to preside. First, issues of general policy would be kept under the domain of the governments. Second, the report raised the need for the institutions to be able to take decisions on certain matters by a method other than unanimity. Finally, parliamentary control was considered. Following the precedent implemented in the mechanisms of the ECSC structure, the report considered four fundamental separate institutions: a Council of Ministers, a European Commission, a Court, which would be the existing ECSC Court, and a parliamentary

Assembly, which would be the existing Common Assembly of the ECSC. Qualified majority votes, based on a weighting of votes, was foreseen in the Council (ibid. 25–6).

On the issue of the customs union, the report recommended the gradual elimination of internal customs duties. Moreover, the elimination of customs duties in the common market would then be accompanied by the establishment of a single tariff for imports from non-member countries. The establishment of this common tariff should be based on the simplest possible calculation methods. Therefore, structural differences between producer countries and importing countries should be considered. Quotas should be slashed.

Regarding services, the report contemplated that the economic output of the member countries included not only goods but also other different areas: transport, insurance, banking and financial activities, distribution, hotels, personal care, the liberal professions and public administration. As a principle, the liberalisation of services should facilitate the implementation of the common market. In tune with the main ever present priorities in the history of the EU, any discrimination based on residence or nationality should also disappear. A common system to accept equivalents in university degrees awarded in different countries should also be set in place.

On the socially sensitive issue of agriculture, the report stated that the establishment of a general common market was not possible without the inclusion of agriculture, a prerequisite for balanced trade. However, special problems existed in the agricultural field and, consequently, the common management of markets would be beneficial. The principles of the future Common Agricultural Policy were set in place.

Regarding competition, it was reaffirmed that the abolition of discrimination based on nationality or residency was considered necessary. Preventing future problems, it was also thought that state aid and monopoly practices should not undermine the basic aims of the common market. On the specific field of transport, considered basic for the functioning of a common market, the report recommended a change in the prevailing charging system and in the conditions governing international transport, as well as the formulation of a common general transport policy.

Two financial instruments were designed to guarantee that the common market developed in a balanced way. For this purpose, an investment fund was to be established to help in developing national budgets; similarly, an adaptation fund was for the conversion of industrial plants and the retraining of workers.

Central to the good functioning of the free movement of labour and capital, it was felt that a system of gradual liberalisation should be based on progressive annual increases, at an agreed rate, in the number of nationals of the other member countries that would be permitted to take up employment. The free movement of capital should be based on the liberalisation of capital transfers. It also required recognition of the right of nationals of member countries to acquire capital from any of the members, and to transfer and use it within the common market. Of the areas needing urgent action, the report emphasised energy, air transport, postal services and telecommunications.

Spaak later paid special tribute to Pierre Uri in his memoirs: 'The "Spaak Report", an important document, is largely the fruit of his efforts. Uri was one of the principal architects of the Treaty of Rome' (Spaak 1971: 231). Uri is not shy about his contributions in his memoires. He went to the south of France together with Von der Groeben and Hupperts to have peace while drafting the text (Uri 1991: 122).

Jean Monnet

Jean Monnet had also been working, in a different manner, behind the scenes. After resigning in November 1954 as chair of the High Authority of the ECSC, Monnet was once more free to act and also to express opinions. He had learned a great deal from the sorry experience of the disaster of the Defence Community. He needed to gather the necessary political forces to promote another step of European reconstruction and integration. At that time, he still believed in the principle of sectoral integration, as in the ECSC, with coal and steel as an axis. He thought that the next move should be to deal with the sectors of transport and energy (gas, electricity). Monnet was even more eager to concentrate on nuclear power, reading the atmosphere and urgency of the times very well. He felt that Europe would lose in a confrontation between the Soviet Union and the United States over nuclear research and development for civilian uses. He was also for cooperation with the United Kingdom.

Personally, Monnet was not really in favour of a horizontal and comprehensive common market, as in fact was later founded and developed, but he took note of the fact that the European partners were aiming for this. He then decided to lobby for a combination of the two complementary paths of integration, the functional sectoral and the wider, horizontal common market approach. In his view, they should work in synergy. Monnet pressed Spaak to work with his partners on that complementary path. It appeared that Monnet had found a new Robert Schuman to act as the political agent for his own idea. Spaak, in turn, rescued Jean Monnet to inspire him in the right and decisive direction (Monnet 1978; Duchene 1994; Featherstone 1994).

Monnet then concentrated his energies in the foundation of the Action Committee for the United States of Europe (ACUSE), an early form of a lobby group that set the trends in the preliminary stages of unifying Europe. Through this entity he managed to obtain the cooperation of different political parties, trade unions and political figures. One of the first 'manifestos' was a call for the governments to form an organisation with supranational profile dedicated to atomic energy, following the model of the ECSC. He also maintained close contact with experts preparing the actual foundational treaties of the EEC and Euratom.

The Venice meeting

On 29–30 May 1956, the ministers for foreign affairs of the six member states of the ECSC convened on the island of San Giorgio Maggiore in the city of Venice to consider the report. The meeting was chaired by French Foreign Minister Christian Pineau and France was also represented by Maurice Faure. The other representatives were Hallstein (Germany), Gaetano Martino (Italy), Spaak (Belgium), Beyen (Netherlands) and Bech (Luxembourg) (Communiqué de Press 1956).

There was an initial agreement to establish a general common market and a treaty creating Euratom. The French government suggested that the transition from the first to the second stage should be subject to the results of the first four-year period. It was also understood that the reduction of customs duties, the harmonisation of social security, equal pay for men and women, and paid holidays should be implemented at the same time.

Overall the main achievement of the Venice meeting was to agreeto adopt the Spaak Report as basis for future negotiations. Jean-Charles Snoy, who worked closely with Spaak, called it a 'miraculous conference' (Spaak 1971: 240).

The final agreement included a number of concrete items. First, there should be a single Intergovernmental Conference (composed of a single representative per nation). This event should take place in Brussels beginning on 26 June, in a process to be ended with the approval of the common market and Euratom treaties. Spaak would be appointed chairman of the conference. It was also decided that the sectors requiring urgent action (energy, aviation, postal services and telecommunications) should be considered alongside the discussion of the common market. Finally, although technical details were avoided at that time, provisions on the arrangements for accession or association by third countries would be simultaneously considered.

Arguably the two most difficult issues at this stage were the association of overseas territories (a French request) and the question of military usage of atomic energy, a possibility that France wanted to keep open, but Germany especially opposed.

The Intergovernmental Conference (Spaak II)

The Intergovernmental Conference (IGC) met for the first time in Brussels on 26 June 1956. This was the forum which would turn ideas into a treaty. The national delegations were headed by Lodovico Benvenuti (Italy), Count Jean Charles Snoy et d'Oppuers (Belgium), Karl Fridrich Ophüls (Germany), Maurice Faure (France), Johan Linthorst Homan (Netherlands) and Lambert Schaus (Luxembourg). Under the presidency of Spaak, two groups were formed to deal with the common market and Euratom. They were respectively chaired by Hans von der Groeben and Pierre Guillaumat (France).A drafting group was also organised to give form to the treaties, chaired by Roberto Ducci (Italy). There were some meetings in July followed by summer vacation in August. The work then resumed in the fall and continued through the winter of 1957 (La Conférence Intergouvernementale pour le Marché commun et l'Euratom 1956–57).

The country creating the most difficulties during the IGC was France. This was partly because French industry was used to protection, but also due to the difficult political situation during the 4th Republic where governments changed regularly. On the left the French Communists were against European integration, so were the Gaullists on the right. For the conclusion of the IGC and the eventual ratification of the treaties negotiated by the IGC the French parliamentary elections in January 1956 and the formation of the Socialist Guy Mollet government on 31 January was to be of decisive importance. After the shocking rejection of the EDC in 1954 the other governments paid much attention to the political situation in France. The Mollet government was in a stronger parliamentary position than the previous Edgar Faure (Radical) government (Willis 1968: 242–5).

Guy Mollet won a crucial vote in the National Assembly getting a mandate for the Euratom negotiations in July 1956 with support mainly from the Socialists and Popular Republicans. Given the relative lack of domestic support for the Common Market France presented six conditions to the IGC on 19 September 1956:

1. The passage from the first to the second stage should only take place after the objectives of the first stage had been attained. The Council of Ministers would make that decision by unanimity.

2. Social charges should be harmonised. At the end of the transition period the total social charges should be equivalent in the member states.
3. Given the differences in French and foreign prices France insisted on maintaining import duties and export subsidies until price disparities disappeared and France got rid of its negative balance of payments.
4. A safeguard clause should be included in the treaty allowing a state with balance of payments problems to introduce appropriate measures.
5. The French delegation would present proposal for inclusion of overseas territories at a future meeting.
6. Concerning the difficult situation in Algeria, which was a drain on French resources, France might have to ask for a postponement of the entry into force of the treaty.

(Note présentée par la delegation française 1956)

Apart from Algeria other geopolitical events should be mentioned at this point. In the fall of 1956 the Suez Crisis, where Israel, the UK and France invaded Egypt after President Gamal Abdul Nasser had nationalised the Suez company, was to influence thinking in France. The fact that the US turned against the invasion of Egypt and the action had to be aborted was a lesson in power politics for France. Arguably it bolstered Guy Mollet's argument in favour of the Common Market (Dinan 2004: 71). At about the same time the Soviet intervention in Hungary confirmed the East–West division of Europe.

The two most difficult issues in the IGC were the question of overseas territories and social harmonisation. The French found support from Belgium on overseas territories but Germany was originally strongly against. None of the Five cared much about the French social policy model, where high social insurance costs were covered by business. Some of the issues relating to the French demands were solved at a private meeting between Adenauer and Mollet on 6 November 1956, including equal pay for men and women and provisional maintenance of French import taxes and export subsidies. This left agriculture and overseas territories still to be solved. The foreign ministers were able to agree on agricultural policy in January and February 1957 (Willis 1968: 248–9).

One way to look at the IGC is to see it as a two-level game. Member of the French delegation Robert Marjolin talked about the 'Battle of Paris' and said:

[I]t would be necessary to do battle on all fronts, in Brussels against our partners, who found it difficult to agree to certain of France's demands, in Paris against officialdom, which was almost unanimously opposed to the idea of the Common Market, and also against a number of industrial and agricultural lobbies that wanted special advantages, guarantees or additional protection.

(Marjolin 1989: 285)

Mollet and his foreign minister Christian Pineau were members of a small group of 'Europeans' in Paris. Marjolin mentions a meeting on 24 April 2956 where he presented the Spaak Report to heads of departments. All except one were against! (ibid.).

According to Marjolin the Suez debacle had a decisive influence on events. Afterwards Mollet wanted to erase the humiliation that France had suffered by concluding a European treaty quickly. At a meeting of the cabinet, where a majority of ministers opposed the continuation of the negotiations in Brussels Mollet ruled in favour of Pineau, Faure and Marjolin, who wanted to continue: 'We are therefore agreed to ask our negotiators to continue the discussions and bring them to a successful outcome as rapidly as possible' (Marjolin 1989: 297).

The job of the negotiators in Brussels was to find language that was satisfactory to both France and the Five. In the end they succeeded, sometimes with the help of Mollet and Adenauer, as mentioned in connection with social policy. The final problems were solved at a meeting of Heads of Government in Paris on 18 and 19 February 1957. Adenauer accepted that Germany would contribute as much as France to the development of French overseas territories. This had Spaak write in his memoirs: 'Once again it was Adenauer who showed himself to be a true statesman' (Spaak 1971: 248).

In Rome on 15 March 1957, the new treaties were signed.[2] The ceremony took place in the Capitoline Palace, built on the Campidoglio hill, overlooking the ancient Roman forum, with the Coliseum visible in the distance. Representing their respective states, the following personalities were signers: Paul-Henri Spaak (Minister of Foreign Affairs of Belgium), Konrad Adenauer (Federal Chancellor of Germany), Christian Pineau (Minister of Foreign Affairs of France), Antonio Segni (President of the Council of Ministers of Italy), Joseph Bech (Prime Minister of Luxemburg), and Joseph Luns (Minister of Foreign Affairs of the Netherlands) (Whitlow 1957–8; Lumb 1963).

Content of the EEC Treaty

In the preamble we read that the states forming the European Economic Community were 'DETERMINED to establish the foundations of an ever closer union among the European peoples.' Later in the history of European integration the 'ever closer union' terminology was to become controversial.

Article 3 outlined the objectives (see Box 3.1). Basically the EEC was about four freedoms: free movement of goods, services, capital and

Box 3.1 Objectives

Article 3 For the purposes set out in the preceding Article, the activities of the Community shall include, under the conditions and with the timing provided for in this Treaty:

(a) the elimination, as between Member States, of customs duties and of quantitative restrictions in regard to the importation and exportation of goods, as well as of all other measures with equivalent effect;

(b) the establishment of a common customs tariff and a common commercial policy towards third countries;

(c) the abolition, as between Member States, of the obstacles to the free movement of persons, services and capital;

(d) the inauguration of a common agricultural policy;

(e) the inauguration of a common transport policy;

(f) the establishment of a system ensuring that competition shall not be distorted in the Common Market;

(g) the application of procedures which shall make it possible to co-ordinate the economic policies of Member States and to remedy disequilibria in their balances of payments;

(h) the approximation of their respective municipal law to the extent necessary for the functioning of the Common Market;

(i) the creation of a European Social Fund in order to improve the possibilities of employment for workers and to contribute to the raising of their standard of living;

(j) the establishment of a European Investment Bank intended to facilitate the economic expansion of the Community through the creation of new resources; and

(k) the association of overseas countries and territories with the Community with a view to increasing trade and to pursuing jointly their effort towards economic and social development.

people. Four specific common policies were mentioned in the treaty: common commercial policy, common agricultural policy, common transport policy and competition policy. There would be co-ordination of economic policies and approximation of domestic policies 'to the extent necessary for the functioning of the Common Market'. The treaty further foresaw the creation of a European Social Fund and a European Investment Bank, as well as association of overseas countries and territories.

The treaty is what French lawyers have termed a *traité cadre* – a framework treaty. In subsequent articles the degree of detail varies. It is relatively specific on free movement of goods, including the elimination of duties between member states, establishment of a common customs tariff and the elimination of quantitative restrictions between member states.

The treaty is less specific on the remaining three freedoms, free movement of persons, services and capital. This section of the treaty has chapters on workers, the right of establishment, services and capital.

The section on agriculture included the listing of objectives:

(a) to increase agricultural productivity by developing technical progress and by ensuring the rational development of agricultural production and the optimum utilisation of the factors of production, particularly labour;
(b) to ensure thereby a fair standard of living for the agricultural population, particularly by the increasing of the individual earnings of persons engaged in agriculture;
(c) to stabilise markets;
(d) to guarantee regular supplies; and
(e) to ensure reasonable prices in supplies to consumers.

A common price policy was foreseen, but detail still had to be worked out in the first years after the entry into force of the treaty.

The section on competition policy was rather specific, including rules applying to enterprises, dumping practices and aids grated by states. The treaty outlawed 'any agreements between undertakings, decisions by associations of undertakings and any concerted practices which may affect trade between the Member States and which have as their object or effect of prevention, restriction or distortion of competition within the Common Market'. Further, 'To the extent to which trade between any Member States may be affected thereby, action by one or more enterprises to take improper advantage of a dominant position within the Common Market or within a substantial part of it shall be deemed to be incompatible with the Common Market and shall hereby be prohibited.' Also state aid was in principle outlawed: 'Except where otherwise provided for in this Treaty, any aid, granted by a Member State or granted by means of State resources, in any manner whatsoever, which distorts or threatens to distort competition by favouring certain enterprises or certain productions shall, to the extent to which it adversely affects trade between Member States, be deemed to be incompatible with the Common Market.' But the treaty then did list some state aid considered compatible with the Common Market.

The treaty assigned important roles to the Commission and European Court of Justice (ECJ) in enforcing competition policy.

Concerning approximation of laws article 100 stipulated: 'The Council, acting by means of a unanimous vote on a proposal of the Commission, shall issue directives for the approximation of such legislative and administrative provisions of the Member States as have a direct incidence on the establishment or functioning of the Common Market.'

The unanimity rule subsequently turned out to be a problem. Different national legislation would often constitute non-tariff barriers (NTBs) to trade, but getting unanimous agreement on common European standards could be difficult. A central aspects of the Single European Act (SEA) introduced in the mid 1980s was to introduce qualified majority voting (QMV) for approximation of laws.

The sections in the treaty on co-ordination of macroeconomic policies were kept in rather general language. The social policy provisions were also relatively weak: 'Member States hereby agree upon the necessity to promote improvement of the living and working conditions of labour so as to permit the equalisation of such conditions in an upward direction.'

The section on commercial policy was the strongest, making it an exclusive competence of the EEC, including a strong role of initiative for the Commission and QMV in the Council.

The section on association of overseas countries and territories included the following:

1. Member States shall, in their commercial exchanges with the countries and territories, apply the same rules which they apply among themselves pursuant to this Treaty.
2. Each country or territory shall apply to its commercial exchanges with Member States and with the other countries and territories the

same rules which it applies in respect of the European State with which it has special relations.

3. Member States shall contribute to the investments required by the progressive development of these countries and territories.

So basically the 'non-European countries and territories which have special relations with Belgium, France, Italy and the Netherlands' would get free access to the Common Market but could protect their own production as long as they did not discriminate among the EEC member states, and all member states committed themselves to aid these countries financially.

The treaty established four main common institutions. The Assembly would basically be a consultative body. It was to be composed by delegates from national parliaments, with the bigger states getting more seats than the smaller states (see Box 3.2).

The Council was the body where government ministers would meet. This was the legislative body. And it included weighted voting for some decisions (Box 3.3).

Box 3.2   The Assembly

Article 137 The Assembly, which shall be composed of representatives of the peoples of the States united within the Community, shall exercise the powers of deliberation and of control which are conferred upon it by this Treaty.

Article 138   1. The Assembly shall be composed of delegates whom the Parliaments shall be called upon to appoint from among their members in accordance with the procedure laid down by each Member State.

2. The number of these delegates shall be fixed as follows:

Belgium 14
Germany 36
France 36
Italy 36
Luxembourg 6
Netherlands 14

Box 3.3   The Council

Article 146 The Council shall be composed of representatives of the Member States. Each Government shall delegate to it one of its members.

The office of President shall be exercised for a term of six months by each member of the Council in rotation according to the alphabetical order of the Member States.

....

Article 148   1. Except where otherwise provided for in this Treaty, the conclusions of the Council shall be reached by a majority vote of its members.

2. Where conclusions of the Council require a qualified majority, the votes of its members shall be weighted as follows:

Belgium 2
Germany 4
France 4
Italy 4
Luxembourg 1
Netherlands 2

Majorities shall be required for the adoption of any conclusions as follows:

- twelve votes in cases where this Treaty requires a previous proposal of the Commission, or
- twelve votes including a favourable vote by at least four members in all other cases.

The Commission was the independent executive, which would have an exclusive right of initiative in most legislative areas (Box 3.4).

The ECJ was given strong independent powers. It would have seven judges assisted by two advocates-general. The court was to have jurisdiction in three main areas: Failure to comply, known as 'infringements proceedings', legality of acts, knows as 'judicial review', and importantly, so-called preliminary rulings, whereby the Court assists national courts in interpreting Community law (Box 3.5).

Box 3.4   The Commission

Article 155 With a view to ensuring the functioning and development of the Common Market, the Commission shall:

- ensure the application of the provisions of this Treaty and of the provisions enacted by the institutions of the Community in pursuance thereof;
- formulate recommendations or opinions in matters which are the subject of this Treaty, where the latter expressly so provides or where the Commission considers it necessary;
- under the conditions laid down in this Treaty dispose of a power of decision of its own and participate in the preparation of acts of the Council and of the Assembly; and
- exercise the competence conferred on it by the Council for the implementation of the rules laid down by the latter.

Article 157   1. The Commission shall be composed of nine members chosen for their general competence and of indisputable independence.

The number of members of the Commission may be amended by a unanimous vote of the Council.

Only nationals of Member States may be members of the Commission.

The Commission may not include more than two members having the nationality of the same State.

2. The members of the Commission shall perform their duties in the general interest of the Community with complete independence.

In the performance of their duties, they shall not seek or accept instructions from any Government or other body. They shall refrain from any action incompatible with the character of their duties. Each Member State undertakes to respect this character and not to seek to influence the members of the Commission in the performance of their duties.

Article 158 The members of the Commission shall be appointed by the Governments of Member States acting in common agreement.

Their term of office shall be for a period of four years. It shall be renewable.

Box 3.5 The Court of Justice

Article 164 The Court of Justice shall ensure observance of law and justice in the interpretation and application of this Treaty.

Article 165 The Court of Justice shall be composed of seven judges.

Article 166 The Court of Justice shall be assisted by two advocates-general.

The duty of the advocate-general shall be to present publicly, with complete impartiality and independence, reasoned conclusions on cases submitted to the Court of Justice, with a view to assisting the latter in the performance of its duties ....

Article 171 If the Court of Justice finds that a Member State has failed to fulfill any of its obligations under this Treaty, such State shall take the measures required for the implementation of the judgment of the Court.

Article 173 The Court of Justice shall review the lawfulness of acts other than recommendations or opinions of the Council and the Commission. For this purpose, it shall be competent to give judgment on appeals by a Member State, the Council or the Commission on grounds of incompetence, of errors of substantial form, of infringement of this Treaty or of any legal provision relating to its application, or of abuse of power.

Article 177 The Court of Justice shall be competent to make a preliminary decision concerning:

(a) the interpretation of this Treaty;
(b) the validity and interpretation of acts of the institutions of the Community; and
(c) the interpretation of the statutes of any bodies set up by an act of the Council, where such statutes so provide.

Where any such question is raised before a court or tribunal of one of the Member States, such court or tribunal may, if it considers that its judgment depends on a preliminary decision on this question, request the Court of Justice to give a ruling thereon.

It was decided in a separate agreement that the Assembly – later European Parliament – and the ECJ would be common institutions for the three Communities, the EEC, Euratom and the ECSC.

But the three Communities would have separate Councils (of Ministers) and executives, the High Authority in the case of the ECSC and Commissions for the EEC and Euratom. The very first reform of the three founding treaties, the Merger treaty in the mid 1960s would create a single executive, the Commission and a single Council for the three Communities.

The European Atomic Energy Community (Euratom)

The Euratom treaty was designed to pool knowledge, infrastructure and funding of nuclear energy (Efron and Nanes 1957; Blumgart 1956). It has as its mission to ensure the security of atomic energy supply and to provide the efficiency of a monitoring system. Following the model of the ECSC, Euratom was also the twin answer to the failure produced by the rejection of the European Defense Community (EDC) in 1954. As outlined above, with the evolution of the EEC, Euratom was designed through a process that began at the Messina conference of June 1955. Its objective was to lessen the damage presented by a shortage of 'conventional' energy in the 1950s. The original members considered nuclear energy as a means of achieving energy independence. Tackling this task individually was seen as a mission impossible. Joint research and production was accompanied by guarantees of high safety standards, keeping in mind civilian use and avoiding at all costs the spill-over to military use.

The preamble was direct and precise. It recognised that 'nuclear energy represents an essential resource for the development and invigoration of industry and will permit the advancement of the cause of peace'. Therefore, Europe needed 'to create the conditions necessary for the development of a powerful nuclear industry which will provide extensive energy resources, lead to the modernization of technical processes and contribute, through its many other applications, to the prosperity of their peoples'. To this end, it needed to find 'conditions of safety necessary to eliminate hazards to the life and health of the public'. Unable to act in isolation, the new entity would seek to 'associate other countries with their work and to cooperate with international organizations concerned with the peaceful development of atomic energy'.

The specific tasks of Euratom were: to promote research and ensure the dissemination of technical information; to establish uniform safety standards to protect the health of workers and of the general public, and ensure that these standards are applied; to facilitate investment and ensure the establishment of the basic installations necessary for the development of nuclear energy in the EU; to ensure that all users in the EU receive a regular and equitable supply of ores and nuclear fuels. The treaty banned practices designed to secure a privileged position for certain users; and established an agency with a right of option on ores, source materials and special fissile materials, as well as having an exclusive right to conclude contracts relating to the supply of ores, source materials and special fissile materials coming from inside the community or from outside.

The essence of the Euratom remains fully in force. It has retained a separate legal personality while sharing the same institutions. In March of 2007, the Commission reviewed the status of the Euratom treaty articles. The result of this examination was positive regarding research, health protection and peaceful use of nuclear material. The current energy crisis of Europe has turned the continent's attention towards this field, with due consideration to the consequences of climate change. However, the treaty and its institutions lost their flair and urgency with the years becoming a sort of clearinghouse for information exchange.

Analysis and legacy

The experience of the negotiation and later implementation of the Treaties of Rome offers several lessons and points for reflection (Roy 2008). First of all, the decision to put together an effective and ambitious organisation implied a continuous process through progressive stages of integration. In the mind of its framers, the EEC was not going to stop its functions with a mere customs union. It was not designed to be a simple reinforcement of a free-trade area. In fact, insiders of the EU process have insisted for decades in correcting a wrong perception that the EU has proceeded from an initial step of a free trade area towards economic and political union. The EU was never a 'free trade area'. In essence, it was at birth already a common market.

In sum, the EEC was based on the same revolutionary concepts as the foundation of the European Coal and Steel Community. The new entity showed that it was possible to evolve from a structure that was placed around a portion of the economy or social life into a collective basket comprising many and potentially all realms of human activity within the confines of the competences of state sovereignty. The 'conversion' from the ECSC to the EEC proved that a change from a vertical (sectoral) to a horizontal experiment of regional integration (a common market and beyond) was highly challenging and problematic, but feasible, according to the historical evidence.

The European Economic Community was early on simply known as the 'common market'. These two words were popularly given to an entire territory. Outsiders of the confines of the geographical boundaries of the EEC, and even today within the EU, talked about 'going to work in the Common Market.' The model was – since very early in its life – copied and imitated, in theory and in practice, on paper and in real life. But the clones were not as authentic as the original.[3] In fact, they have been simple paper copies (African Union), partial failures (MERCOSUR, Andean Community), limited in scope to free trade areas (NAFTA), or with a certain degree of common tariffs (Central America). None has aimed towards the path of economic or political union.

The substantial body of theoretical literature, populated by notable debates, has contributed greatly to the clarification of the nature of the process towards the current European Union. One common understanding has to be admitted: there is no clear consensus as to which theory and approach best explains the road to Rome, its aftermath and legacy. As Laursen says in the introduction to this volume, there is a need 'to combine different theories at the different levels to fully account for reforms'. An attempt to summarise some of the approaches will help to construct, if not a scientific scholarly agreement, at least an understanding of the complexity of the beast created by the Treaty of Rome.

As a preface to this brief review, it would be advisable to pay attention, as Desmon Dinan once did in a pioneer fashion, to the preambles of both the ECSC and EEC. Preambles are usually discarded as unsubstantial verbosity without impact. However, a close reading will reveal that the introduction to the Euroatom treaty 'includes two key words in the lexicon of European integration: peace and prosperity'. The prelude to the EEC treaty refers by implication to peace and prosperity, but that the EEC is a means 'to a greater end: an ever closer union among the peoples of Europe'. Dinan stresses that the preambles 'stood in marked contrast to the utilitarian nature of the treaties themselves' (Dinan 2004: 76).

The first stage of this brief exploration should also pay attention to the lasting impact of both functionalism and neo-functionalism as crafted by David Mitrany and neofunctionalism as proposed by Ernst Haas (1958). Although he does not mention the direct connection with the essence of functionalism, Craig Parsons coins a simple word that is fitting to define the entity we know today as the European Union: 'something'. 'The European Union is, by all accounts a remarkable creation. Its authority and scope resemble those of a weak federal state ... something has led European beyond the political framework of the nation-state. ... This something was a set of ideas that appears in Western Europe after the Second World War. In sum, the "community" method won the initial battle over the vague, old fashion "confederal" option' (Parsons 2003: 1).

However, this 'community' force, as a word of caution, is also questioned by subtle evidence and then by analysis. On the one hand, the 'community ideas' won tactical struggles on several occasions, but critics also point out that the resulting Europe is the product of 'vacillation between community, confederal, and traditional projects' (Parsons 2003: 235). Anyway, evidence also shows that the process of reinforcing and enlarging the community has been stubborn.

Still, the 1957 treaties still can be explained by the legacy of the ECSC in terms the basics of neofunctionalism. In the words of its founder, this is described as 'the process whereby political actors in several distinct national settings are persuaded to shift their loyalties, expectation and political activities to a new center whose institutions possess or demand jurisdiction over the pre-existing national states' (Haas 1958: 16). To large extend, this theory has dominated the scene of explaining the nature of the EEC and to support the base of its extension to its successors.

A fundamental part of the DNA of the 'something' alluded by Parsons is the 'spill over' effect. In the words of a specialist, 'spill-over' refers to a situation in which a given action, related to a specific goal, creates 'a situation in which the original goal can be assured only by taking further actions, which in turn create a further condition and a need for more action' (Lindberg 1963: 10). This essential characteristic was the pivotal base for the work of scholars in the golden era of neofunctionalism. Ernst Hass, the undisputed founder and leader of the movement, defended 'the expansive logic of sector integration'. He predicted, or rightly wished, that the process of the spirit of the Schuman Declaration would continue in the EEC. The liberalisation of trade within the customs union would lead to 'a logic harmonization of general economic policies and eventually spill-over into political areas and lead to the creation of some kind of political community' (Haas 1958: 311).

Other scholars have been more sceptic. Iris Glockner and Berthold Rittberger have pointed out in the preceding chapter 2 of this volume that the expectations that Haas had that the operation of the ECSC 'would engender "spillover" processes were hardly met'. They state that not 'only did the (economic) situations for which the ECSC was created fail to materialise, functional and political "spillovers" equally failed to ensue'. The ECSC did not produce a relationship between public authority and private power, nor did the scope of economic policy change from national state to supranational agency. In essence, the supranationalist project was muted by the accommodation of businesses with the existing markets to avoid competition, and governments were satisfied to subsidise national production. In sum, this line of criticism finds the deterministic sure path to deeper integration and the automatic appearance of a 'closer union' too optimistic, subject to the role and pressure of other actors.

In this context, observing the evolution of the EEC in the 60s, the state-centric theory of inter-governmentalism open up the scholarly scene in an even wider fashion. That meant the 'comeback' of 'eurorealism', in which the states are in command. The crafter of this school, Stanley Hoffmann, recommended a necessary analysis of the role of the state and the observance of national situations. He once argued: 'Every international system owes its inner logic and its unfolding to the diversity of domestic determinants, geo-historical situations, and outside aims among its units' (Hoffmann 1966: 864). Years later than his pioneer work, Haas admitted that he and others at the time were too happy with the rise of the EEC and did not detect 'a rebirth of nationalism and anti-functional high politics'. Hence, other theories had to come to the rescue and explain the behaviour and impact of certain leaders, such was the notorious case of De Gaulle (Haas 1967).

Years later, when the EEC and its Common Market were rescued by the Single European Act of 1986 negotiated in an Intergovernmental Conference (IGC) of 1985, new dynamics appeared that needed to be explained (Laursen 1990). Enter then the theory of 'liberal-intergovermentalism', in which the central argument is that the states (the same protagonists of the realist-intergovernmental approach), saw certain advantages in negotiating the pooling of certain degree of sovereignty. Liberal intergovernmentalism, the exclusive brain child of Andrew Moravcsik is the unavoidable reference in the comparison of different theories of integration. The key concept is 'grand bargains', by which states see the advantages of joining projects in three phases: national preference formation, interstate bargaining and institutional choice. In essence, intergovernmentalism, the theory does not recognise the centrality of the role of institutions. However, while they are like part of a given state, some perform activities and regulate services that are normally under the jurisdiction of a state. Governments evolve with elections and circumstances that influence states' decisions. For example, the French were at time ambivalent towards the process of the EEC, but were convinced by the insistence of the rest of the partners, who saw the unavoidable need to keep France on board. The success was then due to a combination of national interest and effective leadership.

Liberal intergovernmentalism advocates that the governments have enough information to find relatively efficient solutions without a political entrepreneur or intermediary. The costs of bartering and transaction are not as high as the benefits given by serious cooperation. This 'method' ensures the relative efficiency of the agreements made in the negotiations (Moravcsik 1998: 61). Laursen has observed with a certain degree of surprise that Moravcsik does not assign much importance to the new actors put in place in 1957: the community institutions in the 'grand bargains'. This is surprising in an approach called 'liberal intergovernmentalism' which includes 'institutional choice' as an important part in the 'pooling and delegation' of sovereignty. The 'bargains' were made by the member states. However, when the policies have to be implemented the community institutions are crucial (Laursen 2008b).

But Laursen insists in the introduction to this book that the role of the EU institutions, the Commission, the Council secretariat or the Parliament should not be ignored in treaty making. Also the role of the Presidency is sometimes important. As Glockner and Rittberger say in their chapter, 'the ECSC marks the first international treaty in the history of international cooperation to propose a supranational organisation, the High Authority, to which the authority to issue binding decisions was delegated'. However, considering the failure of the EDC, and the subsequent vanishing of the federal dream as proposed in the European Political Community, it was advisable to adopt of a more practical and pragmatic approach to European integration. As an example, the initial decisive power of the High Authority became irremediably eroded; the change of name to the Commission in the EEC lexicon was living proof.

Overall, the long road to Maastricht was only possible by the mechanics pictured by the combination of traditional functionalism and new inter-governmentalism. As Monnet (rephrasing Amiel) used to remind us, 'all is possible by the work of men, but nothing is lasting without institutions'. The institutional framework put in place by the Treaty of Rome made a difference. And the complexity of the new entity gave way for the appearance of middle-of-the-way theories that filled the vacuum left by the Manichean dichotomy presented by the autonomous functioning of the ensuing entity and role of the states. Constructivism and other social-oriented theories managed to shed light to an ever-expanding field.[4] A more traditional approach was also needed to deal with an undisputed protagonist: leadership.

Scholars ask themselves if 'the initial creation then depend on national leadership of some kind' how 'can we explain the creation of the ECSC without looking at the role of leadership by Jean Monnet, Robert Schuman and others? Can we explain the creation of the EEC without the leadership roles played by some Benelux leaders, including especially Paul Henri Spaak from Belgium?' (Laursen: Introduction, this volume, p. 10). The fact is that Monnet played a role in the evolution of the EEC, but not really through his ACUSE, but as an individual. As mentioned above in detail in the preceding sections, the towering figure of Spaak is impossible to miss. Although he is diplomatically modest in his memoirs, his role is recognised as a perfect example of the forces of decisive leadership in certain stages of the evolution of the EU. His views were behind the double strategy for the sectoral Euratom and the wider common market. His imprint is visible in the insistence of the voting method by qualified majority, a trade mark of the EU. Doing justice to his role, Parsons uses one of his quotes for epigraph of one chapter: 'Where there is a political will, there are no insurmountable technical problems. Where there is no will, each technical problem becomes a pretext for the failure of negotiations' (quoted from Parsons 2003: 90).

Leadership has had positive and negative consequences. Benefits have been obtained by good performance and damages have been caused by blunt opposition, by absenteeism and also by a dose of what can be called hyperactivity. As a result of the Luxembourg compromise of 1966, to appease De Gaulle, the use of unanimity threatened the evolution of European integration.

Some critics point out that part of the problem in the rise of the power of the governments was the clash with personalities taking over the role of Jean Monnet in the initial stages of the process. As an example, Walter Hallstein was named the first president of the Commission. A federalist at heart, he aggressively elected to take the road to place the EC on the map. This was one of the causes for De Gaulle's opposition and the beginning of the loss of the Commission in the unbalance battle between supranationalism and intergoverntmentalism (Dinan 2004: 79).

However, the complexity generated by the internal nature of EEC, a 'community of law' (Cotter 1995; Mathijsen 1985) led to a certain alarming sense of incomprehension by the people. This was historically explained by the foundational profile of the ECSC – it was the product of an elite. Was the remedy to get rid of the democratic deficit that, according to observers, still survives today? Was the solution to force major decisions through referendums? Recent disasters like the failed constitution and the near death of its substitute, the Lisbon treaty, seem to send a word of caution (Roy 2009).

In closing

In any event, the new entity seemed to be able to grow steadily in two directions. First, history shows that the open doors left by the treaty of the EEC have led to the perpetual growth of common policies, the result of the unstoppable delegation of sovereignty (not its loss). Not a single area that has become part of the community (or 'federalised') has returned to be fully controlled by the state. The other dimension is the history of progressive enlargements – from six to nine, then to 12 and 15, and finally to 25 and 27 and beyond. Not a single member has ever indicated a desire to leave, while a long line of suitors is waiting.

Part of the impressive success is the original balance of policies and principles presented by a reformed capitalism, based on competition and profit, and an evolved Social Democracy that guaranteed the continuation and correction of the welfare state. Christian Democrats were dominant in the foundational moments; Social Democrats, although initially opposed, were the second part of the equation. Middle-of-the-road liberals contributed to the balance, sometimes making possible coalitions that seemed intractable. Former communists, greens, and others managed to complete the range of ideologies. They are all present in the European Parliament today, and were already visible in the original Assembly.

In a way, one can also say that today's assessment by many observers shows that the Monnet method is now exhausted, in view of the current panorama. This can also be applied in certain terms to what happened in 1954–7 with the limitations of the 'spillover'. The fast travel from Messina to Venice and then back to Brussels was considered a victory for those endorsing intergovernmentalism as a theory to explain the new experiment. In any event, the balance of the EU contribution since the Treaty of Rome is impressive on any comparative base.

Notes

This chapter recognises the editing assistance of Beverly Barrett, the bibliographical gathering of Maxime Larivé, the assistance of the University of Miami's College of Arts and Sciences Computer Support service and the generous reading, comments and editing provided by Finn Laursen, beyond the call of duty.

1. For a selection of studies on the history of the EU, see Asbeek Brusse, 1997; Gillingham, 2003; Hallstein, 1962; Milward, 1992; Young, 1993; Weigall and Stirk, 1992; Heater, 1992; Moravcsik, 1998; Salmon and Nicoll, 1997; Willis, 1975; Lundestad, 1998; Stirk, 1996.
2. For a retrospective account, see Willey, 2007: http://news.bbc.co.uk/2/hi/europe/6480347.stm (accessed April 2012).
3. For a review of the considerations of the nature of the EU, see Roy, 2005 and 2006. For a comparative commentary on the different paths towards regional integration in Europe and Latin America, see Roy, 2007.
4. For selection of studies on the theory of European integration, see Chryssochoou, 2001; Diez and Weiner, 2004; Haas, 1958 and 1964; Nelsen, 2003; Rosamond, 2000; Eilstrup-Sangiovanni, 2006; Burgess, 2000.

4
The 1965 Merger Treaty: The First Reform of the Founding European Community Treaties

Finn Laursen

Historical context

After the entry into force of the Paris and Rome treaties there were three European Communities (EC). They had separate 'executives' in the form of the High Authority of the European Coal and Steel Community (ECSC) and one Commission for the European Economic Community (EEC) and another Commission for the European Atomic Energy Community (EAEC or EURATOM). The three Communities also had separate Councils of Ministers. However, when the Treaties of Rome were negotiated it was decided that the three Communities would share the European Court of Justice (ECJ) and the Parliamentary Assembly. No single Commission was created in 1957 because the negotiators wanted to avoid a re-opening of the discussions of the powers of the High Authority (Houben 1965–6, 71). The Assembly incidentally started calling itself the European Parliament in March 1962 (Gerbet 2007, 194).

There were some important differences between the ECSC treaty and the two Rome treaties. The ECSC treaty was rather detailed and gave important 'supranational' powers to the High Authority to implement the treaty. The Rome treaties were framework treaties depending more on future legislation thus giving more powers to the Council of Ministers, the legislative body, and a less supranational role to the Commissions. Also, due to the failure of the European Defence Community in 1954 the negotiators were more 'pragmatic' in 1957 (Noel 1966, 2).

Suggestions about a possible merger of the 'executives' started emerging soon after the entry into force of the Treaties of Rome in 1958. It clearly got on the agenda in 1960, with proposals from Jean Monnet's *Comité pour les États-Unis d'Europe*, as well as from the existing executives and the European Parliamentary Assembly, but it took five years before the ensuing so-called Merger Treaty was signed at an Intergovernmental Conference (IGC) on 8 April 1965. It entered into force on 1 July 1967 after being ratified by the six member states. From then on the European Communities had a single 'executive', the Commission, and also a single Council.

The Merger Treaty was the first treaty reform in the history of European integration. It normally does not take up much space in the books on the history of European integration. However, being the first, it may be worthwhile to take a look at it. What were the reasons for this reform? How was the treaty negotiated? What was in it? How significant was it?

Since the treaty was negotiated during the first half of the 1960s it is worth remembering that the EC had six member states at the time, France, West Germany, Italy, the Netherlands, Belgium and Luxembourg. Enlargement got on the agenda in 1961 when the UK applied for membership, followed by Ireland, Denmark and Norway. The French President, General De Gaulle had created the Fifth Republic in France in 1958. This happened soon after the entry into force of the Treaties of Rome. He did not really favour supranational integration. He tried early in the sixties to propose an intergovernmental set-up which should include foreign policy cooperation but also be a kind of umbrella organisation which would supervise the Communities. The so-called Fouchet negotiations about this Gaullist scheme collapsed in April 1962 (Dinan 2004, 100). British membership became another contentious issue due to General de Gaulle's veto in January 1963. It was after the collapse of the Fouchet negotiations and French veto of British membership that France started showing flexibility on the proposed merger of the executives, and negotiations started moving relatively quickly in the autumn of 1963. There were a number of rather technical issues to solve, but the most difficult political issue became that of the seat of the institutions, where Luxembourg demanded compensation for the loss of the High Authority. Agreement on the seats was only reached in March 1965. The final Intergovernmental Conference, where the treaty was signed, took place on 8 April 1965.

The first part of the 1960 was also the period where the Common Agricultural Policy was negotiated through several 'marathon' negotiations, where de Gaulle would often issue threats of undoing the EEC, to get his way. Important progress was realised in creating the customs union and the EEC took an active part in the first GATT round since the creation of the EEC, the Dillon Round, which reached an agreement on lowering tariffs in July 1962. The Yaoundé Convention with former colonies in Africa was concluded in July 1964. Association agreements were reached with Greece in 1961 and Turkey in 1963. So the EC was becoming an international actor (Gerbet 2007, 175–88).

Part of the context is also De Gaulle's 'empty chair' policy. In the second part of 1965 France stayed away from Council meetings. It was the response to a set of proposals from the Commission of the EEC, headed by Walter Hallstein. The substance was related to the financing of the Common Agricultural Policy (CAP), the budget, including the question of 'own resources', and the envisaged move to using qualified majority voting (QMV) in areas where the treaty had foreseen this to happen in 1966.[1] The conflict ended with the so-called Luxembourg Compromise in January 1966, where the Six agreed to disagree. France insisted to have a right of veto if important national interests were at stake. The Five other members wanted the treaty rules about QMV applied (Dinan 2004, 104–8). The final ratifications of the Merger Treaty only followed after the Luxembourg Compromise. The Dutch Upper House only approved the treaty on 25 October 1966. The 'empty chair' policy thus delayed the full ratification of the Merger Treaty. A final issue that further delayed the entry into force was the question of who would become the first president on the new single Commission. Walter Hallstein was a candidate, but France was strongly against Hallstein. Eventually Hallstein withdrew his candidature in May 1967 and the Six agreed on the Belgian Commissioner Jean Rey as the first president of the new single Commission (Bitsch 2007, 160).

Treaty content

At the outset there was some debate about how to go about merging the executives and Councils. Two methods were discussed, one called the common trunk and another called harmonisation. The 'common trunk' consisted in writing the applicable rules into the new treaty and deleting the corresponding articles in the initial treaties. 'Harmonisation consisted in modifying the corresponding articles in the three treaties. In the end a combination of these two methods was used' (Noel 1966, 6). The result is that the Merger Treaty is not easy to read, a fate it shares with later 'reform' treaties.

The Merger Treaty, officially called The Treaty Establishing a Single Council and a Single Commission of the European Communities was signed on 8 April 1965. It established a single Council with a rotating presidency of six month in the following order: Belgium, Germany, France, Luxembourg, and the Netherlands (Art. 2) – alphabetic order of the member states' names in their own language. This, according to Emile Noel, was a very limited reform (Noel 1966, 7). The Councils in reality functioned as one Council since 1958, with a single secretariat.

The Committee of Permanent Representatives (COREPER) was now mentioned in the treaty thus becoming a more formal institution (Art. 4). A Coordinating Committee (COCOR) had been created in 1953 under the Paris Treaty without a treaty provision. The treaties of Rome said that the Councils *may* establish a committee of representatives of the member states, and such a committee was set up after the entry into force of the treaties. Mentioning COREPER in the treaty was a French proposal, at first resisted by the Dutch, who felt that this decision should be left to the Council (Houben 1965–6, 53–4).

Voting procedures of the ECSC Council were amended to conform to the procedures of the Rome Treaties. Instead of weighted voting based on coal and steel production the existing weights used in the EEC and EURATOM Councils would apply: Belgium 2, Germany 4, France 4, Italy 4, Luxembourg 1, and the Netherlands 2. For ECSC decisions abstention would not prevent adoption by unanimity. For ECSC decisions requiring a qualified majority the rule of '12 votes in favour, cast by not less than four members' would apply (Art. 8).[2]

The question of the size of the single executive was controversial in the negotiations. The treaty adopted a nine-member solution for the Commission, a number which 'may be amended by the Council, acting unanimously'. The nine should include at least one national of each member state, but not exceed two (Art. 10). The members would be appointed by mutual agreement between the governments of the member states and the term of office would be four years (Art. 11). The president and three vice-presidents would be appointed for two years, renewable (Art. 14). Commission decisions would be by a majority of the number of members (Art. 17).

However, a transition period of three years was foreseen. The treaty stipulated:

> Until the date of entry into force of the Treaty establishing a single European Community and for a period not exceeding three years from the appointment of its members, the Commission shall consist of fourteen members.
>
> During this period, the number of members who are nationals of one and the same State shall not exceed three.
>
> (Art. 32)

The treaty also had detailed stipulations about the budget procedures, based on EEC rules. This meant the disappearance of the Commission of the four presidents, which had existed within the ECSC. It had been composed of the presidents of the four main institutions: the High Authority, the Assembly, the Council and the Court, and it had full budget autonomy. In the EEC and EURATOM it was the councils that had full budget authority. Adopting this procedure in the Merger Treaty meant that the presidents of the Assembly and Court lost their co-decision power. The special revenue for the ECSC, the levy, was maintained for the ECSC as part of a single budget (Noel 1966, 12). The budgetary powers of the Assembly were not reinforced despite proposals for such reinforcement (see also Spierenburg and Poidevin 1994, 573–6). The treaty also included a Protocol on the Privileges and Immunities of the European Communities.

The most difficult issue in the negotiations was the question of the seats. Appended to the treaty was the Decision by the Representatives of the Governments of the Member States relating to the provisional installation of certain Institutions and services of the Communities. According to Article 1 of this decision: 'Luxembourg, Brussels and Strasbourg shall remain the provisional working places of the Institutions of the Communities.' Article 2 continued: 'The Council shall hold its meetings in Luxembourg during the months of April, June and October.' The following articles then listed the institutions that would be in Luxembourg:

> The Court of Justice shall remain in Luxembourg. (Art. 3)
> The General Secretariat of the Assembly and its services shall remain in Luxembourg. (Art. 4)
> The European Investment Bank shall be installed in Luxembourg ... (Art. 5)
> The financial intervention services of the European Coal and Steel Community shall be installed in Luxembourg. (Art. 7)
> An Official Publications Office of the Communities ... shall be installed in Luxembourg. (Art. 8)

Further, it was stipulated that the following departments of the Commission should be installed in Luxembourg:

> The Statistical Office and the Computing Services;
> The Hygiene and Industrial Safety Services of the European Economic Community and the European Coal and Steel Community;

The Directorate General for the Dissemination of Information, the Directorate for Health and Safety, the Directorate for Safeguards and Controls of the Atomic Energy Community. (Art. 9)

This decision about the seats was only reached in March 1965. It could look like a victory for Luxembourg. However, Luxembourg did not succeed in moving the meetings of the Parliamentary Assembly to Luxembourg. France insisted on keeping those meetings in Strasbourg. The Parliament itself preferred Brussels.

Dynamics of the negotiations

Setting the agenda

The question of coordination of the activities of the three Communities emerged quickly in 1958. It was discussed by the Parliamentary Assembly already in May–June 1958. Some common services of the three executives were organised and the three presidents of the executives would meet regularly. A coal sector crisis in 1959 pushed the discussion further. The responsibility for coal, oil and atomic energy were divided between the three Communities. The President of the ECSC High Authority, Piero Malvestiti, said in a debate in September 1959 that an integration of the ECSC into the EEC would be a natural solution, but it would probably take 10, 15 or 20 years, and it would be a condition that the ECSC would retain its independent and direct powers (BAC 25/1980, pp. 2–5).

Jean Monnet's *Comité d'Action pour les Ètats-Unis d'Europe* proposed a merger of the three executives at a meeting in November 1959 (CM 2/1967 No. 176; Gerbet 2007, 193). Among Community actors it was the President of the Commission of EURATOM, Etienne Hirsch, who first officially proposed the creation of a single executive of the three Communities (For a detailed chronology, see Table 4.1). He did so in a speech to the Parliamentary Assembly in Strasbourg on 16 May 1960. He referred to inter-executive cooperation on energy questions and common services, especially the press and information service for which a supplementary budget had been approved by the Councils and talked about the need to assure management with maximum speed and efficiency. Since the three Communities shared a single Assembly and a single Court, it was essential to create, as soon as possible, a single executive. The creation of such a single executive would be an important step towards the formation of the United States of Europe. Hirsch's intervention found support from Christian-Democrat and Socialist members of the Assembly (BAC 25/1980, No. 1079, pp. 6, 12–13).

Table 4.1 Chronology of merger treaty negotiations

Date	Event
November 1959	Jean Monnet's *Comité d'Action pour les Ètats-Unis d'Europe* proposes merger of the executives
16 May 1960	Etienne Hirsch, President of EURATOM Commission calls for single executive
28 June 1960	Dirk Spierenburg, Vice-President of ECSC High Authority calls for single executive
27 June 1960	Walter Hallstein, President of EEC Commission calls for single executive
24 November 1960	European Parliamentary Assembly adopts Maurice Faure Report # 1 in favour of merger
23 January 1961	The Netherlands proposes treaty reform in note to the Council of Ministers
27 June 1961	Dutch project for convention instituting one Council of the European Communities and one High European Commission
25 July 1961	The Council examines the Dutch proposal and decides to consult the EPA and Commissions – some French hesitation
22 September 1961	EURATOM Commission positive opinion
11 October 1961	The Parliamentary Assembly's *Commission Politique* adopts report in favour of merger (Faure Report # 2)
24 October 1961	Assembly gives positive opinion and suggests some modification in the Dutch proposal
10 November 1961	EEC Commission gives positive opinion
11 November 1961	COREPER discussion Luxembourg worried, France hostile, others referring to British membership as an issue to be solved first
3 April 1962	Council discusses project on Dutch demand COREPER is asked to study issue, no deadline given
24 May 1963	COREPER text, supported by Italy, Netherlands and Germany Alternative texts from other Member States
11 July 1963	French support for study of merger in Council meeting
23–24 September 1963	Council gives mandate to COREPER to study issue and make proposal before the end of the year
From October 1963	COREPER discussion of modalities make quick progress: Presidency of 6 months in merged Council, extension of competences of COREPER, 4-year mandate for single Commission, and possibility of Parliamentary Assembly censure any time. Still disagreement about the name of the single executive, France against including the word 'authority.' Also issue of size of Commission: 9 or 14–15 members

(*continued*)

Table 4.1　Continued

Date	Event
18 December 1963	COREPER report Single executive will be called Commission of the European Communities; No cooption of member.
From January 1964	Size of Commission and seats of institutions the main issues: Luxembourg demands compensation if single Commission will be in Brussels
3 March 1964	Draft Convention with 33 articles and protocol on privileges and immunities of 23 articles
May–July 1964	Revised Draft Treaty proposals
28, 29 and 30 July 1964	Council agrees on Treaty text, with a few unsolved questions
18 September 1964	Council agrees on size of single Commission
1–2 March 1965	Council meeting reaches agreement on seats
3 April 1965	Council calls Intergovernmental Conference (IGC)
8 April 1965	IGC: Signing of Treaty and other texts

Source: Compiled by the author.

On 27 June 1960 the Vice-President of the High Authority of the ECSC, Dirk Spierenburg, supported the idea of a single executive in a speech to the Parliamentary Assembly. He talked about a solution that should create a more rational and efficient organisation. The support from the High Authority was conditional upon retaining the existing powers and autonomy of the ECSC (BAC 25/1980, No. 1079, pp. 18–19).

The President of the Commission of the EEC, Walter Hallstein, supported the idea of a single executive in a speech at the Parliamentary Assembly on 28 June 1960. He talked about rationalisation of working methods. He mentioned overlapping competences for commercial policy, energy policy and transport policy. By creating a single executive there would be more cohesion and internal contradictions could be avoided (BAC 25/1980, No. 1079, pp. 14–15).

A written question from the Belgian Christian Democrat member of the Assembly, Jean Pierre Duvieusart, to the three executives received the same answer from the three: support on condition that the institutional patrimony of the three Communities would be preserved. If the political will was available the merger could be realised, even before the problem of the seat of the single executive was solved (BAC 25/1980, No. 1079, pp. 22–5).

So from 1960 the merger of the executives was actively supported by the three executives and it also found wide support in the Assembly. The main motivation was one of coordination and efficiency. At this moment the proposal was not the merge the three treaties or Communities as such. It was a more limited reform that was proposed. This suggests that the main initiative came from the Community institutions.

On 25 October 1960 the Assembly's Committee on Political and Institutional Questions adopted the so-called Maurice Faure Report. Prior to the Committee's adoption of the report the Councils meeting 17–19 October instructed the Committee of Permanent Representatives (COREPER) to study the Maurice Faure Report.

The First Maurice Faure Report

The Maurice Faure Report, which was published on 7 November 1960, proposed the merger of the executives as an institutional simplification. It was argued that this would be a simple operation. It should not be a problem that the single executive would be responsible for three treaties with different competences. After all, the ECJ and the Parliamentary Assembly were already common for the three Communities.

The report proposed that the unified executive should have 15 members, 14 appointed by the member states, maximum three per member state, and a 15th member should be co-opted by the 14 appointed members. This system of co-option existed for the High Authority of the ECSC but not for the Commissions of the two other Communities. The mandate would be for four years.

Concerning the relations between the executive and the Assembly the existing possibility of a vote of no-confidence should be retained on the basis of the EEC Treaty provisions allowing such a vote at any time, not just during the debate of the annual report from the High Authority, as was the case for the ECSC. Further, the report suggested an investiture vote of the new executive. Such vote would be an act of approbation of the choice made by the governments and show confidence in the appointed team.

The reform should take place on the basis of the reform articles in the treaties: article 96 of ECSC Treaty, article 236 of the EEC Treaty and article 204 of the EURATOM Treaty. These rules required a proposal from a member state or one of the executives and consultation of the Assembly followed by a positive opinion from the Council. The calling on an intergovernmental conference (IGC) was foreseen. This IGC would decide by unanimity, and the adopted amendments would have to be ratified by all member states to enter into force.

The Assembly adopted the Maurice Faure Report on 24 November, adding that the merger of the executives should not prejudice the choice of single seat of the European Communities (BAC 25/1980, No. 1079, pp. 47–8).

Prior to the Assembly's adaptation of the Faure Report the Assembly had arranged a colloquium where the merger idea was discussed, on 21–2 November, 1960. In view of preparing the Council's participation in the colloquium COREPER had a first substantive exchange of views on 11 November 1960. Luxembourg was reticent, insisting that the question of the seat of the Communities should be solved before a single executive could be created, France took no position, but the four other member states, Germany, Italy, the Netherlands and Belgium were positive (BAC 118/1986, No. 28).

The Dutch Proposal

The Netherlands was the first member state to formally propose a merger of the executives. In a note to the Councils dated 24 January 1961, the Dutch government reiterated its support for a merger in view of the closest possible coordination of policies and most efficient organisation of the work. Since a first analysis had concluded that a slight modification of the treaties was necessary it was proposed to follow the procedures of the treaties. The executives should work out a proposal, the Assembly be consulted and an IGC called to conclude the negotiations (BAC 25/1980, No. 1079, pp. 51–3).

On 27 June 1961 the Dutch Permanent Representative forwarded a concrete draft to the Councils of the three Communities in the hope of speeding up the process. The French title of the proposal was 'Project de convention instituant un Conseil des communautés européennes et une Haute Commission européenne'. So far the discussion had mainly been about merging the High Authority and the two Commissions. Now the proposal also included the creation of one Council, and the name proposed for the unified executive was High Commission (BAC 25/1980, No. 1079, pp. 68–78).

The Dutch draft had 12 articles. Article 4 stipulated 14 members of the High Commission, at least one, maximum three, per member state. No co-option was foreseen. A vote of no-confidence remained a possibility, but no investiture was foreseen. Expenses would be divided between the budgets of the three Communities.

A restricted meeting of the Councils of the EEC and EURATOM, 24–25 July 1961, discussed the Dutch proposal. France was of the opinion that a merger of the executives was more façade than substance. Given the political context, including the question of enlargement, it would be better to postpone a decision about the merger until later. Luxembourg was the other country that hesitated. Concerning procedure the view was expressed that the Parliamentary Assembly could only be consulted on the opportuneness of calling an IGC, not the substance of the Dutch proposal. This interpretation was disputed by some other member states as well as the EEC Commission, represented by Walter Hallstein. The Netherlands, represented by Foreign Minister Joseph Luns, tried to push the proposal. Belgium, represented by Paul-Henri Spaak, hesitated a little, too, because of the enlargement issue, but in the end would go along with the Dutch proposal. Italy and Germany were in favour of starting the procedures by asking for opinions from the Assembly and Commissions. Commission Presidents Hallstein and Hirsch spoke in favour of speeding up the merger, so that the issue could be solved before enlargement. Luxembourg wanted internal issues such as the Common Agricultural Policy (CAP) as well as enlargement solved before the merger of the executives. In the end the German Presidency put the issue to a vote. The Netherlands, Belgium, Germany and Italy voted in favour and France and Luxembourg abstained. The president then concluded that the Councils had decided to forward the Dutch proposal to the Assembly and the two Commissions for their views (BAC 118/1986, no. 30).

On 27 July 1961 the Presidency asked for the opinions from the Assembly and the two Commissions.[3] President Hirsch of the EURATOM Commission answered favourably on 22 September. Accession of new member states should not delay the merger. On substance the letter only suggested that the budgetary repartition should be established in the proposed convention (BAC 118/1986, No 29, p. 846).

On 24 October 1961 the Assembly gave its favourable opinion, with some suggested modifications of the Dutch proposal, including a High Commission of nine members (BAC 25/1980, No 1079, pp. 85–91).

Finally, on 10 November 1961 the EEC Commission gave its favourable opinion in a letter from Hallstein to Ludwig Erhard, President-in-office of the Council. The EEC Commission also favoured nine members of the new High Commission (BAC 25/1980, No. 1079, p. 103).

Prior to the official opinion from the Assembly its Political Committee had adopted a second Maurice Faure Report on 11 October 1961. This was a response to the Dutch proposal, which was largely accepted. In most ways the Dutch proposal was in accordance with the wishes of the Assembly. It proposed a simple institutional reform which would not touch on the powers and competences of the three treaties. The enlargement perspective made such reform more urgent. The Dutch proposal also included the merger of the Councils. This was supported by the second Maurice Faure report. It would be a very simple operation. The Councils already shared a secretariat. The Assembly's Political Committee also wanted the member states to appoint Ministers of European Affairs to sit on this merged Council, but recognised that it was up to the governments to make such decision. During the deliberations of the Political Committee it was decided to accept that there would be no co-option. The political Committee now suggested nine members of the unified executive. On this they had especially listened to the arguments put forward by Walter Hallstein. Anyway, after enlargement the number of members would increase. The Committee further accepted that there would not be an investiture. It did suggest that the unified executive should present its programme to the Assembly for approval. Finally, the Political Committee did want more precise rules concerning the budgets to be worked out. The second Maurice Faure report was accepted by the Assembly on 9 November 1961 (BAC 118/1986, No. 29 pp. 274–275).

During the remaining part of 1961 and the year 1962 the Dutch proposal was discussed by the Council and COREPER on various occasions. But as long as France was not on board the proposal could not move.

French flexibility from 1963

On 14 January General de Gaulle vetoed British membership of the Communities. In the following period the EC executives and some member states started trying to revive the idea of a merger of the executives.

The French first indicated support for a study of the proposed merger in a Council meeting on 11 July 1963. At this meeting the member states were invited to express their opinions before the end of 1963 on the merger of certain Community institutions, taking the Dutch proposal into consideration. It was also stated that a future merger of the Communities should take place three years after the merger of certain institutions. According to Foreign Minister Couve de Murville France had so far seen the merger of the Communities as the prior step. Now the merger of the Communities was the perspective for three years after the merger of certain institutions (BAC 118/1986, no. 30, pp. 187–9). The same meeting also dealt with the Parliamentary Assembly, including the question of direct elections, as well as contacts with the UK government through the Western European Union (WEU).

Why did France finally move? The explanation given by a leading French historian was that de Gaulle gave in to pressure from the partners who were irritated by his veto of British membership. But the condition was that the merger of certain institutions would be followed by a merger of the Communities within three years (Gerbet 2009, 1019). According to Piers Ludlow the French permanent representative Jean-Marc Boegner acknowledged retrospectively that the new French line was 'a deliberate attempt to appease the Five' (Ludlow 2006, 23).

A Council meeting, 23–4 September 1963 followed up by giving a mandate to COREPER to study the issue of merger of institutions and make proposals before the end of the year (Bull. EEC 1963, No. 9–10, p. 32).

COREPER then had a first analysis of the issues at a meeting on 18 October. Some agreements started to emerge, like a 6-month Presidency in alphabetic order in the single Council, a single Commission appointed by common accord for four years, although other modalities were not completely excluded, and possibility of Parliamentary censure of the Commission at any time. There was still disagreement about the name of the single executive: Commission, High Commission, High Authority or Commission of the European Communities. France was against using the adjective 'high'. The size of the single executive was also still an issue. France, Germany, Italy and the EEC Commission were in favour of a small executive of 9 members. The Netherlands and Belgium were in favour of 14, after having dropped the idea of cooption (BAC 118/1986, No. 31; Bitsch 1998, 338–40).

In a detailed COREPER report dated 16 December 1963 these emerging agreements seemed more or less to hold. The merger of the Councils was seen as a rather simple job. Decisions would have to be made about the length of the rotating Presidency, where the ECSC had three months and the two other Communities six months. The former being rather short the Permanent Representatives went for the latter. Concerning the alphabetic order, the ECSC had based the order on the French language, but the Rome Treaties used the names of the member states in their national language. Here too the Permanent Representatives opted for the EEC and EURATOM solutions. It was argued that the different kinds of legislation and different rules of majorities of the treaties could be maintained. An appendix spelt out these differences.[4]

The merger of the executives raised more problems. The permanent representatives now favoured the name Commission of the European Communities. There was still disagreement on the size of the

Commission, nine or 14 members, but a majority favoured nine members. This would allow for national equilibrium and assure the principle of collegiality. It was also remarked that Community tasks were normally divided between seven to 10 ministries in national governments. Nine members would further allow for increasing the number in connection with future enlargements. Among actors favouring a larger Commission the High Authority still favoured 15 to allow for one cooption. Four years remained the favoured length of the Commission's mandate (BAC 118/1986, No. 31, pp. 211–53).

Concerning the Commission's responsibility vis-à-vis the Assembly the permanent representatives referred to democratic traditions and opted for the possibility of a motion of no confidence at any moment. To rationalise the administration the single Commission should have one single administration with one personnel statute and one regime concerning privileges and immunities. Budget procedures should be harmonised. The Treaties of Rome should be the basis of that harmonisation. The Commission of Presidents that had played a budgetary role in the ECSC would disappear. For this reason the permanent representatives suggested a strengthened role of the Assembly (ibid.).

Successive COREPER and Council Draft Treaty Proposals

As we move into 1964 France had accepted the idea of a merger of the institutions as a first step towards the merger of the three Communities. Luxembourg remained a difficult partner. The issue was the seat of the merged institutions. Luxembourg demanded compensation if the single Commission would have its seat in Brussels (BAC 118/1986, No. 38, pp. 23–31).

On 3 March 1964 COREPER put forward a first draft agreement. The preamble talked about rationalisation and increased efficiency. The proposed merger of the Councils and executives would be a contribution to the unification of the Communities and consequently a closer union of the peoples of Europe. There was still no agreement on the size of the Commission, nine or 14 members. The proposal had 33 articles and there was a protocol on privileges and immunities with 23 articles (BAC 118/1986, no 39, pp. 2–35).

A Council secretariat document dated 19 March 1964 indicated that, apart from disagreement on number of Commissioners and the seats of the institutions, there was also disagreement on the budgetary powers of the Assembly (BAC 118/1986, No. 33, pp. 47–8).

A revised draft treaty proposal, with footnotes giving member state positions, was issued on 20 May 1964 (BAC118/1986, No. 33, pp. 74–116).

The next draft treaty proposal followed on 10 June 1964. The Council had a discussion on 16 June and COREPER spelled out the agreed changes in a document dated 22 June 1964 (BAC 118/1986, No. 33, pp. 216–25).

A new draft treaty proposal from COREPER followed on 2 July 1964 (BAC 118/1986, No. 33, pp. 229–65). Finally, at meetings on 28, 29 and 30 July, the Councils of the EEC and EURATOM agreed on a treaty text, leaving some formulations to COREPER. The political problems remaining at this point included the size of the Commission, the seat of the institutions and strengthening of the Assembly, especially in the area of the budget. At the start of the meetings Belgium and the Netherlands still favoured 14 members of the Commission. Belgium, represented by Paul-Henri Spaak, was now also in favour of a co-opted member representing the trade unions. Spaak told his colleagues that he had been contacted by representatives of trade unions protesting against losing the co-opted member of the High Authority. Dino Del Bo from the High Authority was also in favour of 15 members, including a co-opted member. The Commission of EÚRATOM favoured 14 members because of the specific tasks in the merged Commission. But Walter Hallstein from the EEC Commission maintained that nine members would be enough. The new Commission could rationalise the work, especially on transport, competition policy, social policy and general economic policy coordination. Eventually the idea of a transition period with 14 members, to be reduced to nine, emerged as a compromise and was accepted. The question then was how long this transition period should be, some arguing for a rather short period, others for a somewhat longer period. Eventually it was left to COREPER to draft a text. Concerning the powers of the Assembly Germany had proposed to give the Assembly competence to approve international agreements and the Dutch had been in favour of an investiture of the Commission by the Assembly. Several delegations had mentioned the question of budget powers. Under the treaty of Paris the Commission of Presidents, including the President of the Assembly, had budget powers. This Commission of Presidents was now set to disappear, so in some way the Assembly, or at least its president, would lose some power. However, Couve de Murville, representing France, was against giving the Assembly the suggested powers. The question of the powers of the Assembly was a political question not linked with the merger of the Councils and executives, he argued. It therefore belonged in the context of a different discussion. It was not opportune to deal with that issue in connection with the merger of institutions (BAC 118/1986, No. 34, pp. 126–48).

Final agreement on the size and composition of the single Commission was reached on 18 September 1964 by the Councils (Louis 1966, 846; CM 2/1967 No. 188).

Agreement on the seats of the institutions

After agreeing on the size of the Commission the main remaining issue was that of the seats of the institutions. Council meetings on 19 September, 11 November and 1 December 1964 discussed the merger, especially the question of location of institutions and compensation for Luxembourg (EC Bull. 11-1964 and EC Bull. 1-1965). Finally the Council reached an agreement on the seats on 1–2 March 1965. Luxembourg, Strasbourg and Brussels would be provisional seats of institutions. Luxembourg did not succeed getting the Assembly to meet in Luxembourg because France was against. The ECJ would remain in Luxembourg. The Council would meet three times a year in Luxembourg, and the Assembly secretariat would be in Luxembourg. The new Commission, however, would be in Brussels (BAC 118/1986, No. 35, pp. 3–5; Bull. EC 4-1965).

What was supposed to be provisional still has serious repercussions today especially for the European Parliament.

The Intergovernmental Conference (IGC)

The Council then called an Intergovernmental Conference (IGC) as foreseen in the treaties (BAC 118/1986, No. 35, pp. 25–6). It took place on 8 April 1965. It was a one-day event, where the treaty and other texts were signed. The signing was preceded by speeches by the foreign ministers and representatives from the still existing three executives. All seemed happy that the process was over. Some looked forward to the future merger of the three Communities themselves. Dino del Bo (High Authority), Joseph Luns (The Netherlands), Paul-Henri Spaak (Belgium) and Pierre Werner (Luxembourg) all suggested that it was now time to think about strengthening of the role of the Assembly (BAC 118/1986, No. 39, pp. 114–54). We might call this a 'left-over' problem, a term used later in the history of treaty reforms.

In his closing statement Council president Couve de Murville stated that the merger would allow a considerable improvement in the management of the European Communities at the administrative level and make it possible for the Communities to deal with certain important problems, in particular energy policy. But the merger should be followed by the merger of the Communities themselves. Clearly, for France this was first of all an administrative reform.

Table 4.2 Ratification and entry into force of the merger treaty

8 April 1965	Treaty signed at IGC
18 May 1965	German *Bundesrat* approves treaty
16 and 17 June 1965	French National Assembly approves treaty
26 June 1965	French Senate approves treaty
30 June 1965	German *Bundestag* approves treaty
19 October 1965	Italian Chamber of Deputies approves treaty
23 July 1965	Luxembourg Council of State approves treaty
27 January 1966	Belgian Chamber of Deputies approves treaty
5 April 1966	Belgian Senate approves treaty
29 April 1966	Italian Senate approves treaty
21 June 1966	Dutch Chamber of Deputies approves treaty
30 June 1966	Luxembourg Parliament approves treaty
25 October 1966	Dutch Upper House approves treaty
5 May 1967	Walter Hallstein withdraws candidature for election as first President of the single Commission
1 July 1967	Treaty enters into force

Source: Compiled by the author on the basis of 9th General Report, p. 325, 10th General Report, p. 374, EC Bull 6-1967, p. 14, and EC Bull. 7-1967, p. 24.

Ratification

The treaty went through the obligatory ratifications by the member states, starting with Germany, and finishing with the Netherlands (see Table 4.2). Entry into force further had to await agreement on the new single Commission's members, including first of all its president, Jean Rey.

Perspectives

Afterwards a Dutch official wrote:

> The present Treaty is going to fulfil an important condition for a more effective policy; in all fields concerning more than one Community, such as the common commercial policy, the common energy policy, competition policy, transport policy, social policy and financial interventions, one European and independent body will defend one viewpoint based on the Community interest.
>
> (Houben 1965–6, 72)

He further maintained that the treaty would strengthen the European Parliament:

> The formation of one instead of three institutions responsible to the Parliament will enhance the political significance of the ties between the Assembly and executive. Whereas up till now the 23 members of the various executives were required above all to have expert qualifications, in accordance with the fields covered by the respective Treaties, the existence of the nine member executives will necessitate more political and general governing qualities.
>
> (Ibid., 73)

The merger would also strengthen the position of the Communities *vis-à-vis* the rest of the world, in GATT negotiations for instance.

Emile Noel gave similar evaluations: Creation of a single Commission would improve the efficiency as well as the morale and political authority of the institution. This would also strengthen the European Parliament because it would be controlling an executive with more powers and authority (Noel 1966, 14).

What these officials did not say was that the Luxembourg Compromise, which came between the signing and entry into force of the Merger Treaty, had weakened the Commission and strengthened the intergovernmental aspects of the Communities.

The parameters of this first EC treaty reform were very much set by General de Gaulle's France. France decided the speed and the content of the reform. During the Fouchet negotiations, the first couple of years of the 1960s, France did not allow real negotiations about a merger of the institutions. The change in French policy came after de Gaulle's veto of British membership in 1963, as a way to improve relations with the other member states. But France made sure to limit the reform to the merger of the Councils and the executives, very much on the basis of the Treaties of Rome. Efforts by some member states, Germany and the Netherlands in particular, to open the question of the role of the Parliamentary Assembly were blocked by France. France wanted a merger of the executives to be followed within three years by the merger of the treaties, presumably to create a less supranational Community. Although the linkage was accepted at the time of the merger of the executives the merger of the treaties in the end did not take place. By 1970 the first enlargement was the greatest issue (Gerbet 2007, 236–7).

Luxembourg was the member state that had most at stake in connection with the merger of the executives. It succeeded keeping the ECJ and some other institutions as well as getting new ones, but with the new single Commission in Brussels that city gradually became the 'capital' of the European Communities, now European Union. Although plenary meetings of the European Parliament still take place in Strasbourg the committee meetings largely take place in Brussels. Despite some Council meetings in Luxembourg most Council activities take place in Brussels. So Brussels was the relative winner in respect to seats of institutions.

The size of the new Commission became an important issue in the negotiations. The positions taken by the main actors were fairly easy to explain: the larger member states wanted a relatively small Commission. With nine members they would still have two of their nationals on the Commission. The smaller members had most to lose, so they tended to be in favour of 14. So did the representatives of the two more 'technical' executives, the High Authority of the ECSC and the Commission of EURATOM. But the position advocated by Hallstein's Commission and the three bigger member states prevailed.

Seen in a historic perspective it is worth noticing the important role played by COREPER in negotiating this first treaty reform. It is only from the Single European Act in the mid 1980s that the IGC becomes institutionalised and the main negotiating forum.

Seen from an analytical perspective it is fair to say that 'rational' concerns about efficiency dominated the debate. Issues of democratic accountability and legitimacy came up in the debates but were largely kept off the agenda due to French resistance, only to re-emerge as important issues in the following treaty reforms relating to the budget in 1970 and 1975 as well as the decision to have the European Parliament elected directly from 1979. But those later reforms happened after the departure of General de Gaulle from French politics in 1969.

So in the end the Merger Treaty was an intergovernmental bargain negotiated by the member states in the Council and through COREPER. The Community institutions played an important role setting the agenda and the High Authority and two Commissions were actively engaged in the process, but in the end had no vote. The initiators were the Community institutions, including the Parliamentary Assembly, as well as the most integration friendly member states, the Netherlands in particular. The laggards were France and Luxembourg, the former partly for ideological reasons, the latter having clear material interests in respect to the seats of the institutions.

Rationalist perspectives can largely explain the contours of the outcome. But the fact that the role of the European Parliament kept popping up in the discussions suggest that legitimacy concerns were also on the mind of many of those involved in the process. Given the Gaullist resistance to a strengthening of the European Parliament this became a 'left-over' from this first treaty reform, to emerge again in later reforms.

Notes

Research for this chapter, including visits to the EU historical archives in Florence and Brussels, was made possible by the author's *ad personam* Jean Monnet Chair and the specific grant for this project from the Executive Agency for Culture, Education and Audiovisual (EACEA). The following archives were consulted:

Commission Archives consulted in Florence:

BAC 25/1980 No 1079 (1960–1966): Agenda setting, Dutch proposal, etc.

BAC 118/1986 No 28 (1960–1967): Agenda setting, Faure Report, COREPER docs, etc.

BAC 118/1986 No. 29 (1961–1962): Dutch proposal 1961 and Commission and EP opinions.

BAC 118/1986 No 30 (1961–1963): Mostly COREPER and Council docs.

BAC 118/1986, No. 31 (1963–1964): Mostly COREPER reports

BAC 118/1986, No. 33 (1964): COREPER and Council texts, successive draft treaty proposals

BAC 118/1986 No 34 (1964–1965): Draft Treaty and Council minutes

BAC 118/1986 No 35 (1964–1967): Agreement on seats of institutions, Council minutes, etc.

BAC 118/1986 No 36 (1964–1965): Mostly European Parliamentary Assembly documents

BAC 118/1986 No 37 (1965–1967): EPA reports and resolutions

BAC 118/1986, No. 39 (1964–1965): Draft treaty of 3 March 1964 and final treaty text, 8 April 1965 as well as full text of IGC on same day.

Council Archives consulted in Brussels:

CM 2/1967 No 176: Comité d'Action pour les Etats-Unis d'Europe and Luxembourg perspective

CM 2/1967 No 177: Dutch proposal, Council treatment, 23 January–26 July 1961

CM 2/1967 No 178: Opinions from institutions, Council treatment, 27 July 1961–21 November 1961

CM 2/1967 No 179: Council treatment 30 March 1962–20 November 1963

CM 2/1967 No 180: COREPER proposal and report, 13 December 1963

CM 2/1967 No 181: COREPER report, 21 December 1963–6 January 1964

CM 2/1967 No 182: Council treatment, 20 December 1963–24 March 1964

CM 2/1967 No 183: Council treatment, 22 March 1964–20 April 1964

CM 2/1967 No 184: Council treatment, 7 April 1964–5 June 1964

CM 2/1967 No 185: Draft proposals and Council treatment, 10 June 1964–24 June 1964

CM 2/1967 No 186: Draft proposals and Council treatment, 2 July 1964–24 July 1964

CM 2/1967 No 187: Council treatment, 27 July 1964–17 November 1964
CM 2/1967 No 188: Council treatment, 4 September 1964–24 September 1964
CM 2/1967 No 189: Council treatment, 2 October 1964–8 January 1965
CM 2/1967 No 190: Council treatment, 12 January 1965–16 February 1965
CM 2/1967 No 191: Council treatment, 1 March 1965–9 March 1965
CM 2/1967 No 192: Council treatment, 16 March 1965–6 April 1965
CM 2/1967 No 193: Council treatment, 5 April–26 November 1965 (implementation)
CM 2/1967 No 194: Council treatment, 5 January 1966–28 November 1966 (implementation)
CM 2/1967 No 195: Council treatment, 2 June 1967–1 July 1967 (new Commission)

1. The EEC was first financed by national contributions during a transitional period. Article 201 of the EEC treaty stated: 'Without prejudice to other revenue, the budget shall be financed wholly from own resources.' The idea was to give the EEC revenue independent of the member states. The Commission proposal in 1965 was to transfer customs duties and agricultural levies to 'own resources'. See also Ann-Christina Knudsen's chapter on the Budget treaties.
2. An official English version of the treaty was not published at the time. French, German, Dutch and Italian versions were published in the *Official Journal of the European Communities*, No. 152, 13 July 1967. An English version was published juxtaposed to the French text in *Annuaire européen*, Vol. 13 (1965), pp. 460–85. The English version was also made available as 'Treaty Establishing a Single Council and a Single Commission of the European Communities,' *Journal of Common Market Studies*, Vol. vi, No. 1 (September 1967), pp. 60–87.
3. Article 96 of the ECSC Treaty did not require a formal opinion from the High Authority.
4. A majority in the Treaty of Paris was defined as a majority of the members of the Council including the vote of a State that assures at least one sixth of the production of coal and steel (Art. 28(4)). A simple majority thus was in reality a kind of qualified majority vote. The treaties of Rome had weighted voting giving the three larger members, France, Germany and Italy four votes, the Netherlands and Belgium two votes and Luxembourg one vote. A qualified majority vote (QMV) was defined as 12 votes as long as the Council voted on a proposal from the Commission. If the treaty did not require a proposal from the Commission a QMV should include at least four member states (Art. 148(2) of EEC Treaty and Art. 118(2) of EURATOM treaty). In reality these rules were not very different. A majority vote in the ECSC could not be taken against France and Germany. In the EEC and EURATOM a QMV would have to include two of the three larger states. Concerning unanimity there was a difference. In the ECSC a unanimous vote had to include all members. In the two Rome treaties abstention did not hinder unanimity (Annex B to COREPER report of 16 December 1963).

5
The 1970 and 1975 Budget Treaties: Enhancing the Democratic Architecture of the Community

Ann-Christina L. Knudsen

The treaties signed in 1970 and 1975 are often called the Budget Treaties, and they have so far lived a fairly anonymous life in histories of the EU/EC. Despite their somewhat mundane name, there is good reason to pay closer attention to them because the creation of these treaties can tell us something new about how choices for democratic and institutional design have been made. The 1970-treaty gave the European Parliament (EP) its first new powers since the Rome Treaty in respect of the community's budgetary process, and these were further strengthened in the 1975-treaty. The latter treaty also gave birth to the European Court of Auditors (CoA), called the financial consciousness of the community (Kutchner 1977). We now know that the EP has been granted further powers in every subsequent treaty amendment, a development that reached a zenith with the 2010 Lisbon Treaty where the EP was granted co-decision status in practically all policy areas. But what retrospectively looks like a continuous development could not have been predicted in the first half of the 1970s.

The aim of this chapter is to examine the origins and significance of these treaties by analysing how their relatively technical contents can be understood in a broader perspective, and to trace the political processes shaping the treaties. The chapter argues that there was a normative dimension to the institutional innovations in these treaties that brought a greater measure of accountability and transparency to the community and thus enhanced its democratic architecture. The 1970-treaty was premised on a new way of financing the community through own resources, rather than direct member state contributions, and based on an argument of increasing the parliamentary legitimacy at community level. This 'logical link' (Rittberger 2005: 122) between parliamentary powers and public resources was however not automatically there, but took nearly a decade of inter-institutional debate to become firmly established. By contrast, the 1975-treaty was concluded after the first enlargement, at a time when there were increasing problems of fraud and inefficient management of the community's funds. In this context, the second budget treaty was not complicated to make, but the finalisation of it, paradoxically, stood in the shadow of the British demand for renegotiation over its financial membership terms and principled opposition to own resources (For basic data of the treaties, see Table 5.1).

The chapter emphasises the importance of tracing political processes that led to the treaties not only from the position of those formally empowered to negotiate and sign them, as functional and liberal models of delegation do, but to also take a systematic look at the windows of opportunities for other political actors who could place demands and decisively shape the outcome. The EP played a crucial role in shaping the key premises upon which the treaties were created although it held no formal powers in this respect, and the Commission was at various times key to promoting and delimiting the logical link. By examining the contents and the political processes on the basis of multi-archival historical research, the chapter also provides a stronger historical foundation for understanding the more recent discussions about democratisation of the EU's institutional architecture.

Table 5.1 Basic data of budget treaties

	1970-treaty	**1975-treaty**
Full name	Treaty amending Certain Budgetary Provisions of the Treaties establishing the European Communities and of the Treaty establishing a Single Council and a Single Commission of the European Communities	Treaty amending Certain Financial Provisions of the Treaty establishing the European Communities and of the Treaty establishing a Single Council and a Single Commission of the European Communities
Signatories	Belgium, Federal Republic of Germany, France, Italy, Luxembourg and the Netherlands	Belgium, Denmark, Federal Republic of Germany, France, Ireland, Italy, Luxembourg, the Netherlands, and the United Kingdom
Signed	Luxembourg, 22 April 1970	Brussels, 22 July 1975
In force	1 January 1971	1 June 1977

Source: *Journal Officiel* 2.1.1971; *Official Journal* 31.12.1977.

The political context

The mid-1970s marked the end of *les trentes glorieuses* – the glorious 30 years of growth and prosperity in Western Europe that followed after the Second World War. An atmosphere of political and economic malaise grew in the wake of the monetary turbulence that erupted towards the end of the 1960s. The abolition of the gold standard in 1971 and the first global oil crisis in 1973 led to the worst economic recession in Western Europe since the interwar years, and resulted in a dramatic increase in unemployment and slow economic growth. Political parties struggled to navigate in a domestic environment that seemed ever-more fractured, and the Keynesian doctrine that had informed much of the built-up of the post-war welfare states was questioned. There was an increasing alertness towards new forms of contestation, for instance from violent campaigns by disenchanted domestic groups such as the Red Army Fraction and Baader-Meinhof group in the Federal Republic, the Red Brigades in Italy, and an escalation of the troubles in Northern Ireland. International terrorism escalated such as the 1972-shooting of athletes in the Olympic Village in Munich, and the repeated hostage-taking of airline passengers. International diplomatic relations were fatigued by long-drawn Cold War conflicts such as the Vietnam War, as well as the situations such as the Yom Kippur War of 1973 and the Turkish invasion of Cyprus in 1974.

Political priorities for the community in the 1970s were sandwiched in-between such global and domestic constraints. By the end of the 1960s, the implementation of the community's customs union and the common agricultural policy (CAP) had been completed, and the fundament for the entire project had been monetary stability that was now under pressure. The departure of the notoriously difficult French President Charles de Gaulle in April 1969 seemed to be a good time to address the challenges facing the European project anew. Formally this began with the summit of Heads of State and Government in The Hague in December 1969, and they here expressed their will to deepening, enlarging and widening their common project. The most politically ambitious task to deepen the scope of cooperation was placed in the hands of Luxembourg's Prime Minister, Pierre Werner, who in October 1970 delivered a report for how economic and monetary union could be achieved by 1980. However, launched at a time when the economic recession seemed to worsen continuously, the Werner Plan was eventually abandoned. Eurosclerosis, it is often assumed, did not provide fertile ground for that kind of progress on European integration, though it did result in a strengthening of monetary cooperation. However, to interpret the whole history of the 1970s in the shadow of Eurosclerosis would be to miss out on important nuances of that decade (e.g. Kaiser and Meyer 2010; Mourlon-Druol 2010).

Community enlargement moved ahead as planned. These negotiations were formally begun in mid-1970 with the four countries that had first applied for membership in 1961–2. By January 1972 the formal conditions of accession were concluded. At the ceremony welcoming Britain, Denmark and Ireland into the community in January 1973, Commission President Sicco Mansholt reminded his colleagues that in the fourth candidate – Norway – 53.3 per cent of the electorate had refused accession in a referendum. Mansholt saw this as a 'blunt reminder ... because they simply could not see the point of what we are doing' (Mansholt 1973: 3–4). Often seen as the architect of the CAP, Mansholt had in fact become sceptical of the way the community had developed (Harst 2007). He suggested that the common market and the CAP 'were rather limited, unromantic tasks. By and large, they failed to fire most people's imagination' (Mansholt 1973: 1). With this mix of seriousness and irony, Mansholt highlighted some of the challenges facing the community.

Unlike in Norway and Denmark, Britain had not held a referendum over the question of accession to the community. It was a divisive issue among the country's political elite that had only been passed in Parliament by a small margin (Pine 2007). The deepest cleavage was among Labour's leadership, so much so that its executive committee refused to send its members to the EP; the British trade unions, in turn, also refused to send members to the Social and Economic Committee (Butler and Kitzinger 1976: 21–2). When Labour got back into government in October 1974 – after a debacle over a 'hung parliament' and two rounds of consultations of the electorate – the new Prime Minister Harold Wilson tried to get a renegotiation of the terms of membership. The key demand from British side was to get a correction mechanism in place that would reduce the country's financial contributions in relation to the CAP (Leigh 1975). Against the background of mounting domestic unemployment and strikes, and a popular outcry against rising food prices widely attributed to the CAP, as well as the fact that the country was paying the lion's share of the community's budget, Wilson decided to test the issue of membership with the electorate; in Britain, there was no tradition for referendums (Butler and Kietzinger: xi). The referendum was held on 5 June 1975, and resulted in 67.2 percent in favour, and Labour subsequently resolved to 'normalise' Britain's membership by, among other things, sending delegates to the EP.

The community itself faced financial constraints that were also addressed in the December 1969-Communiqué. On the one hand, the Communiqué encouraged a change in the community's structure of financing and revenue from the direct member state contributions of the Rome Treaty, to the introduction of an autonomous basis of financing called own resources. This shift had been debated since at least 1960, and had in fact already been gradually implemented with the CAP's external dimension along with the decision to apply levies to trade in agricultural products with third countries. On the other hand, the Communiqué pointed to the need to ensure 'better control' of CAP expenditure 'making it possible to limit budgetary charges' (Final Communiqué 1969: Item 6). This was made with reference to a number of problems inherent in the design of the CAP. The CAP was a redistributive policy that provided entitlements to practically all farmers in the community based on the volume of their production (Knudsen 2009a). Technological advances in agriculture meant that the community came to subsidise a mounting agricultural production, and resulted in the stockpiling of food that could neither be consumed nor sold. The institutional capacity of the original Audit Board was vastly insufficient for controlling that payments were made correctly. By the early 1970s, it had become 'common knowledge' that community funds were being wasted 'running into hundreds of million dollars annually' (EP 1973: 16). So while the CAP by many had been seen as the 'engine' of European integration in the 1960s, much of the allure of this policy had waned a decade later. Yet political hopes were still pinned to the promises of the CAP, and so rather than reforming it entirely, it was decided to enhance the parliamentary legitimacy and accountability surrounding it.

The contents of the budgetary treaties

The Budget Treaties were fairly technical in nature, and to make sense of them, it is useful to take a look at what the key questions generally are in relation to budgetary processes in democratic polities (e.g. Laffan 1997; Strasser 1992; Wallace 1980):

- *Revenue:* How is the funding of the common political priorities organised?
- *Expenditure:* Who has the authority to take decisions over budgetary allocations?
- *Implementation*: Who has the right and duty to implement the budget?
- *Control:* Who audits that the common funds are used appropriately?

The founding treaties of the three Communities had given one answer to the questions above, and the 1970 and 1975-treaties made amendments to these; unless otherwise stated, the following will refer to the provisions relating to the EEC (Articles 199–209, EEC) as the set-up for the ECSC and the Euratom was similar.

The 1970-treaty was premised on a new revenue structure for the community that was agreed by the Council on 21 April 1970, the day prior to signing the treaty (Council Decision 1970). So far, the community had been financed through direct contributions from the member states fixed in the founding documents according to a key of distribution (Art. 200.1, EEC); in that respect it looked much like other international organisations. The Rome Treaty suggested that the community could switch to a different financing structure based on 'other resources' such as revenue from the common customs tariff (Art. 201 EEC); the ECSC had been financed in a similar way (Art. 49, ECSC). The April 1970-Decision completed the introduction of own resources based on three different sources:

- The community's agricultural levies.
- The common customs duties.
- A fixed rate based on value added tax.

The first two revenue sources would thus come from the community's trade with non-member states, and the latter would be collected on the basis of national tax revenue. Own resources became fully implemented by 1 January 1975 and the direct member state contributions would be phased out in the meantime.

The 1970-treaty introduced subtle changes to the balance of authority among the community's three main institutions. The key argument was that own resources would create financial autonomy for the community that national parliaments would not be able to control, and this called for the 'strengthening of the budgetary powers of the European Parliament', as stated in the preamble. The original budgetary procedure set out in the Rome Treaty resembled the original consultation procedure used for most policy decisions: the Council would take decisions; the Commission draw up proposals and ensure implementation. The EP was here confined to consultation at the second reading of the draft budget, and the Council could disregard any amendments it proposed without producing any formal justification (Art. 203, EEC). This procedure was revised in the 1970-treaty as illustrated in the five steps below.

Step 1   The Commission draws up a preliminary draft budget, and submits the preliminary draft budget to the Council by 1 July.
Step 2   The Council deliberates and consults with the Commission. The Council submits the draft budget to the EP by 5 October.
Step 3   The EP has the right to amend non-compulsory expenditures in the draft proposal. This must be done within 45 days. If not, the budget is finalised.
Step 4   The Council can modify the EP's amendments.
Step 5   The President of the EP declares the budget finally adopted.

The main amendment in the 1970-treaty thus pertained to the EP's role in the budgetary process. The EP would still only enter at a relatively late stage (step 3), and a crucial distinction was made between 'compulsory' and 'non-compulsory' expenditure. The former related to direct policy spending such as the politically sensitive CAP, and the latter to all other expenditures. In reality, this gave the EP the right to propose amendments to no more than an estimated three per cent of the budget at the time.[1] A further novelty in the 1970-treaty was that the EP's President would have to declare the budget finally adopted; a ritual traditionally performed by parliamentary presidents. In short, the Council remained the primary decision-maker in budgetary matters, and the Commission the main budgetary expert. The EP, still indirectly elected, was kept on the sideline.

In combination with the 1975-treaty, it is however possible to see the 1970-treaty as the start of a systematic increase of the EP's position. The 1975-treaty stipulated that the EP 'may, if there are important reasons, reject the draft budget and ask for a new draft to be submitted to it' (Art. 12.8, 1975-treaty). To do so would take a majority of MEPs and two-thirds of the votes cast. In the event where the budget had not been approved at the start of the new year, the Council would need the EP's approval if it wished to appropriate new funds compared to the previous year (Art. 13, 1975-treaty). With these provisions, the threat of EP sanctions of Council and Commission activities now became omnipresent.

The Commission's original powers to draw up the preliminary draft budget, and to implement it at 'its own responsibility and within the limits of the appropriations made' (Art. 205, EEC) remained untouched in both treaty amendments, but its powers to act autonomously in drawing up the budget were slightly reduced. The 1970-Treaty set up rules for how increases in community expenditure could be made, namely in relation to key economic indicators, and it set up a procedure whereby the Commission would have to consult the relevant EP committees in such matters. While this procedure did not give the EP any further formal powers, it was bound to result in a larger measure of accountability over how the preliminary draft budget was being constructed. The 1975-treaty also tightened the control mechanisms monitoring the Commission's implementation of the budget by requiring it to submit annually its accounts to the Council and the EP.

The 1975-treaty also strengthened the dimension of accountability by creating a new community institution, the CoA, to replace the Audit Board. The new CoA would have the duty to independently examine that all community-related accounts were 'lawful and regular and whether the financial management has been sound' (Art. 16.2, 1975-Treaty). The formulation of the CoA's purpose was in fact not all that different from that in the Rome Treaty (cf. Art. 206a, EEC), and the real novelty related to matters of independence and the recruitment of auditors. The Audit Board's powers were originally subjected to those of the Council that, if dissatisfied, could give its own discharge to the Commission in respect of the implementation of the budget. The 1970-treaty placed the EP on equal footing with the Council in the discharge procedure, and the 1975-treaty went further by establishing that the CoA 'shall assist the European Parliament and the Council in exercising the powers of control over the implementation of the budget' (Art. 16.4, 1975-treaty). The EP now also had the right to discharge the Commission's implementation of the budget based on an examination of the accounts and annual report made by the CoA, if the Council so recommended based on a qualified majority vote.

The CoA would consist of nine members selected in a similar way as the judges of the European Court of Justice, namely persons who had worked with external audits before, whose 'independence must be beyond doubt', and who were 'completely independent in the performance of their duties' (Art. 15.5, 1975-treaty). Appointments were for six years, renewable, and made by a unanimous Council after consulting the EP. The auditors would appoint their president from among their numbers for a term of three years. The 1975-treaty gave the auditors the powers to base their work on written records and, if necessary, performed on the spot in the institutions of the community and in the member states. This essentially created a superstructure of auditing public accounts in areas pertaining to community legislation. Nine auditors would be appointed as of 1 June 1977.

Explaining the treaties

Analysts of the EC/EU have so far not paid much attention to the making of the Budget Treaties. The literature that does exist focuses either on the broader theoretical themes in the contents of the treaties, or the decision-making processes from which the treaties resulted. The former literature rightly argues that there is a normative dimension to issues of parliaments, public budgets and institutions of auditing, and the Budget Treaties should be seen in light of theories of democratic government (Coombes 1972; Laffan 2003 and 1999; Wallace 1980). On the one hand, the 'power of the purse' is a key parliamentary power. Parliaments hold the power to oversee and sanction the executive, to decide over state revenue, and to allocate public spending (Buchanan and Musgrave 1999; Coombes 1976). Independent and external accounting institutions, on the other hand, are part of the structure of the modern, Weberian state where democratic institutions can both be majoritarian and non-majoritarian.

There was no uniform model of parliamentary legitimacy and accountability in budgetary affairs in the community member states (Coombes 1976; Conway and Romijn 2004). Constitutions not only give parliaments right to decide and sanction the executive at will, but they also constrain the parliamentary room to manoeuvre financially due to the wish for assuring a degree of financial autonomy to the executive. In the Constitution of the Fifth Republic, for example, the French National Assembly was only second tier to the strong executive in the domestic budgetary process. National auditing institutions are rarely visible in debates about democratic institutions, but these non-majoritarian institutions in fact have a long history closely tied to the development of democratic states. In Western Europe, they typically trace their roots back to the early or mid-nineteenth century where they were embedded in the new constitutions. The interwar period saw renewed national discussions over the positions of the auditing institution, sometimes referred to as the fourth branch of power (e.g. EP 1973: 131–52). The authority and independence of auditing bodies would vary from one country to another, and they were central to the institutional architecture of the democratic and uncorrupted state. From this perspective, the institutional innovations made with the Budget Treaties may be seen as part of the 'European experiment to democratize political space beyond the state' (Laffan 2003: 762).

Treaties and new institutions do not emerge by themselves, but require political agency. The second strand of literature relevant here approaches treaties as outcomes of intergovernmental bargaining. Functional or liberal approaches to the study of why states delegate powers assume that utility maximation is the key to understanding actors' positions and behaviour (e.g. Pollack 2003; Moravcsik 1998). Generally, such approaches have a hard time explaining delegation to the EP, and reduce non-majoritarian institutions at the European level to regulatory agencies that deal with technical market matters (Majone 1996). Such theoretical positions therefore struggle to account for delegation of a normative nature. The challenge was taken up most convincingly in a major study of delegation to the EP over time (Rittberger 2005). It argued that once questions of delegation are invoked, national leaders in post-war Western Europe were likely to begin worrying about the emergence of a legitimacy deficit, particularly in relation to parliamentary accountability. Political elites may share legitimating beliefs, but do not automatically agree on how to address them. Accordingly, it is necessary to examine how national political elites come to share perceptions of the legitimacy deficit and identify the opportunities for formal and informal communication among them, for instance at intergovernmental conferences.

While this approach is convincing in its accept of normative delegation, it is still formalistic in its approach to how European politics operate, and replicates an intergovernmental view of European integration politics that is not shared in the emerging historical literature that demonstrate how informal and transnational political processes can influence policy outcomes decisively (Kaiser, Leucht and Rasmussen 2009; Ludlow 2006). To appreciate how complex institutional arrangements are made, it is necessary to adopt a less rigid approach to politics. A good example of a puzzle that is left unexplained by the short-term intergovernmental framework is how the 'logical link' between own resources and parliamentary legitimacy for the EP was ever made. This was a key premise for the 1970-treaty, yet these two elements were initially not linked when own resources first appeared in the context of the CAP in 1960 (Knudsen 2009a). Moreover, historical archival evidence also shows that it was often practically impossible to separate the different financial and normative positions of the political actors involved in negotiations over multiple sources of own resources. In contrast to the intergovernmental approaches, this chapter takes inspiration with historical institutionalism that traces the policy process over time to include formal decision-making moments as well as the windows of opportunities where other actors got involved in shaping the treaties (e.g. Pierson 2004; Rasmussen 2009; Knudsen 2009b). The chapter particularly focuses on the lively inter-institutional debates within the community.

In search of the logical link

Own resources roamed around in the community's policy process for many years without being connected to the EP's powers. These emerged on the agenda already around 1959 as part of the CAP's external dimension (Knudsen 2009a). Levies were a kind of tariff that could be adjusted to seasonal changes to the supply of agricultural products, and had been widely used in national agricultural policies where they constituted a source of state revenue (Tracy 1989). The extent of such revenue varied according to the country's overall needs for agricultural imports. If the destination for levies was changed to the community, it was clear that some member states would be surrendering more of such state revenue than others. A basic financial estimate would show that particularly Germany, as a net agricultural importer, stood to lose revenue. The Netherlands was a net agricultural exporter, but because its agricultural production of meat and dairy products was dependent on imports of feed grains and other products from outside the community, own resources were also financially problematic. Own resources would later become a controversial solution to Britain, a country with major agricultural imports and relatively modest agricultural production to attract CAP subsidies. Such overall calculations did inform the basic standpoints on own resources, but their introduction did not result in a direct bargaining situation between net importers and exporters, as liberal intergovernmentalists would assume (Moravcsik 1998).

In December 1960, the Council passed its first Resolution towards establishing the CAP policy framework. It noted that the revenue generated from common agricultural levies should flow to the community rather than to the importing member state (Knudsen 2009a: 183–5). Being a resolution, the document was not legally binding according to the Rome Treaty and it seems that only a few civil servants in the German finance ministry raised concerns about it. However, at community level the Resolution was subsequently interpreted as a political commitment, and became the basis for developing the CAP further. During the coming year, the formulation of the CAP was in the hands of the Commission as the member governments still had no clear visions for what the CAP should look like.

The first stage of implementing the common market was to take place by the end of 1961, and this posed questions about just 'how much' of the CAP would actually need to be realised to be attained 'in substance' (Art. 8.3, EEC). Yet by November 1961, the Council of Agriculture Ministers had hardly ever met, and no CAP regulations had been passed. The few but rather broad political discussions that had taken place so far suggested that it would not merely be about market regulation and protection, but also encompass some form of redistribution for the community's farmers through price interventions. Against this background, the negotiations over the CAP became cumbersome and dragged the last Council meeting of 1961 into overtime (Knudsen 2009a: 195–9). When the Council and the Commission finally surfaced with its financial Regulation 25 in the early morning hours of 14 January 1962, it was merely a temporary agreement due to expire on 30 June 1965 (*Journal Officiel* 1962). It stipulated that at the end of the transition period, agricultural levies from third country imports would finance the CAP, and thus would be channelled to the community.

Regulation 25 had been conceived under somewhat unusual circumstances, and its wording was ambiguous. During the long Council meeting, the issue of financing was seen as secondary to the political goal of giving some substance to the CAP. These two themes had in fact been connected in the Commission's draft proposal, but the connection was removed during the negotiations in order to isolate the political issues pertaining to the CAP (Knudsen 2005). Subsequently, Regulation 25 was drafted towards the end of 1961 and separated from decisions over agricultural prices. It had therefore not been through any consultations outside the narrow group of persons involved in the negotiations. Moreover, it later transpired that there was a legal ambiguity as to whether own resources could indeed be established, as the Rome Treaty required a more cumbersome procedure for this. Regulation 25 nevertheless became known as the basis for the financial solidarity underlying the CAP, but it was an unfinished installation of own resources, and there was no mention of the EP's powers.

The EP did not fail to mention the procedural flaws behind the making of Regulation 25 when discussing the Commission's annual report in October 1962, and in a subsequent Resolution drafted in the EP's budget committee, it formulated the logical link most clearly for the first time.[2] It stated that 'it is essential that the rights that the national parliaments have given up with the ratification of the EEC treaty, notably in the area of legislation and in budgetary power, are soon transferred to the European Parliament'.[3] Hence, rather than rejecting own resources and Regulation 25 altogether, the EP eyed the opportunity to use this issue as a lever to try to enhance its own role in the budgetary process.[4]

The EP subsequently began to issue a steady stream of resolutions and reports arguing that national parliaments had lost legislative and budgetary powers with the institution of the community and own resources, and the only way to restore this would be to grant more powers to the EP. The logical link was now explicated by the EP, and framed as a parliamentary legitimacy deficit. Commissioners were repeatedly summoned to the EP to respond to this demand, and a number of MEPs tried to persuade their national hinterlands – political parties and parliaments – to make similar demands. Yet, none of the other community institutions had accepted the logical link at this point.

The Commission was at first unwilling to accept the logical link. This was clear when Commissioner Robert Marjolin tried to get own resources accepted through the backdoor during the accession negotiations with Britain (for details Knudsen 2005). These negotiations were in no way clear-cut. During late-night meetings, Marjolin tried to pressure the British negotiators to accept own resources. If this financial arrangement was part of the British accession package, so he seems to have reasoned, this would end further discussions about introducing own resources (and not include the EP). Yet the British negotiators were reluctant to accept this, and towards the end of 1962 they were close to leaving the negotiations entirely (Lamb 1995: 174). Shortly thereafter, French President Charles de Gaulle withdrew his support for British accession. The Commission subsequently continued to be obstructive towards accepting the EP's logical link. When in mid-1963 Commission President Walter Hallstein was made to react to the EP's Furler Report demanding that own resources should come along with the strengthening of EP powers, he insisted that this could only happen at the drafting stage of the budget, and that the EP could have no part in implementation.[5] Hallstein thus put a fence around the Commission's powers to execute the budget. Hallstein later addressed the EP and insisted that the problem of financing the CAP and 'budgetary independence' would have to be solved before further parliamentary powers could be installed.[6]

The Council now began to react to the EP's demand in a more open way. In December 1963 it mandated the Committee of Permanent Representatives to compare all available positions of the member governments regarding an increased role for the EP.[7] In anticipation of that report, Hallstein decided that rather than to quell the discussion it was better for the Commission to participate in it. In early November, an internal discussion in the Commission showed that most commissioners actually saw it as desirable if the EP in some cases could overrule the Council.[8] The discussions also transgressed into national politics during 1963 as at least three member governments threw their support behind a revision of the EP's role. The Dutch government had already in late February proposed to reinforce the powers of the EP in connection with the fusion of the institutions that later resulted in the Merger Treaty.[9] Representatives of the Italian government supported this position at different times. And towards the end of the year, the Luxembourg and German governments advanced further suggestions in this direction.[10] Drawing on declarations made in their national parliaments, they argued that the EP should, based on a double-majority, be able to amend the draft budget up to the total amount of expenditure agreed by the Council. Towards the end of the year, the report from the Permanent Representatives moved in the same direction. On 23 December, the Council passed a declaration emphasising the connection between the specific model for financing the CAP and reinforcing the EP's budgetary powers, even though it had not actually had time to discuss the matter at the meeting.

Finding the link

The logical link subsequently became subject of a triangular inter-institutional debate. When the Council in February 1964 had its first real debate about the issues involved in the logical link, a certain hesitance began to transpire.[11] This had largely been provoked by the highly sceptical French foreign minister, Maurice Couve de Murville. While he had strongly supported own resources in Regulation 25, he now made clear that the French government was reluctant to accept any modifications of the budgetary procedure that could affect the financing of the CAP. Several other options for empowering the EP were discussed at Council meetings between March and September 1964 without the Council coming to any clear position. Meanwhile, the EP passed 16 resolutions during that year towards reinforcing its position in the budgetary process.[12] By October, the Commission promised the EP that it would incorporate the revised budgetary procedure into the proposal for financing the CAP that was to replace Regulation 25.[13] And by November, the German government issued a far-reaching call for, among other things, making the competences of the EP 'comparable to those of the national parliaments in areas where the Community has subtracted from the national parliaments', including budgetary and legislative powers to the EP.[14] This German initiative stood in odd contrast to the stubbornness with which this government allowed its powerful farm lobby to block the parallel CAP negotiations towards the common grain price (Knudsen 2009a: 232–60). But once the common grain price was finally settled in mid-December – against a lump-sum pay-off to German farmers – it was time for the Commission to begin drawing up proposals for a permanent financing settlement to replace Regulation 25.

The Commission's proposal from March 1965 integrated CAP financing, own resources and the strengthening of the EP's position in the budgetary procedure.[15] The basic argument was now that own resources for financing the CAP would change the balance of powers among the key political actors of the Communities. As national parliaments' ability to control community financing would diminish, the balance could be restored by giving similar powers to the EP. Yet the Commission's proposal also delimited the EP's role arguing that it would be inappropriate to give the EP too much influence before it was elected by universal suffrage. Once direct elections were in sight – which they were not in this proposal – the Commission promised that it would revise the budgetary procedure again to enhance the EP's standing. In the proposal, the Commission would remain central to the budgetary procedure at all times. In short, those wishing for further budgetary powers to the EP were kept waiting for direct elections in some distant future.[16] About two months later, French President de Gaulle used the proposal as a trigger to withdraw French high-level representation from the community; the Empty Chair Crisis. Yet in light of the debate that had taken place in previous years, the proposal was not radically new.

The EP expressed its severe discontent with the condition of direct elections in the future. In May it demanded further budgetary powers as soon as own resources were introduced.[17] It also wanted direct elections from September 1971 at which time the community budget should be passed in the EP by majority voting. Addressing the EP on 11 May 1965, Hallstein refused to accept the criticism, and responded that the only disagreement he could see was over the date of increased powers for the EP.[18] To the EP, the first problem was exactly the absence of a date for direct elections. The nature of the logical link was now disputed.

A Council debate on 9 June showed that most delegations actually wanted the logical link to go further than proposed by the Commission.[19] Particularly the Dutch and Italian delegations argued for an extension of the EP's powers in legislative matters, while the German and Luxembourg delegations wanted the EP's budgetary powers gradually extended to give it a final say. Yet French hesitation was growing with the proposed new institutional settlement, and as the 30 June deadline for renewing the financial regulation was approaching, practically no progress had been made by the Council. This was when the Empty Chair Crisis erupted on 30 June, at the expiration of Regulation 25. Meanwhile, the Merger Treaty had been signed in April 1965, stripped of anything pertaining to the strengthening of the EP's powers, as Laursen's chapter demonstrates.

When all six governments resumed negotiations in January 1966, the Commission's proposal from March 1965 was dissected into its main elements, and own resources and the empowering of the EP became detached from the financial regulation for the CAP.[20] The negotiators aimed to get another temporary agreement for the latter, set to expire at the end of 1969. It was largely a continuation of the gradual channelling of the revenue from the common agricultural levies to the community as begun with Regulation 25. It did however not solve the final legal status for own resources, or establish the logical link in community legislation. In subsequent COREPER discussions, the Dutch, German and Luxembourg permanent representatives on several occasions made clear that they wished to continue the discussion over the empowerment of the EP in relation to the continued installation of own resources. The French representative however insisted that 'all that needs to be said about the topic had already been said in Regulation 25'.[21] Meanwhile, the EP also continued to force the issue on the community's agenda by issuing further resolutions and reports on the need to overcome the legitimacy deficit. Not surprisingly, the EP focused particularly on its own position in the budgetary procedure, thus accepting that direct elections and further legislative powers would have to come later.[22]

Establishing the logical link

The deadlock was not broken until April 1968 when the Commission – now with a new president, Jean Rey – issued a highly ambitious communication to the Council.[23] The document has to be seen in the context of the administrative reform following the Merger Treaty. Its vision was that the fusion process should lead to political union, direct election of the EP, and the creation of financial autonomy for the community. The Council responded with a renewed commitment to reinforcing the EP's budgetary powers, and the ensuing Resolution referred back in time to various community documents prior to the Empty Chair Crisis as well as the most recent resolution of the EP, as if the Empty Chair crisis had never happened.[24] The Council thus signalled that the dialogue was continuing. In a declaration from 1 July 1968, the Commission argued that progress in the community – especially with the Merger Treaty, the finalising of the common market, and the end of the veto right in the Council – would necessitate further supranational parliamentary legitimacy through the strengthening of the budgetary and legislative powers of a directly elected EP.[25] Needless to say, the EP welcomed these new developments.[26]

The logical link finally appeared logical to all, and it was confirmed in statements from all the community's institutions in the months towards the Hague Summit in December 1969. The EP's role up to that point appears to have been crucial for ever getting the logical link established. It coincided with new challenges such as monetary turbulence, and the spiralling cost of the CAP. Meanwhile, there was a gradual change in certain forms of cooperation within the community such as the beginning of summitry and more frequent meetings of finance ministers (Mourlon-Druol 2009). The latter meant that problems relating to financing the community became divided from discussions of the CAP. Finance ministers thus discussed own resources in Rotterdam on 9 September 1968, and decided to broaden the definition of own resources to include not only agricultural levies but exploring other sources too.[27] The meeting also produced a renewed commitment to reinforcing supranational parliamentary legitimacy as a pre-condition for finally establishing own resources.[28] In this forum, there was no questioning of the logical link.

A new Commission proposal emerged in July 1969 for the reform of the community's financing model.[29] While it generally embraced the full establishment of own resources by January 1974, it proposed an overtly complicated budgetary procedure that hardly left any scope for the EP to manoeuvre. This was a qualitative move away from the signals in April 1968, and the matter divided the Commission.[30] The Council and the COREPER criticised the dilution of the EP's position. It later became clear that this was a misjudgement on the part of the Commission, it delayed progression of the matter, and it was finally shelved temporarily in anticipation of the summit in The Hague.[31] In the autumn 1969, the member governments began to take the lead in the negotiations, and the Commission now had out-played its own role in the remaining policy process leading up to the 1970-treaty.[32] Analysts have typically picked up the negotiations around this time, assuming that the logical link was more-or-less always given (Pollack 2003: 209–15). Yet to understand how the treaty was shaped, it has been necessary to search for how its fundamental premise materialised. That discussion, as has been demonstrated here, had been in the making for nearly a decade.

The December 1969-agenda of completing, deepening and enlarging was accepted by all the member governments though they had different priorities. Financing came under the heading of completion, but there was no consensus as to where the EP's new budgetary powers belonged. As earlier, the issue was carried forward by especially the Netherlands, Germany and Luxembourg, but ultimately resumed second rank at the summit (Rittberger 2005: 126). The Rotterdam agreement to broaden the notion of own resources complicated the discussions over institutional reform. It meant that those member states that originally had promoted the EP's empowerment based on normative arguments began to revise their positions.[33] Inside the Dutch administration, for example, the budgetary restraints had already weakened internal support for the logical link (Molegraaf 1999). Moreover, the fact that enlargement had entered the equation further complicated the picture. In an address to the French National Assembly in November 1969, for example, French foreign minister Maurice Schumann now argued that it would be crucial to cement a permanent financing agreement before re-starting the accession negotiations with Britain (Rittberger 2003: 215). He did not, however, mention the possible institutional reform that would follow the new financing model, and so before this domestic audience, Schumann downplayed the logical link.

A new financial agreement had to be found at The Hague because the 1966-agreement would expire at the end of the year. Most agreed that faced with currency instability, a permanent solution to the community's own financial instability would signal that it had grown strong enough to face the challenges surrounding it.[34] The final Communiqué of the summit has been described alternately as a 'watershed' or as 'vague and evasive' (Harst 2003: 7). From the perspective of the logical link, it was both. While the logical link was reiterated, the summit agreed to separate the subsequent negotiations relating to the financing solution and delegation to the EP. This move had been engineered by the German government, and meant that the EP's new role could be negotiated in a new way (Hiepel 2003: 79). The French government had rejected any talk of direct elections to the EP, but accepted that there was no turning back on a new role for the EP in the budgetary procedure.

It had taken the community a decade to get to the stage when everyone accepted the principle of the logical link. The negotiations after The Hague summit did therefore not have to deal with the basic premises involved in the logical link, but could instead focus on the degree to which delegation and institutional reform should happen (Rittberger

2005: 124). While the Commission remained sidelined in this process, national representatives were now aware that their moves were being scrutinised closely by national parliaments, yet the EP's Spénale Report from December 1969 remained moderate in its demands.[35] It interestingly accepted several limitations to the EP's powers while also suggesting – in line with documents in the Commission and discussions among national representatives – that that national value added tax (VAT) could become own resources.[36] On this basis, the Commission moved to revise its 1969-proposal.[37] The presence of VAT caused a rearrangement of positions of the key players.[38] For instance, the Dutch and Luxembourg representatives began questioning the necessity of granting budgetary powers to the EP over VAT because it was fundamentally a national tax. It became clear that with multiple sources of own resources, a balance had to be found between national and supranational parliamentary legitimacy, and the EP still lacked popular legitimacy.[39]

Between 17 and 21 December, the Council discussed the degree of delegation of budgetary authority to the EP and other nuances of institutional reform.[40] In particular, a more substantial discussion developed over how to distinguish between the common and nationally based own resources.[41] A concern for parliamentary legitimacy was now seen as a potential problem of undermining national parliamentary control also by former proponents of further powers to the EP.[42] In the current proposal the Commission still held a central position in drafting the budget, but with national funds involved, particularly the French delegation began to question whether this was appropriate. These complex discussions led to the invention of the distinction between compulsory and non-compulsory expenditure that found its way into the 1970-Treaty.

By the end of December, the overall framework was practically in place for creating own resources along with the institutional reform of the 1970-Treaty. The COREPER now began working on outstanding technical issues such as how to set limits to spending.[43] Importantly, the Dutch and Italian delegations teamed up behind a German proposal to involve the EP's Budget Committee. Despite objections from the Commission, it was agreed in early February that the Commission would have to cooperate with the relevant EP committees about setting limits to budgetary increases.[44] While this in no way created a genuine supranational power of the purse, opponents to this 'tight circumscription' (Harryvan and Harst 2003) of the EP's role seemed to accept that it was the best deal available at the time for the EP. The final meeting of the Council to sign the Decision and Treaty in April 1970 had more the character of a ceremonial closure than intergovernmental bargaining because the new financing model and the institutional innovations related to it had been settled gradually in the interinstitutional dialogue over the past decade.

Enhancing accountability

The thrust of the second Budget Treaty of 22 July 1975 was the creation of the CoA and the right of the EP to reject the draft budget. The political process towards this result did not pick up directly from where the 1970-treaty had been settled, but also had a separate trajectory.

By creating the CoA, the 1975-treaty reacted to concrete problems in the institutional design of the original Audit Board, namely its lack of competences and resources to exert control, as well as its complete independence. A report from 1969 by the Audit Board drew attention to its own inability to control the accounts and expenditures of particularly the CAP and the European Development Fund (EDF). The EP reacted in October 1969 by 'instruct[ing] the Committee for Finance and Budgets to keep a constant check on the financial management of the Communities' (EP1973: 63). The EP's monitoring of this situation had actually begun much earlier when in 1965 it had first questioned the Commission over alleged manipulations of agricultural levies and refunds on imports of wheat and maize (EP 1973: 80–1). It subsequently continued to push the Commission and Audit Board on the matter. Moreover, there was a problem about the independence of the Audit Board auditors resulting from the statute for recruitment. Appointments to the Audit Board had initially consisted of academic professors and members of national auditing bodies, but towards the end of the 1960s there had been a tendency among certain (unnamed) member states to also nominate officials employed in national administrations (EP 1973: 19). Finally, the EP report pointed to the inadequacy of resources available to make the Board efficient. The Audit Board had around 40 staff when it was dissolved, and to most of them, auditing of community finances was carried out 'more or less as a side-line occupation' (EP 1973: 19). By contrast, the CoA would by 1995 have a staff of 500 (Laffan 1999: 256).

In view of the 1969-report of the Audit Board, and the EP's continuing criticism of the matter, Albert Coppé, commissioner for Budgetary Affairs, presented a plan for increasing internal audit in the Commission, thus avoiding to take position on a new external, independent auditing institution. This led to a dispute between the EP and the Commission, the former accusing the latter of having obstructed external audits by the Audit Board on several accounts (EP 1973: 65–70). The EP's Committee for Finance and Budgets – that following the 1970-treaty now enjoyed the formal right to be consulted by the Commission when drafting budgetary increases – went a step further and in September 1972 held meetings with the presidents or representatives of the six national auditing offices to discuss how financial control of the community's budget could be improved (EP 1973: 152). In this forum, there was broad agreement towards the need for improvements. Against this background, the Audit Board, the EP and – reluctantly – the Commission had already had a long-term exchange of opinions about the pitfalls of the current auditing system when the Heads of State and Government of the enlarged community in October 1972 issued a Communiqué expressing the desire to strengthen the powers of control of the EP.

The introduction of own resources had also led to a number of questions about the control of community revenue on the basis of the figures declared by the member states, and the new member states that joined the community in January 1973 made a further push in the direction of getting control of the community's funds. On the one hand, a working group under the Council of Ministers began discussing the extent to which Commission officials should have access to controlling the national bases for the determination of own resources, and what the authority of the Commission's controllers should be.[45] Powers to the EP or the CoA did not emerge in these discussions. On the other hand, the community's structure of financing and expenditure was a great disadvantage to particularly Britain, something that had been a long-standing controversy in the enlargement negotiations in the 1960s. Moreover, new reform-eager MEPs had come in such as the leader of the British Conservative delegation to the EP, Sir Peter Kirk, who actively engaged himself in matters of efficiency, openness and accountability (Laffan 1999: 254). And as former finance minister in France, the new Commission President François-Xavier Ortoli, was sympathetic towards the idea of creating a respectable external auditing board. In this scenario, it is difficult to judge exactly where the initiative for the CoA came from, as there was broad agreement among experts and politicians that it was necessary to assure good governance of community funds.

The Council's legal service began in 1972 to mention 'good financial management' as an absolute necessary requirement for the functioning of the community.[46] The EP in September 1973 provided further documentation of problems of auditing. Behind the report were three long-term MEPs: Heinrich Aigner, Cornelius Berkhouwer and Georges Spénale. The report noted that it would be 'a grave threat to European integration if the financial management and expenditure of a European bureaucracy more or less responsible only to itself is not brought under an adequate and independent control authority' (EP 1973: 16). It pointed to a 'communications gap' between all parties involved that needed to be solved in view of the complexity of the emerging community legislation. Around the same time, the Commission issued two documents that essentially drafted the 1975-treaty.[47] It was recognised that 'Control over the use of public money by the institutions of the Community is insufficient and must be strengthened. In this connection, Parliament has a key role to play'.[48] It proposed the creation of a 'Court of Auditors', but still insisted that 'the Commission will continue as at present to have the exclusive and heavy responsibility of implementing the budget', and conceded that the EP alone should have the power of discharge upon recommendation from the Council.[49] Moreover, it recommended that the EP be brought into the budgetary process at an earlier stage, particularly in view of the multi-annual budgetary frameworks for community activities, and that the EP's involvement with all types of expenditure be gradually increased to include the entire community budget.

There were thus many commonalities between the EP's suggestions and the Commission's draft treaty as it appeared in June 1973. The EP had a more vivid imagination, suggesting a standing 'flying squad' of auditors to perform unannounced controls, and expecting that there would be 'psychological effects of an auditors' corps capable of working at any time and in any place would assure itself felt in the Member States' administrations ... and would certainly act as a deterrent to potential "agricultural defrauders"' (EP 1973: 28). A consensus seemed to have emerged that the community needed to do something to enforce institutions of good governance. From this time onwards, 'there was no outright opposition from other member states' (Laffan 1999: 254).

It still took another two years before the treaty was signed. While there was no British reluctance per se to the draft treaty, it was primarily the British government that stalled progress. In February 1974, the Labour government returned to office and demanded a renegotiation of its terms of membership, and subsequently announced a referendum over membership. The threat of British dismemberment was in fact taken seriously in many quarters.[50] The Commission issued an analysis of Britain's 'unacceptable situation'.[51] Shortly thereafter came a bulky report from the EP that tried to assess the effects on Britain of community membership.[52] It did not shower Britain with pity over its current situation, but it advised that a correction to its budgetary contributions could bring benefits at the 'psychological level which is particularly important to the Community, than at the level of economic and financial reality'.[53] In March 1975, the first 'correction mechanism' was made setting out the conditions for Britain getting refunds from the community's budget. It was a 'diplomatically contrived package with a number of complex restrictions which made it at first sight difficult to evaluate' (Dodsworth 1975). Yet the rebate, as it became known, helped appeasing the British political leadership and public in the referendum scheduled to take place on 5 June. A referendum in Britain was at the time an alien arrangement, causing controversy that had nothing to do with community membership *per se*, but rather because it would mean a shift away from the Burkeian idea of the MP as the true representative of the people that had underpinned Britain's parliamentary system for centuries (Butler and Kietzinger 1976: 12–13). Less than two months after the referendum, the 1975-treaty was signed. Its negotiations had been shaped in a broad inter-institutional debate, and had not evoked much controversy or need for dramatic negotiations.

Conclusion: The significance of the budgetary treaties

The institutional innovations made in the budgetary treaties made their clear mark on the EC/EU in the longer run in very concrete terms. Firstly, with own resources the EC/EU became 'financially independent'. It did not end budgetary conflicts in the community, but changed the nature of it (Lindner 2006). This opened for new opportunities such as discussions over fiscal federalism and the financial platform necessary for establishing monetary union. Secondly, with the Lisbon Treaty the EP gained co-legislative powers in virtually all policy areas, and in retrospect it seems clear that the 1970-treaty set the fundament for this. Shortly after the passing of the 1975-treaty, the Council accepted to make the EP directly elected; a debate that in fact had been another inter-institutional struggle since the late 1950s. Thirdly, the CoA signalled that the community was willing to enforce good governance, and its mandate was strengthened in the Amsterdam Treaty (art. 188C). The CoA did not however eliminate the problems of fraud and irregularity in relation to community expenditure, but by enforcing these majoritarian and non-majoritarian institutions, the budgetary treaties enforced the democratic architecture of the community. Meanwhile, five countries made other institutional innovations from the toolbox of democratic governance, namely the referendums in Norway, Denmark, Ireland, France and Britain.

The analysis of the contents and origins of the budgetary treaties in this chapter has added further perspectives to how treaties are made. Instead of focusing solely on how member states bargain, it has shown that the shape of treaties was moulded decisively in inter-institutional debates. Particularly the EP's own role in the political process has not previously been identified. By consistently advancing arguments for the logical link and the legitimacy deficit, it persuaded the Council and Commission to respond. This was not only about discursive and normative agenda-setting, but about MEPs' ability to use their multiple political positions. In preparation of the 1975-treaty, for example, MEPs were also able to use their national platforms to establish meetings with national auditing institutions to prepare the ground for the creation of the CoA. The Commission's role was ambiguous throughout. The Hallstein Commission would, it appears, gladly have installed own resources without the logical link. It was only when the Commission saw the need for a counter-balance to the Council in budgetary matters that embracing the logical link became attractive. Yet, the Commission also delimited the EP's future role in its proposals even at times when it claimed to accept the logical link. The activities during 1965 and 1966 illustrated that there were several veto-players in establishing the logical link, particularly the Commission and the French government, but not necessarily out of rejection of the principle of the logical link. The official declarations and communiqués from the member states were often reactions to issues that had been brewing in the community's political system, and the relatively technical matters addressed in the budgetary treaties are a good example of that. To study the making of the treaties on the basis of national leadership positions and intergovernmental bargaining alone would be to misrepresent how the community functioned when the budgetary treaties were made.

Notes

1. Figure from EP, Draft Report, PE 23.807, 23 January 1970, Historical Archives of the European Communities (HAEC), Brussels Archives Commission (BAC), 51/1986, 833.
2. EP, Resolution of 18 October 1962, *Journal Officiel*, no. 116, 12/11/1962, pp. 2669–72.
3. Quote from the EP's Deringer rapport, doc.74/62, reproduced in Commission, Secrétariat Général, Note, 31 March 1969, SEC (69)1250/2, HAEC/BAC, Bxl, 187/1995, p. 1.

4. EP, Resolution, 18 October 1962.
5. Commission's summary in Note, 28 April 1969, SEC (69)1250/3, p. 6.
6. SEC (69)1250/3, p. 5f.
7. Commission's summary in Note, 25 March 1969, SEC (69)1250, p. 2.
8. SEC (69)1250/3, pp. 7–9.
9. Johan H. Molegraaf, *Boeren in Brussel. Nederland en het Gemeenschappelijk Europees Landbouwbeleid 1958–1971*, PhD, Utrecht: University of Utrecht, 1999, Chapter 8.
10. SEC (69)1250, p. 2.
11. SEC (69)1250, pp. 4–5.
12. Secretariat General (SecGen), Note, SEC (69)2786, 11 July 1969, HAEC/BAC, 51/1986, 832.
13. SEC (69)1250/3, p. 9.
14. EP, Doc. 102.
15. Commission, Proposal, COM (65)150, 31 March 1965, HAEC/BAC.
16. EP, Minutes, 24 March 1965, SEC (69)1250/3, p. 10.
17. EP, Resolution, 14 May 1965, Council of Ministers (CM2), 1965, 474.
18. SEC (69)1250/3, p. 12.
19. Council, Rapport, R/622/65 (Agri 254) (Fin 51) (Ass 250), 9 June 1965, HAEC/BAC, Cabinet Marjolin, 1965, 285.
20. For example, Council, Press statement, 29 January 1966, CM2, 1966, 476.
21. Various documents early 1966, HAEC/BAC, Cabinet Marjolin, 1966/1036P.
22. EP, Resolution, 20 October 1966, quote, SEC (69)1250/2, p. 7.
23. Extract, SEC (69)1250/3, p. 21.
24. SEC (69)1250, pp. 16–17.
25. COM (68)550, 1 July 1968, SEC(69)1250/3, pp. 23–4.
26. For example, EP, Report, 3 July 1968, SEC (69)1250/2, p. 9.
27. SEC (69)1250/3, p. 25; Communication, M. Grund, 9 September 1968, SEC (68)3201, HAEC/BAC, Cabinet Mansholt, 38/1984, 18.
28. For example, Comité de politique budgétaire, Report, 12 December 1968, HAEC/BAC. 20/1973, 1.
29. SecGen, Report, SEC (69)1071, 14 March 1969, HAEC/BAC, 7/1973, 28/1; SEC (69)1250/3, p. 31; SecGen, Draft proposal, SEC(69)1071/9, 14 July 1969, HAEC/BAC, Bxl, 20/1973, 2; Commission, Communication, COM(69)1020final, 30 October 1969, HAEC/BAC, 207/1996, 29.
30. SecGen, Report, SEK (69)1071/4, 23 June1969, HAEC/BAC, Cab. Mansholt, 38/1984, 18.
31. Council, Note, R/2077/69 (AGRI 622) (FIN 378), 7 November 1969, HAEC/BAC, Bxl, 207/1996, 29.
32. Council, Note, R/2340/69 (ASS 1223, FIN 449), 3 December 1969, HAEC/BAC, 207/1996, 29.
33. SecGen, Note, 5 December 1969, SEC (69)4638/2, HAEC/BAC, 20/1973, 3.
34. Commission, Bulletin, no. 305, 4 December 1969, CM2, 1969, 1271 (temp).
35. EP, Report, Doc. 174, 8 December 1969, HAEC/BAC, 207/1996, 29.
36. SecGen, Note, SEC (69)4729, 14 December 1969. HAEC/BAC, 187/1995, 15.
37. SecGen, Note, SEC (69)4710, 8–9 December 1969, HAEC/BAC, 187/1995, 15.
38. For example, Council, Questions à examiner, R/2520/69 (ASS 1246), 16 December 1969, HAEC/BAC, Cab. Coppé, 74/1985, 648.

39. Council, Minutes, extract, 17 and 19–21 December 1969, HAEC/BAC, 51/1986, 833; SecGen, Note and Annex II, SEC (69)6989, 19 December 1969, HAEC/BAC, 187/1995, 15.
40. PE 23.807.
41. Sec (69)6989.
42. SecGen, Note, SEC (69)4769, 13 December 1969, HAEC/BAC, 187/1995, 15; Council, R/2520/69 (ASS 1246).
43. Council, Note, R/14/70 (AGRI6) (FIN2), 7 January 1970, HAEC/BAC, 207/1996, 29; Minutes, COREPER, 15–16 January 1970, HAEC/BAC, 187/1995, 15.
44. Council, Minutes, 19–20 January 1970, HAEC/BAC, 51/1986, 833.
45. Referat af møde, 9 March 1973, Udenrigsministeriet; Conseil, Projet, Note, Objet: Règlement financier général applicable au budget des Communautés Européennes. R/724/73 (FIN163) (ATO44); Conseil, Document de Travail, T/168/73 (FIN), and Council, Note, R/600/73 (FIN 132) (JUR 27), both documents 19 March 1973, all in Udenrigsministeriet (the Danish Ministry for Foreign Affairs, UM) 400D9/2.
46. Conseil, Service Juridique, Note, 27 June 1972, UM 400, D9/2.
47. COM (73)999, Practical measures to strengthen the powers of control of the Parliament and to improve relations between the Parliament and the Commission, Communication to the Parliament. Brussels, 30 May 1973; COM (73)1000, Strengthening of the Budgetary Powers of the European Parliament (Project of the Commission presented to the Council on 8 June 1973), 6 June 1973, *Bulletin of the European Communities*, Supplement 9/73.
48. COM (73)1000, p. 2.
49. COM (73)1000, pp. 2–3.
50. For example, letter and appendices, Wendel-Petersen to Erling (Jørgensen), 4 April 1974, UM 400.A.3.
51. COM(75)40, European Commission, The Unacceptable Situation and the Correction Mechanism. Commission communication to the Council. Brussels, 30 January 1975 (aei).
52. European Parliament, The Effects on the United Kingdom of Membership of the European Communities, February 1975 (aei).
53. Find reference in February 1975 report.

6
The Single European Act: Revitalising European Integration

Desmond Dinan

The Single European Act (SEA) is an unassuming name for a far-reaching reform of the Rome Treaty, a reform that helped revitalise political and economic integration in the late 1980s and that paved the way for the launch of the European Union in 1993. Yet when national leaders concluded the SEA at a summit in Luxembourg in December 1985, the title of the accord seemed appropriate for an outcome that greatly disappointed proponents of ever closer union. Hopes that the 1985 intergovernmental conference (IGC) would result in a treaty on European Union crumbled in the face of widespread uncertainty over what, exactly, European Union meant, and over most governments' unwillingness to go beyond seemingly narrow treaty amendments. Even so, the substance of the SEA was impressive, given the difficulty of revising the Rome Treaty and moving the European Community in a more federal direction.

The reactions of most observers and participants reflected the importance attached to the SEA at the time of its negotiation. Commission President Jacques Delors was downcast, believing that national governments had been too timid in the IGC, thus reducing progress to the level of the lowest common denominator. Franco-German leadership had not been decisive; far from pushing a radical reform agenda, French President François Mitterrand had been unassertive and German Chancellor Helmut Kohl had apparently succumbed to British Prime Minister Margaret Thatcher's minimalist position. Thatcher's delight and Delors's disappointment were typical of contemporary responses to the outcome of the IGC. Delors even wondered whether the SEA would suffice to allow completion of the single market by the end of 1992 (Delors, 2004). As the *Common Market Law Review* editorialised in 1986, 'the results [of the IGC] are disappointingly meager. They ... fall short of the expectations ... of the Commission and some of the member states. ... But they reflect the limits of what was possible at the turn of the year [1985–1986]' (*Common Market Law Review* 1986, p. 251).

Few predicted the impact that the SEA would have on the course of European integration, not least because the ostensibly modest treaty reform coincided with the accession of Portugal and Spain. The experience of enlargement so far had not been reassuring. Britain and Denmark seemed ill-at-ease in the community; Greece was obstructionist. Even if they became model members, Portugal and Spain would add to the complexity of Council decision-making. Would the greater scope for qualified majority voting (QMV) provided for in the SEA ensure implementation of the single market program in an enlarged EC? Would the call in the SEA for reform of the structural funds – the instruments of economic and social cohesion – satisfy the poorer member states and remove a potential impediment to completion of the single market? Would the modest extension of the European Parliament's legislative authority come at the expense of efficient decision-making? Would the SEA's other reforms help reinvigorate European integration?

The significance of the SEA soon became clear. Within a year or two, the impact of the SEA delighted Euro-enthusiasts and dismayed Eurosceptics. The SEA sparked an astonishing transformation in the EC, which even enjoyed a brief burst of popularity in the late 1980s, based on widespread support for the single market program.

The SEA also sparked a revival of academic interest in the phenomenon of European integration. Neo-functionalism, the dominant theory of European integration in the late 1950s and early 1960s, had fallen into disfavour as European integration appeared to stagnate following the Gaullist challenge of the mid-1960s and the economic setbacks of the 1970s. Integration no longer seemed an inexorable process driven by a politically powerful Commission, acting as a policy entrepreneur in the European interest. The revival of integration in the post-SEA period gave neo-functionalism, in the form of supranationalism, a new lease on life. More important, it spawned liberal intergovernmentalism, a contending theory of European integration that emphasized the primacy of commercial interests, the leading role of national actors (notably the leaders of the three big member states), and the centrality of intergovernmental bargaining in the development of European integration.[1]

What accounts for the SEA's success? What accounts for the SEA itself? How significant were economic, political, and strategic concerns? How influential were the Commission, under Delors's energetic leadership, and the directly elected European Parliament? What were the inter-institutional and inter-personal dynamics during the negotiations themselves? Was the 1985 IGC a case apart? What lessons does it provide for subsequent IGCs and later rounds of treaty change? What were it theoretical underpinnings? This chapter addresses these questions while recounting the negotiation, ratification, and implementation of the SEA.

Prelude to the Intergovernmental Conference

By the time that major treaty reform was mooted in the mid-1980s, the European Council had become the predominant decision-making forum in the EC. Regular meetings of the heads of state or government, plus the Commission president, were major events in the life of the EC, where big decisions were reached. The European Council had proved its worth in the negotiation and launch of the European Monetary System in the late 1970s and in resolving the protracted British budgetary question in 1984. Similarly, the European Council would be essential for reaching agreement on how to complete the internal market, an objective that had emerged in the early 1980s as essential for economic recovery and resurgence.

The key question revolved around voting in the Council of Ministers. According to the Luxembourg Compromise of 1966, which ended the Gaullist boycott of the Council of Ministers, governments could prevent a vote from taking place in the Council by invoking a 'very important' national interest. Thereafter, legislative decision-making slowed to a crawl as governments succumbed to pressure from vested national interests to block supposedly unfavourable outcomes. Governments were especially prone to invoke the Luxembourg Compromise during the recessionary 1970s, and Britain and Denmark, instinctively wary of supranationalism, saw the Luxembourg Compromise as part of their EC membership deal. By the early 1980s, the Luxembourg Compromise had become a major impediment to completing the single market.

Moreover, achieving a fully functioning internal market would mean tackling non-tariff barriers to trade. Yet Article 100 of the Rome Treaty stipulated that 'the approximation of such provisions laid down by law, regulation, or administrative action in Member States as directly affect the establishment or functioning of the common market' – that is, non-tariff barriers – could happen only on the basis of unanimity in the Council. The Commission's new approach to approximation or harmonisation, based on the principle of mutual recognition, would reduce the amount of legislation needed to tackle non-tariff barriers. To the extent that old-fashioned regulation was still necessary for some harmonising measures, however, the unanimity requirement of Article 100 could prove insurmountable.

Thatcher, a fierce proponent of economic integration, advocated a simple solution to completing the internal market: when it came to enacting single market measures, governments should forego the Luxembourg Compromise or, in the case of Article 100, legislate in the Council on the basis of qualified majority voting. Governments could make a political commitment along those lines, just as they had made a political commitment in the Luxembourg Compromise to renounce qualified majority voting when sensitive national interests were at stake.

Thatcher made the case for a revised Luxembourg Compromise at the Milan summit in June 1985, where national leaders endorsed the Commission's White Paper on Completing the Internal Market, which outlined the legislative measures necessary to implement the single market by the end of 1992 (European Commission 1985). In addition to the White Paper, national leaders considered a report by the Ad Hoc Committee on Institutional Reform, chaired by Irish senator Jim Dooge, which they had commissioned the previous year to consider options for EC reform. Malcolm Rifkind, Thatcher's representative on the committee, had argued vociferously in favour of a revised Luxembourg Compromise and against convening an IGC to negotiate formal treaty change. The personal representatives of the Danish and Greek prime ministers also opposed the IGC option. Nevertheless the Dooge report recommended convening an IGC, while noting the opposing opinions.

Beyond market integration, national governments proposed other EC-related policy initiatives in the mid-1980s, ranging from science and technology, to the environment, to regional policy. Furthermore, in view of the unsettled international situation at the time, many national governments favoured strengthening European Political Cooperation (EPC), the procedure for foreign policy cooperation among EC member states. Thatcher was enthusiastic about EPC, as long as it did not weaken transatlantic relations or acquire a powerful secretariat. Indeed, Thatcher brought to the Milan summit a paper on the EC's future that included proposals for reforming foreign policy cooperation.

A number of factors, therefore, energised the EC in the run up to the Milan summit. Change was in the air. Resolution of the debilitating row over Britain's budget contribution had cleared the decks for new community initiatives. There was strong momentum behind the emerging single market program. EPC reform seemed desirable and possible. Thatcher was amenable to moving things forward. Since his famous economic policy U-turn in 1983, Mitterrand had become a champion of deeper European integration, using his country's Council presidency in 1984 to help resolve the British budgetary question and reanimate European integration.

The Genscher-Colombo initiative of 1981, launched by the German and Italian foreign ministers, had called for more effective decision-making procedures in the EC as well as greater community competence in external relations (Rosengarten 2008). This gave rise to the 'Solemn Declaration on European Union', which national leaders endorsed at their summit in Stuttgart in June 1983. The Stuttgart Declaration covered a range of institutional and policy issues and was a harbinger of the SEA. With regard to the legislative process, it stated that 'Within the Council every possible means of facilitating the decision-making process will be used, including, in cases where unanimity is required, the possibility of abstaining from voting.' On the equally sensitive issue of parliamentary powers, it stated that 'The Council will enter into talks with the European Parliament and the Commission with the aim, within the framework of a new agreement, of improving and extending the scope of the conciliation procedure provided for in the Joint Declaration of 4 March 1975' (although Denmark entered a reservation on this point) (European Council 1983).

Finally, under the guidance of veteran Italian Euro-federalist Altiero Spinelli, the first directly elected European Parliament had produced the Draft Treaty Establishing the European Union. The draft treaty sought to substitute a single European Union treaty for the existing treaties establishing the European Communities. The EU would maintain the basic institutional structure and legal competence of the three communities but strengthen decision-making procedures and add new or expanded authority over certain aspects of economic, social, and political affairs. The purpose of decision-making reform was to improve efficiency and to close what politicians perceived as an emerging democratic deficit at the European level of governance. Sensitive to national concerns about the centralization of power in Brussels, the draft treaty included something that received little attention at the time but became prominent a decade later: the principle of subsidiarity, whereby the EU would be responsible only for tasks that could be undertaken more effectively in common than by governments acting alone. In one of the most famous votes ever taken in the EP, the draft treaty passed by a resounding majority, in February 1984 (*Bulletin of the European Communities* 1984).

The EP's Draft Treaty had less of an impact on national governments than had the Stuttgart Declaration, which national leaders had themselves endorsed. Nevertheless the Draft Treaty was not unimportant.

The timing of the EP vote was auspicious; it gave Mitterrand, then in the Council presidency and boldly championing deeper integration, additional political ammunition. The Draft Treaty, and Spinelli's author-ship of it, emboldened the Italian presidency in early 1985 to push for a decision at the Milan summit to launch an IGC on treaty reform (a desire for Italian leadership of the treaty reform movement led to an unlikely coalition of leading politicians: Spinelli, a Euro-communist; Foreign Minister Giulio Andreotti, a Christian Democrat; and Prime Minister Bettino Craxi, a socialist).

Given the strong momentum for deeper European integration, it is hardly surprising that the Milan summit generated as much attention and excitement as had The Hague summit of 1969, the last occasion on which the EC seemed on the verge of a major advance. As at The Hague 16 years previously, a pro-integration demonstration by members of the European Movement heightened public awareness of an imminent breakthrough. Determined to make the most of the Council presidency and assert its position at the forefront of European integration, Italy wanted an historic decision at the Milan summit to convene an IGC for a new treaty on European Union, or at least a major reform of the existing treaties.

Quick endorsement of the White Paper apparently presaged a success-ful outcome, but the meeting soon descended into acrimony. Mitterrand and Kohl presented a proposal for a treaty on European Union that dealt mostly with EPC. The Franco-German proposal closely resembled a paper that Thatcher had shown to Mitterrand and Kohl months before the summit suggesting more formal arrangements for EPC, including a small secretariat and commitments form national leaders to consult each other before launching foreign policy initiatives (Wall 2008, p. 53). Thatcher was incensed because Mitterrand and Kohl presented their proposal in the form of a new treaty, without reference to her earlier idea. In a cutting aside, Thatcher later remarked that 'the behaviour of Mitterrand and Kohl was the kind of thing that would have got them thrown out of any London club' (Wall 2008, p. 54).

The contretemps among Thatcher, Mitterrand, and Kohl soured the atmosphere at the summit. The situation deteriorated as Thatcher fiercely resisted the idea of treaty change, instead advocating infor-mal arrangements to quicken decision-making in the Council and facilitate completion of the single market. Taking a coordinated posi-tion, Mitterrand and Kohl urged treaty reform. The Italian presidency forced the issue by proposing an IGC to negotiate a possible new treaty on political cooperation and a revision of the Rome Treaty to address institutional and other issues. For reasons of principle (defence of national sovereignty) and pragmatism (awareness of prevailing opinion in their national parliaments), the British and Danish prime ministers objected; their Greek colleague followed suit. Italy further pressed the point by calling for a vote under Article 236 of the Rome Treaty, permitting an IGC to be convened if a majority of member states approved. It was unprecedented for national leaders to vote on anything in the European Council. In the ensuing ballot seven voted in favour of an IGC and three – the British, Danish, and Greek prime ministers – voted against (at that time the EC had ten member states; Portugal and Spain joined in January 1986).

Far from being a glorious reaffirmation of ever closer union, the Milan summit had degenerated into a bitter dispute over whether to convene an IGC. Nor did the fact that an IGC would take place necessarily guarantee a satisfactory outcome. Little wonder that Michael Burgess, a staunch Euro-federalist, saw the Milan summit as an 'opportunity [to endorse the EP's Draft Treaty] squandered by the shared faint-heartedness of Mitterrand and Kohl and torpedoed by the combined obstinacy of the British, Danes, and Greeks' (Burgess 1986, p. 77). In place of the ambitious Draft Treaty, national leaders had merely agreed, with difficulty, to convene what promised to be a bruising IGC.

Given Britain's relative importance, Thatcher's position was especially worrisome. It was nothing new for Thatcher, the lone crusader for reform of the EC budget, to be isolated in the European Council, but she was in a new situation in 1985. The IGC could proceed without the dissenting member states. By adopting an empty chair strategy, Thatcher would risk provoking a crisis in the EC and thwarting implementation of the single market programme, which she keenly wanted. Thatcher faced intense pressure from the Foreign Office to make a virtue of necessity and allow British representatives to participate positively in the IGC. In her post-summit press conference, Thatcher did not say that Britain would never agree to treaty change, only that she would need to be convinced during the IGC of the need for it. From Britain's point of view, 'The search for minimal, acceptable treaty change, avoiding risky isolation … and the possibility of our partners seeking to make progress without us, was to be the work of the next six months' (Wall 2008, p. 61).[2]

The Intergovernmental Conference

Despite the fractiousness of the Milan summit, there was a palpable sense of occasion when foreign ministers launched the IGC opened in Luxembourg in September 1985. Delors caught the mood when he remarked that 'conferences like this one are not convened every five or ten years. There may not be another between now and [the year] 2000' (Gazzo 1986, p. 23). Little could Delors have known that the success of the SEA, combined with the acceleration of globalization and collapse of communism in Central and Eastern Europe, would result in three more IGCs during the next 15 years.

Procedures and positions

The 1985 IGC took place formally at the foreign ministers' level, although national leaders devoted themselves exclusively to the subject at their summit in December 1985. The foreign ministers met for eight sessions of the IGC in all, and concluded their negotiations in Luxembourg in January 1986. Two working parties of high-level officials carried out the detailed negotiations. The first, consisting mostly of permanent representatives, dealt with the Rome Treaty revisions. The second, made up of the political directors of the foreign ministries (the 'political committee'), tackled EPC and also drafted the SEA's preamble. In addition to national ministers and officials, commissioners and Commission officials participated at all levels of the IGC. Yet the Commission did not have the right to veto a decision in the IGC, which – in that sense – remained strictly inter-governmental.[3]

Luxembourg was in the Council presidency during most of the IGC, which came to an end early in the succeeding Dutch presidency. Because the negotiations took the form of an intergovernmental conference, the presidency chaired the proceedings. It was fortunate that a small country such as Luxembourg, with fewer vested interests than its larger partners, was in the presidency for most of the conference. While favouring greater supranationalism in the EC, Luxembourg acted during the negotiations as a neutral chairman and honest broker, confident that Belgium and The Netherlands would advocate positions shared by the three Benelux countries.

The Council secretariat assisted the Luxembourg presidency, as did the Commission. Indeed, the IGC allowed the Council secretariat to assume a more prominent position in the EC system under the energetic leadership of Secretary-General Niels E. N. Ersbøll. Ersbøll's assertiveness – new for a Council secretary-general – helped to keep the Commission's influence in check and irritated Delors. If given a freer hand, Delors might well have succeeded in nudging Jacques Santer, the Luxembourg prime minister, in his role as conference chairman, in a more supranational direction. Santer was indeed a supranationalist, but took a middle-of-the-road position while in the Council presidency.

The procedural problem of parliamentary involvement in the negotiations proved almost as contentious as the substantive issue of increasing the EP's political power. Members of the EP (MEPs), revelling in their status as directly elected representatives, and citing the supposedly pivotal role of the 1985 Draft Treaty in propelling European integration, claimed a moral right to sit at the conference table. Although Article 236 did not provide for parliamentary participation in the IGC, it required the consent of the community's institutions before such a conference could take place. The Commission and the Council gave their approval without difficulty or delay, but the EP used the opportunity to complain about its exclusion from the proceedings. While vainly demanding 'full and equal participation in drafting the new treaty', the EP nonetheless gave its assent to the IGC in July 1985 (*Official Journal* 1985, p. 29).

At the opening session of the IGC, foreign ministers tried to appease the EP by agreeing to 'take account' of the Draft Treaty and any parliamentary proposals and to 'submit' the results of their deliberations to the EP. Pouncing on this statement, the EP put forward a mechanism to consider the results of the conference, suggest amendments, and, if necessary, settle differences by a conciliation procedure. Most national governments had no intention of adopting such an elaborate mechanism, being of the opinion that 'submit' meant no more than 'inform'. The EP was welcome to express opinions on whatever the conference sent to it, but ministers were under no obligation to consider those opinions in turn.

Nevertheless the EP acquired some leverage over the proceedings because the Italian government, wanting to strengthen the role of the EP in the community system and to champion the Draft Treaty, linked its approval of the outcome of the IGC to the EP's approval. This does not seem to have materially affected the substance of the SEA. However, it became an issue at the end of the conference when the Italian government delayed signing the SEA precisely because of the EP's reservations. In the event, the other member states called Italy's (and the EP's) bluff. Was Italy really going to thwart the SEA for the sake of solidarity with the EP, especially as the SEA increased the EP's power (although not as much as the EP wanted)? The answer was obvious: the Italian government duly signed the SEA and the EP duly endorsed it.

The Stuttgart Declaration and the Dooge Report, rather than the EP's Draft Treaty, provided a foundation for the IGC. The negotiations proceeded on the basis of written submissions from national governments (either jointly or separately) and the Commission. One of the Commission's earliest contributions recommended a single concluding document rather than a treaty on foreign and security cooperation and a separate set of Rome Treaty revisions. Most governments saw the advantage of having one document emerge from the IGC. Yet it was only at a late stage of the negotiations, in December 1985, that foreign ministers endorsed the idea of *unicité* and named the eventual outcome of their deliberations the *Single* European Act.

Other contributions to the conference covered foreign and security policy; the internal market, the environment; research and development; economic and monetary policy; economic and social cohesion between rich and poor member states; culture and education; and institutional affairs. Governments adopted their positions on the basis of internal deliberations and national political debates. As in any international negotiation, national positions reflected the views of the parties or coalition of parties in power. Governments were well aware that the outcome of the IGC would require ratification at home, which would require the support of a majority (or possibly supermajority) of the members of national parliaments. Inevitably, domestic political realities determined and sometimes constrained the positions of national governments.

Policies

The scope of QMV, the legislative power of the EP, and the mere mention of monetary policy were the most contentious issues in the IGC. By contrast, despite divergent national positions on the reform of EPC, governments dealt easily and quickly with the question of foreign policy cooperation. Current trends in East-West relations – intensified Cold War rivalry gradually giving way to direct US-Soviet bargaining without European involvement – convinced most governments of the need to assert the EC's international identity by shoring up foreign policy cooperation. All participants agreed on the need to make the EC's external economic policy and the member states' foreign policies more consistent with each other. Specific ideas included formalising EPC in the Rome Treaty, strengthening EPC procedures, establishing an EPC secretariat, and incorporating military and defence issues. Neutral Ireland shied away from going too far down the defence road, as did reluctant (though NATO member) Denmark and idiosyncratic (though also NATO member) Greece. Britain and the Netherlands, strongly Atlanticist in orientation, warned that the EC should not risk alarming a sensitive United States by appearing to undermine NATO with far-reaching treaty changes.

Despite traditional differences between the Atlanticist and Europeanist member states, and the reservations of Denmark, Ireland, and Greece, the negotiations on EPC were not particularly onerous and ended before the Luxembourg summit. Governments were sensitive to each other's concerns; none took an extreme or irreconcilable position on a procedural or substantive aspect of EPC. What became Title III of the SEA dealt exclusively with EPC, which in effect became an intergovernmental pillar of the EC (and in the Maastricht Treaty would formally become an intergovernmental pillar of the EU). To emphasise its distinctiveness from other policy areas, decisions relating to EPC would be taken only on the basis of unanimity and would not be subject to review by the Court of Justice. Nevertheless national governments agreed that the Commission would be 'fully associated' and the EP 'closely associated' with EPC.

The IGC concluded that member states would 'coordinate their positions more closely on the political and economic aspects of security' and 'endeavour jointly to formulate and implement a European foreign policy'. Procedural improvements included ending the distinction between foreign ministers' meetings 'in EPC' and in the General Affairs Council; creating a mechanism for convening the foreign ministers or the Political Committee (senior foreign ministry officials) within 48 hours at the request of at least three member states; and establishing a small EPC secretariat in Brussels. The SEA also stipulated that 'The external policies of the European Community and the policies agreed in Political Cooperation must be consistent' and charged the presidency and the Commission with ensuring such consistency. In deference to presumed American concerns and to those member states – notably Britain and the Netherlands – most sensitive about US opinion, the conference declared that greater foreign policy coordination would not 'impede closer cooperation in the field of security' among relevant member states 'in the framework of the Western European Union or the Atlantic Alliance'.

The political committee's deliberations on EPC were far less fraught than the permanent representatives' negotiations on revision of the Rome Treaty, which subsequently caused deep divisions among the foreign ministers and national leaders. Negotiators had little difficulty endorsing the goal of the internal market and the target date of 1992 for its completion, but found it harder to define the internal market as 'an area without internal frontiers in which the free movement of goods, persons, services, and capital is ensured'. Concerned about illegal immigration, cross-border crime, drug-trafficking, and the possible spread of rabies from across the channel, Britain insisted that such a definition did not mean the abolition of border controls.

During the IGC, Delors returned repeatedly to his pet project of including 'a certain monetary capacity' in the eventual agreement. This would help bring about 'an alignment of economic policies' in the community 'and outside it would enable Europe to make its voice heard more strongly in the world of economic, financial and monetary matters' (Gazzo 1986, p. 9). Finance ministers considered the question at an informal meeting in Luxembourg in September 1985 – the only sectoral Council to discuss IGC issues – after which the Commission submitted a formal proposal, as did the Belgian government in late November. Britain strongly opposed any move towards EMU; France was broadly in favour; and Germany was equivocal, foreign minister Genscher being more inclined at that stage than Kohl towards strengthening monetary policy cooperation in the EC.

Without strong support from a large member state – France was unwilling to go out on a limb and disregard the British and German positions – Delors succeeded only in having a reiteration of the 1972 Paris summit's approval of 'the objective of the progressive realization of Economic and Monetary Union' included in the preamble of the SEA, as well as short chapter on 'Cooperation in Economic and Monetary Policy'. This merely recognised the desirability of converging economic and monetary policies 'for the further development of the Community', and specifically mentioned the European Monetary System and the European currency unit. Crucially, the new chapter specified that 'insofar as further development in the field of economic and monetary policy necessitates institutional changes, the provisions of Article 236 shall be applicable'. In other words, progress towards achieving EMU would require an IGC, in which decision-making was based on unanimity. Thatcher interpreted this as a guarantee that EMU would never happen, at least on her watch.

Cohesion, or efforts to promote economic convergence between rich and poor countries and regions, was another controversial item. Delors and the leaders of the poorer member states (including imminent members Portugal and Spain) exploited uncertainty about the distributional consequences of the single market programme to advocate a significant increase in spending on the structural funds (the instruments of cohesion policy). Fears that the dynamics of market integration would intensify existing regional disparities led to an explicit link in the SEA between cohesion policy and the 1992 programme. Governments would have to go beyond a mere 'solidarity principle'. Otherwise, the single market programme might never be implemented if the poorer member states and their allies held up the necessary legislation. As Greece had shown during the negotiations on Portuguese and Spanish accession, a determined member state could leverage its ability to block a 'big event' unless it received a generous side payment.

Accordingly, the Commission proposed a substantial redistribution of resources via the community budget for the EC's less prosperous countries. Although one of the attractions of the single market program for a financially strapped EC was its relative lack of cost, the Commission's emphasis on cohesion raised the prospect of a sizeable increase in the budget. Thatcher opposed any such increase, let alone financial transfers to poor countries. A devout neo-liberal, she firmly believed that the market would provide the means to improve the plight of less well-off member states. Mitterrand and Kohl were more in sympathy with the solidarity principle, although Kohl knew that Germany would bear most of the burden of enlarging the EC budget.

The compromise was a section in the SEA on economic and social cohesion, which called on the Commission, once the SEA entered into force, to submit a proposal to strengthen the structural funds and for the Council to act unanimously on the proposal within a year. Inevitably, the Commission would propose a hefty hike in spending on cohesion policy. Thatcher was right to think that the requirement for unanimity would allow Britain to block such a proposal, but wrong not to realise that linkage between cohesion and the single market program would nullify the use of the veto in this case.

The IGC addressed a number of other policy areas, notably the environment and research and technological development (R&D). Thatcher was sceptical about incorporating environmental policy into the Rome Treaty, not least because of Britain's poor record of environmental protection. She was especially reluctant to allow QMV for environmental measures, but went along with the wording of Article 130s whereby the Council, acting unanimously, 'shall decide what action is to be taken by the Community', and would then 'define those matters on which decisions are to be taken by a qualified majority'. Accordingly, Britain (and other member states) would be able to limit the scope of environmental policy in the EC through recourse to a national veto. Denmark's concern about environmental policy was that EC standards could undermine higher national standards. For that reason, Denmark won inclusion in the SEA of an article stating that EC environmental measures 'shall not prevent any Member State from maintaining or introducing more stringent protective measures compatible with this Treaty' (Article 130t).

The environment title of the SEA included the first reference in the EC treaty to the principle of subsidiarity, which would emerge as a major issue in subsequent treaty reforms. Without mentioning subsidiarity by name, Article 100r(4) stated that the EC would act on the environment only to the extent that its policy objectives 'can be attained better at Community level than at the level of the individual Member States'.

Most national governments and the Commission favoured including a title on R&D in the SEA. After all, concern about the EC's relative weakness in this area had contributed to the revival of interest in European integration in the early 1980s. Britain was sceptical about the usefulness of community-funded R&D programs and the desirability of QMV for the implementation of R&D policy. As in the case of environmental policy, however, Britain agreed to allow QMV for treaty provisions relating to R&D, such as the implementation of particular programs, as long as the general, multiannual framework program could be adopted only by unanimity.

Institutional issues

Negotiations about the procedural steps necessary to complete the internal market, notably through the use of QMV, were predictably pugnacious. There was widespread agreement on the necessity for QMV, but not on its general or unqualified application. Given the consensus on the desirability of completing the internal market, national governments agreed to revise Article 100 to allow majority voting on harmonisation, but only for approximately two-thirds of the measures outlined in the White Paper; the rest – the least tractable ones – were still subject to unanimity. The IGC also approved a number of national derogations for aspects of the single market programme.

Negotiators did not confront head-on the Luxembourg Compromise. Some governments saw in the agreement to use QMV for most of the single market programme the beginning of the end of the national veto. Others reached the opposite conclusion, citing the continued applicability of unanimity for the White Paper's most controversial proposals. Undoubtedly governments would remain sensitive to each other's special concerns, thus perpetuating 'the very strong inclination of the Council to seek consensus irrespective of the voting rules' (Bieber 1985).

The role of the EP in the community's decision-making process was another highly-sensitive institutional issue. To push the EC more in a federal direction and to increase its democratic legitimacy, Germany and Italy urged greater legislative power for the EP. For a combination of ideological and practical reasons, Britain and France opposed strengthening the EP's legislative role. Eventually, governments agreed to extend the requirement for consultation between the Council and the EP to new policy areas and, more important, to establish a cooperation procedure to involve the EP more fully in legislative decision-making, notably for most single market measures. This fell far short of co-decision by the Council and the EP in the enactment of EC legislation. Moreover, governments agreed to give the EP the right to approve future accession and association agreements. As these measures – the new cooperation and assent procedures – were less than those proposed in the Draft Treaty, the EP, supported by the Italian government, expressed serious dissatisfaction with them.

The IGC addressed the complex issue of 'comitology', or power delegated from the Council to the Commission for the implementation of Council decisions. The Commission pushed hard for the right to acquire implementing power for the single market program. Most member states, jealous of their prerogatives and sensitive to the far-reaching nature of the single market program, resisted giving the Commission unfettered executive authority. While agreeing in the SEA that powers of implementation should generally be conferred on the Commission, governments also agreed that the Council would have to decide, unanimously, on a set of principles and rules to define the exercise of those powers. This was a setback for the Commission.

Two other institutional innovations were largely symbolic, but portentous nonetheless. First, governments agreed to change the name 'European Assembly' to 'European Parliament'. Although 'European Parliament', was already widely used, the formal change of name symbolised the growing stature of the directly elected body, and robbed Thatcher of a way of belittling it. Second, governments acknowledged the importance of the European Council by including in the SEA an article describing its existence and composition, and stating that it 'shall meet at least twice a year'. Though still not formally an EC institution, the European Council was clearly on the ascendant in the EC's overall institutional architecture.

Concluding the IGC

The SEA was a package deal. Although governments had agreed to substantial parts of it before the concluding summit, a number of controversial issues – notably monetary policy, the extension of QMV, and the role of the EP – remained on the table as national leaders and the Commission president convened in Luxembourg on 2 December 1985.

Until these issues were settled, the entire package could have unravelled. Thatcher and Poul Schlüter, her Danish counterpart, came to the summit with reservations on all parts of the package; Thatcher as a negotiating ploy and Schlüter because of limits imposed by the Danish parliament (the *Folketing*).

Thatcher had been careful throughout the ICC not to show her hand until the summit itself (Wall 2008, p. 66). Although she complained about the absurdity of national leaders having to negotiate detailed treaty changes, Thatcher was in her element. She had an unrivalled grasp of complicated negotiating briefs and unparalleled experience in the European Council. Nonetheless Thatcher wanted to conclude the IGC in December; the longer it dragged on, the less advantageous it might be for Britain.

Of the outstanding issues in the summit negotiations, the question of whether to include a reference in the SEA to monetary policy cooperation, and what form such a reference should take, was settled first, when Thatcher and Kohl accepted a compromise proposed by The Netherlands. Secure in the knowledge that further progress on EMU could happen only in an IGC, the two leaders conceded a point of principle – keeping any reference to monitory policy out of the SEA – for the sake of the package agreement. Next, national leaders spent several hours at the summit negotiating specific exclusions from the general rule about using QMV to implement the single market programme, with Britain and Ireland insisting on border controls to protect plant and animal health and Denmark demanding safeguards for higher environmental standards.

The final outstanding issue concerned the role of the EP. Thatcher, Mitterrand, and Schlüter opposed granting the EP significant legislative authority; Kohl, Craxi and others favoured a form of co-decision between the EP and the Council. Both sides settled on the cooperation procedure, while Denmark and Italy issued reservation: Italy because the cooperation procedure did not go far enough and Denmark because it went too far down the road towards co-decision.

The negotiations, lasting nearly 20 hours over two days, ended after midnight on 3 December. The summit included many bilateral and plurilateral sessions, as well as multilateral negotiations involving all participants. Santer, in the presidency, proved adept at bringing the protagonists together and reconciling diverging positions. Each government had conceded something in the course of the IGC and each had gained enough to make an agreement possible and defensible in front of national parliaments.

Given her reputation for intransigence and reputed indifference to the EC, Thatcher's willingness to compromise in the IGC, notably on the questions of monetary policy and the legislative role of the EP, seems surprising. Yet as Thatcher herself wrote with regard to the British budgetary question, 'In every negotiation there comes the best possible time to settle' (Thatcher 1993, p. 540). As it was, Thatcher's concessions seemed limited. Further moves towards EMU and legislative co-decision looked politically unlikely and procedurally improbable in the near future. In return, Thatcher won the much bigger prize of a legally binding commitment to complete the single market.

Kohl and Mitterrand had compromised as well, softening their positions on co-decision (in the case of Kohl) and EMU (in the case of Mitterrand) for the sake of the overall agreement. In effect, the positions of the three major protagonists – Kohl, Mitterrand, and Thatcher – had converged on a determination to complete the single market regardless of their other preferences. There was no question of France and Germany excluding Britain, whose participation in the single market program was essential for the economic success of the venture. Britain's participation in EPC was equally important, and Germany was as keen as Britain to assuage US concerns about the direction of EPC by toning down its security dimension.

The summit came at the end of Delors's first year as Commission president. Indeed, the conduct and outcome of the IGC burnished Delors's image and strengthened his political position in Brussels, despite the predominance of national leaders in the decisive negotiating sessions. Overall, the Commission had been an important but not decisive player in the IGC, notwithstanding supranationalists' assertions to the contrary.

The Luxembourg summit was not quite the end of the IGC. The wording of a new article on social policy caused a last-minute delay. Britain reluctantly agreed to the use of QMV to establish 'minimum requirements for gradual implementation [of measures] having regard to the conditions and technical rules obtaining in each Member State', pertaining to 'the working environment, as regards health and safety of workers' (Article 118a). Thatcher's concern, subsequently justified, was that the Commission and sympathetic governments would use this provision to advance a broader social policy agenda. Whether because of fatigue or undue faith in the restrictive wording of the article, Thatcher went along with it and authorized her foreign secretary to approve, at the final ministerial session of the IGC in Luxembourg on 27 January 1986 the draft SEA put together by the Dutch presidency, the Commission's legal service, and the Council secretariat.

Signing and ratification

The foreign ministers of only nine of the 12 member states signed the SEA in Luxembourg on 17 February 1986, the date stipulated by the IGC. Indicating his disappointment with the SEA, Delors stayed away from the signing ceremony. The Danish foreign minister did not sign because of the Danish parliament's rejection of the SEA on 21 January (a majority of parliamentarians complained that the government had gone too far in the IGC by agreeing to treaty provisions that infringed on national sovereignty). The Italian government decided not to sign out of solidarity with the EP and chose instead to extend the consultation process with the Italian parliament. Greece opted not to sign until and unless Denmark and Italy were able to do so. After the successful outcome of the Danish referendum, held on 27 February, and an Italian parliamentary debate, the foreign ministers of the three remaining member states signed the SEA in The Hague (capital of the rotating Council presidency) on 28 February 1986.

Despite official British and Danish protestations during the IGC, there was little public concern throughout the EC about a possible loss of national sovereignty or an excessive accumulation of power in Brussels. In the absence of widespread apprehension, ratification of the SEA in national parliaments proceeded relatively smoothly. Most parliaments held lively debates on the SEA; all but one (the *Folketing*) voted solidly in favour of it. The positive outcome of the subsequent referendum ensured Danish ratification (the reverse happened in 1992, when a majority of Danes rejected the Maastricht Treaty following the Danish parliament's acceptance of it). In the House of Commons, the Labour opposition voted against the SEA, as did seventeen Conservative Eurosceptics. The vast majority of Conservative parliamentarians followed Thatcher's lead in supporting the SEA, a decision many of them later regretted.

One of Act's final provisions stipulated that the SEA would come into effect the month after the last country ratified it. National governments and the Commission hoped that the process of ratification would be over by December 1986, allowing the SEA to become operational in January 1987. A last-minute delay in Ireland upset this timetable. An Irish citizen, concerned about the impact of the proposed changes to EPC on Ireland's military neutrality, challenged the constitutionality of the SEA. The case ran into early 1987, when the Supreme Court ruled that the SEA was indeed unconstitutional. The chagrined Irish government had no choice but to call a referendum to change the constitution. Held in May 1987 and cast by the government as a referendum on whether Ireland should stay in the EC, the result was 70 per cent in favour, with an unusually low turnout of voters. Eventually, after an unexpected holdup, the SEA came into law on 1 July 1987.

The significance of the SEA

The *Economist* newspaper dismissed the SEA in early 1988 as a set of 'tiny changes' to the Rome Treaty (*Economist* 1988, p. 50). Such a view was not uncommon at the time. Yet within a year or so the SEA came to signify the revival of European integration – the facilitator of the single market and progenitor of EMU – and to connote a commitment by national governments to seek supranational solutions for pressing common problems. What accounts for the elevation of the SEA to such exalted heights? What impact did the SEA really have?

Completion of the single market program might well have been possible without the SEA, but the fact that governments committed themselves in a new treaty to enact the program by the end of 1992, largely by means of QMV, was undoubtedly important. Even so, implementation of the program got off to a slow start. The UK, in the Council presidency in the second half of 1986, made the single market one of its presidential priorities. With the SEA still unratified, governments were not obliged to use QMV for most single market measures, but the political momentum generated by the 1985 White Paper and by growing enthusiasm among the business community encouraged rapid decision-making in the Council of Ministers. Yet progress was slow. By the end of 1986 the Council had adopted 31 of the White Paper's approximately 300 measures. By March 1987, the Council's record was 56 proposals adopted out of 170 submitted by the Commission. Six months later, the Council had adopted only an additional eight proposals.

The problem was not the new cooperation procedure, the 'the institutional core of the SEA' (Fitzmaurice, 1988, p. 290). Many national governments, as well as the Council secretariat, were convinced that the EP would never master the complexity of the procedure, and that legislative gridlock would ensue. To prove otherwise and to strengthen its case for the right to have additional authority within the EC system, the EP decided from the outset to make the cooperation procedure work as quickly and smoothly as possible. In December 1986 the EP radically revised its rules to make the most of the cooperation procedure. It especially appreciated the importance of the first reading stage of the new procedure, using it to apprise the Council of its intentions and to begin to build the coalition of political groups required to amend, or possibly reject, a Council common position.

Thus the SEA, through the cooperation procedure and to a lesser extent through the assent procedure, put the EP at the centre of the EC political system. As a result of the SEA, the EP became a major player in the legislative process. National governments had no choice but to take the EP seriously and lobbyists began to pay close attention to committee meetings in Brussels and plenary sessions in Strasbourg. Within the EP, the dynamics of inter-group behaviour changed appreciably thanks to the cooperation procedure. The precedent of the SEA, the fact that the EP was direct elected, and growing concern about the democratic deficit placed the EP in a powerful position to agitate for additional reform, both treaty- and non-treaty-based.

Initially, implementation of the single market program languished not simply because of the complexity and sensitivity of many of the White Paper's proposals and not because of delays in the EP, but because of a festering dispute over the EC budget. In 1987 the Commission introduced a proposal for the first ever multi-annual financial framework. The purpose of the so-called Delors I package was implicit in its official title: 'Making a Success of the Single Act' (*Bulletin of the European Communities* 1987). The SEA had committed the community to achieve a single market by the end of 1992 and to take a number of measures in other policy areas. One of these pertained to cohesion, including an implicit commitment to increase the amount of money allocated to the structural funds. The ensuing dispute was the biggest obstacle to implementation of the single market program in the immediate aftermath of the SEA, as the poorer member states demanded greater spending on regional development in return for market liberalisation measures. The Commission, Council of Ministers, and European Council became embroiled in a sharp dispute over how much to allocate to the structural funds. Delors himself characterized the proposed new budget as a 'marriage pact between the Twelve' (*Bulletin of the European Communities* 1988, p. 14.) and struggled to bring Thatcher to the altar. The British prime minister strongly opposed increasing the size of the EC budget and was disdainful of cohesion policy.

The row over Delors I festered throughout 1987 before erupting spectacularly at the Copenhagen summit in December. In the meantime, the single market program fell farther behind schedule. Delors had hoped that Germany, coming into the Council presidency in January 1988, would have been able to devote itself exclusively to pushing the single market program. Instead it looked as if the German presidency, like the immediately preceding Danish and Belgian presidencies, would remain preoccupied with the budget question.

The same concern motivated Kohl to call a special summit, in February 1988, to try to resolve the impasse over Delors I. After intensive bargaining, national leaders agreed at the summit to double the structural funds by 1992 and to introduce a new method of budgetary assessment that, at Thatcher's insistence, guaranteed Britain's rebate. The success of the summit hinged on a related issue: the price ceiling for cereals, a key commodity in the Common Agricultural Policy. To everyone's surprise, Thatcher accepted the higher price advocated by other national leaders, which seemed a remarkable climb-down in light of previous budgetary battles. Thatcher may have been grateful for her colleagues' continuing acceptance of Britain's rebate, but most likely a desire to end the dissipating Delors I struggle and proceed with the single market program convinced her to compromise. Whatever the reason, the successful outcome of the summit removed a huge obstacle on the road to 1992.

The significance of the SEA for EC public policy, therefore, went well beyond enactment of the single market program. The SEA resulted as well in a doubling of the structural funds which, together with a major reform in 1988 of how the funds were managed, led to the emergence of cohesion policy as a primary community endeavour. Thanks to the SEA, cohesion policy became a powerful means of addressing the north–south economic divide in the EC, and later the east–west economic divide in the EU.

The institutional implications of the SEA were equally profound, especially with respect to the EP and the Council of Ministers. The new cooperation procedure contributed greatly to the EP's empowerment and internal reorganization. Within the Council, as the legislative logjam eased in the late 1980s and progress improved in implementing the single market programme, governments grew more comfortable with the principle and practice of QMV. Even if votes were rarely taken in the Council, the possibility of taking a vote – the shadow of the vote – helped to concentrate governments' minds and move the legislative process along. This had a knock-on effect beyond the single market programme, which contributed to the withering away of the Luxembourg Compromise. Even though the SEA had set the question of the Luxembourg Compromise aside, in effect the SEA marked the end of the widespread use – or threatened use – of the national veto.

The SEA had another, less consequential, impact: it fed the Delors myth. Delors's visibility and dynamism led people to believe that he was largely responsible for the EC's metamorphosis. As Stanley Hoffmann wrote in 1989, 'Delors is as important to the enterprise today as Jean Monnet was in the 1950s' (Hoffmann 1989, p. 32). Yet Delors's role in helping to negotiate the SEA and in subsequent developments should not be exaggerated. Undoubtedly he was ambitious, competent, and resourceful. But Delors could not have succeeded had the economic, political, and international circumstances been unfavourable. It was his good fortune to have become Commission president at precisely the time when internal developments (resolution of the British budgetary question, agitation for institutional reform, and pressure to complete the internal market) and external factors (intensifying global competition) made a dramatic improvement in the EC's fortunes almost inevitable.

As Moravcsik convincingly demonstrated, national governments – and national leaders in particular – were the decisive protagonists in the SEA story (Moravcsik 1991). Given their countries' preponderance in the EC, the British, French, and German governments and leadership were especially important. Thatcher may have been the most important of all. She had pushed relentlessly for completion of the single market but had resisted a formal treaty change to help bring it about. Once she entered into the negotiations for what became the SEA, she managed to keep the treaty changes within what she thought were acceptable limits. Ironically, Thatcher won the battle of the SEA but, given subsequent treaty changes, lost the war of European integration. The EC that emerged in the late 1980s, not to mention the EU of the 1990s, was far more supranational than what she had expected or intended.

To Thatcher's annoyance, the SEA was much more than a device to launch the single market program. It was a complex bargain to improve decision-making, strengthen democracy, achieve market liberalisation, and promote cohesion in a community of growing economic diversity. It was also a platform to advance other policy areas. The SEA set a precedent procedurally for future IGCs, the first two of which took place only five years later. Little wonder that the SEA, dismissed at the time as a set of 'tiny changes' to the Rome Treaty (*The Economist*, 20 February 1988, p. 50) soon came to be seen as the first in a series of political and constitutional steps that greatly intensified European integration.

The SEA also represented the zenith of public acceptance of the European project. The intensification of integration, to which the SEA gave rise, fuelled growing public concern about political accountability and representation at the increasingly powerful European level of governance. The democratic deficit was already endemic in the EC.

In the aftermath of the SEA, especially in the post-Maastricht period, concern about the democratic deficit became acute and Euro-scepticism became widespread. It is hardly surprising, under the circumstances, that the SEA is such a shining light in the history of European integration.

Notes

1. For the revival of neo-functionalism, see Sandholtz and Zysman 1989; on the birth of liberal intergovernmentalism, see Moravcsik 1991; on the impact of the SEA on European integration theory more generally, see Rosamond 2000.
2. For Thatcher's perspective on the Milan summit and the subsequent IGC, see Thatcher 1993, pp. 551 – On the split between Downing Street and the Foreign Office, see Thatcher 1993, pp. 551–4, and Wall (2008), pp. 57–60.
3. For a description and analysis of the IGC and the SEA, see de Ruyt 1995; Dinan 2004; Moravcsik 1998. For the SEA itself, see *Bulletin of the European Communities* 1986.

7
The Treaty of Maastricht: Designing the European Union

Colette Mazzucelli

Introduction

The decision to create the European Union (EU), a unique achievement in the history of European construction, was a decisive step taken in the Kantian tradition of international relations. In 1991, the member states of the European Community (EC) negotiated the Treaty on European Union (TEU) to establish a single European currency and to create a new supra-national institution, the European Central Bank (ECB). National govern-ments decided to delegate their decision-making in monetary affairs to the ECB and to pool sovereignty in a key sector of domestic responsibil-ity. The landmark agreement to place Economic and Monetary Union (EMU) in the first, or EC, pillar of the newly formed European Union was depicted by Commission President Jacques Delors as the 'tiger in the tank' of European integration. Two other pillars, the Common Foreign and Security Policy (CFPS) and Justice and Home Affairs (JHA) were cre-ated as a result of agreement in the Intergovernmental Conference on Political Union (ICG-PU), which concluded at the same time as that of the Intergovernmental Conference on Economic and Monetary Union (IGC-EMU). Integration did not advance as far or as deep in negotiations on Political Union. The IGC-PU did not benefit from the preparation in the pre-negotiation that characterised its EMU counterpart and, more importantly, lacked a common definition of political union upon which the members states could agree. Distributive bargaining that underlined the lowest common denominator among the member states was evi-dent in most areas owing to the nature of the most important policy dossiers negotiated: treaty structure and 'federal vocation'; the CFSP, especially regarding decisions taken by qualified majority; defence; new competencies; social policy; and cohesion. The last two issues were by far the most difficult in terms of reaching agreement. The cohesion dossier, which linked the two ICGs, was by far the most explosive among state leaders around the table with Spanish Prime Minister Gonzalez threatening to veto the Treaty on European Union unless agreement could be reached to create a new 'cohesion fund' to help poorer member states on the periphery to prepare for monetary union.

The realisation of EMU addressed French concerns about the persistent asymmetry with Germany in monetary questions, as expressed in the longstanding dominance of the *Bundesbank* in policy decisions (Moravcsik 1998). The pooling of national sovereignty gave France a seat at the EMU table with a voice in the new system of monetary integration. The placement of EMU in the first community pillar, not an envisaged fourth intergovernmental one, with a fixed date of transition to the single European currency in 1999, allayed French insecurities once the Yalta system disintegrated. Likewise, provisions in the Treaty on Political Union, particularly related to defence policy, were key in the ambition to give the newly created European Union a voice as a global actor to match its weight in international trade negotiations. The decision to move irrevocably to EMU at the century's end was the answer provided to the French regarding the newly sovereign Germany's role in a Europe from the Atlantic to the Urals. Germany as the linchpin of Economic and Monetary Union precluded the future option of a *Sonderweg*, which Kohl, a leader who vividly recalled the horrors of nationalism in World War II, wanted to make impossible for his successors. This explains why EMU was sold in Germany primarily in a defensive way by the Chancellor: no more war (Mazzucelli 2008) instead of in a manner that emphasised the positive implications of the new European monetary system for the country that had the most to lose in the surrender of its national currency.

This chapter is organised with three objectives in mind. First, there is a brief overview of the key institutional and policy-related innovations of the Treaty on European Union with an emphasis on the EMU agreement. The second part of the chapter sets forth three 'fault lines,' identified by Rittberger and Glockner in the academic debate about the ECSC, which are particularly relevant to the EU. In the concluding section, the legacy of the EU is explored, particularly in light of the actual 2011–12 crisis in monetary affairs, which may be traced back to inadequate political integration in the Treaty on European Union. The existing asymmetry between EMU and Political Union inherent in the Maastricht Treaty design may inspire deeper integration in the years to come or threaten future steps in European construction.

Treaty content: Institutional and policy-related provisions

Institutional provisions

Institutionally, the key component of the Treaty on European Union was the European Central Bank which together with the central banks of the member states formed the European System of Central Banks (ESCB) from the beginning of Stage 3 in EMU. The supranational nature of the ECB was enshrined in Article 107 TEU, which states that 'Neither the ECB nor a national central bank, nor any member of their decision making bodies shall seek or take instructions from Community institutions or bodies, or from any government of a Member State, all of which undertake to respect this principle' (European Social Observatory 1992: 92). The independence of the ECB is guaranteed by the Treaty. It must be independent if it is to attain the objective of price stability, defined in Article 105 TEU, which was set for the system. It is not a guarantee of price stability. The *Reichbank*, nominally independent since 1922, was not able to prevent hyperinflation in Germany.

The question of the ECB's independence stimulated intense ideological debate. Too much value was not to be attached to its legal personality, however, since the ECB was not given any power of sanction or 'impeachment' with regard to policy decisions taken by the Council, just as the *Bundesbank* was powerless to prevent German monetary unification, which it judged premature.

The bank is run directly by a six-man Executive Board of a president, vice-president and four other members, who are appointed by the Heads of State and Government after consulting the European Parliament and the Governing Council of the ECB, the period of office being a single term of eight years. The Governing Council is composed of the executive board and the governors of the national central banks. Voting is on a one man one vote basis, acting on a simple majority except where it refers to the bank's capital when votes are proportionate to the member states' subscribed capital, the executive board having no votes. The subscribed capital is determined by an equal weighting of the member states' shares of community population and GDP at market prices (the latter averaged over the previous five years). The subscription is revised every five years (Britton and Mayes 1992: 26).

The creation of a supranational European central bank was supported by Mitterrand and by those in France who advocated the community model. The French decision to push for this institutional set-up plus the fixed deadline was a question of political will (Parsons 2003: 219). There were numerous voices in France that rejected an independent ECB and echoed German scepticism about the commitment to a strict timetable for EMU.

At the time of German unification, the *Bundesbank* raised interest rates in late 1990 as European growth was slowing. Other central banks also had to raise their rates to maintain EMS parities. As elections loomed in France, unemployment began to climb, which was politically disastrous for the Socialist Party. Those in the business sector argued that French economic fundamentals called for interest rates at 4 per cent instead of the 9–10 per cent dictated by Germany. Those opposed in France to the community model of a single European currency used this context to argue for a common currency with limited influence by a European bank on national policies, which must remain independent.

Throughout the EMU conference, the main institutional questions highlighted the differences between the German ECB design and the French proposal, advanced by Bérégovoy, of a *gouvernement économique*, which rejected the complete subordination of economic policy to monetary policy. The French idea was that it was necessary to distinguish between monetary policy and exchange rate policy, the latter to be determined by political leaders in the European Council (Mazzucelli 1997: 106–7).

In 1991 Mitterrand's domestic autonomy as president gave him the opportunity to decide to move ahead with the community model in the face of the demands to act otherwise made by hesitant French elites, particularly Bérégovoy on the Left and Balladur on the Right. Mitterrand believed that only a supranational European central bank could give France a voice in its own monetary affairs. Competing explanations of this choice for Community Europe at Maastricht have been advanced in that broad economic and geo-political contexts encouraged monetary cooperation. Agreement on EMU was translated by leadership in the European Council into the community equation, 'institutions + fixed dates = politics' during a negotiation process that stood on its own, quite independent of the pressures resulting from German unification (Moravcsik 1998: 403, 437–9; Parsons 2003: 216; Mazzucelli 1997: 202).

Certainly the institutional legacies of the European Monetary System and the Single European Act made the pressures for EMU more acute. None of these pressures changed the dynamics of contestation within the French political spectrum about the institutional design or the fixed deadline to make EMU irreversible. The decision to move ahead was Mitterrand's choice alone to make with Kohl in spite of the opposition from their respective ministers (Parsons 2003: 220).

The negotiations around the institutional design of the ECB revealed that in 1991 member state commitment was insufficient to allow for a great leap to the conceptualisation of national interests through the community. The negotiating strategies of the most important players at the table reflected this reality. The British, central to the talks, were resolved in their ambition to avoid isolation and then resist all efforts to extend the scope of integration to new EC competencies. The French wanted a strongly integrated and 'deepened' albeit con-(federal) community. France's aim was to compensate for economic weakness by its political and administrative leadership, with EMU as the vehicle. The Germans were committed federalists, but hesitant and divided about EMU. The contention of most treaty reform analysts is that while there were other important players, the logic of Maastricht was created largely by interactions among these three member states with others like the Italians falling in behind the French (EMU) or the Germans (Political Union), the Dutch aligning closely with the Germans, and the Danes forming the minimalist coalition with the British (Ross 1995: 192).

This analysis posits that negotiations to achieve European Union, with a supranational EMU in the community pillar, revealed the emergence of Spain as a new type of IGC player, the 'lieutenant country' (Etzioni 1965: 46) whose veto power in the critical issue area of cohesion threatened to derail the entire European project (Beach 2005: 71). Economic and social cohesion was an essential issue in EMU given the adjustment costs inherent in the ECB's commitment to price stability. More importantly, as a parallel issue linking the two IGCs, EMU and Political Union, cohesion, and the protocol agreed to as a result of Spain leading the coalition of the Club Med states (along with Portugal, Ireland, and Greece), pointed towards the 'new grand *rendezvous*' proposals of the second Delors package (Ross 1995: 193).

In addition to a particular role as 'lieutenant country' on the cohesion dossier, Spain's influence was also evident in other areas during the negotiations on Political Union. First, in terms of the extension of community competences, including institutional questions, European citizenship and the subsidiarity principle, Spanish diplomacy was assertive and engaged in the submission of documents to the intergovernmental conference. This was also true in the late stages of negotiations to reach agreement on the Common Foreign and Security Policy when Prime Minister Felipe Gonzalez backed France and Germany by supporting the need to simplify decision-making in this policy area and lent his support to the Belgian Prime Minister's proposal by which a common defence policy would be developed leading eventually to a common defence (Mazzucelli 1997: 179). On additional dossiers in Political Union, particularly Justice and Home Affairs, Spain was not as accomodating with regard to German policy goals, which aimed to advance as far as possible on so-called third pillar issues, such as asylum, owing to domestic constraints. In this policy area as well as on questions of treaty structure, namely the retention of the pillar system, Spain was neither as intransigent as France nor as integrationist as Germany.

For Mitterrand, the French-German tandem was the edifice upon which Europe was built (Parsons 2003: 218). This European conviction in the French interest led him to support an institutional design with a federal orientation. Article 106 TEU states that 'The ESCB shall be composed of the ECB and the national central banks. It shall be governed by the Governing Council and the Executive Board of the ECB. The powers conferred on it may be amended by the Council either by qualified majority on a recommendation from the ECB or unanimously on a proposal from the Commission. The assent of the EP is required.' The direction of the ESCB clearly assigns to its institution a federal nature. Members of this governing Body of the ECB are nominated through procedures from the protocol on its statute (European Social Observatory 1992: 92).

The ECB is subject to audit and is under the jurisdiction of the Court of Justice. Overdraft or other credit facilities by the ECB or national central banks to any community or member state public body are explicitly prohibited. The President of the Council and a member of the Commission may attend the Governing Council of the ECB. The ECB has to make an annual report on its activities which the president will present to the Council and the European Parliament. He and the other members of the Executive Board may be heard by the relevant committees of the European Parliament at either side's request (Britton and Mayes 1992: 26–7).

Policy-related provisions

In the high politics of EMU, Delors saw in the European project a new pooling of sovereignty with tremendous potential for spillover into other policy areas. Of particular significance for the proposed European Union as a whole, EMU would be more beneficial for the more prosperous regions of the community: the adjustment costs would be greater for the EC 'South' with EMU's strong 'price stability' commitments particularly burdensome (Ross 1995: 84).

As Table 7.1 indicates, the policy-related provisions in the Treaty on European Union emerged from two separate IGCs, whose negotiating

Table 7.1 Chronology of TEU negotiations process

Date	Event
June 1988	European Council in Hanover charges a Committee including the governors of the Central Banks – chaired by Jacques Delors – with the responsibility of drafting a report on EMU
26–27 June 1989	European Council in Madrid examines report of Delors Committee and accepts in principle the idea of holding an intergovernmental conference on EMU
11 November 1989	Berlin Wall 'falls'
19 April 1989	Kohl-Mitterrand letter to Irish Presidency supports idea of a second IGC on political union to 'strengthen democratic legitimation,' 'render its institutions more efficient,' 'ensure unity and coherence' and to define a 'common foreign and security policy'
25–26 June 1990	The European Council in Dublin formally examines the ideas discussed by Foreign Ministers and agrees on the principle of a second IGC on political union to run parallel to that of EMU
3 October 1990	German unification Former East German territory therefore becomes part of EC
27–28 October 1990	The European Council in Rome agrees (with UK reservations) that the IGC on EMU should aim to establish a single currency managed by an independent Central Bank, which could be operational in 1997
29 November 1990	John Major replaces Margaret Thatcher as British Prime Minister
14–15 December 1990	Rome II European Council meeting indicates wide agenda for Political Union IGC
15 December 1990	Launch in Rome of the Intergovernmental Conferences on Political Union, Economic and Monetary Union
1 January 1991	Luxembourg takes over Presidency of EC Council
17 January 1991	Gulf War begins
15 April 1991	The Luxembourg Presidency presents a 'non paper' on Political Union
18 June 1991	New version of the Luxembourg 'non paper' on political union, now called 'draft treaty'
28–29 June 1991	The European Council in Luxembourg agrees to take the Luxembourg text as the basis for further intergovernmental negotiations
1 July 1991	Netherlands takes over rotating Council Presidency

(continued)

Table 7.1   Continued

Date	Event
August 1991	The Dutch Presidency prepares a draft treaty which revises certain fundamental points of the Luxembourg text
30 September 1991	Dutch text on Political Union is rejected by a majority of the Twelve in Brussels
8 November 1991	Dutch Presidency presents new draft treaty on Political Union
9–10 December 1991	Maastricht European Council reaches conclusions on all the outstanding points in the IGCs

Source: Corbett 1993: xvi–xx.

dynamics were markedly different. Unlike the EMU conference, which involved extensive preparations, the Political Union negotiations emerged as the Yalta system was disintegrating. The accelerated pace of change in Europe provided the impetus for political union, an idea with antecedents in the requests of the European Parliament for institutional reform (Ross 1995: 89; Beach 2007: 65; Mazzucelli 1997: 63). Delors was focused on the role of the community as an international political actor. After the revolutions of 1989, the road ahead was more difficult to map given the uncertainty about the future, highlighted by outbreak of internal conflict in southeastern Europe and the disintegration of the former Soviet Union. Decisive state-building efforts in the foreign policy realm figured prominently in the strategy of deepening integration, which became a central focus of political union negotiations.

In April 1990, Kohl and Mitterrand asked for a second IGC on Political Union to address four objectives: 'democratic legitimacy; institutional effectiveness; the unity and coherence of the Community across economic, monetary and political areas', and the definition and implementation of a 'common foreign and security policy' (CFSP). Spain proposed another objective in May, which was the elaboration of 'European citizenship' (Laursen 2012). In addition to foreign and security policy, the negotiations on Political Union introduced a wide array of new EC 'competencies' to consider, thereby extending the scope of integration and broadening the areas in which the community would be empowered in the treaty to act. The meaning of 'subsidiarity' was to be defined in the new treaty further delineating relations among different levels of political authority – European, national, regional, and local.

The issue of 'democratic legitimacy' was meant to address an extension of the European Parliament's powers and influence within the EC institutional triangle (Commission, Council of Ministers, Parliament), the reinforcement of the other EC institutions' democratic credentials, and the promotion of greater national parliamentary involvement in EC matters (Ross 1995: 89). Table 7.2 provides an overview of the substantive provisions as defined in the Treaty on European Union.

Table 7.2 The treaty on European Union

Issue-area	Outcome
First Pillar (Provisions amending the Treaty establishing the European Community)	
Introduction of new policies	creates an Economic and Monetary Union (EMU): • three-stage process with a fixed timetable, with the introduction of a single currency in the third stage at latest in 1999 • relatively strict economic convergence criteria during the transition • creation of a weak monetary institution at the start of stage 2 • monetary policy to be determined and conducted in the third stage by the ECB, which is fully independent of both the member states and the EC institutions • temporary opt-outs for member states that do not qualify, and with more permanent opt-outs for Denmark and the UK
Modification of existing policies	• included new policies: developmental, education, public health, consumer protection, trans-European networks, and the competitiveness of industry • strengthened R&D policy, environmental policies, and economic and social cohesion
Institutional changes	• adopted a Social Protocol, strengthening community social policies but with an opt-out for the UK • QMV in Council considerably extended • co-decision introduced • scope of cooperation procedure revised, scope of assent extended • reform of Commission, including EP approval of the Commission • Committee of Regions established • ECJ given ability to fine member states for failing to fulfill treaty obligations

(continued)

Table 7.2 Continued

Issue-area	Outcome
Second Pillar (Common Foreign and Security Policy)	
Scope	• includes all questions of security, even the eventual framing of common defence policies
Institutional issues	• can adopt common positions 'when necessary' • can adopt joint actions by unanimity in the European Council, then implementation by QMV in the Council • EU can request WEU to elaborate and implement defence decisions • non-exclusive right of initiative for Commission, and EP shall be consulted on main aspects and basic choices
Third Pillar (Justice and Home Affairs)	
Scope	• deals with: asylum and immigration policy, 3rd country nationals, combating fraud, immigration and drug addiction, judicial cooperation in civil and criminal matters, customs cooperation, and police cooperation to combat terrorism and drug trafficking
Institutional issues	• joint positions adopted by unanimity • joint actions adopted by unanimity, then can decide that implementing measures to be decided by QMV • can draw up conventions for member states to adopt • coordination between relevant administrative departments

Source: The Treaty on European Union, Official Journal of the European Communities, No. C 224/1, 31.8.92.

The TEU in the academic debate: Three 'fault lines'

Rittberger and Glockner identify three debates or 'fault lines,' which are relevant in the literature analysing the Treaty on European Union. First, analysts differ in their interpretation of the decisive actors in treaty reform. The dominant school of thought is expressed mainly in political science accounts, which privilege the state-centric perspective by emphasising governmental leaders, diplomats, or domestic economic interest groups (Moravcsik 1998). In response to the liberal intergovernmental school, the literature explores whether the influence of supranational actors or transnational networks is decisive in an analysis of intergovernmental conference diplomacy (Ross 1995). More recent analyses in this context put forward a new model that aims to go beyond the either–or dichotomy of intergovernmental versus supranational theories with an emphasis on the importance of leadership (Beach 2005; Beach and Mazzucelli 2007). Secondly, the literature focuses on the origins of actors' preferences concerning treaty reform by contrasting 'materialist' accounts of preference formation, which highlight economic or geopolitical conditions (Moravcsik 1998), with constructivist accounts that stress subjective interpretations of material conditions (Parsons 2003). Third, the literature explores the question of institutional design asking why leaders in the European Council agreed to a supranational institution in the case of EMU. Accordingly, a later section of this chapter contrasts advocates of functionalist and rationalist explanations for institutional design (Pollack 2003) with those of constructivist-inspired institutionalist accounts, which underscore the legitimacy-enhancing influence of institutional choices (Rittberger 2005).

Identifying the key actors in treaty reform: State-centric versus supranational or transnational perspectives

The literature that discusses the Treaty on European Union consistently references Moravcsik's liberal intergovernmental account, which highlights the dominant influence of the three largest member states: France, Germany, and the United Kingdom. Moravcsik utilises a rationalist account to explain international cooperation asking about: (1) the sources of national preferences, weighing economic versus geopolitical interests; (2) the reasons for the efficiency and distributional outcomes of interstate bargains, evaluating asymmetrical interdependence versus supranational entrepreneurship; and (3) the choices to construct particular international institutions, including the transfer of sovereignty, assessing the influence of federalist ideology versus centralised technocratic management versus more credible commitment (Moravcsik 1998: 23–4).

Moravcsik's research is a domestic liberal intergovernmental account in that economic interest, relative power, and credible commitments are underlined in his argument. As he explains:

> Far from demonstrating the triumph of technocracy, the power of idealism, and the impotence or irrelevance of the modern nation-state, European integration exemplifies a distinctly modern form of power politics, peacefully pursued by democratic states for largely

economic reasons through the exploitation of asymmetrical interdependence and the manipulation of institutional commitments.

(Moravcasik 1998: 5)

Parsons emphasises the role of domestic politicians, presidents, ministers, and parliamentarians, in his 'ideational' approach, which suggests that 'structural circumstances rarely dictate a specific course of action, and even institutional constraints may admit of multiple interpretations' (Parsons 2003: 5). As he asserts:

> The cognitive lenses through which actors interpret their surroundings shape how they respond to structural or institutional pressures. Any choice is predicated on assumptions about causal relationships, the prioritization of costs and benefits, and the normative legitimacy of various actions.
>
> (Parsons 2003: 5)

Supranationalists in the tradition of Haas and Lindberg assert that EU institutions, particularly the Commission, are the motor of European integration exploiting the power of initiative in daily EC policymaking, and pushing agreement in IGC diplomacy beyond the point where the majority of member states are willing to go. Analysts who acknowledge the limits neo-functionalist thinking posit that a window of opportunity opened during the years 1985–92 to the extent that treaty reform resulted in a European renewal. As Ross argues:

> As of the mid-1980s new space existed for the Community to do new things. It was the Commission's official job to find ways to use this space. The Commission had the power and institutional right to pick and choose among possible courses of action, to set agendas. The right choices, those which made the most of the new opportunity structures, could set the Community in motion again. Bad political work by the Commission would have wasted the opportunity.
>
> (Ross 1995: 12)

In his analysis that asserts the importance of leadership, Beach maintains that 'EU institutions do matter vis-à-vis governments in the actual intergovernmental history-making decisions, but their influence varies according to the leadership choices they possess, the negotiating context and their choice of strategy in the negotiations' (Beach 2005: 1).

Kaiser's critique of state-centric approaches situates transnational political parties and party leaders at the centre of forward momentum in post-war European integration. His argument is that the position of Christian Democratic parties to shape the post-war European integration agenda was 'hegemonic' (Kaiser 2007). As he asserts:

> As these examples of EEP network activities demonstrate, Christian democracy continued to play an important role in European integration after the signing of the Rome Treaties. They did so not primarily as political parties that pass resolutions at national- and European-level congresses. Instead the EPP network, as the Christian democratic network after 1945, has defined policy agendas, promoted policy solutions, built advocacy coalitions for them and facilitated the entrepreneurial leadership by networked party politicians who, unlike many political scientists, have never made a clear distinction between their overlapping party and governmental roles. In this and other ways, transnational Christian democracy has helped to link the emerging European political society with national and supranational politics and national polities with supranational institutions and policy-making in the complex informal politics of the present day EU. European Union was shaped in crucial ways by political networks, especially transnational Christian democracy.
>
> (Kaiser 2007: 325)

Forming preferences: Material versus ideational worlds

This section addresses the query about the basis of political actors' preferences for treaty reform during the 1991 IGCs. In the literature on European integration, several theoretical perspectives stand out in this context: within intergovernmentalism, the realist strand emphasise the interests of states to maximise security, autonomy, and influence (Hoffmann 1966; Grieco 1996); the liberal strand assumes that states' preferences reflect the interests of dominant (economic) interest groups (Moravcsik 1998). Intergovernmental analyses underscore the 'material' underpinnings of state preferences, highlighting economic and geopolitical conditions. Constructivist accounts emphasise the role societal norms and ideas play in influencing the ways political actors interpret the 'material world' (Rittberger 2005).

In the literature, Pedersen analyses treaty reform from a realist viewpoint with a focus on the roles of Germany and France. His analysis emphasises the prominent role of Germany in the EC's constitutive politics. Pedersen argues that the EU is less a sign of the abandonment of power politics than the product of a new 'soft' great power strategy typical of comparatively weak regional big powers. IGC diplomacy is interpreted with attention to the role of big powers in processes of regional integration. His research introduces a theory of cooperative hegemony and symmetrical federalisation (Pedersen 1998).

Liberal intergovernmental theory not only stresses the relevance of economic interests more generally; it offers a 'liberal' explanation for why commercial interests play a crucial role in the formulation of state preferences. State preferences are considered to be sector-specific and reflect the interests of dominant societal interest groups in a particular sector (Moravcsik 1998).

The literature that challenges materialist approaches to explain governmental preferences focuses on transnational cooperation between Christian Democrats with a shared 'ideological predisposition' (Kaiser 2001), which provided the impetus for supranational integration in postwar Europe. Kaiser's historical research is grounded in the study of Christian Democrats throughout Western Europe after 1945 who shared a set of ideas that complemented the notion of delegating sovereignty to the European level.

In an article that questions materialist accounts, Johansson analyses the Maastricht outcome by examining the role of the European People's Party (EPP) and its member parties. There is particular emphasis placed on the meetings of Christian Democrat leaders. During the 1991 parallel Intergovernmental Conferences, six out of twelve heads of government met in the EPP. Johansson argues that the Treaty on European Union was facilitated by the transnational coalition of the Christian Democrats and by the shared ideological identity of this federalist movement, thereby challenging the intergovernmental approach to European integration (Johansson 2002).

In his study of French elite preferences, Craig Parsons analyses treaty reform by arguing that ideational variables are important. His query focuses on the problem of how to explain that seemingly similar economic or geopolitical conditions led to radically different foreign and security policy trajectories. Ideational approaches rest on the assumption that 'actors interpret their interests through ideas that can vary independently from their objective positions' (Parsons 2002: 50). In his study, Parsons illustrates the ways in which three distinct sets of ideas about European institution-building, traditional, (con)-federal and community models of cooperation, were viable in the French domestic political debate to enter Euroland (Parsons 2003: 202–20).

In her analysis of the preferences of the Dutch Presidency during the 1991 IGCs, Mazzucelli identifies contestation within the Presidency rooted in federalist ideology and the country's historical experience of European integration. Distinct sets of ideas led to competing interpretations of how to act in the Chair in the context of the debate about the treaty structure, which led to the infamous 'Black Monday' standoff that isolated the Dutch Presidency from most of the member states at the table (Mazzucelli 2007: 43).

Choosing institutions: Institutions as credible commitment devices versus legitimate design solutions

In the academic debate about the TEU, the third fault line speaks to the choice by the member states of a particular set of institutions to create the European Union. There are two issues of relevance in this context. The TEU, like its predecessor the Treaty of Paris, established a supranational institution, the European Central Bank, to which authority was delegated by the member states to issue binding decisions in monetary policy. Why, in the face of notable French, British, and Danish opposition, did this supranational delegation occur? The TEU also includes the creation of a new institution, the Committee of Regions. How does the scholarly literature take issue with explaining the broader institutional set-up of the European Union? Here scholars debate the differences between a functionalist 'rational design' approach and explanations based on constructivist social theory.

The major proponent of a functionalist rational design approach to explain institutional delegation is Mark Pollack. As he explains,

> member governments do indeed delegate powers and discretion to the Commission and the Court in order to reduce the transaction costs of EU policy-making. Specifically, I argue that the delegation of discretionary powers to the Commission and the ECJ is motivated largely, although not exclusively, by the demand for credible commitments by EU member governments.
>
> (Pollack 2003: 9–10)

Of particular relevance to the agreement by member states delegating responsibility for monetary policy to the ECB is Pollack's argument that 'member state principals will – depending on the precise nature of the delegation problem – create a set of institutional checks and control mechanisms to limit the discretion of their supranational "agents"' (Pollack 1997, 2003).

Empirical research is necessary to address the limitations of functional rational design explanations as these pertain to the ECB. Scholars must assess why Germany and France perceived the 'control problem' in different ways. In accordance with constructivist arguments, which underline the importance of ideas in forming institutional design preference, the German delegation to the EMU conference opposed any political counterweight to the ECB on normative grounds. Of decisive importance was whether the institutional set-up provided a 'fit' with prevailing domestic (*Bundesbank*) notions of appropriate constitutional design. French proposals for a '*gouvernement economique*' likewise reflected a 'fit' with internal notions of power relations by which the state influences monetary policy.

Explaining how the Maastricht European Council led to the treaty on European Union

The Maastricht European Council was the culmination of negotiation process that was fundamentally unbalanced. The EMU conference was thoroughly prepared at each level of negotiation, working group, civil servant, and ministerial, leaving the most difficult choices to the heads of state and government meeting on 9–10 December 1991 in the capital of Limburg, Netherlands. The political union IGC was a rushed and messy affair, which, for many involved, particularly Commission President Delors, was experienced as a 'nightmare' in terms of process and end result. This analysis focuses on the nine larger issues that dominated the negotiations throughout 1991 as well as the meeting of the Heads of State and Government in Maastricht. The devil was in the detail, which explains how the marathon meeting was likened to a 12-dimensional game of chess and a family tug of war (Mazzucelli 1997: 173). The tables in this chapter give an overview of the major cleavages (see Tables 7.4–7.6) during the negotiations as well as the leadership (see Table 7.3) exercised by the various actors at the table. The nine issues left for the European heads of state and government to decide at the Maastricht European Council were: 1. the transition to the final phase of EMU; 2. decision-making on CFSP; 3. the defence dimension of the CFSP; 4. the powers of the European Parliament; 5. the inclusion of the term 'federal vocation' in the chapeau or general provisions common to both Treaties; 6. new community competencies; 7. interior and justice affairs, including the contentious issue of whether or not to place Article 100c in the first pillar; 8. cohesion; and 9. social policy.

Table 7.3 Leadership in the IGCs on EMU and political union

Issue-area	Outcome

First Pillar – Provisions amending the Treaty establishing the European Community
 	
Introduction of new policies
	• EMU – basic contours of agreement reached in Delors Committee, where the German *Bundesbank* set the broad framework, and where leadership by Delors ensured that agreement was reached
	  – fixed timetable – French-German compromise in endgame
	  – decision-making – Commission prevented creation of intergovernmental 4th pillar, but acceptance was due to French strategy of trade-off between a (semi) supranational EMU in exchange for intergovernmental 2nd/3rd pillars
	  – economic convergence criteria – French/German/Belgian compromise of 'criteria plus trend'
	  – stage 2 institution and independence of ECB – despite French-Italian pressure, issues were firmly controlled by Germany
	  – temporary opt-outs – Commission brokered outcome

Modification of existing policies	• citizenship EP and Spanish advocacy influenced outcome • Commission leadership on other issues such as trans-European networks • environmental policies – Danish/German/Commission leadership • economic and social cohesion – Commission brokered outcome
Institutional changes	• Social Protocol – Belgian/Commission collusion shaped agenda – the Commission with Secretariat assistance brokers compromise with UK in endgame • pillar structure – French backed idea that was fleshed out by Council Secretariat • introduction of 'laws' – Commission kept issue on agenda, but was unable to push governments to accept it • introduction of co-decision – German–led process, backed by EP
Second Pillar – Common Foreign and Security Policy	• EP right of initiative – Commission prevented the introduction of EP right despite German and Italian pressure to do so

(*continued*)

Table 7.3   Continued

Issue-area	Outcome
Third pillar – Justice and Home Affairs	• reform of the EP to approve Commission – EP leadership ensured the creation of non-binding vote of approval • ECJ fines – UK leadership
	• French-German leadership, although 'Atlanticist' countries acted as brake on full incorporation of WEU into EU and UK/Denmark acted as brake in extension of QMV
	• German leadership with France advocating intergovernmental solutions, and UK as brake

Source: Beach, 2005: 112–13.

States versus institutions in treaty reform

Treaty reform is a state-driven process with opportunities for supranational entrepreneurship to exert influence. The parameters of the Maastricht negotiation were established by the dynamics between France and Germany to push for a conclusion that advanced towards a European Union with agreement on EMU. These dynamics were countered by the hard line bargaining of the British to maintain the status quo and to stay in the European game, supported consistently by the Danes in the minimalist camp. In hindsight, the role of Spain as 'lieutenant country' must be factored into respective analyses of IGC diplomacy throughout 1991, the end result in the Treaty, and, most importantly, the legacy of Maastricht today. The Spanish focus on economic and social cohesion revealed a member state that proved 'almost as truculent and stubborn as the British' during the negotiation (Grant 1994: 196). Spain was no 'laggard' (see the Beach analysis in this volume) in that Westendorp's negotiating strategy cleverly linked the momentum on EMU to the further integration of those states on the community's periphery that would be hardest hit by the commitment to price stability inherent in the ECB's institutional design. Spain utilised the threat of veto at Maastricht to realise its objectives in cohesion. This issue at Maastricht is also illustrative of the influence Delors exerted among the heads of state and government. The question of timing during the marathon negotiations was a key factor. On cohesion Delors intervened to bring Spain and Germany together (Ross 1995: 191; Grant 1994: 200; Mazzucelli 1997: 193), which resulted in a protocol attached

Table 7.4 IGC on EMU – major cleavages

Elements of EMU	Distribution and Intensity of Governmental Preferences
Single Currency (EMU)	• Germany – Prefers EMU with no 'opt-outs' but demands a parliamentary vote to 'opt in' (supported in negotiating line consistently by the Netherlands) – Economist approach • France – Prefers EMU with no 'opt-out' (supported in negotiating line consistently by Italy and Commission) – Monetarist approach
Strict convergence criteria ('two-speed' EMU)	• Britain – Opposes EMU; All countries have to opt-in explicitly but cannot be excluded (supported in negotiating line consistently by Denmark – vanguard for the minimalist position) Status Quo orientation
Schedule and procedure for the transition	• Germany – Favours prior but flexible macro-economic convergence criteria; prior autonomy of national central banks; and full capital liberalisation • France – None • Britain – Unclear • Germany – Favours automatic movement in 1999, with QMV to decide which countries qualify; In the interim, a weak EMI, headed by a central banker • France – Favours rapid movement in 1997 or before by simple majority vote; Strong interim EMI starting in 1993, headed by an EU official • Britain – Favours maximal delay; Weak transitional EMI headed by a central banker
ECB autonomy, mandate, and voting procedure	• Germany – Prefers autonomous bank, except for multilateral exchange rate policy, firm anti-inflationary mandate, and simple majority decision making • France – Favours political control, particularly over exchange rates, balanced mandate, and decisions by simple majority (economic government)
Location of ECB and name of currency	• Britain – Opposes EMU but apparently argues that the ECB should be autonomous with a strong anti-inflationary mandate
Domestic budgetary controls with sanctions	• Germany – Frankfurt; Euro • France – Paris, maybe Brussels; ECU • Britain – London; ECU • Germany – Yes, by simple majority • France – No • Britain – No

Source: Moravcsik 1998: 382–3; Beach 2005: 87; Mazzucelli 1997: 173–205; Parsons 2003: 202–30.

Table 7.5   The preferences of the European Commission in the EMU

Issue-area	Commission preferences
Convergence criteria	• relatively weak and not rigidly defined convergence criteria • in the 3rd stage a system of incentives should be used instead of sanctions for member state transgressions
Tasks and organisation of the ECB	• monetary policy to be determined and conducted by the ECB, which is fully independent of both the member states and the EC institutions
Fiscal transfers and other economic policies	• a strong emphasis on price stability, coupled with a focus on high levels of growth, employment and cohesion between the member states • interested in prominent economic-policy pillar of EMU, with EC-wide fiscal transfers, structural adjustment, and EC-wide industrial policy, and certain labour market policies
Institutional issues	• strong role for Commission in EMU policymaking, for example, in multi-annual economic guidelines, and exchange rate policy
Procedures for transition	• strong role for European Council, for example in the decision to start stage 3 of the EMU • fixed timetable • short stage 2 starting on 1 January 1994 • creation of ECB at start of stage 2 • decision on 3rd stage by 1997, with the Commission and Council submitting reports to the European Council, which then decides whether the conditions for the 3rd stage have been met • temporary opt-outs for member states that cannot participate

Source: European Commission 1990a and 1990b; Dyson and Featherstone 1999: 718 (as cited in Beach, 2005).

to the Treaty and a new cohesion fund to aid the poorer member states in the areas of environment policy and transport infrastructure.

As analysed by Beach, the Commission utilised its 'material leadership resources to broker a compromise that prevented a negotiating breakdown'. During the run-up to the Maastricht European Council, Delors met with the foreign ministers of Greece, Ireland, Portugal and Spain to assure them that they would receive increased structural funds in the next EC budget. This initiative ensured Spanish support for including stronger community environmental policies and a commitment to EMU along the lines defined by Germany and France at

Table 7.6 IGC on political union – major cleavages

Issues	Distribution and intensity of governmental preferences
Overall structure	• Germany – Single structure (supported consistently in negotiating line by Dutch Presidency, Belgium, Commission) Supranational, federal solutions • France – Three pillars (for purposes of domestic ratification – interim solution) Intergovernmental solutions • Britain – Three pillars (supported consistently in negotiating line by Denmark) Status quo orientation
CFSP procedure	• Germany – Favours QMV and active Commission role • France – Favours QMV only on implementation, no formal role for the Commission, and independent secretariat • Britain – Favours unanimity, no Commission role, comes to support independent secretariat
WEU and defence cooperation	• Germany – Prefers WEU as a bridge between EU and NATO • France – Prefers WEU subordinate to NATO • Britain – Prefers WEU subordinate to NATO
Justice and home affairs	• Germany – Prefers strong policy with QMV and Commission role (strong initiative from the Chancellor's Office) • France – Prefers weak policy without QMV or Commission role • Britain – Opposes any policy (minimalist position)
Social policy	• Germany – Strong social policy on non-financial issues • France – Strong social policy on non-financial issues • Britain – No social policy
Other new policies or expansion of QMV	• Germany – Favours generalising QMV to economic issues, including environment and research, but with many exceptions: industrial policy, professional qualifications, indirect taxation; seeks to restrict education and culture policy (influence of the *Länder* in domestic ratification) • France – Favours new industrial policy, as well as QMV on research, but restrictive clauses on culture and environment • Britain – Favours no new policies

(continued)

Table 7.6 Continued

Issues	Distribution and intensity of governmental preferences
EP powers and the legislative process	• Germany – Favours Parliamentary initiative at Commission's expense, and advocates both 'co-decision' and limits on the right of the Commission to amend or withdraw proposals • France – Opposes any increase in EP powers • Britain – Opposes any increase in EP powers, except oversight over Commission
Strengthen ECJ	• Germany – Yes • France – Yes • Britain – Yes
Oversight of Commission ('comitology')	• Germany – Status quo • France – Status quo • Britain – Status quo
Financial transfers	• Germany – No bail-outs, no financial transfers • France – No financial transfers • Britain – No financial transfers • Spain – Leader of coalition to create fund for economic and social cohesion (supported consistently in negotiating line by Portugal, Ireland, Greece and Commission) Emergence of the 'lieutenant state' in IGC negotiations

Source: Moravcsik 1998: 384–5; Beach 2005: 88; Mazzucelli 1997: 173–205; Parsons 2003: 202–30.

Maastricht (Beach 2005: 103). Moravcsik identifies the 'side-payments to poorer countries' as the one exception to a French-German bargain on EMU, 'excluding the British and ignoring the Commission,' which was achieved on 'German terms' (Moravcsik 1998: 446).

If we take into consideration that Delors also helped to broker a deal in the waning hours of the Maastricht European Council on a proportionality clause, helping Dutch President Lubbers find a solution satisfactory to all sides in the budgetary conflict, then it is possible to identify distinct and circumscribed ways in which the Commission President was effective at the table pushing the member states beyond the point which they originally intended to go. The result was a specific one: a legally binding TEU protocol (No. 15) that the member states intended to take 'greater account of the contributive capacity of individual Member States in the system of own resources, and of examining means of correcting, for the less prosperous Member States, regressive elements existing in the present own resources system' (Beach 2005: 103).

The influence Delors exerted must be seen in context because as Beach underlines, the Commission had little success overall in providing leadership during the IGC on Political Union. The Commission advocated an extreme policy position to enhance its own powers, especially in its support of a unified treaty structure, which could only come at the expense of member states' powers. National officials saw only the distributive elements in the Commission's strategy. In their perception, the game was defined in zero-sum terms. Nils Ersbøll, the former secretary-general of the Council of Ministers, explains Delors unique deal-making skills as follows:

> No task is too humble for Delors to perform: he's the mechanic who works out the lowly details which make an agreement possible. He is brilliant at satisfying a country by finding tiny changes in a text, or a sum of money, which others would not have thought of because they would not have known the details.
>
> (Grant 1994: 240)

Social policy as deal breaker at Maastricht

The issue of social policy was the most divisive among the heads of state and government during the Maastricht European Council. British intransigence threatened to prevent agreement on a treaty. Disagreement was evident on two points: the scope of qualified majority voting (QMV) and a provision that provided for binding European-level, labour management negotiations under threat of community legislation (the 'negotiate or we'll legislate' clause). Relatively wealthy member states, including France, Belgium, Luxembourg, Italy, and Denmark plus the Commission, were supportive of QMV. Lower income countries, led by Britain and Spain, and discreetly backed by Ireland, Portugal and Greece, were against a strongly worded treaty article on social policy (Moravcsik 1998: 452–3).

Major's strategy at Maastricht was to subject all social policy to unanimity, which Kohl rejected. This issue provided the most successful occasion for the Commission to exercise influence through a combination of prior brainstorming, quick action from the institutional support team, and smart politics from Delors. The talks on social policy lasted until the early morning hours on the last day of the European Council by which time, Kohl, looking for a graceful way to close the negotiation, placed the proposal on the table (Ross 1995: 191). The arrangement on social policy, which allowed the eleven other member states to move ahead within the community structure to adopt measures not applicable to Britain, was discussed with Mitterrand in advance and brokered by the Dutch Presidency. Significantly, the 'deal by 11' meant that the 'negotiate or we'll legislate' provisions might energise social dialogue (Ross 1995: 300).

Once Major agreed to the opportunity for the eleven others to opt-in to social policy, the recalcitrant member states were faced with a stronger policy than expected and the pressure to conclude the negotiations without delay. The 'Club Med' states were won over by Delors with promises of more substantial structural funding (Moravcsik 1998: 453). In the case of Spain, the appeal to Socialist solidarity did not confirm the decisive influence of transnational actors.

The necessity to reach agreement on cohesion and social policy offered Delors circumscribed opportunities to exert influence among the heads of state and government on issues central to the political union negotiations. The real key to the Maastricht negotiations for Delors was EMU.

Making EMU irreversible: The response to German unification

The EMU process began well in advance of 1989 not in response to German unification. The decision made late in 1991 by EC state leaders to commit to the automatic transition in 1999, which sought to assure passage to Stage 3 of EMU, was a direct response to pressures resulting from German unity. As the literature attests, negotiations on EMU were influenced markedly by positive timing, capitalising on the momentum of the internal market initiative, and by the search for common solutions in which Delors was able, within strict parameters set by the member state leaders in the European Council, to exercise a mediatory role (Thiel 1995: 14; Mazzucelli 1997: 202). There are scholars who emphasise that the result at Maastricht was a poor one for a Germany that was saddled with Economic and Monetary Union without achieving the commensurate gains its diplomacy aimed for in the Political Union negotiations (Baun 1996: 97; Grieco 1995: 34–8). For those analysts whose focus is the intensity of distributional bargaining at Maastricht, what stands out is Germany's inability to translate its structural power at the EMU table into substantive progress on Political Union (Moravcsik 1998: 467).

The empirical findings overwhelmingly support the argument that member states were the key actors throughout the Maastricht process from pre-negotiation through decisions reached in the European Council, and culminating in national ratifications. While the economic conditions to realise EMU were dictated by the constraints of Germany's win-set, geo-political changes as well as Kohl's own beliefs as a source of ideological support for EMU (Moravcsik 1998: 403) led to the decision taken by the Maastricht European Council to make progress to Stage 3 irreversible.

Analysts point to the arrangements to set up the procedures for the transition to EMU's final stage as the most crucial issue in the negotiations. France and Germany's roles, situated at the core of EMU, drove the process to solve the problems that stood in the way of the final agreement, namely: the openness of member state participation, which depended on the fulfillment of the convergence criteria according to a fixed timetable; and the extent of participation with no member state able to prevent others from implementing the transition to Stage 3 of EMU (Thiel 1995: 15). These arrangements underlined the French President's material objective to secure a strong French voice in EMU to address the persistent monetary asymmetry in its relationship with Germany. Mitterrand decided on the formula for transition over the objections of his own ministers and advisors to realise his longstanding goal of EMU. This achievement was the cornerstone of France's Maastricht diplomacy in spite of the fact that German EMU conditions went against the French idea of an 'economic government', in which leaders in the European Council played the key political role to determine exchange rate policy.

The decision to make EMU irreversible was possible because Mitterrand alone had the domestic authority to define France's geo-political interests in a way that prompted him to put all his political capital behind the European project. Mitterrand's aim was to provide a further incentive for Kohl to commit fully to European unification, thereby pre-empting other future options for a unified Germany. Mitterrand made the choice for Europe to maximise his domestic autonomy in the European Council by embedding France deeper in a Union designed for the member states to realise joint gains. Kohl was likewise able to instrumentalise the Maastricht process, thereby assuring his internal freedom to choose among competing options: witness Kohl's commitment to the automatic transition in 1999, which sought to assure passage to Stage 3 even in the face of domestic opposition (Moravcsik 1998: 443). The fact that Germany conceded equal votes in the ECB during the Maastricht negotiations and the way in which Kohl sold EMU in Germany, with an emphasis on the need to prevent a return to the nationalism of the World War II era, each illustrates that the Chancellor's personal convictions, buttressed by his historical experience and interpretation of the geo-political changes on the Continent after 1989, were decisive in his definition of the German interest at Maastricht.

Delors' understanding of Germany's internal problems, his efficient management of the process integrating the former East Germany into the European Community (Moravcsik 1998: 460–1), and the way in which Delors helped Mitterrand to understand the German domestic context each contributed to his specific, albeit circumscribed, role, which may be defined as 'pivotal' in a triangular relationship mediating between Mitterrand and Kohl (Mazzucelli 1997: 202).

The relevance of domestic 'fit' to the TEU's institutional design

France's insistence to the present day on the necessity for political influence to set monetary policy underlines the relevance of the constructivist approach in the design of institutions. The right 'fit' with prevailing domestic notions of appropriate constitutional design remains as important to France under President Nicolas Sarkozy in defining its choices for EMU today as German insistence on independence for the European Central Bank during the Maastricht negotiations. The realisation of EMU, as defined by the Maastricht design, in no way crowded out the French idea of an 'economic government' as a competitor to German emphasis on ECB independence (Mazzucelli 2007). Moreover, Pollack's argument that 'member state principals will – depending on the precise nature of the delegation problem – create a set of institutional checks and control mechanisms to limit the discretion of their supranational "agents"' (Pollack 1997, 2003) does not makes sense in the analysis of German EMU diplomacy without a consideration of 'fit' given the nature of a tightly constrained German win-set during the entire Maastricht process (Moravcsik 1998; Mazzucelli 1997). This narrow win-set allowed questions related to ECB autonomy to be decided on German terms. In fact, the Treaty on European Union 'went even further than German domestic law in insulating the central bank from political control' in order to offset the potential influence of pan-European societal pressures on ECB autonomy (Moravcsik 1997: 445).

The German ability to translate structural power into gains at the table was not a given in negotiations on Political Union at Maastricht owing to the intensity of distributional bargaining. Kohl's strategy was to include as much as possible in the substance of the Political Union treaty to move in the direction of a federal Europe despite British opposition and French reluctance to cede additional powers to the European Parliament. In this context, there were a number of issues grouped together during the Maastricht European Council, particularly the inclusion of Article 100c pertaining to visa policy in the community pillar, the federal vocation in the Treaty, the extension of the Parliament's powers, and expanding the scope of community competences, on which Germany wanted to make substantial progress. Although the advances were modest, negotiations on Article 100c illustrated Kohl's determination, the limits of Major's strategy to play for time on the issue that ended discussions at the Maastricht European Council, and the extent to which French leaders understood the explosive nature of asylum policy in German domestic politics. More importantly, this issue was indicative of France's intention to proceed gradually in the transfer of internal and justice affairs policies from intergovernmental cooperation to community decision making (Mazzucelli 1997: 193).

Maastricht's fatal asymmetry?: Weak political integration

Gains on Political Union were meant to be a first step to deepen political integration over several decades by opening the door for transfers in time of justice and home affairs articles from pillar III to the community sphere, by increasing the powers of the European Parliament relative to the Commission and the Council, and by extending the scope of new competences, particularly those subject to qualified majority voting. The minimal progress highlighted the increasing difficulty for member states to define a vision of political integration as the intensity of distributional bargaining among Germany, France, and Britain set the parameters of agreement and as interests diverged more with each successive enlargement.

The negotiations pertaining to the Common Foreign and Security Policy (CFSP) focused on sensitive questions, including the extent of involvement by European institutions as well as the scope of qualified majority voting (QMV) in decision-making. The minimalist countries, led by the United Kingdom, Denmark, and Ireland, set the tone to limit the involvement of the Commission and Parliament by including CFSP in the second pillar, which privileged intergovernmental cooperation, and to restrict the scope of QMV to those cases in which member state governments had voted unanimously to approve its use. The triumph of the three-pillar design reflected the preferences of France and the United Kingdom and effectively strengthened the role of the European Council, which was involved in decision-making in the European Community (EC), CFSP, and Justice and Home Affairs (JHA) pillars.

On defence policy, the role of the Western European Union (WEU) was a divisive one among the member states. Britain led the pro-NATO coalition, with backing from the Netherlands, Portugal as well as the support of Denmark and a neutral Ireland, by advocating a primarily symbolic link between the EU and the WEU. Germany led the camp that sought a commitment for the WEU as the eventual defines arm of the European Union, in a coalition that included Italy, Spain, Greece, and Luxembourg. France, with the backing of the Commission and Belgium, asked to establish a European attack force and urged the rapid integration of the WEU into the Union even though a direct challenge to NATO was avoided (Moravcsik 19998: 451).

In the closing day of negotiations at Maastricht, France and Germany maintained a negotiating line that advanced the ideas stated in their joint paper submitted to the Presidency on 15 October 1991. The French-German position agreed to establish the WEU as a 'component of the European Union' that would also 'reinforce the European pillar of the Atlantic Alliance' (Whitney 1991: A20). The language on defence was interpreted by many as a significant advance secondary only to the agreement on EMU at Maastricht (Mazzucelli 1997: 191). Others interpreted the result as indicating a lack of consensus regarding the newly created Union's relationship to NATO or the degree of institutionalisation with respect to the roles of the Commission and Court in foreign policy (Moravcsik 1998: 451).

The empirical findings suggest that lessons drawn from the overwhelming US presence during operations in the Gulf War, the planned US decrease in soldier force levels on the Continent at the end of the Cold War, and the changes inside the USSR led Spain, along with Greece, which became a member of the Western European Union as a result of Germany's support at Maastricht, to advocate the French-German line calling for the emergence of a European defence policy within the Atlantic Alliance.

Shrinking financial resources for defence expenditures in an era of globalisation underlined the need to maximise national capabilities in the European context. This evolution was not lost on President Mitterrand who already began to contemplate France's eventual re-integration into NATO's integrated military command (IMC) structure. French diplomacy, the outlier in terms of its stated objectives to max-imise the European presence as a Union vis-à-vis NATO, emphasised the state-driven nature of the IGC process as well as the intent to rationalise shrinking resources to allow the Europeans to weigh more heavily within the Atlantic Alliance. Even French thinking about the eventual institutional reintegration in NATO was about maximising national influence within existing transatlantic structures. The agree-ment on defence in the Treaty on European Union should be analysed in this broader context. The member states created a European Union with a qualitative leap in monetary integration as well as an agreement on defence that opened the door at Maastricht to further advances in the area where Europeans sought to maximise their collective weight on the world stage.

Legacy of the TEU

More than 20 years after the fall of the Berlin Wall, scholars continue to assert a causal relationship between the achievement of German unity, which transformed Europe's relations between the superpowers, and the agreement at Maastricht to realise the single European currency (Sarotte 2009: 145–9). As one more recent study argues:

> Kohl fundamentally agreed with the goal of a common currency, although he had previously indicated that it should be accomplished in future decades. Nevertheless, he understood that West German voters, a majority of whom favored European integration and wor-ried about the costs of rebuilding East Germany, would resist a go-it-alone reunification process that alienated the EC. Given France's weight in the EC, this meant that Kohl needed Mitterrand's approval to proceed.
>
> In return, Mitterrand asked that Germany assent to move towards a single currency as soon as possible, with the crucial IGC conven-ing by the end of 1990. Mitterrand further insisted that the open-ing of the IGC be announced in December 1989 during the French Presidency of the European Council. If the French President could preside over a significant declaration about the future of European

integration on French soil, Mitterrand would advocate within the EC for German unification. In the interest of success, Mitterrand acceded to German wishes for the full independence of a future ECB. Mitterrand's offer was well framed – Germany would get a currency union largely on its terms, but Kohl would have to compromise on timing. Kohl agreed to Mitterrand's bargain.

Consequently, the 1989 Strasbourg summit announced both the opening of the IGC and the EC's favorable attitude toward German unification.

(Sarotte 2010: 2 [online])

Journalistic reports of secret government documents also make the case that Bonn was forced to sacrifice the German national currency: 'Giving up the D-Mark for the (equally) stable Euro was one of the concessions that helped pave the way for German unification' (*Der Spiegel* 2010: 1 [online]). These recent accounts lend credence to the Euro's detractors, particularly in the Federal Republic of Germany, whose celebration of national unity two decades later is matched by popular discontent with the financial difficulties within the European Union, especially the Greek bailout.

Scholars of the treaty assert that 'the EMU bargain was stable on its own (Moravcsik 1998: 403). Empirical findings support the fact that French insistence on the IGC as well as Kohl's support for the EMU process were established well before events during fall 1989 (Parsons 2003: 216). These findings in no way deny this chapter's emphasis on treaty reform as a state-driven process, with the parameters of negotiations set by interactions among the largest three members of the community: France, Germany, and the United Kingdom. The EMU process afforded a circumscribed role for Commission President Jacques Delors. The linkages between the parallel intergovernmental conferences, which negotiations on the cohesion issue brought to the fore, offered Gonzalez the opportunity to wield his influence at the table negotiating, and obtaining, extraordinary side payments with Kohl's acquiescence. A legacy of Maastricht is the emergence, with successive enlargements, of Spain as the example *par excellence* of the 'lieutenant country', which sought consistently to assert its material interests in the face of dominance by the Big Three.

Yet, the crisis of 2010–11 reveals that anchoring cohesion in the Treaty on European Union as a cornerstone of solidarity in the European integration process creates persistent tensions in the domestic politics of member states. Germany, despite considerable public discontent, is ready to pay to keep Greece from exiting the Euro-zone. This point is particularly salient in view of the decision agreed by state leaders in the Maastricht European Council, made in direct response to German unity, to commit to the automatic transition in 1999 assuring the passage to Stage 3 of Economic and Monetary Union. Kohl's decision, spurred by Mitterrand's diplomacy, aimed to make EMU irreversible by forcing a commitment to a union ahead of member state readiness to join. Likewise, German fears are now grounded in the calculation that a Greek defection could result in a breakup of EMU, thereby eliminating the fixed exchange rate that is a benefit for German exporters and the Federal Republic's economy in a more general sense. Greece, by accepting the funds Germany provides, faces stiff domestic opposition to the austerity measures that are the price to pay for the German subsidies. Looking ahead, it is evident that integration cannot rest on the principle of solidarity defined as the consistent transfers of funds to prevent a Greece that plays by its own budgetary rules from leaving monetary union.

Further reflection indicates that institutional provisions agreed to in the creation of the ECB, as well as the enduring French insistence on the contrasting idea of an 'economic government' made clear that the 'fit' with prevailing domestic notions of appropriate constitutional design explain the outcome as well as the legacy of Maastricht. The different strategies to deal with the prospect of default by several European member states speak to this fact in the present context. As Feldstein explains, one strategy, which France advocates, requires the European Central Bank to buy the bonds of Italy, Spain and other highly indebted countries, thereby keeping their interest rates low. In other words, the strategy asks the ECB to expand on its previous limited actions in this regard in an attempt to prevent Greek and Italian rates from reaching levels that are unsustainable. To ask the ECB to expand this policy would be a contradiction of the 'no bailout' terms in the Treaty on European Union. Given its experience during the Weimar Republic, Germany opposes this strategy because of 'its inflationary potential and the risks of losses on those bonds' (Feldstein 2012: 110).

Another strategy, favoured by Chancellor Merkel, involves the tracing of 'fault lines' to explain the agreement at Maastricht, which points consistently, over time, to the qualitative difference in the progress on EMU as opposed to Political Union. In 2011, the most enduring legacy of the Treaty on European Union was the inability to deepen political integration, along the lines advocated by German diplomacy in 1991, as monetary union advanced. Presently, the German Chancellor's calls for a fiscal union would result in the transfer of funds each year by those member states with budget surpluses to assist others running budget deficits as well as trade deficits. These transfers would give the European Commission authority to review national budgets and compel member states to adopt policies leading to a reduction of their fiscal deficits, an increase in their growth, and a rise in their international competitiveness. The respective situations in Greece and Italy to date illustrate the internal turmoil caused by this strategy leading in 2011 to the installation of a technocratic government in Rome, which is committed to resolve the country's fiscal difficulties (Feldstein 2012: 110–11).

Instead of the expulsion of member states, the challenge the European Union now faces is governance reform. The crisis in the Euro-zone leaves the member states with starkly contrasting options. A breakup of the Euro in its current setup would allow Greece and Italy 'to manage their own currencies to match their fiscal policies' (Grygiel 2012: 2 [online]). Greater political centralisation among EMU members, in contrast, would lead to the concentration of fiscal power in the hands of technocrats in Brussels and decision makers in Berlin without popular consent in member states across the Euro-zone. This scenario is likely, in time, to generate further social unrest, frictions among member states, and possible further stagnation in economic terms (Grygiel 2012: 2 [online]).

No analyst of treaty reform has a crystal ball to predict that present difficulties may provide the impetus among a group of member states to form an *avant-garde*, which chooses political union as the next step in European construction. The alternative of sacrificing the Euro to revert back to national currencies is likely to undermine Germany's export competitiveness as well as its employment with collateral damage to the European Union and its single market. As power shifts to the centre and Berlin becomes the new Brussels, the Maastricht experience of integration remains anchored in the post-war ideology of 'no more war', which is how EMU was originally sold to Germans, as the metaphor of two-level games explains. The lesson to retain from the legacy of the Treaty on European Union two decades hence is that harmony cannot be imposed by any one national capital to save Europeans from themselves. As the Union undertakes a future enlargement to Croatia, it is the member states that must re-evaluate their material interests in the European project to ascertain if, and how, the crisis of 2010–11 may provide the momentum to integrate further. It is for member state leaders, who meet jointly as the European Council, to decide whether or not to realise joint gains, and greater legitimacy, from a deeper integration achieved through policymaking and institutions that 'fit' with prevailing domestic notions of appropriate constitutional design.

Note

The author thanks Miss Saghar (Sara) Birjandian, MSGA, Center for Global Affairs at New York University, for her assistance in the initial editing of this chapter.

8
The Amsterdam Treaty: Modest Reforms

Sophie Vanhoonacker

After Maastricht, the Treaty of Amsterdam was the second Treaty that was concluded under the aegis of the Dutch Presidency (first half of 1997). The organisation of the Intergovernmental Conference (IGC) leading to this new treaty had already been agreed upon in 1991. It was a concession to those who had hoped for a more ambitious outcome in Maastricht. Amsterdam was therefore in the first place a follow-up treaty rather than an agreement leading to historic steps. This does not mean however that one should downplay its results. It laid the foundations for the development of the European Security and Defence Policy (ESDP) and allowed for the integration of Schengen into the Treaty on European Union. It was also a first attempt to prepare for the upcoming enlargement to a EU of more than 20 member states. Following the 1993 Copenhagen Council it had become clear that the countries of Central and Eastern Europe had the ambition to become full EU members. Seen the differences in economic and political development, several Western European capitals started to question to possibility to always move ahead jointly and flexible integration became a hotly debated issue.

The IGC leading to the Amsterdam Treaty lasted for 16 months (March 1996–June 1997) and was successively chaired by the Italian, Irish, and the earlier mentioned Dutch Presidency. It was the first IGC where also Austria, Finland and Sweden participated, bringing the total number of negotiating states to 15. Since all three were neutral or non-aligned, this brought new perspectives to the debate on European security. Also with regard to questions such as transparency and the environment they introduced novel ideas.

In line with the general focus of this volume, this chapter will try to come to a better understanding of the negotiation process and the role of various 'actors and factors' in the final outcome. Following a brief introduction on the actors and the agenda-setting process, we will successively examine how the treaty tried to bridge the gap with the European citizens, and examine its role in strengthening the EU's international role, the results on institutional reform, and the outcome of the debate on flexible integration. The conclusion tries to make sense of the negotiation process.

The actors

As the name suggests, an Intergovernmental Conference is in the first place a meeting of governments. Through a process of domestic bargaining and coordination, every member state determines its preferences and core priorities. The only supranational body that is a full member is the European Commission. Contrary to the member states however, its representative does not have a veto right. The European Parliament is only an associated member. It is regularly informed and can try to indirectly influence the process through its reports and resolutions but is not a direct participant in the negotiation process. The Council General Secretariat is present at all meetings in a supporting role but formally does not have any position.

Since decisions in an IGC are taken by consensus, all national delegations formally have the same weight. In practice however size matters and some countries are more equal than others. Through their role as motor of European integration, France and Germany have traditionally always occupied a key position and it is always difficult, if not impossible, to move ahead without having them on board. During the Amsterdam IGC, the Franco-German axis was led by the French President Jacques Chirac and the German Chancellor Helmut Kohl. Paris and Berlin submitted two joint letters, closely coordinated positions on reforming the Common Foreign and Security Policy (CFSP) and submitted a common proposal on flexibility. The disagreements on questions of institutional reform due to the French reluctance to strengthen the EU's supranational bodies and their plea give a bigger role to national parliaments complicated the deliberations. And so did domestic factors. The unexpected victory of the French socialists in the parliamentary elections of May 1997 further reinforced the French opposition to the Stability Pact and Germany's lack of attention to social issues (Deloche 2002). In Germany Chancellor Kohl was under heavy pressure of the German *Lander* who after Maastricht had managed to introduce a new article in the German constitution, requiring that any transfer of sovereign powers required the consent of the *Bundesrat*, the body composed of their representatives (Beuter 2002). The combination of these different developments made that the Franco-German couple carried less weight on the negotiation than in Maastricht.

Also in the case of the UK, domestic politics played a major role. As all public opinion polls pointed in the direction of a defeat of John Major's Conservative government, the UK found itself in a weak and relatively isolated position. The prospect of a more European friendly Labour government under the leadership of Tony Blair (May 1997) made that the decision on several sensitive issues was stalled. While one may dispute the extent to which the new government constituted a real step change, it remains that it made an end to the British opt-out on the social charter and allowed for the inclusion of an employment chapter into the Treaty (Best 2002). On questions of subsidiarity, the role of national parliaments and the continuing autonomy of the Western European Union (WEU), it indeed continued to defend the line taken by its predecessor.

The 1996–7 IGC was the first Conference taking place with 16 delegations around the table: the former Twelve; the three new members Austria, Finland and Sweden, and the European Commission. The larger the number of players, the bigger the chance for diversity and the more difficult it is to get once voice being heard. The obvious strategy for member states is therefore to look for possible alliances. Especially for the smaller member states who run a higher risk to be marginalised, this is of utmost importance. A classic example is the cooperation between the Benelux on matters of institutional design. As small countries they have an interest in strong supranational institutions defending the European interest. In the 1996 IGC they submitted a joint Benelux memorandum on the reform of the Council voting system and the extension of qualified majority voting (QMV). The three also submitted a joint proposal on the free movement of persons (Kerremans 2002). Other examples are the coalition between the Nordic countries Denmark, Sweden and Finland in areas of the environment, employment and fundamental rights (Devuyst 1998). It is important to note that depending on the topic, coalitions can vary. On flexibility Portugal joined forces with Greece, Sweden and the UK while on institutional matters it forged an alliance with Ireland, Luxembourg and the Nordic counties (Marinho 2002).

One delegation that has a very particular position in any IGC negotiation process is the country holding the rotating Presidency of the Council. Seen the relatively weak position of the European Commission which in the case of an IGC, only has a co-right of initiative, its role is potentially much more influential than in day-to-day EC policymaking process. As chair of the meetings at all levels, the rotating chair is at the centre of the information and in a privileged position to put forward new proposals and to formulate compromises. While operating as a broker it has however to be careful not to breach the trust of the other delegations by pushing too much for its own preferred position (see also chapter on Nice and the role of the French Presidency). To avoid a conflict of interests and a blurring of functions, the country at the helm is also represented by a national delegation in charge of articulating the national position. During the 1996–7 IGC, the Presidency was held by three medium-sized to small countries, all of them being strong supporters of the European integration process. Italy opened the negotiations in the first half of 1996, followed by Ireland (second half of 1996) and The Netherlands (first half of 1997). The role of Italy consisted mainly in mapping the different positions and presenting a summary of the state of the art at the Florence European Council (21–22 June 1996) (Corrado 2002). Ireland started the brokering process and by the end of its period at the helm it had prepared an outline draft treaty on all questions on the agenda and including concrete articles on various issues (McDonnagh 1998). The most sensitive issue such as the reform of the Council voting system, the integration of Schengen into the Treaty, the transitional regime for migration and asylum were all left to the Dutch Presidency.

The only non-member state with a right to speak around the IGC negotiation table is the European Commission. Its main task is to defend the European interest. During the Amsterdam negotiations the European Commission was led by Jacques Santer, who was much less pro-active than his predecessor Delors. The Council General Secretariat is not a formal participant of the negotiations but it is present at all meetings to support the Presidency in its heavy task. Its task is in the first place organisational but since it also helps the chair in the drafting of compromise proposals, it can sometimes also influence the final outcome (Beach 2004). The reliance of Presidencies on the Secretariat however varies heavily. Small member with limited resources tend to make more use of their services than the bigger ones.

Setting the agenda

An important part of the Amsterdam agenda had already been set during the 1991 IGC. In order to buy the support of countries that were disappointed with the poor progress in the security field and the limited areas of parliamentary co-decision, it had been agreed that these questions would again be discussed at a new IGC starting in 1996. Also policy fields such as energy, tourism, civil protection and the hierarchy of norms were mentioned as areas for further discussion.

The Maastricht Treaty had barely entered into force (November 1993) when the preparations for the next IGC were already taking off. Between June and December 1995, a Reflection Group under the chairmanship of the Spanish Secretary of State for European Affairs Carlos Westendorp regularly met to brainstorm about the agenda. Besides the personal representatives of the foreign ministers, also the European Commission and the European Parliament (EP) were represented. It was a first opportunity to get a grasp of the different positions and hobbyhorses. In the final report, adopted in December 1995, the following three priorities were identified: (1) bringing Europe closer to its citizens; (2) enabling the Union to function better and preparing it for enlargement; (3) endowing the EU with a greater capacity for external action (Reflection Group 1995).

The choice for these issues did not come as a surprise. The difficult ratification process of the Maastricht Treaty in countries ranging from Denmark and the UK to founder member states such as France and Germany had shown that support for the European integration process could no longer be taken for granted (Laursen and Vanhoonacker 1994). National governments realised that it was important that the new treaty addressed issues of direct interest to the citizens. The second priority was related to the upcoming enlargement. Never before had the Union faced such a massive number of applications and it was widely agreed that in order to prevent paralysis, a substantial reform of the EU's institutional architecture was required. The emphasis on the EU's external action was inspired by the Twelve's poor performance in the Yugoslav crisis. Instead of becoming 'the hour of Europe', the crisis had become a symbol of the Union's incapacity to speak with one voice and had painfully illustrated its lack of foreign policy resources.

The Reflection Group did not take any decisions on specific issues. It however allowed the member states to clarify positions and get a feeling for the concerns and priorities of the different delegations. It also helped in bringing the IGC on the radar of the national governments and administrations (McDonagh 1998).

Bringing Europe closer to the citizens

The Amsterdam negotiations took place at a time where public support for European integration had become increasingly under pressure and all heads of state and government agreed that it was primordial to come with results of direct relevance for the daily life of the European citizens. The result was the tabling of a wide scope of issues ranging from employment, social policy, fundamental rights as well as migration, asylum and the fight against crime.

Trying to address the criticism that the private sector had been the prime beneficiary of the European liberalisation process, the Amsterdam Treaty strengthened the Union's social policy and introduced a new Title on employment. Under the latter the member states and the European Community agreed to develop a coordinated employment strategy. A high level of employment became a formal EU objective and had also to be taken into account in the elaboration of other community policies. Under the social chapter it was agreed to introduce measures on combating social exclusion. The treaty furthermore introduced a legal basis for action in the field of equal opportunities and equal treatment of men and women at work. The Social Democratic government of Sweden, a country with a deep-rooted support and pride of the welfare state played a leading role in the debate (Johansson and Svensson 2002). Stockholm presented two detailed position papers on employment and forged alliances with others such as Austria, Belgium, Ireland, Denmark and Finland. As in Maastricht, the biggest opposition came from the UK. Although the Blair government accepted to join the social chapter, it remained reluctant to give up unanimity in this sensitive area (Best 2002). Following the victories of Blair (UK) and Jospin (France) there were twelve countries where Social Democratic parties formed part of the government. They proved however insufficiently organised and coordinated to heavily impact on the final outcome in the social field (Dehousse 1999).

Fortunately the results were more impressive in the areas of asylum and migration, a question that was high on the agenda at a moment where several member states such as Germany were facing strong migratory pressures from Central and Eastern Europe. Asylum, migration, judicial cooperation in civil matters as well as customs fraud and fraud against the community budget all moved to the (first) community pillar, leaving the intergovernmental third pillar with police cooperation and judicial cooperation in criminal matters. Despite the concession of a transitional period of 5 years whereby the Council and the Commission still shared the right of initiative, the communautarisation of several sensitive third pillar policy areas was a bridge too far for Denmark and the UK. Together with Ireland, with whom the UK has a passport union, these countries obtained an opt-out (McDonagh

1998; Petite 1998). The progress made in the free movement of persons had clearly come at a price and illustrated well how difficult it had become to always move ahead with the entire EU cohort.

A third important decision of direct relevance to the citizen relates to the integration of the so-called Schengen *acquis* into the Treaty. By the time of the Amsterdam negotiations, all member states, with the exception of Ireland and the UK had joined the Schengen agreement on free movement of persons and especially in The Netherlands, there were critical voices about the exclusion of the supranational community bodies from the Schengen policymaking process. The final agreement, only reached at the last phase of the negotiations contained a so-called lock, stock, and barrel approach, implying that all decisions adopted under Schengen would at once be integrated into EC legislation. Depending on the topic, the acts would be legally based on the first (free movement) or third pillar (police cooperation). There were again special provisions for Denmark, Ireland and the UK. The latter two were allowed to maintain their border controls. Denmark was only bound by the measures taken prior to Amsterdam and the new measures taken in the framework of the third pillar, not those falling under the first one (Den Boer 2002; Petite 1998).

The integration of Schengen, realised through the adoption of a Protocol, is a good example of how the rotating Presidency can have an important impact on the IGC negotiation process. Already during the Reflection Group meetings, the Dutch Secretary of State for European Affairs Michiel Patijn had invested much effort to put the question on the agenda. Initially there was little interest but the Dutch systematically kept the issue on the agenda, forging alliances with Belgium and the European Commission. Also the Council Secretariat played an important role in the drafting process. Once they were in the chair, the Netherlands invested a lot of time and resources to convince the opponents, if necessary by making concessions on other issues (Langendoen and Pijpers 2002; Mazzucelli 2003).

Greater capacity for external action

The IGC debate on the development of the EU's international role was a further attempt to come to grips with the radically changed European security situation after the end of the cold war. The difficulties to play a meaningful role in the Yugoslav crisis had made it clear that the gap between the EU's ambitions and its performance was still huge. The debate in Amsterdam centred on two major questions: how to increase the effectiveness of the foreign policy process and secondly how to strengthen the security and defence dimension of CFSP (Vanhoonacker 1997).

The most important innovations aimed at making the Union more responsive to international developments were the introduction of constructive abstention and, stemming from a French proposal, the creation of the new post of a High Representative (HR) for the Common Foreign and Security Policy (CFSP). The institutional home for this new player was heavily debated (McDonagh 1998). The spectrum of options discussed included an upgrade of the position of the Secretary General of the Council, the integration of the HR into the European Commission or, as suggested by Paris, the creation of a new function outside the existing institutional structures. The first and least ambitious option ultimately made it.

In contrast to the Lisbon Treaty where the HR has the right of initiative, the post created in Amsterdam was meant to be merely supportive. The role of the High Representative was to assist the Council and the rotating Presidency with the formulation, preparation and implementation of foreign policy decisions.[1] For his day-to-day work he could rely on a small Policy Planning and Early Warning Unit (PPEWU), composed of officials of the Council Secretariat, the European Commission and the member states. Given its composition it can be seen as the nucleus of the future European External Action Service (EEAS). For the first time, the Council Secretariat received more than a merely supportive role and started to also provide analyses of foreign policy challenges.

The debate on decision making once again was dominated by the perennial request for the introduction of Qualified Majority Voting (QMV). Advocated by Germany, it was strongly opposed by France, traditionally defending an intergovernmental approach to foreign policy cooperation. The compromise consisted in introducing QMV for implementing measures based on an earlier unanimous decision. This was also the case for the implementation of the new European Council instrument of common strategies, setting out general guidelines for a certain country or region. In addition, the treaty also introduced the possibility of constructive abstention. Member states abstaining would not be obliged to apply the decision but at the same time accept that it was binding the Union.[2] It was a first concrete attempt to introduce a certain degree of flexibility in the ponderous foreign policymaking process (Duke 2002).

Not surprisingly the most sensitive debates revolved around the further development of the security role of the Union. A key question was the future relation with the Western European Union (WEU), the body that the Maastricht Treaty had put in charge of implementing the Union's security decisions. Inspired by the gradual character of the EMU model, Europeanists such as Belgium, France, Germany, Italy, Luxembourg and Spain proposed the WEU's progressive integration into the EU in three steps. This was inacceptable for Atlanticists such as the UK and Portugal, who feared that this would undermine NATO's central position in the European security architecture. They also had the support of the neutral and non-aligned countries, opposing a strong EU security role. Besides Ireland, this group now also included the three new member states Austria, Finland and Sweden. The result was that the WEU remained an autonomous body but that the institutional relations with the EU were further strengthened. The full integration of the WEU into the EU would only be realised under the Nice Treaty after the Kosovo disaster in 1998–9.

The Finnish-Swedish proposal to incorporate the WEU Petersberg tasks into the Treaty was less controversial. There was consensus that the EU's future security role laid in the first place in the implementation of 'humanitarian and rescue tasks, peacekeeping tasks, and tasks of combat forces in crisis management, including peace-making'. Implicitly this reference to the EU's role as crisis manager was also a recognition of the fact that NATO would remain the principal organisation for questions of collective defence.

The rather modest results in European foreign policy can be explained through a variety of factors. An important obstacle was the malfunctioning of the Franco-German motor due to disagreements about the introduction of QMV and on the role of the High Representative. The continuing British conviction that European security initiatives should in the first place be taken in the NATO framework and the above mentioned reluctance of the neutral and non-aligned countries hindered any substantial progress in the field of European security and defence. Still the decade following the signature of the Amsterdam Treaty would see major developments in CFSP. This however mainly had to do with pressure from external events and Blair's decision in Saint Malo (June 1998) to give up its resistance against autonomous European action in the security field, backed up by military capabilities (Howorth 2007). Also Xavier Solana's maximalist interpretation of his job as first High Representative made that the new position had much more impact than many had expected.

Institutional reform

The debate on institutional reform was triggered both by the rather unsatisfactory outcomes in Maastricht as well as by the prospect of the upcoming 'big bang' enlargement with the east. Meant to be one of the top IGC priorities, it became the issue with the least results. Trying to come to a more efficient and legitimate policymaking process, the member states discussed a wide variety of issues ranging from the extension of QMV, the scope of parliamentary co-decision, the re-weighting of votes in the Council and the composition of the European Commission.

As in Maastricht the legitimacy question was in the first place addressed by further enhancing the powers of the European Parliament. Parliamentary co-decision was extended to provisions that were so far subject to the consultation, cooperation or assent procedures as well as to a number of new treaty provisions such as incentive measures for employment and several others.[3] Agriculture however, accounting for more than half of the EU budget, remained excluded. The co-decision procedure itself was simplified by abolishing the third reading.[4] The member states furthermore also strengthened the parliament's role in the nomination of the European Commission: the EP's right to approve the European Commission already introduced in Maastricht was extended to the right to approve the Commission President (Maurer 2002). At the instigation of France, the member states also adopted a protocol on the role of the national parliaments. They were to be better informed about EU legislative proposals and given a six-week period between the launching of a proposal and its discussion or adoption by the Council (Maurer 2002).

In terms of efficiency the balance sheet is much less positive, not to say poor. Both the question of the Council voting procedures as well as the composition of the European Commission were postponed to a next IGC. The extension of Qualified Majority Voting was much more limited than many had hoped for. While under the Irish Presidency there were still 19 articles on the list, in Amsterdam the member states only withheld five (Brinkhorst 1997). Sensitive areas such as social security, indirect taxation, culture and professional services were kept under unanimity (Moravcsik and Nicolaïdis 1999). Also for the new treaty articles the list proposed by the Dutch Presidency in Amsterdam was considerably reduced.[5] The limited progress can partly be explained by the rigidity of Chancellor Kohl who in the light of upcoming elections and under pressure of the German *Länder* was very careful not to alienate public opinion (Beuter 2002). In light of the upcoming enlargement to a Union of more than 20 member states, the prospect of the continuing prevalence of unanimity in so many important policy areas was problematic and therefore again put on the agenda in Nice.

Linked to the future influence of the member states, the questions of the size of the European Commission and the weighting of votes proved even more difficult to reach a consensus. Part of the problem was that these issues opposed large and small member states. Arguing that with every enlargement the population represented in QMV was declining, the five largest member states asked to be compensated for their losses. In a Union of Fifteen, a qualified majority vote still represented 58.3 per cent of the EU population while in a Union of 26, it only stood for 50.29 per cent (Laursen 2002b). While France, Italy, Spain and the UK advocated a reweighting of the votes of individual member states, Germany pleaded for a dual majority system. Besides a majority of votes, a 'yes vote' in such system would also be based on a majority of the EU population. The negotiations were further complicated by the fact that the 'weighting of votes' dossier was linked with the question of the size and the composition of the European Commission. At the time of the Amsterdam negotiations the five largest member states still had two Commissioners, while the small ones only nominated one. Big member states were ready to give up their 'second' Commissioner and accept a capped college with less Commissioners than member states based on the principle of rotation. Fearing that the rotation would only apply to them, the small member states rejected the idea of a Commission where not all countries would have a representative of their nationality. The argument was that from a legitimacy point of view it was important for the college to have at least one member with a strong sense of national sensitivities. At a time that the EU was being criticised for not listening enough to its citizens, such national presence was considered to be all the more important.

The linkage between the different institutional questions and their high sensitivity implied that member states left the cutting of a deal to the Amsterdam summit on 16–17 June 1997. One of the key questions was how exactly the revised Council voting system would compensate the larger member states for giving up their second Commission member. By that time, a majority supported the dual majority system but some like France continued to advocate a simple re-weighting of the votes. The negotiations went on until the early hours of 18 June but no agreement was reached (McDonagh 1998). In a protocol attached to the Treaty, the member states agreed to organise another IGC at least one year before the EU was exceeding the number of 20 member states carrying out 'a comprehensive review of the provisions of the Treaties on the composition and functioning of the institutions' (Protocol No. 7). It is also stipulated that upon the date of the entry into force of the next enlargement, the Commission will comprise one national per member state on the condition that the weighting of votes in the Council has been modified. It was up to the next IGC to decide whether this would be by a re-weighting of the votes or through a system of dual majority. The so-called leftovers of Amsterdam would ultimately be tackled under the French Presidency in Nice (December 2000) (Schout and Vanhoonacker 2006b).

Trying to explain the postponement of a decision on what many saw as the key priority of IGC, Moravscik and Nicolaïdis (1999) point to the changed position of the German Chancellor Kohl who, under domestic pressure and upcoming elections, had become much more reluctant to support radical institutional reforms. The realisation that enlargement was still several years away, made the reaching of a deal less pressing.

Flexible integration

One of the big challenges of the upcoming enlargement was how to combine the widening of the EU with a further deepening. Integrationists feared that the increasing diversity would make it very hard to always move ahead with all EU member states. The Maastricht opt-outs for the UK (EMU, social policy) and Denmark (security) were already first indications that in certain cases the only way forward was to allow for differentiation and permit reluctant countries to stay – at least temporarily – on the side-line. Although flexible integration was not one of the three core objectives of the negotiations, it was present throughout the debate leading to heated discussions until the final stages of the IGC.

As in so many IGC questions, Berlin and Paris set the tone. In September 1994, a document prepared by the parliamentary group of Germany's ruling Christian Democrats, better known as the Schäuble-Lamers paper, put forward the idea of a hard core Europe of five member states consisting of France, Germany and the Benelux countries (Schäuble and Lamers 1994). Shortly before, in an interview with the French newspaper *Le Figaro*, the French Prime Minister Edouard Balladur had presented his notion of a Europe of concentric circles (30 August 1994). Although both proposals got a rather hostile reception especially by those not included in the hard core, they had the merit of putting the issue of flexible integration squarely on the agenda. Both countries further pushed the issue by putting forward joint proposals, both at the level of the heads of states and government (December 1995) and at ministerial level (February 1996) (Deloche 2002).

The fact that 'flexibility meant different things to different people' and wide-ranging disagreements both about its purpose and form made the negotiations very difficult and time-consuming (McDonagh 1998). The UK for example advocated an *á la carte approach* where countries could 'pick-and-chose' their areas for further integration. This formula was fiercely rejected both by the European Commission and the Benelux countries seeing it as a potential source of incoherence and disintegration. Southern countries such as Spain, Portugal and Greece firmly opposed the idea of differentiation as they feared that it might lead to their marginalisation. A further complication was the interlinkage between the flexibility question and other issues on the IGC agenda. Since the ultimate need for flexibility depended to a large extent on the progress made in other IGC issues (such as the extension of QMV for example), it could only be settled once there was clarity on the final package (McDonagh 1998).

While one can argue that the decision to include treaty provisions on 'enhanced cooperation' was a revolutionary step, the scope provided by the TEU to initiate it among a number of member states within the EU's institutional framework was rather limited. Rather than discussing specific policy areas, the member states defined a general enabling clause defining the conditions under which the cooperation could take place. The new title of the TEU specified a list of no less than seven of them. These included *inter alia* respect for the TEU's single institutional framework and the *acquis communautaire*, as well as its use as an instrument of last resort, the involvement of the majority of member states and openness to all of them. In addition there were separate provisions on the conditions and decision-making mechanisms in the first and the third pillar. The decision on enhanced cooperation was to be taken by QMV and it was up to the European Commission to check the compliance with the flexibility criteria and to formulate a proposal. While in the first pillar the Commission opinion on member states proposals was binding, this was not the case in the third pillar. A further protection was that member states could always refer a matter to the European Council for a unanimous decision. The second pillar was excluded from enhanced cooperation. Through constructive abstention, CFSP however disposed of its own form of flexible cooperation (Stubb 1998).

Associated with risks of marginalisation, lack of coherence and even disintegration, the overall tone of the debate on flexible integration was very defensive and by the end of the IGC there was not much left of the original Franco-German idea of a hard core (Stubb 1998). While one may be critical of the very cautious approach and the many conditions attached to the application of the flexibility clause, it remains an important step that for the first time the notion is institutionalised and formally enshrined in an EU Treaty.

Making sense of the Amsterdam IGC

The negotiations leading to the Treaty of Amsterdam lasted for 16 months, covered a wide range of issues and involved a broad variety of players at different levels from diplomats to ministers of foreign affairs and heads of state and government. Although it was impossible to give a full account of the IGC in all its richness, our account nevertheless allows us to draw some interesting lessons on the negotiation process.

Firstly, in line with liberal intergovernmentalism, it is clear from our analysis that the member states, particularly the big ones, play a predominant role. Especially the positions of France and Germany were again key, although their motor role was less performing than in Maastricht. In cases of disagreement between the two, such as on institutional reform or the use of QMV in the second pillar, the negotiation process suffered and the outcome was negatively affected.

The impact of the UK was entirely different as it often weighed in a negative rather than in a positive way. With its minimalist positions, the British delegation managed to block progress in a number of key areas such as the integration of the WEU into the EU. In other cases such as the integration of Schengen, the others moved forward without London. The upcoming elections and the expected change of government put the British negotiators in a difficult situation and some of the most sensitive issues were only tackled after the new Blair government had come to power (in May 1997). Despite the ambitions of the new Foreign Secretary Robin Cook, the big member states that really mattered in Amsterdam were only two in number and not three.[6]

The pivotal role of the big member states does not mean that the smaller ones did not matter. Amsterdam again illustrated that, when well prepared and able to forge alliances with others, small countries can definitely have an impact. A case in point is Sweden playing a leading role in the adoption of the employment chapter, and supported by others such as Austria, Belgium, Ireland, Denmark and Finland but strongly opposed by Germany. Another example was Denmark who managed to strengthen the environmental guarantee in the Treaty article on the internal market. Although there was initially not much support, the Danish delegation nevertheless managed to get it through by skilfully playing out the upcoming ratification referendum (Beach 2002).

One group of countries in a particularly privileged position are those holding the rotating Presidency. While Italy and especially Ireland did a lot of the preparatory work, it were the Dutch who were in charge of orchestrating the endgame. The example of the integration of

Schengen, a Dutch hobbyhorse, is a clear example of how a position at the helm puts the rotating chair in a strategic position to impact upon the final outcome.

Does the pivotal role of the member states imply that the IGC is a purely intergovernmental affair or was there also scope for an impact by the supranational institutions such as the European Commission, the EP and the Council General Secretariat? During the Maastricht negotiations the European Commission under the leadership of President Delors had been criticised for overplaying its hand. In Amsterdam the Santer Commission took a pragmatic approach and operated more behind the scenes by closely cooperating with the Presidency and by forging alliances with member states on particular issues (Gray 2002). Our analysis however did not find any clear examples that through its contributions the Commission significantly altered the outcome of the negotiation process. The same applies for the European Parliament. The fact that the Treaty brought extended co-decision and further strengthened the role of the EP had as much to do with the general willingness to increase the legitimacy of the EU as with the EP's contribution to the IGC.

The role of the Council General Secretariat is undoubtedly the most difficult to assess. Since both the Irish and the Dutch Presidencies heavily relied on the Secretariat to draft the Treaty articles, Beach (2004) in earlier research has identified it as an invisible hand. While we don't want to downplay its impact, it remains that the Secretariat is not an autonomous actor and any of its drafts are always subject to the approval of the chair and the other delegations.

A final element, which deserves attention, as it has been present throughout this account is the broader political and institutional context of the negotiations. Factors such as the time horizon of the negotiations, the broader European and international context, particular domestic developments, are all factors going beyond the control of the member states but nevertheless contribute to the structuring of the debate (Christiansen and Reh 2009). In the case of the Amsterdam treaty negotiations, several issues can be mentioned, starting with the fact that the 1996–7 IGC did not start from scratch. The Maastricht Treaty had already defined institutional reform and strengthening CFSP as priority areas for revision. Since it was clear from the start that the negotiations would be concluded at the end of the Dutch Presidency, it was obvious that the most sensitive issues such as institutional reform and flexibility would not be concluded prior to the European Council of 16–17 June. Examples of domestic, European and international contextual factors playing a role are the declining public support for the European integration process, eastern enlargement and the ongoing crisis in the Balkans. There was a general consensus that the IGC needed to give priority to the direct concerns of the citizens such as employment, transparency and migration (McDonagh 1998). The poor EU performance in the Yugoslav crisis gave impetus to the debate on strengthening CFSP and the upcoming enlargement was in the back of everybody's mind in the discussions on institutional reform and flexibility. At the same time the fact that accession was still several years ahead made that the European Council had the luxury to postpone a decision on the reweighting of votes and the composition of the Commission. Also purely domestic factors such as the British expected change in government and the imminent German elections were elements impacting to a bigger extent than many have appreciated.

Concluding we can say that an IGC, as the name suggests, is to a large extent an intergovernmental affair with a crucial role for the bigger member states. However, it has to be emphasised that even if the national delegations will in the first place be led by what has been agreed domestically, they are not immune to what is happening in the broader political and institutional context. Any account of an IGC should therefore also include an examination of how such factors have shaped the final outcome.

Notes

1. The day-to-day management of the Council Secretariat was entrusted to the Deputy Secretary General of the Council General Secretariat.
2. The new mechanism of constructive abstention did not apply when adopting joint actions, common positions or decisions on the basis of a common strategy. Other derogations included the appointment of a special representative or the adoption of a decision implementing a joint action or common position.
3. Besides incentive measures for employment policy, the new Treaty provisions covered by co-decision also included: social policy (equal opportunities and treatment); public health.
4. In the third reading, the Council could impose the common position after conciliation had failed unless the EP could overrule the Council by an absolute majority of its members.
5. Examples include employment guidelines, equal treatment of men and women, public health, transparency, countering fraud, statistics.
6. See Robin Cook, quoted in E. Best (2002), p. 375: 'We want to make sure that from now on there are three players in Europe, not just two.'

9
The Treaty of Nice: The Inadequate Preparation of Enlargement

Finn Laursen

Historical context

The Treaty of Nice was negotiated by an Intergovernmental Conference (IGC), which ran through most of the year 2000. The European Council in Nice, France, concluded the negotiations in December 2000. An important part of the historical context was the expected eastern enlargement, which eventually had six central and eastern European countries (CEECs) joining the EU in 2004 – namely, Poland, the Czech Republic, Slovakia, Hungary, Slovenia together with the three Baltic states (Estonia, Latvia and Lithuania), as well as Malta and Cyprus. Bulgaria and Romania followed in 2007.

Many of the existing members felt that a relatively substantial enlargement would require some institutional changes. The Amsterdam treaty negotiations had tried to deal with these changes, but largely failed. Nice then dealt with three related issues known as the Amsterdam 'leftovers' because the Treaty of Amsterdam in 1997 had failed to solved them (Laursen, 2002a):

1. Re-weighting of votes in the Council.
2. Increased use of qualified majority voting (QMV) in the Council.
3. Size and composition of the Commission.

Changing the voting in the Council involved both legitimacy and efficiency issues. It was the large member states that demanded a re-weighting of votes; these states claimed that they were relatively underrepresented according to the old weighting, and that this would become a bigger issue in a much enlarged Union since most new member states were relatively small, with the main exception of

Poland. A re-weighting of votes, they argued, would increase the legitimacy of the system.

An increased use of QMV should improve the decision-making capacity
of the Union. As long as unanimity is required, one single member state
can veto decisions. With a QMV, it will take a small group of states – a
so-called blocking minority – to block a decision. The size of this group
depends on the definition of the QMV, which in Nice was closely linked
to the re-weighting of votes.

The third issue, the size and composition of the Commission, was
also difficult because most member states wished to be represented in
the college of commissioners. At the time, in the EU-15, there were 20
commissioners, two from each of the big five and one from each of the
ten smaller member states. But was the Commission not already becoming too large to both function as a collegial body and leave meaningful portfolios for all members? This was an efficiency issue, but to the
extent that the smaller members wanted to be represented, it was also
a legitimacy issue.

It took a lot of 'horse-trading' (Norman, 2000) in Nice in December
2000 to reach agreements on these issues. In the end, most of the heads
of state or government that met in Nice were rather unhappy about the
outcome.

In many ways Nice was unique. Past treaty reforms, except the Merger
treaty, had usually dealt with both substantive policy and institutional
issues. This time the agenda was largely limited to institutional issues.
These issues were to include a fourth matter that was added during the
conference: 'closer' or 'enhanced' cooperation, as it was eventually to
be called in the Treaty of Nice. The Treaty of Amsterdam had introduced clauses allowing a group of member states to go further in the
integration process than the more hesitant and slow member states, but
the conditions for such 'closer cooperation' were rather strict (Stubb,
2002). The issue in the Nice negotiations was whether the conditions
should be made less strict. This would make it easier for pro-integration
members to move faster than integration-sceptical member states and
possibly form an *avant-garde* group.

Treaty content

Re-weighting of votes

A re-weighting was eventually agreed. The four biggest states, which used
to have ten votes, would get 29. If we only concentrate on population,
Germany should have had more votes. Spain, which had eight votes, got 27,

which was a very good result for that country. Spain then pulled Poland up to the same level. There was a differentiation between the Netherlands getting 13 and Belgium getting 12 votes, respectively (see Table 9.1).

The Treaty of Nice also assigned new numbers of seats in the European Parliament. Here, a differentiation between Germany and France had existed since a mini-reform had taken place after the Maastricht treaty negotiations in 1992. In the future, Germany would retain its 99 seats, while France, Italy and the UK would go down from 87 to 72 seats (see Table 9.2).

Extension of qualified majority voting (QMV)

The second main issue was the increased use of QMV. When the IGC 2000 started, there were about 70 areas left that still required unanimity according to the treaty. The IGC discussed about 45 of these with a view to a possible transfer to QMV. In the end it was decided to transfer 23 areas to QMV from the entry into force of the treaty and 12 areas later. More than 20 areas, mainly constitutional or quasi-constitutional provisions, were considered too sensitive from the outset so it was agreed early on not to touch them.

The more controversial areas in these discussions about increased use of QMV included visa, asylum and immigration, where some issues would be transferred to QMV in 2004 and others later. Another controversial area was trade policy, where the introduction of QMV for trade in services and trade-related aspects of intellectual property rights (TRIPS) took place with some exemptions, including 'culture' and the 'audiovisual' area. France insisted on that exemption.

Social policy was also controversial. This included Article 42, where no change was adopted, and Article 137, where a limited move to QMV was to be decided by unanimity later. The UK and Denmark were among the countries that had problems with the proposed changes in these two articles. The treaty also left taxation policies untouched, which satisfied the UK, among other states.

Co-decision

The European Parliament argued that policy fields moved to QMV in the Council should also fall under co-decision with the European Parliament. This rule was only followed in a relatively small number of cases. The new cases of co-decision were the following:

Article 13 TEC, incentive measures to combat discrimination.
Article 62 TEC, external border controls.

Table 9.1 Council votes in EU-27 (as of 1 January 2005 and onward)

	Present votes	Future Votes	Population (mio.)	% of Union population
Germany	10	29	82,03	17.05
United Kingdom	10	29	59,25	12.31
France	10	29	58,97	12.25
Italy	10	29	57,61	11.97
Spain	8	27	39,39	8.19
Poland		27	38,67	8.04
Romania		14	22,49	4.67
Netherlands	5	13	15,76	3.28
Greece	5	12	10,53	2.19
Czech Republic		12	10,29	2.14
Belgium	5	12	10,21	2.12
Hungary		12	10,09	2.10
Portugal	5	12	9,98	2.07
Sweden	4	10	8,85	1.84
Bulgaria		10	8,23	1.71
Austria	4	10	8,08	1.68
Slovakia		7	5,39	1.12
Denmark	3	7	5,31	1.10
Finland	3	7	5,16	1.07
Ireland	3	7	3,74	0.78
Lithuania		7	3,70	0.77
Latvia		4	2,44	0.51
Slovenia		4	1,98	0.41
Estonia		4	1,45	0.30
Cyprus		4	0,75	0.16
Luxembourg	2	4	0,43	0.09
Malta		3	0,38	0.08
Total EU-27	87	345	481,18	100
Qualified majority of votes	62	258 (as well as a majority of members if proposed by Commission, otherwise two-thirds of members)		Furthermore, at least 62% of the Union population if a member state asks for control of this criterion
Blocking minority	26	88		

Source: According the 'Declaration on the Enlargement of the European Union' of the Treaty of Nice, see Treaty texts and European Parliament, 'Draft Treaty of Nice (initial analysis)', Brussels, 10 January 2001. Galloway, 2001, p. 88. The final version of the Nice Treaty was published in the *Official Journal of the European Communities* C. 80, 10 March 2001.

Table 9.2 Seats in the European Parliament (EU-27)

	Population (mio.)	Population as % of EU	Seats per member State under the present system	Seats per member State under the Treaty of Nice	Reduction in numbers	Reduction in %	Number of inhabitants per seat
Germany	82,04	17.05	99	99	0	0	828.667
United Kingdom	59,25	12.31	87	72	15	17.24	822.875
France	58,97	12.25	87	72	15	17.24	818.972
Italy	57,61	11.97	87	72	15	17.24	800.167
Spain	39,39	8.19	64	50	14	21.88	787.880
Poland	38,66	8.04		50			773.340
Romania	22,49	4.67		33			681.485
Netherlands	15,76	3.28	31	25	6	19.35	630.400
Greece	10,53	2.19	25	22	3	12	478.773
Czech Republic	10,29	2.14		20			514.500
Belgium	10,21	2.12	25	22	3	12	464.227
Hungary	10,09	2.1		20			504.600
Portugal	9,98	2.07	25	22	3	12	453.636
Sweden	8,85	1.84	22	18	4	18.18	491.889
Bulgaria	8,23	1.71		17			484.118
Austria	8,08	1.68	21	17	4	19.05	475.412
Slovakia	5,39	1.12		13			414.846
Denmark	5,31	1.1	16	13	3	18.75	408.692
Finland	5,16	1.07	16	13	3	18.75	396.923
Ireland	3,74	0.78	15	12	3	20	312.000
Lithuania	3,70	0.77		12			308.417

Latvia	2,44	0.51		8			304.875
Slovenia	1,98	0.41		7			282.571
Estonia	1,45	0.3		6			241.000
Cyprus	0,75	0.16		6			125.333
Luxembourg	0,43	0.09	6	6	0		71.500
Malta	0,38	0.08		5	0	0	75.800
Total EU-27	481,18	100		732			657.351

Source: According the 'Declaration on the Enlargement of the European Union' of the Treaty of Nice, see European Parliament, 'Draft Treaty of Nice (initial analysis)', Brussels, 10 January 2001, European Union. Some seat numbers were amended by the 2003 Act of Accession (see European Union, 2006).

Article 63 TEC, asylum.
Article 65 TEC, judicial cooperation in civil matters (except family law).
Article 137 TEC, use of *passerelle*, rights of third-country workers.
Article 157 TEC, specific measures in support of action by member states
  in the field of industry.
Article 159 TEC, specific actions outside the structural funds.
Article 191 TEC, status of and financial rules governing political parties
  at the European level.

At the same time, the assent procedure was extended to Articles 7 (fundamental rights) and 11 (initiation of enhanced cooperation under the first pillar). All in all these steps were not necessarily impressive, but they constituted yet another step towards empowerment of the European Parliament. As we shall see later, the EP also increased its powers in other ways.

Size and composition of Commission

Concerning the third issue – the size and composition of the Commission – the Treaty of Nice only found a partial solution. From 1 January 2005, the Commission would consist of one national from each member state. When the EU reaches 27 members, a reduction in the size of the Commission would have to be agreed and a system of rotation found, and all of this by unanimity.

Nice further strengthened the role of the President of the Commission. In the future he/she was to decide the internal organisation of the Commission and he/she could reallocate responsibilities among the commissioners during the Commission's term of office. The President can also call on a member of the Commission to resign after obtaining the collective approval of the Commission.

Enhanced cooperation

Nice made 'enhanced cooperation' easier by only requiring an absolute minimum number of states of eight, whereas the Treaty of Amsterdam had required a majority of the member states. The exact rules, however, varied between the three pillars and remained rather complex: the Treaty of Amsterdam had enabling clauses for closer cooperation in the first and third pillars, which provided the possibility of using a veto against such cooperation. This veto was now removed for those two pillars. Nice further introduced enabling clauses for enhanced cooperation in the second pillar but with a veto possibility. The general conditions remained rather restrictive.

Dynamics of the negotiations

Agenda setting

The meeting of the European Council in Luxembourg in December 1997 decided to start membership negotiations with six applicant states – namely, Estonia, Poland, the Czech Republic, Hungary and Cyprus (Laursen, 2001). Enlargement was under way. Given the protocol on institutions from Amsterdam, which allowed for enlargement with up to five new members on the condition of a reduction of the size of the Commission to one member per member state and some modification of the weighting of votes in the Council, it looked as if the number of five might be exceeded in the first enlargement. The Amsterdam protocol foresaw a new IGC 'to carry out a comprehensive review of the provisions of the Treaties on the composite on and functioning of the institutions' before the EU could take in more than five new members (Galloway, 2001: 27).

The meeting of the European Council in Cologne in June 1999 therefore decided to convene an IGC in 2000 to deal with the 'Amsterdam leftovers':

> In order to ensure that the European Union's institutions can continue to work efficiently after enlargement, the European Council confirms its intention of convening a Conference of the Representatives of the Governments of the Member States early in 2000 to resolve the institutional issues left open in Amsterdam that need to be settled before enlargement. The Conference should be completed and the necessary amendments to the treaties agreed upon at the end of 2000.
>
> (European Council, 1999a)

Preparation this time was left to the Finnish presidency during the second half of 1999. The Commission also had a report prepared by Jean-Luc Dehaene, Richard von Weizsäcker and David Simon on 'The Institutional Implications of Enlargement'. The report was presented to the Commission on 18 October 1999. The Commission issued its own communication on 10 November 1999 (European Commission, 1999).

The meeting of the European Council in Helsinki in December 1999 confirmed the relatively narrow agenda of the IGC, leaving open the possibility of adding other topics later. In the presidency conclusions, we read:

> Following the Cologne Conclusions and in the light of the Presidency's report, the Conference will examine the size and composition of the

Commission, the weighting of votes in the Council, as well as other necessary amendments to the Treaties arising as regards the European institutions in connection with the above issues and in implementing the Treaty of Amsterdam. The incoming Presidency will report to the European Council on progress made in the Conference and may propose additional issues to be taken on the agenda of the Conference.

(European Council, 1999b)

The idea was now to convene the IGC in February 2000 and complete it by December 2000. It thus was to run through the Portuguese and French presidencies of that year.

As for organisation of the IGC, the foreign ministers would have the 'overall political responsibility'. Preparatory work was to be the responsibility of 'a Group composed of a representative of each Member State's Government' (ibid.). The Commission would take part in the IGC at both the political and preparatory level, and the Council Secretariat would provide support.

The European Parliament would be 'closely associated and involved' in the IGC. The EP would have two observers in the preparatory group. Sessions of foreign ministers were to be 'preceded by an exchange of views with the President of the European Parliament, assisted by two representatives' of the EP. 'Meetings at the level of Heads of State or Government dealing with the IGC will be preceded by an exchange of views with the President of the European Parliament' (ibid.).

Helsinki also called for the start of accession negotiations with the next six applicants – Latvia, Lithuania, Slovakia, Romania, Bulgaria and Malta – which increased the pressure for institutional changes. The Helsinki meeting of the European Council further gave Turkey the status of an applicant without setting a date for the start of negotiations. Candidate states would be regularly briefed during the IGC.

Parallel negotiations: Defence and fundamental rights

Helsinki decided to follow up on another decision from Cologne, namely to develop the Union's defence policy. The summit underlined the 'determination to develop an autonomous capacity to take decisions, and, where NATO as a whole is not engaged, to launch and conduct EU-led military operations in response to international crises' (European Council, 1999a). In particular, the European Council agreed that 'cooperating voluntarily in EU-led operations, Member States must be able, by 2003, to deploy within 60 days and sustain for at least one year military forces of up to 50,000–60,000 persons capable of the full range of Petersberg tasks', which included, for example, various peace-keeping and peace-enforcing activities.

The idea of consolidating 'the fundamental rights applicable at Union level' in a charter had also been accepted at the Cologne summit. It was decided: 'a draft of such a Charter of Fundamental Rights of the European Union should be elaborated by a body composed of representatives of the Heads of State and Government and the President of the Commission as well as of members of the European Parliament and national parliaments'. This body, later known as a Convention, should present a draft document 'in advance of the European Council in December 2000' (European Council, 1999a).

So these two issues, defence policy and fundamental rights, were kept separate from the IGC and dealt with in parallel processes: in the end, a Charter of Fundamental Rights was adopted in Nice as a political document, not legally binding, and the process of getting the European Security and Defence Policy (ESDP) in place made relatively quick progress.

IGC 2000

The formal initiative for the IGC went out from the Finnish presidency on 14 December 1999. The proposal went to hearings in the Commission and European Parliament on 17 December as required by Article 48 TEU. The Commission issued its positive recommendation on 26 January 2000 in the form of an opinion entitled 'Adapting the Institutions to make a Success of Enlargement' (European Commission, 2000a). The European Parliament followed on 3 February with the required resolution. Objecting to the 'excessively narrow agenda adopted in Helsinki', the EP called for 'an ambitious reform of the Treaty' (European Parliament, 2000).

Having heard from the Commission and the European Parliament, the Council could formally call the IGC, which started 14 February 2000. During the following ten months, the group of representatives met about twice a month and the foreign ministers met approximately once a month. The heads of state or government met in Santa Maria da Feira, Portugal, 19–20 June; in Biarritz, France, 13–14 October; and finally in Nice, 7–10 December 2000. The concluding negotiations in Nice actually finished at 4.15 a.m. on Monday, 11 December.

By the time of the Feira summit in June, the Portuguese presidency had put forward a report on the IGC, giving an overview of the discussions, listing options and some concrete proposals (CONFER 4750).

In the presidency conclusions, the heads of state or government talked about 'significant headway', and said, '[t]he European Council considers in particular that the provisions on closer cooperation introduced into the Treaty of Amsterdam should form part of the Conference's future work, while respecting the need for coherence and solidarity in an enlarged Union' (European Council, 2000a). So closer or 'enhanced cooperation', as it was eventually to be called in the Treaty of Nice, was now on the agenda.

The question of increased application of QMV was one of the issues debated during the Portuguese presidency. In their report to the Feira summit, the Portuguese mentioned 39 areas that might be moved to QMV and eight areas where QMV could be considered for only certain aspects. This latter group included measures to provide freedom of movement for workers and self-employed workers (Art. 42 TEC), certain tax measures (Art. 93 TEC), certain specific provisions on social matters (Art. 137 TEC), and arrangements for participation by the EU in World Trade Organization proceedings, where a new protocol was suggested (Annex 3.1 in CONFER 4750). Also listed were 24 constitutional, quasi-constitutional or organic provisions for which unanimity is required in the Council, and for which no QMV was envisaged (Annex 3.7).

When the French presidency put forward its first progress report on 3 November, the 'List of Provisions to be examined with a view to a possible move to qualified majority voting' had been increased to 47, including articles 42, 93 and 137 (CONFER 4790). It also included articles 133(1) and (4) TEC – the conclusion of international agreements on intellectual property and services. A draft protocol would include the sectors covered by the WTO's General Agreement on Trade in Services (GATS) and the Agreement on Trade-Related Aspects of Intellectual Property Rights (TRIPS) under Article 133(4), which would introduce QMV for these new areas of international commercial policy. The French proposal for QMV also included several of the Justice and Home Affairs (JHA) areas to be transferred from Pillar III to Pillar I according to the Amsterdam treaty (parts of articles 62, 63, 65 and 66) as well as structural funds (Art. 161).

Since some of these proposals were unacceptable to some member states, the politics of QMV became an important part of the IGC endgame in the lead-up to Nice. As mentioned earlier, in the end about 30 areas were moved to QMV.

Size and composition of the Commission also turned out to be a very controversial issue. It pitted smaller member states, who insisted on retaining a Commissioner of their nationality, against larger member states, led by France, who insisted on a smaller Commission in the future and some system of rotation.

Most dramatic was the issue of weighting of votes in the Council. The French presidency put forward its first proposal on 9 December in Nice. The proposal was to triple the number of votes for the big four to 30 votes and double the votes for most medium-sized and smaller member states. Spain would move from eight to 28, more than a tripling. Luxembourg, however, would move from two to three, less than a doubling.

Since the first proposal was violently criticised by the medium-sized and smaller member states, the French put forward a second proposal on 10 December. Most smaller and medium-sized members would get an additional vote in this proposal, but the Netherlands would get two extra, thus creating a differentiation between Belgium and the Netherlands. In the end, the presidency had to offer the medium-sized members one additional vote and reduce the big member states' votes by one (SN 511, SN 522 and SN 533; for more see Laursen, 2006b).

All kinds of linkages were brought into the negotiations. Portugal felt that Spain was treated too generously. The treatment of the Netherlands upset the Belgians. Some of the dissatisfied countries then got extra seats in the European Parliament, and Belgium was promised that future meetings of the European Council would take place in Brussels. Germany was won over by the stipulation that a QMV must also represent 62 per cent of the population in the EU, if a member requests a check of this criterion. Germany further avoided a reduction in the number of seats in the European Parliament, which all other member states except Luxembourg had to accept.

Ratification

The adopted treaty then had to be ratified by all member states to enter into force. The first to deposit the ratification instrument was Denmark on 13 June 2001. Denmark this time ratified without a referendum. The last to finish the ratification process was Ireland. In the Irish case, a referendum was considered necessary. The Irish voters surprised many by voting 'no' in a referendum on 7 June 2001, with 53.87 per cent of 'no' votes. Eventually a second referendum took place on 19 October 2002. This time there was a 'yes' vote of 62.89 per cent (Tonra, 2006).

The Treaty of Nice entered into force on 1 February 2003 and it remained in force until the entry of the Lisbon Treaty in December 2009. But the system of weighted voting adopted in Nice, slightly adapted through accession treaties, will remain in force until 2014.

Analysing the Treaty of Nice: Explanations and assessments

Explaining preferences

In line with liberal intergovernmentalism (Moravcsik, 1993 and 1998), IGCs can be seen as two-level games. Governments have to be concerned about the domestic ratification of an agreement negotiated at the EU level (Putnam, 1988). In most member states, ratification is authorised by national parliaments; the two main exceptions to this are Denmark and Ireland, where ratification normally has taken place through the use of referendums. In the case of the Treaty of Nice, Denmark avoided a referendum because of an interpretation of the treaty, which concluded that it did not extend the policy scope and thus did not fall under Article 20 of the Danish constitution; however, Ireland did need a referendum – two referendums, in fact, to be able to ratify the treaty (Laursen, 2006; Tonra, 2006).

Given the fact that political elites tend to be more pro-European than the wider public, a parliamentary ratification will usually be easier than ratification by referendum. However, sometimes a parliamentary ratification can also be difficult, as was the case in the British ratification of the Maastricht treaty, 1992–3. In the case of the Treaty of Nice, the Labour government had a comfortable majority and ratification was fairly easy. Nonetheless, governments have to anticipate parliamentary reactions to the agreements they bring home. For Spain this was the case with Nice (Basabe, 2006): despite the Aznar government's parliamentary majority, the government felt that it needed to return with a 'victory'. So even if criticism back home does not threaten ratification, governments have a wider concern to limit criticism and maintain a good reputation. A government with weak parliamentary support will be particularly sensitive to such concerns.

Various domestic institutional factors can play a role in preference formation. One domestic-politics factor that had some impact on the Nice negotiations was the fact that during the French presidency, France had *cohabitation* with a Gaullist President and a Socialist Prime Minister. This situation contributed to making it difficult for President Chirac to be a neutral president of the negotiations among the heads of state and government in Nice (Schout and Vanhoonacker, 2006).

In negotiations like the Nice meetings, where formal EU institutions are changed, symbols and national prestige can play a great role. France wanted to stay on par with Germany in the re-weighting of votes in the Council. Belgium compared itself with the Netherlands, Portugal with Spain, and so on. Since leaders had to return to their national capitals and defend the outcome, they could not ignore these factors. As Bart Kerremans has suggested, the Belgian leaders had to be aware of the public's reaction to the front-page news 'Netherlands – Belgium, 12-10' (Kerremans, 2006). This all suggests that liberal intergovernmentalism's focus on demands from economic actors is too limited.

However, with respect to one of the issues on the Nice agenda – the extended use of qualified majority voting (QMV) – liberal intergovernmentalism retains some explanatory power. Where member states insisted on retaining unanimity they often did so for economic reasons. This was clearly the case when Britain resisted QMV for taxation and social policy issues. Austria wanted to retain unanimity for some issues related to environmental policy. This included water resources, an important concern in Austria, and energy, as there is strong opposition to nuclear energy in the country (Blanck, 2006). Denmark's insistence on unanimity for certain aspects of social policy was due to a fear that migrant workers and their dependants might undermine the tax base of the social welfare system. France's insistence on unanimity for the audiovisual and cultural sectors was a defence of the French film industry as well as a defence of the French language. But countries favouring a large extension of the scope of QMV, such as Belgium, did so at least partly because of pro-European or federalist ideology. Interestingly, however, as pointed out by Kerremans, the Belgians sided with the French on the cultural part of trade in services, language being an important element of the Belgian federal system (Kerremans, 2006).

Other countries that favoured a much extended use of QMV included Italy, the Netherlands and Finland. In the Italian case, a pro-European ideology played a role. In the Dutch case, such an extension was promoted by the foreign ministry with some opposition from other ministries. But the expectation was that other member states would limit the extension, as indeed happened (Luitwieler and Pijpers, 2006). That Finland too was in this group indicates that Finland, contrary to the two other Nordic EU member states, had moved to a core position in European integration. But still Finland wanted to keep certain budgetary decisions and the defence sector outside QMV (Antola, 2006).

Greece's defence of unanimity for maritime transportation and structural policy fits in with liberal intergovernmentalism. On maritime transportation, Denmark was an ally of Greece, and on structural policy Spain and Portugal were allies of Greece (Tsakaloyannis and Blavoukos, 2006). That Ireland defended national rights to determine taxation levels can also be explained by Moravcsik's approach (Tonra, 2006): Ireland's low corporate tax had been an important element in the country's impressive economic growth.

Spain had a fairly long list of demands for unanimity: structural and cohesion funds, external borders (because of Gibraltar), taxation (low corporate taxes), social security, water resources (aspects of environmental policy). The United Kingdom also had an extensive list. Apart from treaty reforms and enlargements, where there was wide support for retaining unanimity, the British wanted to retain unanimity for taxation, border controls (the Schengen opt-out), social security, defence and 'own resources' (Larsen, 2006). Liberal intergovernmentalism can explain most of this, but Gibraltar and defence take us into high politics, where sovereignty issues dominate and realism has the most explanatory power.

In the case of member states having federal systems – such as Germany, Austria and Belgium – the regional governments also made some demands. It was the German *Länder* that formulated the demand for a declaration attached to the Treaty of Nice about the post-Nice agenda, including in particular the issue of the delimitation of competences (Engel, 2006). Belgium and Italy joined Germany on this.

The German *Länder* also had some influence on Germany's policy on the scope of QMV. A couple of issues falling under the *Länder's* competence were affected. Germany insisted on unanimity for cultural support programmes (Art. 151(5)), and training and conditions of access for self-employed persons (Art. 47(2)). The threat of non-ratification – given the representation of the *Länder* in the *Bundesrat* – was sufficiently credible to secure the retention of unanimity for these two articles (Engel, 2006).

The role of extreme right-wing parties in some member states was to have a special influence on the Nice negotiations. In the case of Austria, which had been exposed to sanctions from the EU-14 when Jörg Haider's party (FPÖ) entered the Austrian government, this led the Nice IGC to give high priority to getting Article 7 TEU amended to avoid a similar case in the future. On the other hand, Belgium had been a driving force in the decision to impose sanctions against Austria because the Belgian political elite feared their own extreme-right party, the *Vlaams Blok*. This issue almost became a personal crusade for Louis Michel, the Belgian foreign minister at the time (Kerremans, 2006). The issue of sanctions against Austria also became a problem in Denmark, where it was exploited by EU-sceptical parties and groups in the euro referendum in 2000, which in turn affected the Danish determination to avoid a referendum on the Treaty of Nice. What we have seen then is that specific domestic events can reverberate through the whole EU system.

Although liberal intergovernmentalism seems able to explain much about the extension of the scope of QMV, the same approach faces greater difficulties for positions on other aspects of the Nice agenda.

Although there were cracks in the groups of large and small member states, the issues of the re-weighting of votes in the Council and the composition of the Commission were very much small-versus-large-member-states issues, especially the question of the Commission's structure.

These issues were about influence and relative power. Member states did compare themselves with other states of comparable size. They all approached the issue with a sense of fairness. Relative gains and losses did matter and the leaders were concerned about the domestic reaction to a bargain. Defining the 'national interest' in these matters did not depend on demands from interest groups. Politicians did not need the help of experts. It was simply a matter of maximising future influence in an enlarged EU, and governments could easily calculate gains and losses. 'Realist' scholars can explain interests in this area without resorting to more complex theories.

Explaining the bargaining process

Concerning the bargaining process, we have to ask about influence. Was it asymmetric interdependence that formed the basis of influence? Some countries were more eager about enlargement than others. Which threats of veto or exclusion existed and were they credible? What influence did EU-level actors have?

Moravcsik mainly studied France, Germany and the UK in *The Choice for Europe* (1998). Is that sufficient? Shouldn't we at least include Spain in the case of the Treaty of Nice as well as the small member states that formed a large coalition in support of retaining a member of the Commission and avoiding too much re-weighting of votes in the Council in favour of the larger members? It seems fair to say that just studying the three big ones would be very inadequate for the Treaty of Nice. After all, treaty changes require unanimity, so in a way all member states formally have equal power, and the number of votes they get is quite salient for all of them. The reason larger states may have more power is the fact that their threat of veto is more credible. This is a realist explanation, not one based in dependence on outcomes.

Looking at the question of extended scope of QMV, the UK was an important 'minimalist' country insisting on unanimity on many issues.

The UK's power may have increased after the St. Malo bilateral summit with France in 1998, which started the development of European Security and Defence Policy (ESDP), which in turn made the UK a more important actor in the EU (Larsen, 2006). So threats of excluding Britain were less credible than they had been during the Single European Act (SEA) negotiations in 1985. And on most issues, the UK had a number of allies – so the bargain on the scope of QMV was very much a lowest common denominator agreement where the UK got most of what it demanded.

The bargaining process with respect to the Commission saw two coalitions facing each other. Neither side could use threats of exclusion, but both sides could use threats of veto. A compromise had to be found, one where both sides could claim to have won, which in reality largely postponed the decision.

The bargaining process on the re-weighting of votes was the most difficult one and it cannot be explained without an analysis of the role played by the French presidency. Rational institutionalist theory attaches importance to leadership (Beach, 2005; Beach and Mazzucelli, 2006). With France insisting on parity with Germany, Belgium could rightly expect parity with the Netherlands. The process was further complicated by the Spanish problem[1] and the French decision to treat Spain well – possibly to have an influential southern ally in the future eastward-enlarged EU, but possibly also to silence a difficult negotiation partner (Basabe, 2006). The French treatment of Spain had repercussions for the position of neighbouring Portugal. In the end, veto threats from Portugal and Belgium had to be seen as credible. The two countries were partly bought off with more seats in the European Parliament, each getting 22 seats, while two future members of comparable size, the Czech Republic and Hungary, only got 20.

So the third ingredient in Moravcsik's inter-state bargaining, linkage strategies, was used at the margin. However, the narrow agenda limited the possibility of linkages.

Explaining institutional choice

Was institutional choice then because of 'credible commitments'? Yes, to some extent, it can be argued. To the extent that the concern was to have credible institutions after the impending eastern enlargement, such an explanation can be used. And there is no doubt that many member states saw Nice as an enlargement treaty.

The expanded scope of QMV, in particular, can be explained by 'credible commitments'. But Nice was more than a question of credible commitments. It was also about legitimacy. The extended use of co-decision – albeit limited to relatively few cases on this occasion – can only be seen as a response to the 'democratic deficit'. The EP's powers were also increased by giving the EP the authority to bring actions before the ECJ concerning the legality of acts (Art. 230 TEC) and to seek an opinion from the ECJ concerning the validity of international agreements (Art. 300(6) TEC). Further, the EP could henceforth take the initiative in charging a member state with breach of fundamental rights (Art. 7(1) TEU) (Neuhold, 2006). Increased influence for the European Parliament, however, does not fit with Moravcsik's 'credible commitments'. Here we need to look at European norms concerning democratic rule and, thus, legitimacy (Rittberger, 2005; Schimmelfennig and Rittberger, 2006).

Nor is it easy to see the re-weighting of votes as a question of credible commitments. It was a question of relative power that enlargement forced on the agenda. It has a rational explanation – not a liberal but a realist version of intergovernmentalism.

The limits of liberal intergovernmentalism

Overall it can be argued that liberal intergovernmentalism still retains some explanatory power in relation to QMV when we study the case of the Treaty of Nice. But we have also seen some shortcomings. Some national preferences did have economic roots, but others were due to geopolitics and ideology. Pro-European ideology still plays a certain role in some member states, including Belgium, Italy and possibly, to a lesser extent, Germany and the Netherlands. In the bargaining process there were elements of asymmetrical interdependence and linkages were made to find compromises. But given the narrow agenda of the Nice IGC, the use of linkage strategies was somewhat limited. Threats of exclusion may not have been used in the negotiations, but neither were they necessarily very credible.

Liberal intergovernmentalism is especially limited when it comes to the study of the role of the Commission, the European Parliament and the Council Secretariat. The Commission has been involved in IGCs since the beginning. The European Parliament is not formally involved but has increased its informal involvement and had two observers take part in the preparatory group in the Nice negotiations (Neuhold, 2006). The Council Secretariat – to the extent it assists the presidency – has been able to gain some influence through drafting some of the provisions. In the case of Nice these non-state actors were somewhat handicapped because of the way the French presidency tried to control the process from

Paris. This reduced the opportunity for third-party entrepreneurship and brokerage (Beach, 2006). Nevertheless, the Commission did have some influence on the reform of the judicial system, the strengthened internal role of the President of the Commission, Article 133 TEC on commercial policy, Article 7 TEU on the early warning system in cases of breach of democratic principles by a member state, and the new provision on European political parties. The Council Secretariat also contributed to the compromise on the services part of commercial policy, which was required by France, and the declaration on the future venue of European Council meetings – a bargaining chip to Belgium in the endgame in Nice.

Liberal intergovernmentalism fares especially poorly when we study the parallel process of ESDP. ESDP can first of all be explained by geopolitics. It was very much a response to the unfolding of events in ex-Yugoslavia, including disagreements with the US on how to handle the crisis in Kosovo in 1998–9 (Rynning, 2006).

Nor can the other, parallel process, the Charter of Fundamental Rights, be explained by credible commitments. The concern for fundamental rights must be seen as a question of legitimacy, as the process of European integration was becoming more political after the end of the Cold War (Pineda Polo and den Boer, 2006).

There is a further criticism: liberal intergovernmentalism sees preference formation and inter-state bargaining as sequential processes. In reality, member states do not always have clearly defined preferences when they go into inter-state negotiations. This also implies a certain amount of uncertainty during the negotiations, which makes it impossible to define the bargaining space. Especially when new issues are placed on the agenda, like 'closer cooperation' in the Amsterdam talks, negotiations can become a long learning process, where preferences are formed during the process (Stubb, 2002). Also, during the Nice IGC we saw that preferences with respect to 'enhanced cooperation' changed during the negotiation process (Olsen, 2006).

The limits of liberal intergovernmentalism can thus be found at both the level of national preference formation and at the level of inter-state bargaining. At both levels there is a need to include institutions, such as political parties and parliaments, at the national level and the community institutions at the level of bargaining. Sometimes individuals and ideas must also be brought into the picture – such as national diplomats, like the Italian ones who have been involved in a number of IGCs and who have traditionally been fairly pro-European (Bindi, 2006). Even ministers and other representatives of the member states taking part in European negotiations may go through a socialisation process. However, the nature of the issues, especially a re-weighting of votes in the Council, and the way the French presidency handled the endgame in Nice, made the Nice IGC a hard zero-sum bargaining game where 'national interests' triumphed.

Assessments

Nice was supposed to solve the perceived institutional issues before the big eastern enlargement. To the extent that ten new members were able to join in 2004, it could be seen as a partial success at least. But in reality, many of those negotiating the Treaty of Nice were not happy with the outcome.

Afterwards, Peter Norman in the *Financial Times* called Nice 'a horse-trading marathon'. It was, he said, 'a power play in which the five big members were determined to secure more clout' (Norman, 2000). Suzanne Daley in *The New York Times* commented: 'the leaders of the 15 countries which gathered in this Riviera city seemed unable to lift their heads above their own national political agendas' (Daley, 2000).

Many of the leaders were disappointed. They left Nice feeling that next time it had to be done in a different way. British Prime Minister Tony Blair said, 'as far as Europe is concerned, we can't do business like this in the future. How we take these decisions has to be part of the agenda for the future' (quoted from Rafferty, 2000).

Many observers criticised the French presidency for the confusion at the end of the negotiations in Nice. Peter Ludlow said:

> Prime responsibility for the disorderly proceedings, however, undoubtedly lay with Chirac. His misjudgements included: fixation with formal parity between Germany and the other three large states; the decision to give the Spaniards everything they wanted before the negotiations started, thereby destroying any rational basis for the reallocation of votes and skewing the arithmetic at every subsequent point in the proceedings; a serious underestimation of the determination of the small states to safeguard their position; and above all the apparent desire to be all things to all men.
>
> (Ludlow, 2001)

Maybe one of the wisest remarks came from Luxembourg's Prime Minister, Jean-Claude Juncker, who said: 'I think we are going to scale down our ambitions and then, in the great European tradition, call it a success' (quoted from Hughes, 2000).

The dissatisfaction with the way the Nice Treaty negotiations were handled was a major factor in the subsequent decision to have the next reform prepared through a Convention. The next chapters will explore that approach further.

Notes

This chapter relies partly on some of the author's contributions to Laursen, 2006b.

1. The Spanish problem refers to the fact that Spain had a choice between two commissioners and eight votes in the Council or one commissioner and ten votes in the Council when the country joined in 1986. Spain chose the first solution. When it was decided to limit the number of commissioners to one per member state, Spain claimed compensation in the Council.

10
The Constitutional Treaty: The Failed Formal Constitutionalisation

Derek Beach

Historical context

The negotiation and ratification of the Constitutional Treaty is the longest period of treaty reform that the EU has to date experienced, stretching from the initial discussions in the final days of the 2000 IGC until the decision in 2007 to salvage parts of Constitutional Treaty in a revamped form; the Treaty of Lisbon.

As with the two previous rounds of treaty reform, the agenda of the Constitutional Treaty was set by the need for preparing the institutions of the EU for an enlargement with up to ten new member states. The sensitive institutional triangle questions had not been solved in either the 1996–7 or 2000 IGCs, involving: (1) reweighting of votes in the Council of Ministers, (2) revising the number of Commissioner's and MEPs, and (3) extending the use of majority voting in the Council.

What was unexpected was the addition to the agenda of the question of the 'future of Europe'. This magniloquently named debate was sparked by a speech by German Foreign Minister Joschka Fischer on 12 May 2000, halfway through the 2000 IGC. Speaking in a personal capacity at Humboldt University in Berlin, Fischer shared his thoughts on how to move the integration process forward (Fischer 2000). He argued that it would be increasingly difficult for a Union of 30 members to work, but that further movement forward was not possible within the existing framework. Fischer therefore called for the drafting of a constitution that would involve a more fundamental reform of the Union's institutional set-up, including 'full parliamentarisation' through the creation of two European parliaments. The first chamber would include MEPs who would also have national seats. The second chamber would be a European senate, with directly elected senators from each member state. Echoing demands from the German *Länder*, Fischer saw the need for a clearer-cut division of competences, and envisioned the creation of a 'lean European Federation' – stronger in the areas of exclusive competence and acting in ways that are understandable to citizens, but also with a strong role for nation states. Fischer's remarks were subsequently commented on by many heads of state and government, including French President Chirac and UK Prime Minister Blair. For example, and not surprisingly, Blair's vision was very nation state oriented, and merely called for the strengthening of the European Council, and upgrading foreign and JHA policies (Blair 2000). Blair did not want a constitution, but merely a 'statement of principles'.

As the 2000 IGC ground to a close, several unsatisfied governments pressed for another round of treaty reform. Under pressure from the German *Länder*, German Prime Minister Schroeder called for a future IGC to look at the question of the division of competences between the Union and the national and regional levels (Ludlow 2002: 51; Galloway 2001: 169–74). Second, several governments wanted to adopt the Charter on Fundamental Rights that had been drafted by a Convention parallel with the IGC 2000 as a legally binding document, but were blocked by a British/Danish veto (Galloway 2001: 174). Finally, two issues were on the agenda in an attempt to democratically legitimise the Union: the questions of the simplification of the treaties to allow citizens to actually understand the treaties; and an increased role for national parliaments in European decision-making.

These demands led to the adoption of declaration 23 on the future of the Union attached to the Treaty of Nice. The declaration addressed the four questions of the division of competences, the legal status of the Charter, the simplification of the treaties, and the role of national parliaments. An IGC was scheduled to be convened in 2004, prior to which the Swedish and Belgian Presidencies were to encourage 'wide-ranging discussions' in cooperation with the Commission and EP. The Belgian Presidency was entrusted with negotiating a declaration in December 2001 for the continuation of the process. The debate resulted in the adoption of the Laeken Declaration at the Laeken European Council in December 2001 (European Council 2001; Ludlow 2002: 53–74). Beyond fleshing out the four points of the Nice declaration, the debate centred on finding a new method for preparing the coming IGC. After the failings of the traditional IGC-method[1] became all too apparent in Nice, a core of key actors said 'never again' (Ludlow 2002: 52; Closa 2004). At the same time, the parallel Convention on the Charter on Fundamental Rights was widely perceived to have been relatively successful. Pushed by federalist-oriented governments and the Commission and the EP, the Laeken European Council in December 2001 decided that a European Convention would be used to prepare the agenda of the next IGC (Ludlow 2002: 57, 59; Interview 1; Jonsson and Hegeland 2003; Norman 2003: 24–5). The Convention was to be composed of representatives of each national government and two from the European Commission, 16 MEPs, and two national parliamentarians from each member state, along with governmental representatives and national parliamentarians from the accession states.[2] Representatives of each of the groupings were to form the Praesidium, which was envisioned to play a steering role similar to the EU Presidency in IGC negotiations. The Convention Secretariat was to be provided by seconded officials from the secretariats of the Commission, Council and EP.

The mandate for the Convention was relatively modest, namely, 'to consider the key issues arising for the Union's future development and try to identify the various possible responses' (European Council 2001: 24). However, once the Convention started this modest goal was replaced by the much more ambitious goal of replacing the existing EU Treaties with a single, more effective and simplified Constitutional Treaty (Closa 2004; Norman 2003). It was hoped by many of the members of the Convention, the so-called conventionnels, that this new Constitution would then be accepted as is by national governments in the following IGC. The course of the negotiations and explanations of the outcome will be discussed in section 3.

Treaty content

The major innovations of the Constitutional Treaty are listed in Table 10.1. On the institutional side (vertical integration), several major reforms were adopted, including the reduction of the size of the Commission, the revision of the voting weights in the Council of Ministers, and the creation of an EU Foreign Minister that merges the existing High Representative and the Commissioner for External Affairs. There were also changes in the policies of the EU (sectoral integration). First, the content of the existing EU treaties was cut and pasted into a more logical, single 'pillar' Constitutional Treaty composed of four parts. The scope of policies that the EU deals with was not significantly expanded, but there was an increase in the use of QMV and co-decision. Other innovations included the consolidation of the constitutional nature of the EU treaties with many symbolic provisions such as the title of the document, the inclusion of a 'bill of rights', and the codification of EU legal principles such as supremacy.

Table 10.1 A treaty establishing a constitution for Europe

Issue-area	Outcome
Vertical integration (institutional change)	• Commission size to be reduced to two-third of the number of member states in 2014; • European Council established as separate institution, chaired by a permanent President appointed to two-and-a-half year terms; • six-month rotation of Presidency preserved within a form of team Presidency held by three governments; • Council voting procedure changed to a simple double majority with a majority being 55 per cent of the states representing 65 per cent of the Union's population, although it must also represent at least 15 member states. Blocking minority must consist of at least four states; • creation of Union Foreign Minister, merging the tasks of the High Representative and the Commissioner for External Affairs. The minister is assisted by a new European External Action Service;
Sectoral integration (functional scope of EU)	• Constitutional Treaty replaces existing EU Treaties with a single Union, where the pillar structure is merged into a single pillar with special provisions for sensitive sections on foreign, security and defence, along with certain aspects of the area of freedom, security and justice; • Constitutional Treaty includes four parts: I – Institutions, II – Charter of Fundamental Rights, III – The Policies and functioning of the Union, IV – General and Final Provisions; • clarification of Union competences, and simplified set of legal instruments; • QMV made general rule, with exceptions in several issues, including taxation and foreign policy; • co-decision extended to most Union law-making, and the EP is given increased powers in the budgetary procedure, including for agricultural spending; • Charter of Fundamental Rights incorporated as a legally binding text; • adoption of a general *passerelle* clause, allowing for a unanimous decision by the European Council to transfer a policy area in Part III to QMV; • increased transparency of Union law-making; • increased role of national parliaments in law-making, for example by allowing 1/3rd to raise objections to the breach of the subsidiarity principle by a Commission proposal; • the Union is given a single legal personality; • allows the Council to create by unanimity a European Public Prosecutor to combat crimes affecting the financial interests of the Union; • increased the possibility of 'permanent structured co-operation' in field of defence, enabling group of states to co-operate more closely.

Source: OJ, 16 December 2004, C Series, No. 310.

Dynamics of the negotiations

This section first develops three competing theoretical explanations of the dynamics of the negotiation process and why the outcome looked the way it did. Theories are here used in a pragmatic and heuristic fashion, used as analytical tools to understand the single case (Jackson 2011; Humphreys 2010). Each theory is used to create an analytical 'story' of the negotiations, which is then evaluated to see whether it can account for the major dynamics of the case.

Liberal intergovernmentalism

The basic argument of Liberal Intergovernmentalism (LI) is that governments which are representing society-based preferences that reflect patterns of asymmetric interdependence dominate treaty reform negotiations. Power in treaty reforms is a function of how dependent a given government is upon securing a cooperative outcome. In economic issues preferences reflect economic interdependence (those that stand to gain from liberalisation favour opening of markets and vice versa), whereas in political issues governments that are only able to achieve their preferred policy goals through cooperation are more dependent (and therefore less powerful) than those with attractive unilateral options.

When a government has attractive alternatives to a negotiated settlement, they have few incentives to compromise. Given that constitutional reforms in IGCs are enacted by unanimity this results in a final outcome that reflects the preferences of the actor least dependent upon an agreement. The only exception to this lowest common denominator scenario is the situation where other governments are strongly interested in a deal and possess a credible threat of excluding the laggard government from the EU. When governments possess a credible 'nuclear option' the outcome will transcend the lowest common denominator.

Unfortunately, as LI was developed during the late 1980s and early 1990s, it is only able to explain governmental power in the types of issues that dominated EU debates up until that point. Power is based upon actor dependence upon an agreement, but in institutional balance-of-power issues all actors are equally dependent upon maximising their relative weight in EU decision-making. LI therefore offers no predictions regarding actor power in institutional balance-of-power issues such as how many votes each country should have in the Council of Ministers; issues that have been central since the mid-1990s. Here I suggest that LI can be supplemented with predictions from realist theory in a manner that is conceptually valid. In realism actor power is based upon variations in the material capabilities of actors (Waltz 1979; Walt 1985, 1988; Zakaria 1998). In these issues realism can be utilised to supplement LI in a manner that is conceptually faithful to the intergovernmental nature of LI theory. Material capabilities should here be defined in economic terms, and in particular the importance of a country's economy for well-functioning EU markets.

We should therefore expect following LI to see that the negotiating process is dominated by EU governments, and that the laggard actor will be the pivotal actor in the discussions. Outcomes should reflect the preferences of the least dependent actor in substantive issues, whereas drawing upon realist theory, we should expect that in institutional balance-of-power issues outcomes will reflect the materially strongest actor.

Rational Institutionalism (RI)

The basic insight of RI is that institutions are tools used by actors to overcome collective action problems (Hall and Taylor 1996; Tallberg 2006). However, while they increase the efficiency of negotiated settlements, they also have consequences for the outcomes that result (Tallberg 2006; Beach 2009). RI accounts of politics indicate that when faced with the same pressures or demands, two different institutional arrangements will therefore produce different results, other things equal.

In the following the impact of specific actors possessing privileged institutional positions will be evaluated, drawing upon two variants of RI: principal-agent theorisation and leadership theories. In these theories the reason why a given actor is delegated a privileged position is in order to provide leadership in situations where collective action problems hinder cooperation such as agenda failure or lack of effective brokerage (Tallberg 2006; Beach 2009). For instance, giving the chairmanship of a negotiation to a single actor is a rational and efficient solution to the problems of agenda failure that are endemic in complex, multiparty negotiations (Tallberg 2006: 21–2). The leader can then act as a centripetal force, utilising agenda-management techniques such as deciding what issues are to be debated and proposing a focal point around which negotiations coalesce. Yet principal-agent leadership models also theorise that the gains of delegating leadership functions come at a price, as a leader can exploit his or her delegated powers for private gain.

Critical for this chapter are the expectations of RI theory for the size of these 'costs of delegation'. The size of delegation costs vary according to the strength of the procedural powers delegated to the leader and the ability of governments to detect slippage that varies according to the level of technicality of the issue.

Leadership alone is naturally not *sufficient* for a negotiation to reach a mutually acceptable, Pareto-efficient outcome: there must be some form of political demand for agreement among the parties. Yet, as I develop in the following, the provision of leadership is a *necessary* condition for efficient outcomes when institutional bargaining is affected by high transaction costs, impacting upon how between governmental preferences and power are translated into outcomes.

Following logically from RI theory, we should expect that the change from the IGC method to what has been termed the 'convention method' has privileged certain actors and put others at a disadvantage. Whereas the IGC relies on negotiations behind closed doors and requires the capacity to formulate and broker compromises as a result of the unanimity requirement, the new method generated a demand for leadership in order to:

(i) successfully manage the very complicated agenda due to the assembly-like setting of the Convention,
(ii) build and sustain large coalitions due to the requirement for a 'broad consensus' between the *composantes* of the Convention.

Therefore, we should expect that the final outcome of the Convention not only reflects patterns of governmental preferences (the LI baseline), but that who provided leadership also mattered. In particular, I will examine the ability of the EP to provide leadership in the Convention.

Social constructivism

Social constructivist theories shift our attention away from purely instrumental actors, and instead suggest that social interaction and norm-based logics of behaviour also matter. While there are many different social constructivisms out there, the following will focus upon the importance of what Schimmelfennig has termed 'rhetorical action', where actors appeal to shared standards of legitimacy within open, deliberative settings in order to 'shame' opponents, delegitimising their goals and behaviours (Schimmelfennig 2001).[3] For example, it is difficult for a government to be *publically* opposed to arguments for 'democratic openness' and representation within the EU.

The idea of 'rhetorical action' was developed to explain state behaviour in the enlargement of the EU and NATO, but the theory can potentially provide analytical leverage in explaining EU constitutional negotiations, as it takes as its starting point what can be termed 'weakly socialised' actors. In line with LI, Schimmelfennig argues that governments follow their egoistic, material interests. At the same time, EU governments do hold certain shared values, or what can be termed a standard of legitimacy, based upon norms of democratic participation and representation and the public good (Schimmelfennig 2001: 62–3).

In negotiations, actors that are able to use the standard to justify their own goals while delegitimising the goals of others are able to 'shame' actors into accepting outcomes they otherwise would not have agreed upon (ibid.). Through shaming in public, actors can make the promotion by a government of naked, egoistic self-interest in ways that conflicts with the standard of legitimacy into an 'an embarrassing contradiction for most' (Elster 1998: 12; Schimmelfennig 2001: 63–4).

We should expect that the more open, deliberative setting of the CT negotiations would give bargaining advantages to actors who could appeal to shared standards of legitimacy such as 'democratic representation' and 'openness', and that could offer explicit value-based answers to the question of 'what kind of Europe do we want'. In the glaring light of public deliberations, national interest based arguments were simply more difficult to defend by governments, resulting in a more value-laden debate and a symbolic 'constitutional' outcome than would have resulted from a traditional EU diplomacy-based IGC.

The course of the negotiations – The European Convention

There were no formal voting procedures in the Convention. The rules of procedure stated that the final product of the Convention shall be adopted by consensus (CONV 9/02), but despite there being no votes held in the Convention plenary, there was a minority text produced (CONF 773/03). However, a sizable majority of members indicated that they supported the final draft on the final day of the Convention plenary. Within the steering Praesidium, decisions on questions such as tabling draft texts were based upon consensus, although serious disagreements within the Praesidium did erupt during the endgame, and some members were opposed to the some of the final texts distributed by the Praesidium (see below).

The work of the Convention was divided into three phases: a listening phase that stretched from the start to the summer of 2002; a study phase during which working groups deliberated in the fall of 2002; and a final deliberation phase, which lasted from early January 2003 to the final sessions in June 2003. Debates in the Convention revealed two overall cleavages. One was the supranationalist/intergovernmentalist cleavage, and the other was the large/smaller member state cleavage on institutional issues that had developed during the 1990s.

The Praesidium tabled a skeleton text of the draft Constitutional Treaty in October 2002 (CONV 369/03). The text was drafted within the Convention Secretariat under the guidance of Chairman Giscard d'Estaing. The draft outlined a three-part treaty; an institutional part, a section outlining Union policies, and a final section of general and final provisions. The draft included proposed brief texts for some of the first 46 articles in the institutional section. The articles set out the definition and objectives of a Union, including proposed names for the Union ranging from United States of Europe to the European Community. Innovations included stating that the Union would administer common competences 'on a federal basis' (draft Article 1); the Union had a single legal personality (draft Article 4); the conferral principle that competences not conferred on the Union rest with member states (draft Article 8); the pillar structure would be removed (draft Article 14), and legislative debates in the Council would be public (draft Article 36). Several of Giscard's own personal priorities were controversially included in the draft, including a Congress of Peoples of Europe (draft Article 19).

The plenary welcomed the skeleton text, with key EP representatives especially excited (CONV 378/02 and verbatim summary). But the cleavage on the balance of power between the supranational community and governments was very apparent in the debates on the draft.

The reports from working groups were presented to the plenary and debated in the fall and winter of 2002–3. The reports were not intended to be final conclusions, but merely a basis for discussions and a source of inspiration for the Convention Secretariat when producing draft texts.

The final deliberation phase was kick-started by a key Franco-German proposal on institutions in January 2003 (CONV 489/03). The proposal attempted to bridge the gap between the German position of strengthening the Union through stronger supranational institutions, and the French goal of a strengthened government-based Union. The text spoke of creating a long-term Union President heading a stronger European Council, the creation of a foreign minister sitting in both the Council and Commission, majority voting in most foreign policy matters, a Commission President elected by the EP, and the extension of the legislative co-decision procedure.

The proposal met with strong negative reactions from many conventionnels (*Agence Europe*, 16 January 2003: 5–6, 17 January 2003: 4, 18 January 2003: 4, 21 January 2003: 4; *Economist* 18 January 2003: 27–8).

MEPs were especially vehement in their comments, seeing for example the creation of a permanent President of the European Council as a strongly intergovernmentalist element that would in the words of Elmar Brok 'be the beginning of the end of Community Europe' (*Agence Europe* 16 January 2003: 5). Yet the Franco-German proposal set the parameters for further debates on institutional questions (Norman 2003: 180). The proposal was then echoed in a more intergovernmentalist British-Spanish paper in February (CONV 591/03).

By early 2003 there was broad support in the Convention for an extension of co-decision and QMV, and maintaining the general institutional balance between EU institutions and member states (Norman 2003: 181). Another development in early 2003 was the decision to create a team of legal experts drawn from the secretariats of the Commission, Council and EP to make so-called technical adjustments to the policy section of the draft Constitutional Treaty – what would become Part III (CONV 529/03). While the overall structure of the EU Treaties and the institutions would be dramatically overhauled, the actual policy sections of the existing treaties would be merely re-ordered and transposed into the Constitutional Treaty's Part III without significant revisions.

The drafting of articles for Part I and the general and final provisions of Part IV took place in two stages. First, draft texts that fleshed out the components of the October skeleton draft were tabled from February to April. After debates in the plenary and a flood of proposed amendments from conventionnels, the Convention Secretariat and chairmen drafted a third generation of texts that incorporated changes backed by strong majorities in Convention.

Most of the elements of the draft Constitutional Treaty had been agreed by April. Consensus had been reached on issues such as: clarifying and categorising Union competences; incorporating the Charter as a legally binding document; simplifying and consolidating the Union's legal instruments; giving national parliaments a stronger role; granting the Union a single legal personality; and replacing the pillar structure with a single treaty structure with special exceptions for sensitive areas of the former second and third pillars. But the sensitive debates on institutional questions and foreign policy loomed on the horizon.

Giscard had postponed the institutional debate until April to grant governments the opportunity to debate institutional questions prior to his tabling of draft texts in the Praesidium. Giscard had planned to do this at the March European Council Summit, but the start of the Iraq war dominated the Summit, forcing the debate to be postponed to the Athens Summit on 16 April 2003 (Interview 2). On the institutional question, key questions were: how leadership would be provided in the European Council and Council; what the size of the Commission and the method for appointing the Commission President should be; what powers were to be given to the foreign minister, and the degree to which he/she would operate within the Commission; and other questions such as whether a Congress of People's should be created.

Giscard's draft institutional articles were given to the Praesidium for approval on 22 April 2003 (the texts are reproduced in Norman 2003: 343–8). The text was close to the Franco-German and British-Spanish proposals. Giscard called for the creation of a strong President of European Council that would 'prepare, chair and drive', and would be supported by a powerful cabinet (draft Article 15a). The Vice-President would chair the Council, replacing the rotating Presidency (draft Article 17a). The draft also called for the creation of a Legislative Council,[4] and the creation of a foreign minister that had a seat both in the Council and Commission, but was closest to the Council (draft Articles 17a, 19). The draft called for the creation of a system of simple dual majority based upon 50 per cent of member states representing 60 per cent of the Union's population (draft Article 17b). The idea of a Congress of Peoples popped up again, although by titling it 'Article X to be inserted into the title on the Union's democratic life', it looked like the article was a negotiating ploy that could be jettisoned when opportune. Finally, on the size of the Commission, Giscard's draft echoed earlier French proposals for a small Commission, but it also gave the EP the ability to approve by a 3/5th majority a candidate for Commission President that had been chosen by the European Council (Article 18a).

The strong negative reaction within the Praesidium towards Giscard's draft will be discussed in more detail below. Suffice it the say here that the MEP and Commission representatives in the Praesidium succeeded in removing the most intergovernmental elements from the draft texts approved by the Praesidium and put to the plenary on 23 April 2003 (CONV 691/03), including weakening the European Council President, and re-introducing the rotating Presidency of the Council. The Spanish governmental representative in the Praesidium complained about the changes to the Nice compromise on voting weights, but only succeeded in getting the objection mentioned in the introductory text of the proposal (Norman 2003: 230; CONV 691:03, p. 1). Not surprisingly, the Congress of People's was shot down, once again.

The draft institutional text generated a plethora of proposed amendments from conventionnels, many of which argued for the preservation of the status quo on points such as the rotating Presidency and size of the Commission (see CONV 709/03). But most also agreed that the text was 'negotiable', although the smaller governments were uneasy about certain elements (Norman 2003: 240–1).

After a three day Praesidium meeting held on 21 to 24 May 2003, the third generation of Praesidium draft texts were tabled in late May in the form of revised Parts I to IV (CONV 724 to 727/03). Significantly, the section on the institutions in Part I was unchanged from the April draft due to splits within the Praesidium on whether to keep the Nice compromise or not (Norman 2003: 248). Important changes to Part I included: the removal of the 'F-word' from the first article; opening for the possibility for creating European taxes or other new forms of revenue (draft Article I-53); and giving the multi-annual financial framework a treaty base (draft Article I-54). The Charter of Fundamental Rights was to be attached to the Constitutional Treaty as Part II, although the UK was still concerned about the impact of the Charter on its legal system.

Both Poland and Spain made their concerns regarding the revision of the Nice compromise known in Convention. In early 2003, then Spanish representative Palacio tabled an amendment to the provisions on qualified majority voting that called for keeping the Nice formula, which was echoed by other conventionnels, including the UK government representative (CONV 709/03). After Palacio was replaced by Dastis in March as the representative of the Spanish government, he clearly stated in both the 15 May plenary and the 21–24 May Praesidium meeting that Spain could not accept a revision of the Nice compromise, and that any revision would lead to a 'long and difficult Intergovernmental Conference' (Norman 2003: 262; Interview 3). Dastis succeeded in mobilising the support of nine governments for a proposal against tampering with the Nice compromise (CONV 766/03).

But Giscard, backed by a strong majority in the plenary, pushed for revising Nice. Giscard stated that 'If we stick with Nice, the constitutional part of the Convention is pointless' (in Norman 2003: 271). In the revised institutional draft of 31 May 2003, the simple double majority proposal was kept despite Polish and Spanish protests (CONV 770/03).

As the Convention went into its final weeks in June 2003, the two key questions were whether the Nice compromise on institutions would be kept, and whether the UK would stay on board. First, a broad majority in the plenary, led by the triumvirate chairmen pushed for the revision of Nice that made its way into the final draft Constitutional Treaty (Interview 2; Norman 2003: 290–3; Brown 2003). Second, the UK started clearly signalling that it had 'red-lines' on issues such as the 'F-word', along with the introduction of majority voting on foreign, tax and social policy (Menon 2003; *Guardian* 28 May 2003; *Le Monde* 30 May 2003:4; Norman 2003: 269–71). While the final draft Constitutional Treaty did open for majority voting, the word 'federal' was kept out.

In the final days of the Convention, national and European parliamentarians organised along party lines attempted to push the draft towards a slightly more pro-integrative outcome, including proposals for making treaty revision easier and making QMV the general rule in *all* policy areas (*EU Observer* 12 June 2003; Halligan 2003; Norman 2003: 290–3). The final texts did not make QMV the general rule nor was treaty revision made easier. But to please the pro-integrative majority in the Convention, Giscard introduced a *passerelle* (general bridging clause), whereby the Council could agree by unanimity to transfer a policy area to qualified majority voting (CONV 797/03, 802/03, 811/03). The final draft landed between the large government position by creating a permanent President of the European Council, and the smaller government position by keeping a form of rotating Presidency for the Council and introducing an equal rotation within a downsized Commission.

After governmental representatives from Poland, Spain and the UK laid down their swords in the Convention's final days, choosing instead to fight for their red-lines in the coming IGC, the Convention accepted the final draft Constitutional Treaty (Interviews 4, 5, 6; *Financial Times* 16 June 2003; *Agence Europe* 14 June 2003: 3–6; *Le Monde* 15–16 June 2003: 2; *Guardian* 19 June 2003). The final text was then approved by the Thessaloniki European Council Summit as a 'good starting point' for the IGC (European Council 2003: 2; *Agence Europe* 21 June 2003: 3–4). Yet in reality, with the exception of the handful of sensitive Nice-related issues and the British 'red-line' issues, the IGC would in effect merely accept a tidied-up version of the Convention's text (Interviews 3, 6, 7).

The course of the negotiations – the 2003–4 IGC

The IGC 2003–4 was convened by the Italian Presidency on 4 October 2003. The IGC was conducted among governmental representatives from the then 15 member states and 10 acceding states, along with observers from the three candidate states (Bulgaria, Romania and Turkey), two observers from the European Parliament, and the European Commission as a non-voting participant.

The Italian Presidency planned for the IGC to be concluded in December 2003 at the Brussels European Council Summit meeting, and then after translation to all Union languages and a judicial cleaning-up, the Constitutional Treaty was planned to be signed in a pompous ceremony in Rome in May 2004.

In contrast with previous IGCs, most of the negotiations in the IGC 2003–4 were held at the political levels of Foreign Ministers or heads of state and government. The Italian Presidency, backed by a German-led coalition of the six founding member states, used the draft Constitutional Treaty as the basic text for the IGC, and only tolerated serious negotiations on issues where governments were prepared to veto the whole treaty (Interviews 3, 6, 7, 8; *Le Monde* 04 October 2003: 6; *Agence Europe* 9 September 2003: 5, 03 October 2003: 6–10, 7 October 2003: 5–7). In order to legally clean-up the draft Constitutional Treaty, the Italian Presidency created a working group of legal experts chaired by the head of the Council Secretariat's Legal Services, Jean-Claude Piris. A 'Focal Points' group of senior officials was later created to prepare the ministerial meetings in the IGC.

Debates in the IGC only took place on a handful of contentious issues, primarily related to the size of the Commission and the re-weighting of Council votes. Smaller governments were strongly interested in keeping 'their' Commissioner and the rotating Presidency (*Agence Europe* 9 September 2003: 5; *FT* 03 October 2003: 3; *EU Observer* 24 September 2003), while Poland and Spain wanted to go back to the Nice compromise on Council voting weights, which disproportionally favored them (European Parliament IGC Monitoring Group; *Agence Europe* 1 October 2003: 5, 3 October 2005: 6–10; *Le Monde* 4 October 2003: 6). The UK was concerned about the extension of majority voting in several sensitive issues, including taxation and foreign policy, and the incorporation of the Charter into the Constitutional Treaty (*Le Monde* 11 September 2003: 7; *Agence Europe* 3 October 2005: 6–10).

Most issues on the IGC agenda were minor second-order issues dealing with tidying-up the draft Constitutional Treaty text, for example, by fleshing out the incomplete text from the Convention on matters such as the powers and position of the Foreign Minister, and the formations and form of Presidency for the Council (Interview 9). The negotiation of these issues was not contentious, and took place in a problem-solving environment. Another cluster of minor issues dealt with removing unwanted EP fingerprints from the text. This was especially evident as regards the budgetary powers of the EP, where ECOFIN ministers attempted to reduce EP powers in October and November.

During the first two months of the IGC, the Italian Foreign Ministry together with the Council Secretariat guided the negotiations effectively on the minor points (Interview 6, 9). The idea of creating a Legislative Council was the first element of the Convention's text that was removed in the IGC (CIG 1/03; Interviews 3, 8). Paralleling the political meetings, the Piris group undertook the legal 'tidying up', but the group did not deal with political questions (Interview 8). The group concluded its work in November with the production of a revised Constitutional Treaty, where minor inconsistencies and repetitions were removed (CIG 51/03).

In what was planned to be the IGC endgame, the Italian Presidency tabled a compromise proposal on most of the minor issues prior to an informal Foreign Minister conclave meeting to be held on 28–29 November 2003 (CIG 52/1/03 REV 1). The Naples conclave tied up agreement in most of the minor issues (Ludlow 2004; *EU Observer* 29 October 2003), which were then set down as draft treaty text by the Presidency (CIG 60/03 ADD 1). But the handful of contentious institutional issues was bypassed, with the strategy of the Italian Presidency being to put governments under the gun in the final European Council Summit on 12–13 December 2003.

There were no real negotiations during the Italian Presidency on the contentious issues (Interview 9; *Agence Europe* 17 October 2003: 4–6). Luxembourg Prime Minister Juncker clearly saw the danger with the Italian strategy when he stated that, 'What particularly worries me is that meeting after meeting, the different positions become even more rigid because of the repetition' (*Agence Europe* 17 October 2003: 5). Positions hardened in the week prior to the Summit, with France and Germany warning that they wanted to keep the Convention text, and that they would go forward with ad hoc co-operation if the text was not approved by the IGC, whereas both Spain and Poland had backed themselves into a corner and were unable to step down on their insistence that the Nice compromise on vote re-weighting should be preserved (*Süddeutsche Zeitung* 9 December 2003; *EU Observer* 13 December 2003; *The Observer* 14 December 2003: 16–17; *FT* 10 December 2003).

Italian Prime Minister Berlusconi took over the reigns of the Presidency in the final two weeks, utilising Rome-based officials who had not followed the IGC, and he decided to *not* utilise the Council Secretariat as a source of advice and assistance (Interview 8). Berlusconi did not produce different compromise options for leaders prior to the Summit, and instead chose to keep a 'secret solution in his pocket' (Ludlow 2004). The Presidency paper only listed a summary of positions on the contentious issues prior to Brussels (CIG 60/03 ADD 2).

As the heads of state and government arrived in Brussels, the Italian Presidency had no game plan (Ludlow 2004). In confessionals held by the Presidency in the afternoon with delegations, the Italian Presidency did not even have a schedule for meetings, forcing delegates to hang around for hours waiting (Interview 10). A scheduled 6 p.m. plenary meeting started at 6.30 p.m. and lasted only 45 minutes, in which Berlusconi offered no compromise solutions or suggestions to move forward (Ludlow 2004). After another wave of confessionals that lasted until 1.30 a.m., it became increasingly clear that neither side would compromise on the question of the re-weighting of votes (ibid.). After Berlusconi did not even show up to lead further meetings on Saturday morning, the Italian Foreign Minister took over the confessionals (ibid.). At 11 a.m. Italy convened a small ad hoc group of 'friends of the Presidency' numbering Denmark, Greece, Hungary, the Netherlands and the UK. The group was asked to find a compromise (Interview 10). Compromises that were floated included retaining the Nice formula while giving Germany two extra Council votes, deferring a change until 2014, and raising the blocking thresholds (*Independent* 15 December 2003: 10). Parallel with this, French President Chirac and German Chancellor Schröder began holding bilateral meetings, where France met with Spain, and Germany with the Polish. After the two leaders saw that there was no way forward they met with Blair, and the three then asked Berlusconi to close the Summit in a dignified way instead of letting it degenerate into a Nice-like brawl (Ludlow 2004; *Independent* 15 December 2003: 10; Interview 7).

The collapse of the IGC talks in the Brussels European Council Summit of 12–13 December 2003 clearly illustrated the importance of leadership, or more correctly the lack of it in an EU of 25. There are conflicting accounts of reasons for breakdown, with many pointing to Berlusconi as the culprit. But behind his tragicomic handling of the negotiations were fundamental disagreements on the key institutional questions that had not been reconciled prior to the Summit (Interviews 3, 9; *Economist* 20 December 2003: 71–3).

After the Christmas break, the Irish Presidency took up the baton and started quiet consultations with other governments to see whether the pieces could be picked up after the Italian job (Irish Presidency 2004; *EU Observer* 19 January 2004, 21 January 2004; Interview 9). The Irish Presidency worked closely with the Council Secretariat (Interview 8, 9).

After a series of meetings with governments, and especially after the newly elected Spanish government and the Polish government sent signals that they could agree a compromise in February and early March (*EU Observer* 17 March 2004, 19 March 2004), the Irish Presidency suggested to the March 2004 European Council Summit that the IGC should be re-launched, with the Irish assessment of the state-of-play being that agreement was possible by June (Interview 9; *Irish Times* 25 March 2004, 26 March 2004; see CIG 70/04).

The Irish Presidency produced a series of papers for ministerial meetings in May and June that further cleared up several minor issues (CIG 79/04, 80/04, 81/04), including opening for the possibility of future further reforms of the Council Presidency (draft Article I-23, CIG 79/04), weakening the powers of the European Public Prosecutor and strengthening the veto option in CFSP due to British concerns (draft Article III-175, III-201(2), CIG 80/04), and narrowed the scope of possible QMV in taxation (draft Article III-62(2)), social security (III-21), and in the common commercial policy (draft Article 217(7), CIG 80/04).

On the main sensitive institutional issues, the Irish Presidency in April and May continued with its quiet consultations, attempting to find possible compromises (Interview 9). The Irish Presidency did not allow the negotiations to degenerate into a repetition of positions, but sought to narrow the parameters for compromise by testing different draft compromise texts with key delegations (ibid.).

The EU leaders arriving in Brussels for the final Summit in June 2004 were more determined to reach agreement after the poor results in the EP elections held on 10–13 June 2004, which saw both low turnout and success for Eurosceptics in many countries (*FT* 15 June 2004: 1). In the final tinkering on the issue of re-weighting of votes, additional thresholds were introduced along with numerous qualifications to the simple double majority principle. For example, to prevent Germany together with two other large states from forming a blocking minority, the final article states that a blocking minority must encompass at least four states (Article I-24). Despite protests from the smaller states, it was clear in the spring of 2004 that the solution on the size of the Commission would be a reduced Commission (Interview 8). The Irish Presidency landed on the size of two-third of member states from 2014, which proved to be digestible by all.

Due to careful preparations from the Irish Presidency, the parameters for a compromise agreement were already set, and when the final text landed on the table at 10.30 p.m. on 18 June, the text was met with a mere nod of approval (Interview 9). Three years of debate on the future of Europe ended almost in silence, and the press was more interested in the battle over the appointment of the next Commission President than in the new Constitutional Treaty.

Theoretical explanations – the story according to LI and realism – the power of laggards

Was the CT negotiation process dominated by governments and, in particular, laggard actors? Throughout the process there are signs that governments were firmly in control of the Convention, in particular in the key institutional issues. Evidence supporting this included the safeguards inserted into the Laeken mandate, the appointment of Giscard as chairman, and the lack of a working group on institutional issues to prevent governments from 'losing' control of the issue to the deliberative dynamics of the Convention.

For instance, in the Laeken declaration sceptical governments installed a range of institutional 'safeguards' to ensure that a possible federalist majority in the Convention did not 'run riot' (Ludlow 2002: 59). Ministers ensured that national delegates outnumbered EU institutional delegates, and that the Convention would only produce 'options' instead of a ready-made constitution. Further, after the Convention, the Declaration envisioned a six-month 'cooling-off' period in order to prevent the Convention's text from achieving unstoppable momentum.

On institutional questions, as with many constitutional reforms of the past, a Franco-German compromise dominated the debate, although the proposal did not bridge all of the relevant cleavages as past compromises had, as it landed on the pro-big side of the large-small cleavage (see Mazzucelli, Guérot and Metz 2007). Furthermore, the UK government played the role one would expect of a strong laggard actor, with the British 'red-lines' dominating the end-game of the Convention (and most of the IGC). Finally, governments demonstrated that they were firmly in control of the process in sensitive issues, and were able to use the IGC to remove unwanted elements from the Convention Draft Constitutional Treaty, including the Legislative Council, the slight weakening of EP powers in the budgetary procedure, and preserving a member state right of initiative in police and justice cooperation (Beach 2007).

If we look at the outcome, we would expect to see according to LI that the outcome reflected the preferences of the least dependent actor. Here there are many indications that laggards that possessed credible threats of veto were indeed able to dictate the terms of the deal on the most sensitive issues. The overall agreement, while being quite ambitious *symbolically*, did not involve major *substantive* changes either in the legal nature of the EU, the policy-areas dealt with by the EU, or in the way EU decision-making work. When we compare Fischer's visions at Humboldt University and the final Constitutional Treaty, we clearly can see that governments ring-fenced the substance of the treaties. In particular, Part III of the Constitutional Treaty (policies) was cut-and-pasted from the existing treaties with only very minor revisions. The 'major' changes that were adopted were arguably only symbolic, codifying existing practices. For example, calling the treaty a 'constitution' merely reflected existing ECJ case law.[5]

Realist predictions of outcomes in institutional issues were also partially validated. On the big-small cleavage the final deal favoured the bigger member states regarding the reweighting of Council votes, although the smaller governments were able to insert certain safeguards, and the reform of the rotating Presidency was far from what the larger governments wanted. Germany, as the materially strongest actor, was unable to push through the revision of Council voting weights that it favoured, suggesting that LI's focus on decision-making rules (unanimity) is more important.

However, the basic question of why a more ambitious deal (at least symbolically) was adopted in 2004 by the same actors that had rejected such suggestions out of hand in 2000 is inexplicable using LI. Further, while the overall contours of the deal reflected lowest-common-denominator dynamics, there are so many significant exceptions that suggest that the LI baseline explanation needs to be supplemented. It is to this task that I now turn.

Theoretical explanations – the Rational Institutionalist story – EP leadership?

How the negotiations were structured did matter. In the following I focus upon how the shift in the rules of the game impacted upon the ability of the EP to provide leadership in the Convention and influence the outcome. The selective focus on the EP is chosen as the EP role in the Convention arguably was the greatest change in how treaty reform negotiations are organised.

The EP was a formal party to the Convention, and there were 16 representatives along with an equal number of alternates, along with two seats on the steering Praesidium. The Praesidium seats were especially important, as it played a role similar to the Presidency during a normal IGC, controlling the agenda and the drafting of texts. These seats allowed the EP to gain a significant voice, evident for example when MEP de Vigo helped push through the revisions of the budgetary procedure in the Praesidium. Another example was in vetoing the most intergovernmental elements of chairman Giscard d'Estaing's draft texts on institutional issues which included proposals on the creation of a strong European Council President backed by France, Germany, Spain and the UK, and the Congress of Peoples (*EU Observer* 24 April 2003; 25 April 2003; Interview 1). In the Praesidium meeting on 22–23 April 2003 the Commission and EP representatives in the Praesidium threatened to veto, forcing the chairman to remove the most intergovernmental elements of his proposals in the draft, including provisions calling for a strong institutional backup for the President of the European Council, and removing wording that called the European Council the Union's 'highest authority' (Interview 1; Norman 2003: 229–35). Further, EP representatives were able to pressure Giscard to upgrade the role of the EP in the appointment of the Commission President (see CONV 691/03; Norman 2003: 234), although the final result was far from the election wanted by key MEPs.

Besides gaining seats at the table itself, the most important aspect of the change in the rules of the game was the shift from unanimity in the IGC method to 'consensus' in the Convention, where agenda management, deliberation and coalition-building became more important. The shift to consensus meant that laggards could no longer block progress by threatening to veto the final outcome. For example, in the end game of the Convention protests from Poland and Spain on the formula for QMV in the Council were ignored, with the result that the final Convention text adopted was arguably more Pareto-efficient than the lowest-common-denominator outcome that resulted from the subsequent IGC.

Another good example was also in the negotiation of the European Public Prosecutor (EPP). The question of creating an EPP was brought up during the 2000 IGC but was quickly shot down by sceptical governments in a representatives meeting on 30 October 2000. In the Convention the issue was brought up in Working Group X on Freedom, Security and Justice. Instead of dying due to ardent opposition from several governmental representatives (notably the UK, Ireland), the EPP was included as an option in the final Working Group report (CONV 426/02). Later the Praesidium proposed granting the Council the ability to create an EPP by unanimity. The proposal was the subject of heated debate in the plenary session on 3 April 2003 and was the subject of numerous amendments. MEP's like Brok and Duff tabled supportive amendments backed by large number of signatures and succeeded in preventing the heated opposition from several governments from succeeding.

Further, the need to forge consensus in the diverse parliament-like Convention with 207 members granted EP representatives comparative advantages over other delegates, as MEP's were familiar with negotiating European issues in a parliamentary-like framework (Jonson and Hegeland 2003; Interviews 11, 12). In particular, MEP's had extensive experience with 'grand coalition' politics from the EP, where decision-making at the time was primarily about forging majority coalitions between the EPP and PES or liberals (Hix, Noury and Roland 2007). In the Convention this was most evident in the final six months, where numerous EP-led coalitions, organised along party lines with national parliamentarians, tabled ambitious joint texts that ensured a more ambitious outcome than otherwise would have occurred (Interview 2, 4; Norman 2003). For example, a paper was tabled in February signed by 67 members and alternates that attempted to establish a 'minimum catalogue of reform', including co-decision in all areas where QMV was used, and that also preserved the rotating Presidency and the introduction of the Legislative Council (CONV 590/03).

The impact of the change to consensus and the comparative advantages that EP representatives enjoyed in coalition-building was evident throughout the final text. In the dying days of the Convention, MEP's built a coalition of like-minded members that succeeded in ensuring that the draft Constitutional Treaty revised the Nice compromise on institutional matters, including adopting the controversial double simple majority in the Council that was a direct cause of the breakdown of IGC negotiations in December 2003 (Norman 2003: 280–96; Ludlow 2004; Brown 2003).

If we turn our attention to the outcome of the Convention there are numerous instances of EP fingerprints that would not have been included if the document had been negotiated in a normal IGC. Arguably the largest EP fingerprint was the name of the document itself – a constitution. While the EP had been arguing for a constitution-like document since the early 1980s, the continual advocacy since mid-2000 and the support that they built for it prior to and during the Convention was successful, although laggard governments ensured that the term 'treaty' was also inserted (Interviews 1, 2, 4). Further, the adoption of a single treaty text that removed the pillar distinctions was a result of EP advocacy, although here also laggard governments made sure that special provisions were kept for the common foreign and security policies (Interview 1). In particular, MEP Duff's short constitution tabled in September 2002 (CONV 234/02) showed the Convention Secretariat and Praesidium that it was possible to draft a short Part I with a single pillar structure (Interview 3, Norman 2003: 65–6). On the question of competences, the EP's report from the Constitutional Affairs Committee in April 2002 provided a focal point for the debates, and influenced the final outcome (Norman 2003: 90–1, 195).

As regards expanding of the EP's budgetary powers, one particularly sensitive issue was extending EP powers to also include so-called compulsory expenditure (i.e. agricultural spending in the CAP). France and Ireland were the most prominent objectors to a removal of the distinction, but the EP succeeded in extending EP budgetary powers in the final Convention text to all areas of the budget. The EP was also influential in the creation of the European Public Prosecutor, although the Convention's text was subsequently slightly watered down in the IGC as it moved the decision from the Council of Ministers to the European Council (Norman 2003: 209, 258–9). The EP also rallied for an extension of the co-decision procedure, coupled with QMV in the Council, to all policy-areas of the Union. While the final text kept unanimity in several areas that were 'red-lines' for laggard governments, the final outcome was significantly influenced by the EP representatives, and a *passerelle* or bridging clause was introduced into the final text as a concession to MEP's and other pro-integrative *conventionnels* in exchange for preserving unanimity in several sensitive policies, although MEP's would have liked to see the use of a form of 'super-majority' instead of unanimity (Interviews 3, 7, Norman 2003: 366; *Agence Europe*, 13 June 2003: 4). On institutional provisions, the EP representatives, together with the Commission, were in the Praesidium able to kill the most intergovernmentalist elements of Giscard's institutional ideas that he drafted in the spring of 2003, including his hobby-horse; the Congress of People's (Interview 1; Norman 2003: 150, 279).

But in sensitive issues for governments, the EP had notably less success in the Convention, suggesting that the LI baseline theory is more applicable when analysing the most sensitive issues. On the issue of the ratification of the Constitutional Treaty, MEP Duff for example had called for either a pan-European referendum, or approval by a 5/6th majority of member states before the Constitutional Treaty would go into effect (CONV 234/02, also CONV 658/03). The final draft Constitutional Treaty only included a declaration to the effect that if 4/5th of the member states have ratified it two years after its signature, and one or more governments have difficulties, the matter 'will be referred to the European Council' (European Communities 2003). MEP's were also not successful in ensuring that all justice and home affairs policies were under the community method. Coalitions of MEP's had called for the deletion of a member state right of initiative in police and judicial cooperation in criminal matters alongside the Commission, but were unsuccessful (Norman 2003: 208–9; Interview 4. See the final Article I-41.3). The EP was unable to ensure that it had a role in all legislative proposals despite repeatedly calling for this. And the EP had little success in foreign and defence issues, with the final outcome far from what key MEP's had called for (*European Voice*, 12–18 June 2003: 6; Interview 4).

However the overall picture is a more ambitious agreement than would have been negotiated in a normal IGC. Further, given that unanimity was required to depart from the Convention draft in the following IGC, most of the EP's fingerprints survived the IGC. Revealingly, when governments met in a normal IGC to 're-negotiate' on the same issues after the rejection of the Constitutional Treaty in the 2007 IGC, they left out most of the symbolic elements that had been included due to EP leadership in the Convention.

Theoretical explanations – social constructivism and the future of Europe debate

To what extent did the shift to a more open, deliberative setting for constitutional reform matter? Did it give bargaining advantages to actors who could appeal to standards of legitimacy? The post-Nice agenda on the 'future of Europe' openly called for explicit value judgements and political vision. While the EP's calls since the early 1980s for a stronger, more federal Union had fell on deaf ears prior to the 2000 IGC, the terms of the debate shifted during the 2000 IGC. Here the German Länder-led debate on 'less Europe' but 'more federalism' agenda neatly overlapped with long-held EP positions on issues such as competences and the simplification of the treaties. More importantly, the new debate was not about technocratic fixes to the Union, but dealt with value-laden political judgements about the nature of 'Europe'.

Many participants noted that the debate in the Convention was different, with legal details not the prime focus of debate as in an IGC. Rather, the debates often centred on political principles (Interviews 3, 6; Maurer, 2003). Here politicians had an advantage over the civil servant representatives sent by many governments, as well as the Commission representatives. In the words of one Convention Secretariat official interviewed, politicians 'can reach agreement on more vague ideas' than civil servants' (Interview 8).

In this respect EP representatives had comparative advantages over member state civil servant representatives, who spoke the technical discourse but were not as 'fluent' in the more value-charged political discourse in the Convention that involved appealing to standards of legitimacy. This granted EP representatives many comparative advantages in the open Convention debates. These advantages were strengthened by the experience that EP representatives had in discussing the issues, especially through their membership in the EPs Constitutional Affairs Committee, where key issues regarding the shape of the Union, its competences, and so on had been debated for years. Key EP representatives to the Convention such as Brok, Corbett, Duff, Hänsch, Lamassoure, and de Vigo were all members of the Constitutional Affairs Committee. This also supplied them with a ready-made source of proposals and inspiration, as they could draw upon reports from the committee on issues such as competences (Interview 10).

One illustrative example where public debate shifted the terms of debate was on EP powers in the budget. Although the debate was more about symbolism than actual substance, as the 1999 Inter-institutional Agreement on the budgetary procedure had weakened the distinction in actual practice,[6] any change in past treaty rounds had been effectively blocked by the French government. It was a priority area for the EP, and the subject of numerous individual proposals by MEP's (CONV 189/02, CONV 392/02, CONV 325/1/02 Rev 1, 487/1/03 Rev 1).

The issue was first debated as part of the Simplification Working Group chaired by Convention Vice-President Amato in the fall of 2002. Here it became clear that the proponents of an increase in EP budgetary powers had a much easier sell for their argument. Whereas opponents put forward sometimes quite complex and confusing arguments for maintaining the institutional balance-of-power as it was (e.g. Roche (gov-IRL) in WD25, WGIX), EP proponents were able to link increased EP powers with bringing Europe closer to the people, and that it would increase democracy and transparency in the Union, thereby shaming opponents (de Vigo and Weurmeling, EP, WD 20, WG IX; also Maij-Weggen, WD 15, WG IX).

Continued EP advocacy in the Working Group resulted in a final report that suggested removing the distinction while also giving the EP the final say on the budget 'in the context of cooperation already consolidated by practice', although in a concession to laggard governments it was agreed that the financial perspective should also be given legal force in the treaties (CONV 424/02). The Working Group report met heated resistance in the plenary session of 5 December 2002, where governmental representatives from Denmark, France, Ireland, Sweden and the UK all opposed change.

While this governmental resistance would have doomed the proposals in a normal IGC held behind closed doors, governmental resistance was overcome in the Convention by a combination of coalition-building by MEP's and the ease with which arguments about increasing democracy and transparency trumped ideas about the institutional balance-of-power in the open Working Group and plenary debates. However, given that the Convention text would have to be approved by an IGC afterwards, government arguments did have to be taken into consideration, and therefore the final Convention text was a compromise that gave governments sole power over the now legally binding multi-annual Financial Perspective while granting the EP the final say over the annual budget. The final text was drafted by MEP Praesidium member de Vigo and the Convention Secretariat, supported by the continued pressure of a large coalition led by key MEP members (Interviews 2, 3, 4. See Article III-310 in the draft Constitutional Treaty).

The shift in the terms of the debate was also clearly indicated by the difference in the Convention text between issues that were heavily debated in Working Groups and plenary sessions, and those that were given only a cursory hearing. Examples of the first type of issues include the symbolic provisions that were incorporated in the final Convention text, such as incorporating the supremacy principle into the treaties, legal personality and the simplification of the treaties by removing the pillar structure. All of these issues had been debated in past rounds of treaty reform but had been rejected.

Given the strong impulse of the 'constitutional moment' initiated by Joschka Fischer's Humbolt speech in 2000, the terms of the debate were now tilted towards proponents of change in these symbolic issues. While changes such as incorporating the already established supremacy principle into the treaties were only minor substantive changes, their symbolic impact should not be discounted. Indeed, it can be argued that it was the incorporation of these types of ideas that eventually doomed the Constitutional Treaty in public referendums as citizens perceived the text as more far-reaching that it was in substantive terms, as they could not discern between symbolic and legally meaningful reforms.

The impact of the shift to a more deliberative setting is best illustrated by looking at the lack of reform in issues that were subject to little debate and discussion in the Convention. For example, the text on the final provisions was not dealt with in a Working Group and was only treated to a cursory treatment in plenary sessions. Therefore, not surprisingly, despite strong support by a large majority of *conventionelles* for making treaty ratification easier by removing the unanimity requirement, no change was made in the final text. In this and similar issues, Convention President Valery Giscard d'Estaing avoided reform pressures by *not* subjecting such sensitive issues to the glaring light of public debate and discourse. In contrast, more ambitious reforms than would have been agreed in a normal IGC were undertaken in issues that were subject to extensive debate in the Convention, illustrating the impact of the change in the terms of the debate due to the public nature of the deliberations on many issues in the Convention that enabled proponents of change to 'shame' opponents.

Conclusions

This chapter analysed the negotiation of the Constitutional Treaty using three different theoretical 'stories'. It was found that the Liberal Intergovernmentalist (LI) baseline was primarily able to explain what was *not* adopted; in particular that the major reforms envisioned by Fischer and the EP were not adopted. The Constitutional Treaty did not significantly change what the EU did nor how it did it. However, the LI baseline needs to be supplemented in order to account for the changes that were adopted. Two contrasting stories were told: a Rational Institutionalist-based account focusing upon how the changes in the institutional structure of the negotiations that resulted from the use of the 'convention method' mattered, and a Social Constructivist account that analysed the impact of the change in the terms of the debate in a more normative, value-laden direction and the importance of 'rhetorical action'. In both instances support was found that especially the EP was the major 'winner' due to the use of the 'convention method', although the limits to EP influence were clearly set by governments as we would expect following LI.

The importance of both Rational Institutionalism and Social Constructivist factors can also be seen when we compare the more encompassing and symbol-laden Constitutional Treaty and the Treaty of Lisbon. The Treaty of Lisbon was an attempt to salvage the substance of the Constitutional Treaty, but as it was negotiated using the traditional IGC-method, it was a very minimalistic and lowest-common-denominator outcome in contrast to the Constitutional Treaty. These findings suggest that we need further work on developing supplementary theoretical frameworks, where the LI baseline is supplemented with additional explanatory factors in order to provide satisfactory explanations of treaty reform outcomes.

List of interviews

1 = Member of the Commission team on the Future of Europe, Brussels, 18 February 2003.
2 = High level official of Convention Secretariat, London, 2 February 2004.
3 = Official in UK Cabinet Office, European Secretariat, London, 16 December 2003.
4 = Advisor to Irish parliamentary delegation to the Convention, London, 17 December 2003.

5 = Official in UK Cabinet Office, European Secretariat, London, 17 December 2003.
6 = Official in Convention Secretariat, Brussels, 27 January 2004.
7 = Member of UK negotiating team in the 2003–4 IGC, Brussels, 27 January 2004.
8 = High level official of Legal Service of the Council Secretariat, Brussels, 28 January 2004.
9 = Official in Convention Secretariat, Brussels, 17 October 2005.
10 = Official in Foreign and Commonwealth Office, European Secretariat, London, 2 February 2004.

Notes

1. The IGC-method can be defined as negotiations between governmental representatives using unanimous decision-making under ex Article 48 EU, and with the negotiations concluding in a final make-or-break Summit.
2. There were also to be an equal number of alternates, but when the Convention started the alternates took part as full participants.
3. The theory of 'rhetorical action' is actually an eclectic hybrid version of social constructivism, as it attempts to bridge the gap between rationalist and social constructivist accounts.
4. The Legislative Council would be a new configuration of the Council that would have a monopoly on adopting legislative actors in co-decision, giving the EP a sole counterpart instead of numerous sectoral Councils. If created, it would have forced governments to designate a permanent minister to represent them. See Piris (2007): 109–10.
5. From the case *Les Verts*, Case 294/83. See Piris (2007) for more on the codification of existing legal practices.
6. The Interinstitutional Agreement of 6 May 1999 on the budgetary procedure (Official Journal C 172 of 18/06/1999) weakened the distinction between compulsory (primarily CAP spending) and non-compulsory expenditure, as the EP was given a say over compulsory (CAP) spending in the ad hoc conciliation procedure. Therefore, the decision to formally extend the budgetary co-decision procedure to compulsory expenditure was not a major departure from de facto budgetary practices.

11
The Treaty of Lisbon: Constitutional Treaty, Episode II

Jacques Ziller

Historical context

It may be argued that – using the concept of cinematographic art – the Lisbon treaty is a 'remake' of the Constitutional Treaty, which would only be worth an appendix to the chapter by Derek Beach on the Constitutional Treaty. The term 'remake' applies most certainly to the content of the Lisbon Treaty, which only differs marginally from the content of the Constitutional Treaty. Taking into account the historical context and the dynamics of negotiations, it appears, however, that while the path to the signature and entry into force of the Lisbon Treaty has been a continuation of the Constitutional Treaty saga, it nevertheless shows several features of its own: therefore, this chapter on the Treaty of Lisbon bears as subtitle 'Constitutional Treaty – Episode II', as happens with films.

As indicated by Derek Beach, there has never been a unanimous enthusiastic endorsement of the Constitutional Treaty of 2004 by all governments, be it only because the 'convention method' forced a number of them to accept innovations that they might have vetoed in the framework of a classical Intergovernmental Conference (IGC) negotiation. On the other hand, the enthusiasm of a number of *convention-nels*, among other factors, gave prominence to a treaty reform exercise that caught the attention of rather wide sectors of the public in many member states.

Referendums and the failed entry into force of the Constitutional Treaty of 2004

The first event that eventually led to the Lisbon treaty was, in my view, the announcement made by the British Prime Minister, Tony Blair, on

20 April 2004 that a referendum would be organised by his government for the approval of the Constitutional Treaty. During the European Convention of 2002–3 and during the IGC that followed, governments had avoided making statements on the process of ratification – let alone adopt a common statement in the form of some declaration. Many government representatives had indicated that they did not think a European referendum would be feasible – or even a series of coordinated national referendums – and some of them indicated that they were not in favour of a concentration of ratifications in the same period, an idea suggested by some *conventionnels* and commentators in order to avoid ratification debates being dominated by domestic issues. The announcement made by Blair came as a double surprise: First, the negotiations on the Constitutional Treaty were not yet finished. Second, although there had been the precedent of Harold Wilson winning the 1975 referendum on the UK's continuing membership in the European Economic Community (EEC), it seemed a very difficult bet for the British government to try to win a referendum on Europe in 2005.

Once Tony Blair had announced that a referendum would be held in the UK it appeared difficult not to hold a referendum in France – where the authorisation to ratify the Maastricht Treaty had been made by way of referendum in 1992. It was therefore not a surprise when President Jacques Chirac announced on 14 July 2005 that a referendum would also be held in his country. There were two precedents to his move: both presidents George Pompidou – who decided to hold a referendum on the first enlargement treaty in 1972 – and François Mitterrand – who decided to hold a referendum on the Maastricht Treaty in 1992 – made their decision in a situation where the European issue was a dividing factor among members of opposition parties and they hoped, therefore, that a positive referendum would not only enhance the legitimacy of their European policy choice, but also reinforce their domestic political position; Jacques Chirac was apparently in the same situation in 2005.

Referendums on amending treaties had been a common practice since 1986 in Denmark (although not systemically for all amending treaties) and in Ireland; it was therefore difficult not to organise a referendum on the Constitutional Treaty in those two countries. Most of the new member states that acceded in 2004 had organised a referendum on their accession to the EC or EU; however, there were other countries where a referendum on Europe had never been organised – like four of the founding member states: Belgium, Germany, Luxembourg and the Netherlands (see Table 11.1). In some cases there were constitutional impediments that explained why a referendum had never been held,

Table 11.1 Referendums organised by member states on the Constitutional Treaty of 2004 and on other European treaties

Member state	Constitutional Treaty	Previous referendums on European integration
Austria	No	Accession treaty, 1994
Belgium	No	No
Bulgaria	No	No
Cyprus	No	Accession, 2002
Czech Republic	Possibility debated	Accession, 2003
Denmark	Announced, not held	Accession treaty, 1972; Single European Act, 1986; Maastricht treaty: 1992 (*negative*) and 1993; Amsterdam treaty, 1998
Estonia	No	Accession, 2003
Finland	No	Accession treaty, 1994
France	29 May 2005	First enlargement treaty, 1972; Maastricht treaty, 1992
Germany	No	No
Greece	No	No
Hungary	No	Accession, 2002
Ireland	Announced, not held	Accession treaty, 1972; Single European Act, 1986; Maastricht treaty: 1992; Amsterdam treaty, 1998; Nice treaty, 2001 (*negative*) and 2003
Italy	No	Constitutional mandate for the European Parliament, 1998
Latvia	No	Accession, 2002
Lithuania	No	Accession, 2000
Luxembourg	10 July 2005	No
Malta	No	Accession, 2003
The Netherlands	1 June 2005	No
Poland	Possibility debated	Accession, 2000
Portugal	Announced, not held	No
Romania	No	No
Slovakia	No	Accession, 2003
Slovenia	No	Accession, 2000
Spain	20 February 2005	No
Sweden	Possibility announced	Accession treaty, 1994, accession treaty; joining the euro 2003 (*negative*)
United Kingdom	Announced, not held	Staying in the common market, 1975

Source: Compiled by the author.

especially in Germany, while in most cases the absence of a referendum had been due to the contingencies of national politics. All these factors explain why a series of governments announced, after the political agreement of 18 June 2004, that they would organise a referendum on the Constitutional Treaty.

The Netherlands had no experience with referendums at all: the proposal for a referendum had been made already at the time of the European Convention, and had led the Council of State to advise that a such a referendum could only be organised if it was not binding to the Dutch legislator and if it did not amount to a revision of the fundamental laws of the Netherlands (Ziller, 2008).

The first referendum on the ratification of the Constitutional Treaty of 2004 was held in Spain on 20 February 2005 and it had a positive outcome.

In France, there had already been a referendum among the members of the Socialist Party in October 2004, in order to overcome internal party divisions; although the option in favour of the treaty won with a very good margin, the minority, including former Prime Minister Laurent Fabius, announced that they would continue campaigning against ratification. Eventually, the referendum held on 29 May 2005 had a negative outcome. So did the referendum held on 1 June 2005 in the Netherlands.

Some surveys based mainly on exit polls have been published in order to try to explain the results in both countries. Nevertheless, I submit that, as there was no deep study by sociologists in the following months, any explanation of these results is only based on anecdotal evidence, and cannot therefore be considered as conclusive about the reasons that led a majority of voters to vote no or to choose abstention. Such inquiry had been organised both by the Danish government after the unsuccessful first referendum on the Maastricht treaty in 1992, and by the Irish government after the unsuccessful first referendum on the Nice treaty in 2001. The comments pointing to a high level of participation in the French and Dutch referenda on the Constitutional Treaty of 2004 are not sufficiently grounded by facts (see Table 11.2). Other comments have pointed to the fact that, unlike for the precedents of Denmark in 1992 and Ireland in 2001, the two negative referendums were held in founding member countries, and that European integration would not be imaginable without France. Neither of these comments are satisfactory – not because they are not 'politically correct', but because they do not tell the whole story.

Comparing the situation in 2005 after the negative referendums in France and the Netherlands with the situations in 1992 and 2001 reveals a number of specific features. First, the Danish and Irish governments

Table 11.2   Turnout and outcomes of referendums on the Constitutional Treaty of 2004 and previous amendment treaties

	Turnout	**Outcome**
Maastricht Treaty		
Denmark 1992	82.90%	52.07% NO
France 1992	69.70%	51.05% YES
Denmark 1993	85.50%	56.77% YES
Amsterdam Treaty		
Denmark 1998	74.80%	55.10% YES
Ireland 1998	54.90%	61.27% YES
Nice Treaty		
Ireland 2001	34.80%	53.90% NO
Ireland 2003	49.50%	62.89% YES
Constitutional Treaty		
Spain 2005	42.30%	76.70% YES
France 2005	69.30%	54.70% NO
The Netherlands 2005	62.80%	61.60% NO
Luxembourg 2005	98.20% (obligatory vote)	56.58% YES

Source: Compiled by the author.

announced immediately after the vote that they would do their best to find out the reasons for such a vote and to search for a possible solution to the worries, doubts and oppositions expressed by the electorate. The French and Dutch governments – and all national politicians in both countries – only said that 'the People had decided' and they were bound by the results of the referendums. Second, the presidents of the European Council – Portuguese Prime Minister Anibal Cavaco Silva and British Prime Minister John Major in 1992; Belgian Prime Minister Guy Verhofstadt and Swedish Prime Minister Carl Bildt in 2001 – announced the continuation of the ratification process and their support to the governments in searching for a solution; likewise, the respective presidents of the European Commission – Jacques Delors in 1992 and Romano Prodi in 2001 – immediately stated that the Commission would try to help the governments of Denmark and Ireland to come to a resolution. In 2005 the President of the European Council – Luxembourg's prime minister, Jean-Claude Juncker – announced his support of the continuation of the ratification process and his personal commitment to withdraw from politics if the referendum to be held in Luxembourg had a negative outcome; however, his successor as of 1 July, British Prime Minister Tony Blair, did not even congratulate Juncker for the results of the referendum of 10 July. Commission President Manuel

Durão Barroso's first public statement after the referendums in France and in the Netherlands was to declare that the Constitutional Treaty of 2004 was dead.

This being said, the main and conclusive difference between the situations of 1992 and 2001 on one side, and that of 2005, is that while in the first case all governments were determined to do their best to bring the treaty into force, such was not the case in 2005. The British government had to face the very uncomfortable prospect of a referendum, and so did a number of the other governments that had announced they would hold a referendum; furthermore, both the new President and new Prime Minister of Poland – the twin brothers Lech and Jarosław Kaczyński – were opposed to the Constitutional Treaty of 2004, as was Czech President Václav Klaus, since the beginning of the Convention's work.

The 'reflection period'

In the days following the French and Dutch referendums of 29 May and 1 June 2005, there was some confusion as to what would happen next. On 6 June, the British foreign secretary, Jack Straw, announced at the House of Commons that the debate on the ratification bill – which had already been approved in its first and second reading – was postponed *sine die*. It might be worthwhile noting that the bill did not contain any indication of a date for the referendum to be held before its entry into force: this meant that the referendum could very well have been held after the completion of all domestic ratification processes (Church, 2007).

President Juncker announced that a common attitude on the ratification process should be decided at the meeting of the European Council on 15–16 June. Some governments had indicated their preference for a halt in the ratification process in order to take the time for reflection, while others wanted to go on with the ratification process they had already started. Juncker managed to get a compromise: those governments who wanted to stop their domestic ratification process could do so, while the others could go on. This was announced as a 'reflection period', often misleadingly presented as a 'pause for reflection' by the governments who had decided in favour of such a break, and by the press. The assumption of the latter governments seemed to be that the Constitutional Treaty of 2004 would never enter into force, and they seemed happy with that, while others hoped that a continuation of the ratification process would show that an overwhelming majority of member states remained in favour of the Constitutional Treaty.

The domestic ratification processes went on in many member states. Before the French referendum, 11 member states had already obtained the approval of their Parliament (and by referendum in Spain) for ratification; by December 2006, a total of 18 out of 27 member states had achieved such endorsement, while four governments announced that they were in favour of ratification but were waiting to see what the others did before organising the necessary procedures (see Table 11.3). Meanwhile, the French and Dutch governments, albeit not officially opposed to the Constitutional Treaty, indicated that their countries had 'difficulties' in the ratification process.

Between the European Council of 15–16 June 2005 and the end of the Finnish presidency (31 December 2006), Bulgaria and Romania became members of the EU – and this included a ratification of the Constitutional Treaty. There was no debate in France on the consequences of the negative referendums before Nicolas Sarkozy, leader of the majority party, UMP, and candidate in the presidential election to be held in May 2007, announced in September 2006 that he was in favour of a 'mini-treaty' to replace the Constitutional Treaty. In the Netherlands, discussions on the future of the Constitutional Treaty of 2004 were resumed towards the end of 2006 after parliamentary elections and in view of the constitution of a new government coalition. The successive presidencies of the European Council did not achieve anything else on the issue other than postponing the end of the 'reflection period' to the second semester of 2008.

In the meantime, a coalition of pro-Constitutional Treaty governments had started taking shape, backed by a number of members of European Parliament (MEPs) and former prominent politicians in the member states. These resulted in, among other things, different alternative projects that all tried to revive the Constitutional Treaty. The British government did not succeed in creating a coalition of Constitutional Treaty opponents – and, as a matter of fact, it did not even attempt to do so; the only ones to declare themselves contrary to the whole Constitutional Treaty remained the Polish President and Prime Minister and the Czech President. It appeared, anyway, that time itself was playing against possibilities to revive the Constitutional Treaty of 2004.

Three options for a follow-up to the Constitutional Treaty

During the 'reflection period' there seemed to exist three options: first, remaining with the European treaties as amended by the Nice treaty, an option that was favoured overtly by Eurosceptic politicians; second, start new negotiations in order to adopt some changes deemed as technically necessary, but which were not considered as politically salient on the basis of the European treaties as amended by the Nice Treaty – an option

Table 11.3 Domestic procedures for the ratification of the Constitutional Treaty

Country	Approval	Difficulties
	2004	
Lithuania	Parliament 11 November	
Hungary	Parliament 20 December	
	2005	
Slovenia	Parliament 1 February	
Spain	Referendum 20 February; confirmed by Congress 28 April and Senate 18 May	
Italy	House of Deputies 25 January; Senate 6 April	
Greece	Parliament 19 April	
Slovakia	Parliament 11 May	Case filed with Constitutional Court by opponents in order to request holding a referendum
Bulgaria	Parliament 11 May	
Romania	Parliament 17 May	
Austria	Federal Assembly 11 May; Federal Council 25 May	
Germany	Federal Parliament 12 May, Federal Council 27 May	Case filed with Constitutional Court by opponent on the constitutionality of ratification authorising act
France	Referendum 29 May	Negative result
The Netherlands	Referendum 1 June	Negative result
Latvia	Parliament 2 June	
United Kingdom	House of Commons 6 June	Withdrawn from Parliament's agenda during third reading
	European Council 15–16 June	**Beginning of 'reflection period'**
Cyprus	Parliament 30 June	
Malta	Parliament 6 July	
Luxembourg	Referendum 10 July; confirmed by Parliament 25 October	

(continued)

Table 11.3   Continued

Country	Approval	Difficulties
Belgium	Federal Senate 28 April; Federal House of Deputies 19 May; Brussels Regional Assembly 17 June; German Community Assembly 20 June; Wallonia Regional Assembly 29 June; French Community Assembly 20 June 19 July; Flemish Assembly 8 February	
Denmark Ireland Portugal		Referendum announced, but decision on holding it postponed to outcome of reflection period
Sweden		Decision on holding a referendum or not postponed to outcome of reflection period
Poland		New President and parliamentary majority hostile to Constitutional Treaty
Czech Republic		President hostile to Constitutional Treaty and lack of clear majority in Parliament
	2006	
Belgium	Flemish Assembly 8 February	
Estonia	Parliament 9 May	
Finland	Parliament 5 December	
	2007	
	European Council 21–22 June	Constitutional Treaty abandoned

Source: Compiled by the author.

favoured by the British government; third, try to get 'the substance' of the Constitutional Treaty of 2004 approved in the form a new treaty, the position favoured by the governments of member states that had already ratified, the European Parliament and the European Commission, albeit President Barroso did not show much enthusiasm for that option. The supporters of the third option were not necessarily convinced that the whole content of the Constitutional Treaty of 2004 was necessarily to be kept, nor that it was sufficient in reforming the EU institutions, but they were convinced that the second option would either lead only to very minor reforms or to a very long IGC where everything that had been agreed in 2004 would be discussed again.

In order to get a treaty approved and into force before the new parliamentary elections of June 2009, and taking into account that the Czech Republic – with an overtly Eurosceptic head of state – was to chair the European Council in the first half of 2009, it appeared that a possible new treaty had to be agreed by the beginning of 2008 at latest.

As will be explained in the next section, the dynamic of the negotiations that started in early 2007 led to the success of the third option, in the form of the Treaty of Lisbon.

Treaty content

The content of the Lisbon treaty clearly appears as a 'remake' of the Constitutional Treaty. The reader should therefore take into account what has been explained in the chapter by Derek Beach before reading the following lines.

The Treaty of Lisbon of 13 December 2007

Formally speaking, the content of the Lisbon Treaty itself – that is, of the document signed on 13 December 2007 in Lisbon – seems very different from the document signed in Rome on 24 October 2004. The latter was a fully fledged treaty of 448 articles bearing the title of *Treaty establishing a Constitution for Europe* (accompanied by 36 protocols, 2 annexes and 50 declarations). The *Treaty of Lisbon amending the Treaty on European Union and the Treaty establishing the European Community* contains a total of only seven articles: Article 1 contains all amendments to the EU treaty and Article 2 has all amendments to the EC treaty – in the versions resulting from the entry into force of the Nice Treaty on 1 March 2003. Article 3 states that the Lisbon Treaty is being concluded for an unlimited period, as with all preceding treaties except the ECSC treaty of Paris of 1951. Article 4 refers to the protocols amending the previously existing protocols, annexes and the Euratom Treaty, while Article 5 foresees the renumbering of the treaties that result from amendments. Articles 6 and 7 contain the usual clauses on ratification, entry into force and authentic languages. This being said, Article 1 covers 42 pages of the *Official Journal* and Article 2 120 pages. As was already the case with the Single European Act as well as the Maastricht,

Amsterdam and Nice treaties, the content of the Lisbon Treaty can only be understood through simultaneously checking the text of the EU and EC treaties in their previous versions, and the Charter of Fundamental Rights in the version that was re-proclaimed in Brussels at the European Parliament on 12 December 2007 – hence the often-expressed suspicion that the Lisbon Treaty was purposefully written in a way intended to deceive citizens and to hide its real content.

In institutional practice, political declarations, and in the wider public, references to the Lisbon Treaty have since then become references to what is technically known as the 'consolidated version of the treaties'. It has become common practice for practitioners, politicians and the wider public to refer to 'the Lisbon Treaty'; in reality, the reference is to the EU/EC treaties as amended by the Lisbon Treaty, which have been published in a so-called consolidated version of the treaties. Comparing this 'final version' with the previous treaties enables the reader to see what changes have been introduced by the Lisbon Treaty with respect to the Nice Treaty. In order, however, to see the differences between the Lisbon Treaty and the Constitutional Treaty, a comparison with the latter has to be made, taking into account that the Constitutional Treaty of 2004 itself was made largely – and not only for the content of Part III – of treaty clauses which already existed in the previous versions of the EU and EC treaties. Few people have indulged in this latter exercise: the legal experts of the Council's general secretariat and of member states' governments, and a handful of academics who did not even have to wait for the Lisbon Treaty to be signed in order to do this task: applying the instructions contained in the mandate of the IGC annexed to the presidency conclusions of 21–22 June 2007 was enough to check what was taken up from the Constitutional Treaty, what was left out, and what was added to it by the Lisbon treaty (Ziller, 2007).

Comparing the Treaty of Lisbon to the Constitutional Treaty

Compared to the Constitutional Treaty, the Lisbon Treaty contains the following two sets of changes.

First, a number of words, expressions or clauses of the Constitutional Treaty of 2004 have been abandoned: the name 'Treaty establishing a Constitution for Europe'; most of the text of the preamble, the clause on primacy of EU law (contained in Article I-6 CT); the article on the symbols of the Union (Article I-8 CT), the name of 'Minister of Foreign Affairs', the expressions 'European laws' and 'framework laws'; also, the possibility to extend the European Court of Justice's competence to deal with intellectual property (Article III-364). Furthermore, the reference to 'free and undistorted competition' does not appear anymore in the article on the Union's objectives (Article 3 TEU), but it has been taken over into a protocol, which has the same value as the treaties, as will be explained in the following section. The reference to 'mutual confidence' between members states in the framework of the Area of Freedom, Security and Justice, which appeared in Article I-42 CT, has disappeared; this has gone unnoticed by experts and is most probably due to an over-sight that resulted from the technique used to draft the Lisbon treaty, a technique that will also be explained in the following section.

The structure of the resulting treaties is also different: whereas the Constitutional Treaty of 2004 was a single document with four parts (and a number of annexed protocols), the consolidation results in three documents: the Maastricht Treaty ('Treaty on European Union' as amended by the Lisbon treaty); the Rome Treaty (EEC/EC treaty as amended by the Lisbon Treaty), renamed 'Treaty on the Functioning of the European Union'; and the Charter of Fundamental Rights of the EU, with its official 'explanations', to which Article 6 TEU is referring.

Furthermore, the entry into force of the new system for calculating qualified majority has been postponed to 2014, and in some cases to 2017; as well, the reduction of the size of the European Commission has been postponed *sine die* after the failed referendum of 2008 in Ireland.

Almost all these changes – with the exception of the reference to free and undistorted competition and the article on intellectual property, which each have their own *raison d'être* – may be explained as the result of a decision to drop implicit references to the possible future develop-ment of the EU into some kind of federal state. These modifications with respect to the Constitutional Treaty of 2004 do not change the content of EU law in any significant way, but they do have a symbolic impact, the lasting or passing effect of which nobody can foresee.

Second, a number of clauses that were not included in the Constitutional Treaty of 2004 have been added in the Lisbon Treaty. Some of them, while being a step towards more integration with respect to the treaties in their version resulting from Nice, are a step back with respect to the Constitutional Treaty: the protocol on subsidiarity and proportionality sets up a mechanism whereby a coalition of member states' parliaments, representing one third of the total votes (two votes for each member state) and of the simple majority of member states' governments, may block a proposed piece of EU legislation before it starts being debated in the Parliament and Council; a single member state can oppose new legislation in matters of family law and in some matters of social policy. But these 'steps back' are more than compensated by a number of 'steps forward' – elements that enhance or facilitate integration and which were not present in the Constitutional Treaty: more precise objectives for the Union, including an explicit mention of the Economic and Monetary Union (EMU) based upon the euro, and a number of better worded treaty clauses.

On the whole, a non-expert reaction to these changes can only be 'much ado about nothing'. Expert EU lawyers are able to detect quite a number of useful and sometimes significant changes that have little political salience. Whoever is looking for changes with political salience will only find them in the symbolic changes that were agreed to during the June 2007 meeting of the European Council: the words, expressions and clauses that have been abandoned, and an obsessive insistence on the principle of conferral (see below).

Dynamics of the negotiations

In order to explain the dynamics of the negotiations and to draw conclusions on what happened from January 2007 to November 2009, it is indispensable to refer once again to Derek Beach's chapter, Chapter 10. His analysis of the dynamics of negotiations of the Constitutional Treaty of 2004 has been confirmed by the negotiations for the Lisbon Treaty. This being said, the negotiations leading to Lisbon have differed from a simple remake of the previous negotiations in the European Convention 2002–3 and the following IGC of 2003–4. The negotiations shed some light on a dimension that has been so far neglected by rational institutionalism – and totally omitted by other theories of political science applied to European integration. What has been until now neglected is the importance in EU policymaking and especially in treaty negotiations of the epistemic community of legal experts and, more precisely, of experts of EU law. Their significance in turn is due to the importance of legally enshrined rules in EU policymaking, often underestimated by political science theories.

Legally enshrined rules and the epistemic community of legal experts

There is a reason for the specific importance of legally enshrined rules in EU policymaking. Unlike other systems of international policymaking, the EU has an institutional system, including courts and specific remedies, which makes it possible for interested individuals – businesses, NGOs, and even individual citizens – to become active players in policymaking, either by addressing directly the ECJ, or by prompting member states' courts to make references for preliminary rulings to the ECJ. These characteristics of EU policymaking make it comparable to the policymaking of many modern states, such as most of the EU member states and the US. It goes even beyond the role that law plays in a number of states – including EU member states – where access to justice is not as easy as in the EU. As with constitutional rules in a modern state setting, enshrined EU legal rules act as constraints to the political players.

The main constraint is due to the principle of conferral, which has been laid down in black letters with the Treaty of Lisbon but has always been at the centre of EC/EU law – as expressed in Article 4 para. 2 TEU: 'Under the principle of conferral, the Union shall act only within the limits of the competences conferred upon it by the Member States in the Treaties to attain the objectives set out therein. Competences not conferred upon the Union in the Treaties remain with the Member States'. In practice, this means that before undertaking any action at the EU level, the legal feasibility of such an action – that is, the presence of an appropriate 'legal base' in the treaties – has to be checked. Legal bases in the treaties do not only limit the possibility to undertake an action to those fields covered by them, they also limit the choices of instruments to be used, such as directives, regulations or decisions; they indicate the procedures that have to be followed, like unanimity or qualified majority in the Council, co-decision or mere consultation for the European Parliament; and they often set precise policy goals for an action (Héritier, 1999). If no appropriate legal base can be found, there is always a high risk that an interested party – which may be a private person, a business or other body – could go to the ECJ and get an annulment of the directive, regulation, decision, and so on adopted on a legally unsound basis.

A second constraint is due to the rules for treaty amendment; this constraint has been growing in importance with the adoption of ever more detailed legal bases, which has accompanied the extension of qualified majority voting since 1986: the absence of an appropriate legal base in the treaties leaves no other option than treaty amendment, as demonstrated by the Maastricht, Amsterdam, Nice and Lisbon treaties.

As specialists know, enshrined legal rules are not only constraints for political action. They may become resources in light of often-unforeseen events, as demonstrated through the constitutional review by the US Supreme Court since *Marbury v. Madison*, 1803, or by the evolution of the position of the President of the Republic in France between 1875 and 1882. Experienced legal experts are therefore usually well equipped to insert potential resources in legal texts. The most obvious example in the framework of the Constitutional and Lisbon treaties is the wording of the last sentence of Article 15 TEU on the President of the European Council: 'The President of the European Council shall not hold a national office'; the mention of a 'national' office only – and not of another 'EU' office – was made on purpose after discussion in the Convention's Praesidium, in order to leave open the possibility to have one and the same person be in charge of chairing the European Council and the Commission – something that might very well be seen as the only reasonable solution in the future in case of a deep crisis between the presidents of the European Council and the Commission.

The presence of legal constraints and the possibility to build legal resources into the treaties has an important consequence: the epistemic community of EU law experts therefore has a role to play in policymaking and treaty making. The consistence and influence of this epistemic community is under-researched – with the exception of some political science literature on courts in the EU (Magnette, 2003 and 2005; Pollack, 2003; Stone Sweet, 2004; Vauchez and Madsen, 2005; Vauchez, 2005). The epistemic community of EU law experts is mainly known to EU law scholars, on the basis of their own participation in this epistemic community and upon anecdotal evidence, sometimes published in legal literature, where it mainly appears in footnotes. It is not a homogeneous community: while most EU lawyers are usually favourable to European integration as a goal and to EU law as one of the means to achieve it, there are also excellent lawyers, experts in EU law, who have no problems with a more Eurosceptic approach, as demonstrated by the excellent technical work done for the UK government in all treaty negotiations, including and especially the negotiations for the Lisbon Treaty.

The importance of the epistemic community of legal experts is particularly significant in the framework of IGCs, where negotiations occur on the basis of a document that is usually prepared by the legal experts of the Council's general secretariat, lead by the head of the Council's legal service; this has been the position of Jean-Claude Piris, a French lawyer and diplomat, from 1992 (when a solution had to be found to the Danish negative referendum) until November 2010 (Piris, 2006 and 2010). The epistemic community of EU law experts also includes some high-profile members: the European Convention's vice-chairman Giuliano Amato, twice prime minister of Italy and a professor of constitutional law who turned into an expert of EC competition law when he became the first head of the newly established Italian competition authority in 1994; and Antonio Vitorino, also a former professor of constitutional law and the Portuguese member of the European Commission from 1999 to 2004. Vitorino was in charge of implementing the new provisions on justice and police cooperation introduced by the Amsterdam Treaty, and he therefore was a member of the Praesidium of the Convention of 2000 on the Charter of Fundamental Rights and of the European Convention of 2002–3 (Ladenburger, 2007). Amato is also the editor of a book in which many of the authors have been members of the secretariat of the European Convention, and most of the other authors are academics who worked in rather close relationship with members of the European Convention (Amato, Bribosia and De Witte, 2007).

I submit that, on the whole, the epistemic community of legal experts has been thriving in the direction of an EU institutional system that would make it easier to develop common policies. Their role has been fundamental in the negotiations leading to the Lisbon Treaty, first in demonstrating that it was legally feasible to take over the agreement of 2004 in another form, and, second, in counteracting the cumulative effect of initiatives taken by governments and other stakeholders that were mainly driven by a short-term fear of the electorate or by genuine Eurosceptic convictions.

The course of the negotiations

The analysis presented in this sub-section is based on my notes taken during the first semester of 2007 while working for the Action Committee for European Democracy, a group of European politicians chaired by Giuliano Amato, who played an active role in the efforts to re-launch the Constitutional Treaty in 2006–7 (ACED, 2010).

The first semester of 2007 clearly departs from the usual scenario of treaty negotiations, as analysed in the other chapters of this book. Instead of a multilateral negotiation with some elements of bilateral initiatives – especially between France and Germany – there was a series of bilateral negotiations, between the German presidency and the Council legal service on one side, and each of the 26 governments of the other member states on the other. What followed is the usual pattern of preparation of European Council meetings, which culminate in the adoption of the conclusions of the presidency at the end of each semester. The basis for bilateral talks has been a series of proposals prepared by the Council legal service for the writing of a new treaty.

These negotiations have generally been led with utmost discretion, until the publication on the Internet by some insiders of European institutions of a letter addressed on 17 April 2007 by German Chancellor Angela Merkel to her colleagues, members of the European Council, which asked their opinion on (i) whether or not to abrogate the existing treaties and replace them with a single new treaty; (ii) sticking to the consolidated approach of Part I of the Constitutional Treaty; (iii) changing the terminology without changing the substance for the title of the treaty, the names of legal acts, etc.; (iv) not including an article on the symbols of the EU; and (v) replacing the incorporation of the text of the charter in the treaty with a short reference to its legally binding value. In retrospect, the letter of 17 April demonstrates that the shape of the compromise between the member states was settled at that time.

Nothing more could be done before the presidential elections, which were to be held in France on 22 April and 6 May: while Nicolas Sarkozy had clearly indicated during his electoral campaign that he would not organise a referendum on a new treaty, his two main contenders, Ségolène Royal and François Bayrou, promised on the contrary that they would organise a new public vote. With the election of Nicolas Sarkozy, the preparation for the European Council of June could be resumed. The legal experts worked on the mandate of the future IGC, keeping in mind the conditions set by the incoming Portuguese presidency, represented by Antonio Vitorino: the mandate had to be precise enough to allow for an IGC to be concluded during the Portuguese presidency – that is, during the second semester of 2007 – without opening any new negotiation. The Portuguese Prime Minister, Jose Socrates, clearly did not want to experience the same difficulties as the Italian Prime Minister, Silvio Berlusconi, in 2003. These issues were again presented in a note from the presidency to the Council on 'Pursuing the treaty reform process' of 14 June 2007 with 'attached a number of questions drawn up by the Presidency in order to help guide the discussion at the Council on the evening of 17 June' (Note from the Presidency, 2007). A few days before the European Council of 21–22 June, the text of the future mandate was ready.

Only a few points were negotiated during the European Council itself: the main contentious issue was the refusal of the Polish Prime Minister and President to agree to the opening of an IGC. Chancellor Merkel seemed to be prepared to go on without unanimous approval, on the lines of the precedent set by Bettino Craxi and Giulio Andreotti in the Milan summit of June 1985, which launched the IGC that negotiated the Single European Act. Eventually, Nicolas Sarkozy managed to get the Polish President to agree; prior to that, the French President had also succeeded in getting the reference to 'free and undistorted competition' out of the article on the EU's objectives, a move that was counteracted by other members of the European Council with the proposal to adopt a special protocol, which has become Protocol No. 27, on the internal market and competition. The purpose of Sarkozy's action was to be able to show the French electorate that he was not a supporter of neoliberalism in EU matters, while nothing was changed in substance. The European Council meeting lasted until about four o'clock in the morning on 23 June: this seems quite dramatic, but it has to be said that the discussions on the ICG's mandate were the last point on the agenda of a meeting where a whole series of other matters had to be discussed. Reading the mandate that was contained in the presidency conclusions, it was easy to get a clear and precise idea of the shape and content of the future treaty.[1]

The formal opening of the IGC took place on 23 July, at the level of ministers of foreign affairs. The time that had elapsed since the European Council, one month, was not due to the need for supplementary negotiations, but simply to the technical needs imposed by the treaty amending procedure: a formal proposal by the presidency, opinions of the Council, the Commission and European Parliament. After having set the agenda for meetings and having examined the draft treaty proposed by the German presidency at the legal experts' level, the IGC adjourned for the summer holidays and resumed work on 29 August, again at the legal experts' level. They proceeded together to two readings of the proposed treaty text, concentrating on issues of wording and translatability – the number of treaty languages was 23 as of 1 January 2007. From 12 September to 3 October their work concentrated almost exclusively on the negotiation and drafting of the response to the British 'red lines' – that is, specific provisions relating to matters of justice and internal affairs, namely the opt-out provisions for the UK and Ireland, which are now contained in Protocol No. 21, and the provisions on the powers of the Commission and ECJ regarding the *'acquis'*, focusing mainly on the judicial review of framework decisions adopted before the entry into force of the Lisbon Treaty, which are now contained in Title VII of Protocol No. 36, on transitional provisions (Piris, 2010).

Some of the so-called red lines were mere declarations to reassure Eurosceptic voters, like the rejection of further constraints due to the Charter of Fundamental Rights. The text of the *Protocol (No. 30) on the application of the Charter of fundamental rights of the European Union to Poland and to the United Kingdom* had already been agreed during the bilateral negotiations that led to the European Council in June, and it was in line with what had already been incorporated in the Constitutional Treaty. The text of the protocol is presumably due to drafts prepared by Lord Goldsmith for the British government, which were negotiated with legal experts of the Council. Lord Goldsmith was the representative of the UK prime minister in the Convention of 2000, which drafted the Charter of Fundamental Rights. At the time of the June meeting, the Polish and Irish governments had indicated their interest in having the protocol also applied to them, but the Irish government renounced this a few weeks later, due to the opposition of trade unions to a part of the text that seemed to negate the application of fundamental social rights. A detailed analysis of the protocol shows that it has very little legal impact, as could be guessed in view of the declarations of members of the British government, some stating that it was an 'opt-out' for the UK on the charter, while the state secretary stated the contrary in the House of Lords (Barnard, 2008).

The following evaluation of the Lisbon Treaty by an insider, legal expert and diplomat is worth quoting:

[O]n the whole, the Lisbon Treaty:

- on the one hand, gives to the EU a new legal framework which offers better potential to progress. Most, if not all, of the substantive reforms envisaged in the Constitutional Treaty have been preserved. The Treaty brings forward structures, procedures and mechanisms which will potentially allow the Union to develop further in the future. Therefore, without giving significant new competences to the EU, it strengthens the possibility, if there is a political will for it, of more integration of the policies of the Member States and of greater visibility of the EU in the world.

- on the other hand, the Lisbon Treaty is a political backlash for the integrationists. For the first time, they have been obliged to retreat and to accept that their retreat is visible. They have been obliged to accept the disappearance of any word or symbol which aimed at stressing that the Union could be compared to an entity having more and more elements in common with a state. This is an important political event, and the ideal of a federal European entity has been seriously damaged. (Piris, 2010, p. 48)

The author of this balanced analysis, Jean-Claude Piris, has been a prominent member of the aforementioned epistemic community of EU lawyers. I submit in this chapter that it is precisely due to the combined efforts of practitioners in the EU institutions and member states, and of academics working with them, that 'the Treaty brings forward structures, procedures and mechanisms which will potentially allow the Union to develop further in the future' (ibid.). The word 'potentially' is probably the most important: such a potential is very difficult to see without expert knowledge in reading the relevant texts; it might or might not be the basis for unexpected future developments.

The ratification process

The signature of the treaty on 12 December 2007 in Lisbon was not the end of the story, although the ratification process went quite smoothly in 23 out of 27 member states. It might be useful to underline that the text had been agreed at an informal European Council meeting on 15 October. The remaining two months were used to further check the compatibility of the 23 language versions.

The biggest issue to solve, which was not really expected at the moment of signature, was the referendum in Ireland, the only country where a public vote was held: on 12 June 2008, 53.4 per cent voted 'no', with a turnout of 53.13 per cent. In order to understand the result, one has to take into account the impact of the Irish Supreme Court's case law on referenda (Barret, 2009). Since the Supreme Court's ruling in the *Crotty* case of 1986 on the Single European Act, Irish governments held it necessary to amend the constitution – which needs a referendum – for every treaty amending the EC/EU treaties. The subsequent case law on referendums (not only EC treaty referendums, but all kinds of public votes) impeded government from taking part in the electoral campaign, and even political parties from using broadcasting for their campaigns – however, private corporations or rich independent individuals did have access to TV and radio. Anglo-Irish multi-millionaire Declan Ganley thus used *Libertas*, a previously unknown corporate entity that largely represented his views, to mount a remarkably well-resourced campaign on the 'no' side in the 2008 referendum on the Lisbon Treaty.

The reaction of the Irish government and of the EU institutions and other member states was the same as in 1992 and 2001 – as opposed to 2005 (see the first section). In order to do its best to secure a favourable vote in a new referendum, the Irish government managed to get a number of 'guarantees' on the points that seemed sensitive to the Irish electorate at the European Council of 18–19 June 2009 – that is, the solemn reaffirmation that the Lisbon Treaty did not introduce any changes in relation to taxation, to Ireland's traditional policy of neutrality and to its position on abortion, and the reaffirmation of the importance of workers' rights. The European Council also promised to maintain the overall number of commissioners so as to guarantee: 'it shall continue to include one national of each Member State'. No change in the Lisbon Treaty was necessary, as Article 17 para. 5 TEU – as it would be amended by the Lisbon Treaty – was already allowing for the Council to 'alter the number' of commissioners set down in the treaty as from 1 November 2014. An identical wording was already present in the Constitutional Treaty, in Article I-26, para. 6; the idea, however, was not to maintain one commissioner for each member state but to adapt the overall number of commissioners to new situations deriving from enlargement. A new referendum, held on 2 October 2009, had a positive outcome: 67.13 per cent of 'yes' votes, with a turnout of 59 per cent.

In the meantime, the Czech and Polish heads of state had made their agreement to ratification of the Lisbon Treaty by their country dependent on the outcome of the new Irish referendum. Polish President Lech Kaczyński signed the necessary documents immediately after the outcome of the poll, but Czech President Václav Klaus – an overt Eurosceptic – took pretext from a request for constitutional review which had been filed by his political friends in parliament to try to further delay ratification. He clearly hoped that there would be parliamentary elections in the UK, and that the leader of the Conservative Party, David Cameron, would maintain his promise to organise a referendum on the Lisbon treaty. The Czech Constitutional Court did not allow these delaying tactics to succeed, and it gave its ruling on 3 November. In a first ruling, however, one year before, the court had already decided that there was nothing contrary to the Czech constitution in the Treaty of Lisbon. In the meantime, President Klaus made a statement according to which he conditioned the completion of ratification 'upon granting of a guarantee that an opt-out, similar to that which Poland and the United Kingdom have been granted' (Piris, 2010, p. 61) would be offered to his country. As the protocol to which Klaus was referring does not in reality contain an opt-out, it was not difficult for the other member states to agree to an extension to the said protocol to the Czech Republic in the future, which they did during the meeting of the European Council on 29 and 30 October. Eventually, Klaus signed the instrument of ratification, which was deposited in Rome on 13 November. Article 6 para. 2 of the Lisbon Treaty provides that 'This Treaty shall enter into force on 1 January 2009, provided that all the instruments of ratification have been deposited, or, failing that, on the first day of the month following the deposit of the instrument of ratification by the last signatory State to take this step'; hence, the Lisbon treaty entered into force on 1 December 2009.

Only a minority of academics and legal experts outside of Germany had been aware that ratification was also depending upon the outcome of a request for constitutional review that had been filed with the German Federal Constitutional Court in October 2008; the court gave its ruling on 30 June 2009, requiring a change in the content of the bills that were accompanying the ratification law; these changes were adopted mid-September, allowing for Germany to ratify before the Irish referendum; almost the same situation had occurred in 1993 with the ratification of the Maastricht treaty.

Only a handful of specialists know that the ratification saga finished only on 25 November 2009, when the Parliament of the Åland Islands gave its consent to the ratification of the treaty by Finland. This country had already ratified the treaty, but the lack of consent for the autonomous region of the Åland Islands would have created an unprecedented situation: this consent was indispensable according to Finnish constitutional law. Whereas some of the rare specialists who were aware of the need of a special agreement of the Åland Islands' Parliament considered that a negative vote would only create a problem for Finland, there might have been a real legal problem due to the existence of a treaty between Finland and Sweden that implemented a recommendation of the Council of the League of Nations of 25 June 1921. The positive vote on 25 November prevented a situation whereby the President of the Czech Republic might have wanted to experiment whether it was possible to withdraw the act of ratification of his country before the entry into force of the Lisbon Treaty on 1 December 2009.

Perspectives

At the moment of publication, time has not yet come to write on perspectives, be it one would want to indulge in a fortune teller's work. Two series of events in the years 2010 and 2011 need, however, to be commented upon, because they have given birth to new treaties.

On 23 June 2010, an IGC approved a first treaty change since the entry into force of the Lisbon treaty – that is, a protocol modifying Protocol No. 36 on transitional provisions. The issue settled by this protocol was to solve the situation created by the fact that the Lisbon Treaty entered into force after the 2009 election to the European Parliament and added

18 seats for MEPs for the rest of the 2009–14 legislature. The IGC was in fact part of the regular COREPER meeting, where the permanent representatives signed the text that had been prepared by the Spanish presidency of the Council, supported by the legal service of the Council, and discussed with the European Parliament, the Commission and the member states' governments in the previous months. The event shows that if the topic of treaty revision is well circumscribed and politically not contentious, it is not even necessary to use one of the simplified amending procedures provided for in Article 48 TEU to produce a treaty change.

This being said, whereas the protocol foresaw its entry into force on 1 January 2011 – or on the first day following the deposit of the last instrument of ratification – it only entered into force on 1 December 2011, after Belgium had given notice that it had concluded the procedure of ratification. Since the constitutional amendments of 1993, which have transformed Belgium into a federal state, EU-related treaties necessitate approval not only by the two houses of the federal parliament, but also by the Flemish Parliament and the assemblies of the Walloon region and of the German-speaking community, as well as separate approval by the two linguistic sections of the Assembly of the Brussels capital region. Belgium, however, was not the only cause for delay: on 1 March 2011 only 15 member states out of 27 had deposited their instrument of ratification: Bulgaria, Denmark, Estonia, Finland, Hungary, Ireland, Italy, Latvia, Luxembourg, Malta, the Czech Republic, Slovakia, Slovenia, Spain, Sweden. This illustrates the technical difficulties of ratification, which has led experts to think that a minimum of a year-and-a-half is needed between the date of signature and the entry into force of treaty amendments.

With the financial crisis of spring 2010, experts were confronted with the so-called no bail-out clause that was part of the provisions on the EMU introduced in the EC treaty by the Maastricht Treaty (Art. 125 TFEU). A closer look at the relevant treaty provisions showed that the 'no bail-out' clause was not impeding lending to a member state in the situation of Greece, and that there was a provision that could be used for an emergency situation. This permitted the adoption of Regulation No. 407/2010 of 11 May on the mechanism for financial stabilisation. Together with the creation by member states of a company of Luxembourg law, on the basis of a specific treaty between the 17 euro zone member states, Regulation No. 407/2010 allowed for the initial rescue of Greek public finances and, in November, of the Irish public finances, and later of those of Portugal. This seemed to show that the

EMU provisions were flexible enough to permit important changes in the whole system of economic governance of the EU.

A treaty change was later requested by Germany, backed by France and by the other member states at the European Council of October 28–29 2010, in order to reinforce multilateral surveillance beyond the provisions of Article 121 TFEU. Eventually, the European Council adopted on 11 March 2011 a draft decision amending Article 136 TFEU with regard to a stability mechanism for member states whose currency is the euro. For the first time, the European Council has been using the simplified amendment procedure of Article 48 para. 6 TEU – a procedure that was not available for the aforementioned protocol, as this procedure is only applicable for clauses on EU policies, not for institutional clauses of the treaties. The clause foresees entry into force on 1 January 2013 or on the first day following the deposit of the last instrument of ratification. On 1 December 2011, only Slovenia had ratified. There might be some confusion in the wider public, due to the fact that in the meantime a revision of the 2010 intergovernmental agreement on the European financial stabilisation funds had been adopted, which led to the dramatic succession of votes in Slovakia in October 2011, enabling eventually this revision to enter into force. The event confirmed that treaty revisions are still on the agenda after the entry into force of the Lisbon treaty, as long as they are clearly delimited.

At the European Council of 8–9 December 2011, the UK tried to condition a further reform of the clauses of the European EMU upon a specific opt-out for the UK of the EU regulations on financial services, hence leading the 17 euro zone members to declare that they intended to go ahead with a separate treaty without the UK, following the precedent of the Schengen agreement of 1984. On 2 March 2012, this led eventually to the signature by 25 member states (all but the UK and the Czech Republic) of a 'Treaty on Stability, Coordination and Governance in the Economic and Monetary Union' – also known in practise as 'fiscal compact' – which complements the TFEU with stricter conditions and mechanisms for oversight of economic policies, as far as the signatory states are concerned. Article 16 of the fiscal compact' states that 'Within five years at most following the entry into force of this Treaty, on the basis of an assessment of the experience with its implementation, the necessary steps shall be taken, in compliance with the provisions of the [TEU] and the [TFEU], with the aim of incorporating the substance of this Treaty into the legal framework of the European Union'. It is not risky to bet that, in the meantime, other treaty reforms will be undertaken.

Notes

1. This is an exercise that I undertook during the month of August 2007 in order to write a book on what became the Lisbon Treaty; this was published in November, before the signature of the Lisbon Treaty (Ziller, 2007), and the changes that resulted from the IGC itself were few enough to be added to the typescript on the second proofs.

12
Conclusions: So What do we Know about EU Treaties and their Reforms? And Where May we be Going?

Finn Laursen

Trying to summarise what we know about IGCs and EU reforms is a huge and difficult task and important disagreements remain among scholars, partly based on different ontologies and epistemologies. The following summarises some points based on existing research, including the chapters in this book.

Actors

The member states: Constrained masters of the treaties

The member states are legally speaking the masters of the treaties, and this is also very much a reality. They dominate the IGCs which always conclude the treaty-making process. They have also, at least until the Convention preparing the Constitutional Treaty, tended to dominate preparatory bodies. The Treaty of Paris was prepared by the French government, Jean Monnet and his associates in particular. They put forward a *document de travail* when the conference started (Gillingham, 1991, p. 239). The Treaties of Rome were prepared by the Spaak Committee (July 1955–May 1956) (see for example Keesing's Report, 1975). The SEA was prepared by the Dooge Committee (July 1984–March 1985) (De Ruyt, 1987, pp. 51–9). The Economic and Monetary Union part of the Maastricht Treaty, however, was prepared by the Delors Committee, which included heads of national central banks and a couple of independent economists (Dyson and Featherstone, 1999), but the Political Union part of the Maastricht Treaty had not gone through comparable joint preparation (Laursen and Vanhoonacker, 1992). The Amsterdam Treaty was prepared by a so-called Reflection Group with representatives from the governments (June 1995–December 1995) (Laursen, 2002, pp. 4–5). Whatever preparation the Treaty of Nice had it was mainly carried out by the Finnish Presidency in the second part of 1999 (Laursen, 2006b, p. 3). Overall we find heavy national input in treaty reform preparations.

More controversially I would further maintain that rational models, like liberal intergovernmentalism, go a long way in explaining the behaviour of member states in IGCs. They have their preferences and interests which they pursue in hard bargaining processes. These interests depend on demands from domestic constituents as well as supply of initiatives and proposals from governments and political parties to overcome collective action problems. The domestic politics part is somewhat underspecified in liberal intergovernmentalism. It matters what kind of government the member states have: how strong it is vis-á-vis the Parliament, how united it is, how strong the opposition is, and how controversial European integration is in the member state in question? This may not always have emerged in the chapters in this book because space has not allowed for deep analyses of national preferences. To the extent that identity issues are involved it may require deep historical analyses to answer these questions. History may help explain national identity as well as party-political games and conflicts. Most EU governments, caught in a two-level game, normally face important domestic constraints. Understanding these domestic constraints is an important part of doing research on EU reforms.[1]

During the process of negotiations there are important bargaining exchanges. In the end all member states must find the proposed agreement better than, or at least not worse than, the existing treaty. The bargaining issues are of two main kinds, issues of efficiency (reaching the Pareto frontier) and distribution (where you end up on the Pareto frontier). Pareto-efficient solutions are not always easy to find. Leadership can assist member states in overcoming these collective action problems (Beach, 2005).

The member states are also constrained by international commitments and the bargaining situations in IGCs. Scholars have been interested in influence in interstate negotiations. Do the bigger member states have more influence than smaller member states? Is the intensity of preferences an important factor as suggested by Moravcsik's asymmetrical interdependence concept? Can small powers also be influential? How does the need for a referendum to ratify an agreement affect the influence of a member state? According to Schelling, binding your hands can increase your influence (Schelling, 1960; Putnam, 1988). This, arguably, has given smaller member states that regularly require a referendum to ratify a new treaty, like Ireland and Denmark, greater influence than one might otherwise have expected.

Leadership

Initiating reform: Leaders and laggards

The question of agenda setting may deserve further study. But there are certain things we can say. Behind the first community treaty we clearly find Jean Monnet and Robert Schuman. It was a French initiative with five other European countries joining quickly. It is fair to talk about French leadership, also because of the determined way Jean Monnet and his team drove the Paris IGC forward. In the case of the Treaties of Rome, arguably, the Benelux countries played a leading role, including Paul Henri Spaak who chaired the preparatory committee and subsequently the IGC which finalised the treaties. But again France was a major player (Parsons, 2003).

The very first reform treaty, the Merger Treaty in 1965, was put on the agenda by the High Authority of the ECSC and Commissions of the two other Communities in 1960, and the European Parliamentary Assembly, as the Parliament was called at the time, also pushed for reform. The Dutch were the first to put forward a draft treaty proposal in 1961. It found support from the other member states except Gaullist France. Once the French dropped their opposition the new treaty could be negotiated.

From the beginning there have been leaders and laggards. As the community expanded some of the newer member states were often not convinced that easily by the proposals for reform which usually came from the original core group of members. In the case of the SEA the European Parliament and the Commission put the reform on the agenda which was supported by the original six member states. The laggards at this point in time were the UK, Greece and Denmark (De Ruyt, 1987). The Commission played an important role in getting Maastricht on the agenda, especially the EMU part, which was also very much a Franco-Italian project. The Political Union part was to some extent driven by the Franco-German tandem. The laggards again included the UK and Denmark (Laursen and Vanhoonacker, 1992).

Some reforms have been initiated because the previous reform foresaw it. The Amsterdam IGC was foreseen by the Maastricht Treaty. The Treaty of Nice was the response to the so-called Amsterdam left-overs, the unsolved institutional issues. But the Treaty of Nice was widely considered insufficient and a post-Nice agenda was established already in Nice in December 2000. This led to the negotiation of the Constitutional Treaty and after its demise the Lisbon Treaty (Laursen, 2006a).

In the current post-Lisbon situation, where there have been calls for limited treaty reforms to deal with the eurozone crisis, Germany has been the leading force for treaty reform despite widespread treaty reform fatigue.

Importance of leadership contributions

Leadership can be required to reach agreements in complex international negotiations. The theory behind this assertion is quite clear (Beach, 2006; Tallberg, 2006). Let me mention some examples of such leadership in EC/EU IGCs.

The first of the original community treaties, the Treaty of Paris, creating the ECSC, was negotiated by the six original member states in Paris from 20 June 1950 to 18 April 1951. Jean Monnet, who was the intellect behind the Schuman Plan of 5 May 1950, chaired the conference. Two members of the French delegations, Etienne Hirsch and Pierre Uri, had prepared a text, which became the basis of the negotiations. Basically, the treaty emerged through the negotiations as representatives from the other future member states suggested changes and additions. It seems fair to talk about French leadership. Foreign Minister Robert Schuman appeared personally during the conference and he delivered the required parliamentary majority for ratification at the end of the process. Monnet's ideas and tenacity played an important role (Parsons, 2003, pp. 50–66; Haas, 1958, pp. 240–51).

After the plans for a European Defence Community failed to be ratified by the French National Assembly in 1954 European integration was re-launched by a meeting of foreign ministers in Messina in 1955. The pro-community Belgian politician Paul Henri Spaak was asked to chair a committee which would outline plans for a common market (and an Atomic Energy Community) from July 1955 to spring 1956. 'Spaak was well suited by temperament and conviction to draft the necessary report. His enthusiasm for integration had already won him the nickname "Mr. Europe"' (Dinan, 2005, p. 32).

An intergovernmental conference started in Brussels on 26 June 1956. It was chaired by foreign minister Spaak (Küsters, 1987). The two treaties of Rome, establishing the EEC and the EURATOM, were signed on 25 March 1967. Parsons argues that pro-community French leadership again was decisive (Parsons, 2003, p. 116). But it would be fair to mention Benelux leadership, too. It was a Dutch politician Johan Willem Beyen who first suggested a plan for a customs union in 1953, and the Dutch kept pressing for a common market as distinguished from more limited sector integration. It was a Beyen-Spaak agreement that led to a

'Memorandum from the Benelux Countries to the six ECSC Countries' which defined the notion of an Economic Community in May 1955 and which formed the basis of the Messina decisions (Monnet, 1978, p. 403). During the IGC bilateral meetings between German Chancellor Konrad Adenauer and French Prime Minister Guy Mollet also contributed to sorting out some of the disagreements in November 1956 and February 1957 (Moravcsik, 1998, p. 144). But writing about the Brussels IGC the French historian Pierre Gerbet says, 'L'arbitrage politiques était exercé par le président Spaak'[2] (Gerbet 1983, p. 213). So the role of the President or the chair of the negotiations can be and is often important.

Since the negotiation of the Treaty of Paris in an IGC in 1950–1 and the Treaties of Rome in an IGC in 1956–7 there have been a number of treaty reforms as covered in the chapters of this book. The first reform treaties, the Merger Treaty of 1965 and the Budget Treaties of 1970 and 1975, were negotiated through the Committee of Permanent Representatives (COREPER) and the Council and then confirmed in brief IGCs at the end (Smith 2002, p. 7; Edwards and Pijpers 1997, p. 5). The High Authority and the Commissions of the two other Communities, and subsequently the single Commission from 1967, were pressing for these reforms, assisted by the European Parliament. This suggests that community institutions started playing a role rather early.

The SEA was negotiated in an IGC during the Luxembourg Presidency from July to December 1985. The Commission had taken part in the preparatory work in the Dooge Committee, which prepared this reform. When the IGC started the Commission continued to take part in the negotiations, even if this was not foreseen in article 236 of the EEC Treaty. The Commission's participation was accepted by the member states that had got used to its role in day-to-day business. The European Parliament, on the other hand was not allowed to take part. The Draft Treaty on European Union adopted by the European Parliament in 1984 under the leadership of federalist member of the European Parliament (MEP) Altiero Spinelli implied much 'more Europe' than the member states were willing to contemplate at the time. So the EP was only to be consulted, and that is largely the way it has been since then, although with the Convention they succeeded in getting more involvement and influence. However, the rejection of the Constitutional Treaty by the French and Dutch people in referendums afterwards does raise questions about that influence.

The Commission, it has been argued, played an important role in the SEA IGC, the first quasi-constitutional IGC (Budden, 2002). More than half the proposals considered during the IGC had been put forward by the Commission (Corbett, 1987). It is probably fair to say that most of the SEA was originally drafted by the Commission. Even if the EP was not directly involved in the IGC it should be recognised that the EP contributed by putting reform on the agenda because of Spinelli's leadership in the EP (Schmuck, 1987).

A number of treaty reforms followed the SEA. First, it was the Maastricht Treaty which established the European Union, followed by reforms in the Amsterdam and Nice treaties and finally the Lisbon Treaty (Laursen and Vanhoonacker, 1992 and 1994; Laursen, 2002, 2006b, 2008a, 2012a and b). The IGCs negotiating these reforms were organised on similar lines, member states negotiating, chaired by the Presidency but assisted both by the Commission as well as the Council secretariat. The EP was only consulted. Many scholars have argued that the Commission played a less important role in the reforms that followed the SEA (e.g. Beach, 2005). Certainly the Presidencies played important roles in producing negotiating drafts and brokering agreements, occasionally playing controversial role such as the Dutch in the second part of 1991 (Wester, 1992) and the French in the second part of 2000 (Schout and Vanhoonacker, 2006). In the IGC that concluded the negotiations of the Constitutional Treaty in 2004 the Italian Presidency had less success that the Irish Presidency (Dür and Mateo, 2006; Bindi, 2008). The German Presidency during the first part of 2007 played a very important role in getting an agreement on a detailed mandate to the IGC that finalised the Lisbon Treaty (Laursen, 2012a).

By definition, intergovernmental conferences have member states as the most important actors. The Presidency plays an important role. Some Presidencies rely a lot on the Council secretariat, others less. The Council secretariat has a useful institutional memory. The Presidency can arrange 'confessionals' with member states to try to find the bottom lines and thus locate possible agreements. Occasionally, the Commission can also contribute to the process (for a sophisticated discussion, see Beach, 2005).

Preferences

Interests vs. ideational and normative factors

According to liberal intergovernmentalism demands from societal groups, mostly economic groups, have been decisive in the process of European integration. It has been argued above that domestic politics matters. Governments want to stay in power. Politicians want to be elected and re-elected. So politicians have to listen to their constituents. But more than economics enter when citizens and politicians decide whether European integration is a good thing or a bad thing. Political interests and attitudes are often rationalised in the form of ideologies. Ideas concerning the future of Europe vary, from pro-integration federalists to anti-integration nationalists. If economic interests are clear and strong they may triumph. If not ideational factors may become more important. In the end all actors have certain ideas of what is good and legitimate.

In liberal democracies people share certain ideas about legitimate governance, including free elections, protection of human rights, etc. These ideas are also projected onto the European stage. These ideas have played a role in the making and changing EC/EU level institutions from the very beginning. Since the very first IGC in Paris in 1950–1 ideas of efficiency and legitimacy have battled. The institutional system invented then included both a relatively autonomous executive (High Authority, later Commission), a Council to represent the member state governments, a parliamentary assembly (later known as the European Parliament) to represent the citizens and a judiciary (the European Court of Justice), thus imitating the divisions of powers found in the member states and other liberal democracies. Creating a strong executive and court as well as applying qualified majority voting in the Council may have contributed to creating 'credible commitments', as argued by Moravcsik, but these considerations cannot explain the continuous strengthening of the European Parliament. To understand that part of the process you need to look at normative factors relating to procedural legitimacy (Rittberger, 2005; Rittberger and Schimmelfennig, 2007).

Among scholars emphasising the role of ideas we should also mention Parsons. He studied the role of a 'certain idea of Europe' in French European policy. When European integration progressed there was a political coalition in France in favour of the community idea. Interestingly, Parsons points out that the support for the community idea increased over the years while support for more traditional and confederal approaches diminished (Parsons, 2003).

Outcomes

We can study various dimensions of the integration process in Europe. From the beginning integration scholarship has at least been interested in three dimensions: the functional scope, institutional capacity and the geographical area covered by the process. All of these dimensions depend on the treaties. Clearly membership and functional scope have expanded over time. A major purpose of successive treaty reforms has been to keep the institutions good enough so that common policies could be developed and implemented. These linkages have been discussed as 'deepening vs. widening' from the very beginning. The Merger Treaty and first Budget Treaty were adopted in the shadow of future British membership. The SEA was adopted as Spain and Portugal were about joining the EC. Maastricht allowed for the three former members of the European Free Trade Association (EFTA), Austria, Finland and Sweden, to join in 1995. Amsterdam and Nice were about preparing the Union for the big eastern enlargements that followed in 2004 and 2007. Since these reforms were considered inadequate, the Constitutional Treaty followed. When it failed the member states produced the Lisbon Treaty, which many hoped would be the last new treaty for many years.

Expanding policy scope

The policy scope expanded over time, starting with coal and steel in the early 1950s. From the Treaties of Rome a general common market was created, with common commercial, agricultural, transport and competition policies, as well as macro-economic cooperation. The flexibility of the treaties allowed for new policies to be developed as long as the member states could agree and find some justification in the treaties. Environmental policy is an example. It subsequently got a treaty base in the SEA. So did economic and social cohesion, read more money for the poorer regions. Maastricht continued, adding a fairly long list of new or improved policies: Economic and Monetary Union (EMU), social policy (with UK opt-out), public health, industry, European networks, education and culture. And the two new pillars added Common Foreign and Security Policy (CFSP), including defence, and Justice and Home Affairs (JHA) cooperation. This allowed the Union to deal with nearly any policy problem in the Union. Still, Amsterdam could add employment, Nice strengthen defence, and Lisbon even add space policy.

Increased institutional capacity

The treaties founding the EC/EU are formally speaking treaties concluded between sovereign states. Changes in these treaties require the consent of all member states. But these treaties have created a system that is different from classical intergovernmental organisations. There has been a certain delegation and pooling of sovereignty. These are the terms used by Andrew Moravcsik (1998). The Commission and ECJ have certain 'supranational' powers. They can make decisions that are binding on the member states and their citizens. Also, an increasing number of decisions in the Council of Ministers can be taken by a qualified majority vote (QMV). Some scholars talk about 'supranational governance' (e.g. Sandholtz and Sweet, 1998). This, it can be argued, has taken the EC/EU in the direction of a federal system, especially because of the interpretation given by the ECJ of the treaties (Laursen, 2011).

The EC/EU treaties have a strong constitutional character. Even Moravcsik talks about 'quasi-constitutional institutions' (Moravcsik, 1998, p. 2). They define vertical and horizontal divisions of powers and include various checks-and-balances. Treaty reforms have changed the institutional balance somewhat over time. The EP has increased its powers and the use of QMV has increased. But the basic structure has remained largely the same over time.

The ECJ has made important contributions to the process of constitution building in the EC/EU. Early on in the 1960s the ECJ made decisions about direct effect, *Van Gend en Loos v. Nederlandse Administratie der Belastingen* in 1963, and supremacy of community law, *Costa v. ENEL* in 1964. Various ECJ rulings contributed to the consolidation of the internal market, thus driving economic integration forward. The treaties themselves have state-like properties. Internally the member states must adapt national rules to the requirements of EC rules (see for instance Hix, 2005, pp. 121–6). The EC had formal powers to make treaties with third parties. Since the entry into force of the Lisbon Treaty it is the EU as such that has legal personality (Griller and Ziller, 2008; Piris, 2010).

The constitutional character of the EC treaties was noticed by legal scholars early on, including for instance Eric Stein (1981), and in 1986 the ECJ described the founding treaties as a 'constitutional charter' (Hix, 2005, 121). Later on Joe Weiler and other legal scholars have contributed to this debate (e.g. Weiler, 1999).

When it comes to defining constitutionalisation Weiler quotes Alec Stone approvingly:

> [T]he process by which the EC treaties evolved from a set of legal arrangements binding upon sovereign states, into a vertically integrated legal regime conferring judicially enforceable rights and obligations on all legal persons and entities, public and private, within [the sphere of application of EC law].
>
> (Quoted in Weiler, 1997, p. 97)

Primacy and direct effect of EC/EU law are important parts of this process of constitutionalisation. But constitutionalisation is more than legal integration spurred by the ECJ. It is also about fundamental rights, separation of powers, democracy, including the roles of parliaments (Rittberger and Schimmelfennig, 2007). Concerning fundamental rights the ECJ has recognised these as part of the EC legal system since 1969 (Rittberger and Schimmelfennig, 2007, p. 213). The SEA for the first time mentioned them in the Preamble.

When the Maastricht Treaty added references to Citizenship of the Union (Article 8) and fundamental human rights were mentioned in a specific article (Article F) this process of constitutionalisation clearly continued (Council of the EC, 1992). Amsterdam added: 'The Union is founded on the principles of liberty, democracy, respect for human freedoms, and the rule of law, principles which are common to the Member States' (Article 6) (European Union, 1997). The EU Charter of Fundamental Rights incorporated in the Constitutional Treaty was a logical extension of this development. Now, through a reference in the Lisbon Treaty, the Charter has become legally binding.

But should the EU have a (real) Constitution? This question was formulated for the first time officially by the Laeken summit in 2001 in the Declaration adopted then. The Draft Treaty subsequently developed by the European Convention was entitled 'Draft Treaty Establishing a Constitution for Europe' a title retained by the IGC that concluded the negotiations (European Convention, 2003; Council of the European Union, 2004). This Draft Treaty was still a treaty though, but it could be seen as a step in the process of constitutionalisation without creating a 'real' constitution.

In the end the Constitutional Treaty did not survive national politics in France and the Netherlands and its replacement, the Lisbon Treaty, first ran into a 'no' vote in Ireland in June 2008. Eventually the Irish accepted it in a second referendum and it could enter into force. It has strengthened European-level constitutionalism without 'constitution' in the name (Laursen, 2012a and b).

At the early stages of European integration many scholars insisted on the *sui generis* nature of the institutional set-up. Haas, for instance (1958, 526), saw 'a symbiosis of inter-ministerial and federal procedures'. In the early 1980s William Wallace argued that the EU is more than an international regime (or international organisation), but less than a federal state (Wallace, 1983).

Writing about the EC in 1991, just before the creation of the EU, Robert Keohane and Stanley Hoffmann echoed William Wallace's conclusion:

1. The EC is best characterised as neither an international regime nor an emerging state but as a network involving the pooling of sovereignty.

2. The political process of the EC is well described by the term 'supranationality' as used by Ernst Haas in the 1960s (although not as often
used subsequently).

(Keohane and Hoffmann, 1991, p. 10)

The main deficiency of the EU from a federalist perspective is the intergovernmental nature of CFSP (Laursen, 2011). The Union has no real
autonomy in foreign and security including defence policies. Justice
and Home Affairs (JHA) was intergovernmental under the Maastricht
Treaty set-up, but the transfer of a number of these areas from the third
pillar to the first pillar by the Amsterdam Treaty can be seen as a part
of a federalising process. The federalisation of JHA is largely completed
by the Lisbon Treaty. But CFSP has remained too sensitive seen from a
national sovereignty perspective for federalisation.

Expanding membership

Looking at the third dimension, again we see impressive change over
time. It all started with six members negotiating and ratifying the Treaty
of Paris (1951) which established the first European Community, the
European Coal and Steel Community (ECSC) from 1952. There were
still only six members when the two next communities were created
by the Treaties of Rome signed in 1957. But soon the UK applied for
membership, followed quickly by Ireland, Denmark and Norway. Due
to resistance from France's President De Gaulle it was only in 1973 that
the UK, Ireland and Denmark could join.[3]

So the first enlargement was controversial. So were the following
Mediterranean enlargements. At first the Commission was against
Greek membership. But the member states overruled the Commission
and Greece joined in 1981. Spain and Portugal had to go through long
negotiations before they could join in 1986.

The next enlargement, with the three former EFTA countries in 1995,
was less controversial. These were advanced industrial states that would
not have costly budget implications. The main question was whether
these formerly neutral or non-aligned countries could take part in the
development of CFSP.

After the end of the Cold War the Central and Eastern European
Countries (CEECs) quickly indicated their interest in joining the EU. It
was only in Copenhagen in June 1993 that the European Council said
that the CEECs could join once they fulfilled certain economic, political
and administrative criteria. It took more than a decade and a couple of
treaty reforms before the big enlargement in 2004, followed by Romania

and Bulgaria in 2007. The Lisbon Treaty, as a delayed substitute for the Constitutional Treaty, entered into force in December 2009.

Concluding remarks

Studies of IGCs and treaty reforms go in many different directions. The literature is vast. There are important contributions from historians, lawyers and political scientists. The latter tend to favour theories more than the former but all can contribute with important perspectives, as seen also in this book.

The number of studies using political science theories in a systematic fashion is rather limited. The best overall effort to produce theory-based qualitative research, arguably, remains Moravcsik's *The Choice for Europe* (1998). Among rational choice institutionalists the contribution by Derek Beach must be singled out as very important, too (Beach, 2005). Historical and sociological institutionalists have also contributed important studies, including especially Christiansen and Reh (2009).

Rittberger's study of the empowerment of the EP deserves special mentioning (2005). It combines rationality with the use of rhetoric. When pooling and delegation create concerns about procedural legitimacy domestic political elites will respond to alleviate the legitimacy deficit. Empowering the EP has been a way to deal with that deficit. In the IGCs member states will face normative constraints.

At the theoretical level the debate between rationalists and social constructivists is a challenge. Do we have to choose one or the other position? It can be argued that a full understanding of European integration require a dialogue between or a combination of the two. This possibility was discussed in an interesting fashion by Schimmelfennig (2003) in relation to the EU's latest enlargements. In a more recent article Rittberger and Schimmelfennig (2007) came up with the concept of 'normative spillover':

> In a nutshell, we argue that functional supranational integration has regularly undermined existing democratic and human rights institutions at the national level and thereby created a democratic legitimacy deficit of European integration. This legitimacy deficit triggered arguments, in which interested or committed actors drew on the shared liberal-democratic community norms in order to create normative pressure in favour of the constitutionalization of the EU. We propose to term this process 'normative spillover'.
>
> (Rittberger and Schimmelfennig, 2007, p. 216)

Shared norms of a community can be used strategically, thus in a rational way, to shame recalcitrant actors to move. Arguably, this has been an important ingredient of interstate bargaining which has been ignored by liberal intergovernmentalism.

Still, it can be argued that liberal intergovernmentalism can go a long way towards explaining central aspects of EU treaty reforms, especially the reforms from Rome to Maastricht, where economic issues were important, including the Internal Market in the SEA and the Economic and Monetary Union (EMU) in the Maastricht Treaty. However, as argued already, a rationalist approach cannot explain the empowerment of the European Parliament. Further, after the end of the Cold War the process becomes more politicised, and accountability issues come even more to the fore. The days of the so-called permissive consensus were over (Laursen, 1994). Issues of legitimacy became more important.

Another challenge for research is the fact that it is impossible to cover the preferences of all actors in detail. Some selection is necessary. Moravcsik chose to study the three big actors, France, Germany and the UK. But this will sometimes be insufficient. Italy and Spain have also played important roles, and Poland has been a key actor in connection with the Constitutional and Lisbon treaties. Even smaller actors have played important roles, including the Benelux countries, Denmark and Ireland, the latter two partly because of the use of referendums. Seen from a two-level perspective (Putnam, 1988; Evans et al., 1993; Milner, 1997), it can be argued that the use of referendums to ratify a new treaty will strengthen that state in the negotiations. The German Presidency listened attentively to the Danish government in 2007 in order to avoid a referendum in Denmark (Laursen, 2012a, see also contributions to Carbone, 2010).

The debacle of the Constitutional Treaty raises the question, what went wrong with the Constitutional Treaty? Has a constitutional equilibrium or settlement been reached, as argued by Moravcsik (2006 and 2007)? Is he right, when he argues that the premises behind the Constitutional Treaty, basically that more participation and deliberation would create greater common identity, institutional trust and political legitimacy, were wrong? It is a telling comment on Moravcsik's argument that the Lisbon Treaty was negotiated in a very secretive way without much public debate. The member states returned with a vengeance.

Notes

1. The books I have been involved in editing on treaty reforms from Maastricht to Lisbon, have had chapters on the member states. The books I co-edited

with Sophie Vanhoonacker on Maastricht had chapters on all 12 member states at the time (Laursen and Vanhoonacker, 1992 and 1994). The books I edited on the Amsterdam and Nice treaties had chapters on the 15 member states after the 1995 enlargement that added Austria, Finland and Sweden as members (Laursen, 2002 and 2006b), but in the book on the Constitutional Treaty, where the future members from Central And Eastern Europe got involved, I only included case studies of seven current and future member states (Laursen, 2008a). The book I have edited on the role of member states in the case of Lisbon included the cases of Germany, France, the UK, Italy, Spain, the Czech Republic, Poland, Denmark and Ireland (Laursen, 2012a).

2. 'The political mediation was carried out by President Spaak.'
3. In Norway the people rejected membership in a referendum in 1972.

References

Abelshauser, W. (1994) 'Integration à la carte: The Primacy of Politics and the Economic Integration of Western Europe in the 1950s' in S. Martin (ed.) *The Construction of Europe – Essays in Honour of Emile Noël* (Dordrecht: Kluwer Academic Publishers).

Action Committee for European Democracy (2010) The European Union Institute, http://www.eui.eu/DepartmentsAndCentres/RobertSchumanCentre/Research/ArchivesInstitutionsGovernanceDemocracy/ACED/Index.aspx (accessed February 2012).

Alter, K. (1998) 'Who are the "Masters of the Treaty"? European Governments and the European Court of Justice', *International Organization*, 52(1), 121–47.

Alter, K. and D. Steinberg (2007) 'The Theory and Reality of the European Coal and Steel Community' in S. Meunier and K. McNamara (eds) *Making History: European Integration and Institutional Change at Fifty. The State of the European Union. Volume 8* (New York: Oxford University Press).

Amato, G., H. Bribosia and B. De Witte (2007) *Genèse et destinée de la Constitution européenne* (Brussels: Bruylant).

Amsterdam Treaty (1997) *Treaty amending the Treaty on European Union, the Treaties Establishing the European Communities and Certain Related Acts* (Luxembourg: Office for Official Publications of the European Communities).

Antola, E. (2006) 'Finland: 'We have to Live with the Results' in F. Laursen (ed.) *The Treaty of Nice* (Leiden: Nijhoff).

Asbeek Brusse, W. (1997) *Tariffs, Trade and European Integration, 1947–1957: from Study Group to Common Market* (New York: St Martin's Press).

Aspinwall, M. and G. Schneider (2001) 'Institutional research on the European Union: Mapping the Field' in G. Schneirder and M. Aspinwall (eds) *The Rules of Integration: Institutionalist Approaches to the Study of Europe* (Manchester: Manchester University Press), pp. 1–18.

Assemblée Parlementaire Européenne (1960) Documents de Séance (1960–1961) Document 84, 7 Novembre 1960.

Barker, E. (1973) *The Common Market* (London, Wayland/NY: G. P. Putman).

Barrett, B. (2009) 'Taking the Direct Route – The Irish Supreme Court Decisions in Crotty, Coughlan and Mckenna (No. 2)', *UCD Working Papers in Law, Criminology & Socio-Legal Studies, Research Paper No. 08/2009*, http://ssrn.com/abstract=1400029 (accessed February 2012).

Barnard, C. (2008). 'The "Opt-Out" for the UK and Poland from the Charter of Fundamental Rights: Triumph of Rhetoric over Reality?' in F. Griller and J. Ziller (eds) *The Lisbon Treaty – EU Constitutionalism without a Constitutional Treaty* (New York–Vienna: Springer).

Basabe Lloréns, F. (2006) 'Spain: The Need to Sell a Victory' in F. Laursen (ed.) *The Treaty of Nice* (Leiden: Nijhoff).

Baun, M. (1996) *An Imperfect Union: The Maastricht Treaty and the New Politics of European Integration* (Boulder: Westview Press).

BBC News (2012) 'EU Summit: All but Two Leaders Sign Fiscal Treaty', 2 March. http://www.bbc.co.uk/news/world-europe-17230760 (accessed 15 March 2012).

Beach, D. (2000) 'Bringing Negotiations Back into the Study of European Integration: How Negotiations Affect the Ability of Supranational Actors to Gain Influence in IGC's', dissertation submitted for the degree of Doctor of Philosophy, Department of Political Science, University of Southern Denmark, 4 October 2000. Published by the University Press of Southern Denmark in 2003.

Beach, D. (2002) 'Negotiating the Treaty: When Theory Meets Reality' in F. Laursen (ed.) *The Amsterdam Treaty. National Preference Formation, Interstate Bargaining and Outcome* (Odense: Odense University Press), 593–693.

Beach, D. (2004) 'The Unseen Hand in Treaty Reform Negotiations: The Role and Influence of the Council Secretariat', *Journal of European Public Policy* 11, no. 3, 408–39.

Beach, D. (2005) *The Dynamics of European Integration: Why and When EU Institutions Matter* (Basingstoke: Palgrave Macmillan).

Beach, D. (2006) 'The European Commission and Council Secretariat: How They Gained Some Influence' in F. Laursen (ed.) *The Treaty of Nice* (Leiden: Nijhoff).

Beach, D. (2007) 'The European Parliament in the 2000 IGC and the Constitutional Treaty Negotiations: From Loser to Winner', *Journal of European Public Policy*, Vol. 14, No. 8, pp. 1271–92.

Beach, D. (2009) 'Leadership and Intergovernmental Negotiations in the European Union' in M. Egan, N. Nugent and W. E. Paterson (eds) *Research Agendas in EU Studie* (Houndmills: Palgrave Macmillan), pp. 92–116.

Beach, D. and C. Mazzucelli, eds (2007) *Leadership in the Big Bangs of European Integration* (Basingstoke: Palgrave Macmillan).

Beach, D. and R. B. Pedersen (2012) *Process-Tracing: An Introduction* (Ann Arbor: University of Michigan Press).

Beckerleg, B. (1978) *EEC Competition Law* (Oxford: ESC).

Bellamy, C. (1973) *Common Market law of Competition* (London: Sweet & Maxwell).

Best, E. (2002) 'The United Kingdom: From Isolation towards Influence' in F. Laursen (ed.) *The Amsterdam Treaty: National Preference Formation, Interstate Bargaining and Outcome* (Odense: Odense University Press), 359–78.

Beuter, R. (2002) 'Germany: Safeguarding the EMU and the Interests of the Länder' in F. Laursen (ed.) *The Amsterdam Treaty: National Preference Formation, Interstate Bargaining and Outcome* (Odense: Odense University Press), 93–120.

Beyen, J. W. (1968) *Het spel en de knikkers. Én kroniek van vijftig jaren.* Rotterdam: Ad. Donker.

Bieber, Roland, Jean-Paul Jacqué, and Joseph Weiler, eds (1985) *An Ever Closer Union: A Critical Analysis of the Draft Treaty Establishing European Union,* European Perspectives Series. Luxembourg: Office for Official Publications of the European Community.

Bindi, F. (2006) 'Italy: When Individual Actors Make a Difference' in F. Laursen (ed.) *The Treaty of Nice* (Leiden: Nijhoff).

Bindi, F. (2008) 'Italy and the Treaty Establishing a European Constitution: The Decline of a Middle-Size Power?' in F. Laursen (ed.) *The Rise and Fall of the EU's Constitutional Treaty.* (Leiden: Nijhoff).

Bitsch, M. T. (1998) 'La création de la Commission unique: Réforme technique ou affirmation d'une identité européenne?' in M. T. Bitsch, W. Loth and R. Poidevin (eds) *Institutions européennes et identités européennes* (Brussels. Établissements Émile Bruylant) pp. 327–47.

Bitsch, M. T. (2007) *La construction européenne: Enjeux politiques et choix institutionnels* (Brussels: P.I.E. Peter Lang).

Blanck, K. (2006) 'Austria: Between Size and Sanctions' in F. Laursen (ed.) *The Treaty of Nice* (Leiden: Nijhoff).

Blumgart, J. D. (1956) *Euratom and the Common Market: Report on European Unity* (New York: American Committee on United Europe).

Bodenheimer, S. J. (1967) *Political Union: A Microcosm of European Politics 1960–1966* (Leyden: A.W. Sijthoff).

Boer, M. Den (2002) 'A New Area of Freedom, Security and Justice: The Shaping of a Hybrid Compromise' in F. Laursen (ed.) *The Amsterdam Treaty. National Preference Formation, Interstate Bargaining and Outcome* (Odense: Odense University Press), 509–35.

Brinkhorst, L. J. (1997) 'Efficiency and Democracy' in *Making Sense of Amsterdam* (Brussels: The European Policy Centre), 57.

Britton, A. and D. Mayes (1992) *Achieving Monetary Union in Europe* (London: Sage Publications).

Buchanan, J. and R. Musgrave (1999) *Public Finance and Public Choice* (Cambridge MA: MIT Press).

Budden, P. (2002) 'Observations on the Single European Act and "Relaunch of Europe": A Less "Intergovernmental Reading" of the 1985 Intergovernmental Conference', *Journal of European Public Policy*, Vol. 9, No. 1 (February), pp. 76–97.

Bulletin of the European Economic Community (1960) 10-1960: 'The Merger of the Executives', pp. 20–1.

Bulletin of the European Economic Community (1961) 12-1961: 'Debate on the Merging of the Councils and the Executives', p. 66.

Bulletin of the European Economic Community (1964) 11-1964: 'Institutions and Organs: The Merger of the Executives', pp. 42–51.

Bulletin of the European Economic Community (1965a) 1-1965: 'Institutions and Organs: Merger of the Executives', pp. 58–77.

Bulletin de la Communauté économique européenne (1965b) 4-1965: 'La fusion des exécutifs', pp. 11–12.

Bulletin of the European Economic Community (1965c) Vol. 8, No. 7, July 1965: 'Resolution on the Social Aspects of the Merger of the Executives of the Communities', p. 64; 'Resolution on the Effects of the Merger of the Executives on the Problems of Industrial Health and Safety Hygiene and Health Protection within the Framework of the European Communities', p. 65.

Bulletin of the European Economic Community (1967a) Vol. 10, No. 6, June 1967: 'Implementation of the Treaty on the Merger of the Institutions', pp. 14–15.

Bulletin of the European Economic Community (1967b) Vol. 10, No. 7, July 1967: 'Entry into Force of the Treaty establishing a single Council and a single Commission of the European Communities', p. 24.

Bulletin of the European Economic Community (1967c) Vol. 10, No. 8, 1967: 'The Commission of the European Communities takes up its Duties', pp. 5–9.

Bulletin of the European Communities (1984) 2-1984, point 1.1.1.

Bulletin of the European Communities (1986) S/2-1986.

Bulletin of the European Communities (1987) S/1-1987.

Bulletin of the European Communities (1988) S/1-1988.

Burgess, M. (1986) review of Bieber, Jacqué, and Weiler (1985) in *Journal of Common Market Studies*, 25/1, p. 77.

Burgess, M. (2000) *Federalism and European Union: The Building of Europe, 1950–2000* (London: Routledge).

Butler, D. and U. Kitzinger (1976) *The 1975 Referendum* (London: Macmillan).

Camps, M. (1964) *Britain and the European Community 1955–1963*. London: Oxford University Press.

Carbone, M., ed. (2010) *National Politics and European Integration: From the Constitution to the Lisbon Treaty* (Cheltenham: Edward Elgar).

Charter of Fundamental Rights of the European Union (2010) *Official Journal of the European Union*, 30 March 2010, No. C 83/02, first published in the *Official Journal of the European Union*, 14 December 2010, No. C 302/01.

Christiansen, T. and C. Reh (2009) *Constitutionalizing the European Union* (Houndmills: Palgrave Macmillan).

Christiansen, T., G. Falkner and K. E. Jørgensen (2002) 'Theorizing EU Treaty Reform: Beyond Diplomacy and Bargaining', *Journal of European Public Policy*, Vol. 9, No. 1 (February), pp. 12–32.

Chryssochoou, D. (2001) *Theorizing European Integration* (New York: Sage).

Church, C. (2001) 'Intergovernmental Conferences and Treaty Reform: The Nice Experience' in M. Bond and K. Feus (eds) *The Treaty of Nice Explained* (London: Federal Trust and Kogan Page).

Church, C. (2007) 'The United Kingdom: A Tragi-Comedy in Three Acts' in A. Albi and J. Ziller (eds) *The European Constitution and National Constitutions: Ratification and Beyond* (Cheltenham: Edward Elgar Publishing).

Closa, C. (2007) 'The Value of Institutions: Mandate and Self-Mandate in the Convention Process', *Politique Européenne*, Vol. 13, Printemps 2004.

Corbett, R. (1987) 'The 1985 Intergovernmental Conference and the Single European Act' in Roy Pryce (ed.) *The Dynamics of European Union* (London: Croom Helm), pp. 238–72.

Cohen, D. M. (1964–5) 'The Association of Third Countries with the European Economic Community Pursuant to Article 238', *University of Pittsburg Law Review*, 26, 521–31.

Comité Intergouvernemental creé par la Conférence de Messine (1956). Rapport des Chefs de Délégation aux Ministres des Affaires Etrangères [Spaak Report]. Brussels 21 April. http://aei.pitt.edu/996/1/Spaak_report_french.pdf (accessed 20 May 2012).

Common Market Law Review (1986) 'Editorial Comment: The Single European Act', 23/2.

Communique de presse (Venise, 30 mai 1956) http://www.cvce.eu/viewer/-/content/848cdc9d-cabe-40bf-9527-a5942a9b5edf/en (accessed 21 May 2012).

CONFER (2000) 4750/00: Conference of the Representatives of the Governments of the Member States, 'Intergovernmental Conference on Institutional Reform: Presidency report to the Feira European Council', Brussels, 14 June.

CONFER (2000) 4790/00: Conference of the Representatives of the Governments of the Member States, 'Summary: Progress report on the Intergovernmental Conference on institutional reform', Brussels, 3 November.

CONFER (2000) 4795/00: Conference of the Representatives of the Governments of the Member States, 'Presidency Note: Extension of Qualified Majority Voting', Brussels, 9 November.

CONFER (2000) 4810/00: Conference of the Representatives of the Governments of the Member States, 'Revised Summary', Brussels, 23 November.

CONFER (2000) 4815/00: Conference of the Representatives of the Governments of the Member States, 'Revised Summary', Brussels, 30 November.

CONFER (2000) 4816/00: Conference of the Representatives of the Governments of the Member States, 'Draft Treaty of Nice', Brussels, 6 December.

'La Conférence intergouvernementale pour le Marché commun et l'Euratom 1956–57' http://www.cvce.eu/viewer/-/content/06c7e43a-6eca-4f3a-80eb-8581e43a6470/4d6edb33-1bf4-4e2b-98b0-ac02a892b3e9/fr (accessed 20 May 2012).

Consolidated versions of the Treaty on European Union and the Treaty on the Functioning of the European Union, *Official Journal of the European Union*, 30 March 2010, No. C 83/01; first published in the *Official Journal of the European Union*, 9 May 2008, No. C 115/01.

Conway, M. and P. Romijn (2004) 'Introduction', *Contemporary European History*, Vol. 13, No. 4, pp. 377–88.

Coombes, D. (1972) *The Power of the Purse in the European Communities* (London: Chatham House).

Coombes, D. (1976) *The Power of the Purse: The Role of European Parliaments in Budgetary Decisions* (London: Political and Economic Planning).

Corbett, R. (1987) 'The 1985 Intergovernmental Conference and the Single European Act' in Roy Pryce (ed.) *The Dynamics of European Union* (London: Croom Helm), pp. 238–72.

Corbett, R. (1993) *The Treaty of Maastricht* (Essex: Longman Current Affairs).

Corrado, L. (2002) 'Italy: From the Hard Core to Flexible Integration' in F. Laursen (ed.) *The Amsterdam Treaty. National Preference Formation, Interstate Bargaining and Outcome* (Odense: Odense University Press), 225–53.

Cotter, S. (1995) *The Law of the European Community: A Commentary on the EEC Treaty* (New York: Bender).

Council Decision, 28 April 1970, *Journal Officiel des Communautés Européennes*, 28 April 1970, L94:19–22.

Council of the European Communities (1992) *Treaty on European Union*. Luxembourg: Office for Official Publications of the European Communities.

Council of the European Union (2004) General Secretariat, *Draft treaty Establishing a Constitution for Europe as Approved by the Intergovernmental Conference on 18 June 2004*. 2 volumes (Luxembourg: Office for Official Publications of the European Communities).

Council of the European Union (2010) 'Council Regulation Establishing a European Financial Stabilisation Mechanism', Brussels 10 May. http://register.consilium.europa.eu/pdf/en/10/st09/st09606.en10.pdf (accessed 15 March 2012).

Creswell, M. and M. Trachtenberg (2003) 'France and the German Question, 1945–1955', *Journal of Cold War Studies*, 5(3), 5–28.

Daley, S. (2000) 'European Union Reform: After 5 Days, a Yawn', *New York Times*, 12 December, http://www.nytimes.com/2000/12/12/world/european-union-reform-after-5-days-a-yawn.html (accessed February 2012).

De Ruyt, J. (1987) *l'Acte unique européen* (Bruxelles: Editions de l'Université de Bruxelles).

Dehousse, F. (1999) *Amsterdam: The Making of a Treaty* (London: European Research Centre).

Dehousse, F., P. Horion, A. Fettweis, L. Dabin and P. Pescatore. (1965) *La fusion des Communautés européennes*. Colloque organisé à Liège les 28, 29 et 30 avril 1965. Collection scientifique de la Faculté de droit de l'Université de Liège No. 22 (The Hague: Martinus Nijhoff).

Dehousse, J. M. (1967) *La fusion des communautés européennes au lendemain des Accords de Luxembourg*. Colloque organisé à Liège les 27, 28 et 29 avril 1966. Collection scientifique de la Faculté de droit de l'Université de Liège. No. 24 (The Hague: Martinus Nijhoff).

Deloche, F. (2002) 'France: A Member State Loosing Influence?' in F. Laursen (ed.) *The Amsterdam Treaty: National Preference Formation, Interstate Bargaining and Outcome* (Odense: Odense University Press), 139–57.

Deloche-Gaudez, F. (2001) *The Convention on a Charter of Fundamental Rights: A Method for the Future*. Notre Europe, Research and Policy Paper No. 15, November 2001.

Delors, J. (2004) *Mémoires* (Paris: Plon).

Deniau, J. F. (1967) *The Common Market* (London: Barrie and Rocliff).

Deringer, A. (1962) *Some Practical Aspects of the Antitrust Provisions of the Treaty of Rome* (London: British Institute of International and Comparative Law).

Diebold, W. Jr. (1959) *The Schuman Plan: A Study in Economic Cooperation 1950–1959* (New York: Frederick A. Praeger).

Diez, T. and A. Wiener (2004) *European Integration Theory* (Oxford: Oxford University Press).

Dinan, D. (2004) *Europe recast: A History of European Union* (Basingstoke and New York: Palgrave Macmillan).

Dinan, D. (2005) *Ever Closer Union: An Introduction to European Integration*. Third edn (Houndmills: Palgrave Macmillan).

Dodsworth, J. (1975) 'European Community Financing. An Analysis of the Dublin Agreement, *Journal of Common Market Studies*, No. 2, pp. 129–39.

Doutriaux, Y. and C. Lequesne (2010) *Les institutions de l'Union européenne après le traité de Lisbpone* 8th edn (Paris: La documentations Française).

Duchene, F. (1994) *Jean Monnet: The First Statesman of Interdependence* (New York: W.W. Norton and Company).

Dür, A. and G. Mateo (2006) 'Bargaining Efficiency in Intergovernmental Negotiations in the EU: Treaty of Nice vs. Constitutional Treaty', *Journal of European Integration*, Vol. 28, No. 4 (September), pp. 381–98.

Duke, S. (2002) 'The Common Foreign and Security Policy: Significant but Modest Changes' in F. Laursen (ed.) *The Amsterdam Treaty. National Preference Formation, Interstate Bargaining and Outcome* (Odense: Odense University Press), 473–508.

Dumoulin, Michel (1989) 'Les travaux du Comité Spaak (juillet 1955 – avril 1956)' in Enrico Serra (ed.) *The Relaunching of the Treaties of Rome* (Brussels: Bruylant), pp. 195–210.

Dyson, K. and K. Featherstone (1999) *The Road to Maastricht: Negotiating Economic and Monetary Union* (Oxford: Oxford University Press).

Edwards, G. and A. Pijpers, eds (1997) *The Politics of European Treaty Reform: The 1996 Intergovernmental Conference and Beyond* (London: Pinter).

Efron, R. and A. S. Nanes (1957) 'Common Market and Euratom Treaties: Supranationality and the Integration of Europe', *International Law and Comparative Law Quarterly*, October, 670–84.

Egenhofer, C., S. Kurpas, P. M. Kaczyński and L. van Schaik (2011) *The Ever-Changing Union: An Introduction to the History, Institutions and Decision-Making Processes of the European Union.* 2nd edn (Brussels: Centre for European Policy Studies).

Eilstrup-Sangiovanni, M. (2006) *Debates on European Integration* (New York: Palgrave Macmillan).

Eilstrup-Sangiovanni, M. and D. Verdier (2005) 'European Integration as a Solution to War', *European Journal of International Relations*, 11(1), 99–135.

Elster, Jon, ed. (1986) *The Multiple Self* (Cambridge: Cambridge University Press).

Engel, C. (2006) 'Germany: A Story of Saving Face' in F. Laursen (ed.) *The Treaty of Nice* (Leiden: Nijhoff).

Etzioni, A. (1965) *Political Unification* (New York: Holt, Rinehart and Winston, Inc.).

Europa Publications (2003) *The Rome, Maastricht, Amsterdam and Nice Treaties: The Treaty on European Union and the Treaty Establishing the European Community, Amended by the Treaty of Nice: Comparative Texts* (London: Europa).

European Coal and Steel Community, The High Authority (1965) *13th General Report on the Activities of the Community (February 1, 1964 – January 31, 1965).* Luxembourg, March. 'Matters Relating to the Merger of the Executives and Councils', pp. 45–9.

European Coal and Steel Community, The High Authority (1966) *14th General Report on the Activities of the Community (February 1, 1965 – January 31, 1966),* Luxembourg, March: 'The Merger of the Executives and the Councils', pp. 49–51.

European Coal and Steel Community, European Economic Community, European Atomic Energy Community, Commission (1968) *First General Report on the Activities of the Communities 1967.* Brussels-Luxembourg, February: 'Entry into force of the Merger Treaty', pp. 25–30.

European Commission (1985) *Completing the Internal Market,* COM(85)310, June.

European Commission (1999) 'Adapting the Institutions to make a success of enlargement: Contribution by the European Commission to preparations for the Intergovernmental Conference on institutional issues. Presented by the President and Mr Barnier', 10 November, http://www.esi2.us.es/~mbilbao/pdffiles/preigc99.pdf (accessed February 2012).

European Commission (2000a) 'Adapting the institutions to make a success of enlargement: Commission Opinion in accordance with Article 48 of the Treaty on European Union on the calling of a Conference of Representatives of Governments of the Member States to amend the Treaties', COM 34, 26 January, http://eur-lex.europa.eu/LexUriServ/LexUriServ.do?uri=COM:2000:0034:FIN:EN:PDF (accessed February 2012).

European Convention (2003) *Draft Treaty Establishing a Constitution for Europe* (Luxembourg: Office for Official Publications of the European Communities).

European Council (1983) 'Solemn Declaration on European Union, Stuttgart, June 19, 1983', *Bulletin of the European Communities*, 6-1983, Brussels.

European Council (1999a) 'Presidency Conclusions. Cologne European Council, 3 and 4 June 1999', http://www.consilium.europa.eu/ueDocs/cms_Data/docs/pressData/en/ec/kolnen.htm (accessed February 2012).

European Council (1999b) 'Presidency Conclusions: Helsinki European Council 10 and 11 December', http://www.consilium.europa.eu/uedocs/cms_data/docs/pressdata/en/ec/ACFA4C.htm (accessed February 2012).

European Council (2000a) 'Presidency Conclusions. Santa Maria Da Feira European Council 19 and 20 June 2000', http://ue.eu.int/ueDocs/cms_Data/docs/pressData/en/ec/00200-r1.en0.htm (accessed February 2012).

European Council (2000b) 'Presidency Conclusions. Nice European Council Meeting 7, 8 and 9 December', http://www.consilium.europa.eu/uedocs/cms_data/docs/pressdata/en/ec/00400-r1.%20ann.en0.htm (accessed February 2012).

European Council (2001) *Presidency Conclusions: European Council Meeting in Laeken. 14 and 15 December 2001*. SN 300/1/01 Rev 1, Brussels, 14 December 2001.

European Council (2007a) Note from the Presidency to the Council on 'Pursuing the treaty reform process' of 14 June 2007 (10837/07 – POLGEN 69) (accessed January 2012), http://www.statewatch.org/news/2007/jun/eu-treaty-10837-07.pdf (accessed January 2012).

European Council (2007b) Brussels European Council 21/22 June 2007 Presidency Conclusions Brussels, 20 July 2007 (11177/1/07 Rev 1 Concl 2), http://www.consilium.europa.eu/ueDocs/cms_Data/docs/pressData/en/ec/94932.pdf (accessed January 2012).

European Council (2010a) Protocol No. 36 on transitional provisions concerning the composition of the European Parliament for the rest of the 2009–2014 parliamentary term, see Decision of the European Council of 19 May 2010 (EUCO 11/10), http://register.consilium.europa.eu/pdf/en/10/st00/st00011.en10.pdf (accessed January 2012).

European Council (2010b) Brussels European Council 28–29 October 2010 Presidency Conclusions, Brussels (Euco 25/1/10 Co Rev 1 Eur18 Concl 4), http://www.consilium.europa.eu/uedocs/cms_data/docs/pressdata/en/ec/117496.pdf (accessed January 2012).

European Council (2010c) Brussels European Council 16/17 December 2010 Presidency Conclusions, Brussels (Euco 30/10 Co Eur 21 Concl 5), http://www.consilium.europa.eu/uedocs/cms_data/docs/pressdata/en/ec/118578.pdf (accessed January 2012).

European Council (2011a) European Council 24/25 March 2011 Conclusions, Brussels (Euco 10/1/11 Co Eur 6 Concl 3), http://www.consilium.europa.eu/uedocs/cms_data/docs/pressdata/en/ec/120296.pdf (accessed 15 March 2012).

European Council (2011b) European Council Concludes Discussion on the New Fiscal Compact, http://www.european-council.europa.eu/home-page/highlights/european-council-concludes-discussion-on-the-new-fiscal-compact (accessed 15 March 2012).

European Council (2012) Treaty on Stability, Coordination and Governance in the Economic and Monetary Union, signed at Brussels on 2 March 2012, http://european-council.europa.eu/eurozone-governance/treaty-on-stability (accessed January 2012).

European Economic Community, Commission (1961) *Fourth General Report on the activities of the Community (16 May 1960–30 April 1961)*. May. 'The Work of the Institutions', pp. 225–34.

European Economic Community, Commission (1964) *Seventh General Report of the Activities of the Community (1 April 1963–31 March 1964)*, June. 'Work of Community Institutions and Organs: The Merger of the Executives', pp. 293–5.

European Economic Community, Commission (1965) *Eighth General Report on the Activities of the Community (1 April 1964–31 March 1965)*. June. 'The Merger of the Executives', pp. 23–6.

European Economic Community, Commission (1966) *Ninth General Report of the Activities of the Community (1 April 1965–31 March 1966)*. June: 'The merger of the Executives', pp. 324–5.

European Economic Community, Commission (1967) *Tenth General Report on the Activities of the Community (1 April 1966–31 March 1967)*. June: 'The merger of the Executives', p. 374.

European Parliament, Resolution, 18 October 1962, *Journal Officiel des Communautés Européennes*, no. 116, 12/11/1962, pp. 2669–72.

European Parliament (1973) The Case for a European Audit Office. European Parliament, Selected Documents, Directorate-General for Research and Documentation (September).

European Parliament (2001) 'Resolution of the European Parliament on the convening of the Intergovernmental Conference (14094/1999 – C5-0341/1999 – 1999/0825(CNS))' http://www.europarl.europa.eu/igc2000/offdoc/pdf/res03022000_en.pdf (accessed February 2012).

European Parlament, Commission des Affaires Constitutionelles (2001) 'Projet du Traité de Nice (première analyse)' PE 294.737. Bruxelles, 10 January.

European Parliament (2011a) 'Parliament approves Treaty change to allow stability mechanism', http://www.europarl.europa.eu/news/en/pressroom/content/20110322IPR16114/html/Parliament-approves-Treaty-change-to-allow-stability-mechanism (accessed 15 March 2012).

European Parliament (2011b) 'Ratification of Parliament's 18 Additional MEPs Completed' (29 November) http://www.europarl.europa.eu/sides/getDoc.do?type=IM-PRESS&reference=20100223BKG69359&language=EN (accessed 15 March 2012).

European Social Observatory (1992) *Synoptic Analysis of the Treaties before and after Maastricht* (Brussels: Observatoire Social Européen).

European Union (1997) *Consolidated Treaties* (Luxembourg: Office for Official Publications of the European Communities).

European Union (2001) *Treaty of Nice* (Luxembourg: Office for Official Publications of the European Communities). Also in *Official Journal* C80 (10 March 2001), downloadable from http://www.europa.eu.int/eur-lex/en/treaties/index.html (accessed February 2012).

European Union (2006) *Consolidated Treaties (November 2006)* (Luxembourg: Office for Official Publications of the European Communities).

Evans, P. B., H. K. Jacobsen and R. D. Putnam, eds (1993) *Double-Edged Diplomacy: International Bargaining and Domestic Politics* (Berkeley: University of California Press).

Explanations Relating to the Charter of Fundamental Rights (2010) *Official Journal of the European Union*, 14 December 2010, No. C 302/02.

Falkner, G. (2002) 'Introduction: EU Treaty Reform as a Three-Level Process', *Journal of European Public Policy*, Vol. 9, No. 1 (February), pp. 1–11.

Featherstone, K. (1994) 'Jean Monnet and the "Democratic Deficit" in the European Union', *Journal of Common Market Studies*, 32(2), 149–70.

Feld, W. J. (1967) *The European Common Market and the World* (Englewood Cliffs, NJ: Prentice-Hall).

Feld, W. J. (1964) 'The Judges of the Court of Justice of the European Communities', *Villanova Law Review*, 37, 37–58.

Fenwick, C. G. (1952) 'Treaty Establishing the European Defense Community', *The American Journal of International Law*, 46(4), 698–700.

Final communiqué of the conference of Heads of State and Government on 1 and 2 December 1969 at The Hague, http://ec.europa.eu/economy_finance/emu_history/documentation/compendia/19691202fr02finalcommuniqueofsummit conference.pdf (accessed 27 May 2010).

Fischer, J. (2000) 'From Confederacy to Federation – Thoughts on the finality of European Integration', Speech by Joschka Fischer at the Humboldt University in Berlin, 12 May 2000. Available on http://www.auswaertiges-amt.de/www/en/index_html.

Fitzmaurice, J. (1988) 'An Analysis of the European Community's Cooperation Procedure', *Journal of Common Market Studies*, 26/4, pp. 389–400.

Frishauf, S. H. (1961) 'The Present Status of Antitrust Laws in the Countries Forming the European Economic Community, Revised to September 1, 1961', *Antitrust Bulletin*, 245, 245–99.

Galloway, D. (2001) *The Treaty of Nice and Beyond: Realities and Illusions of Power in the EU* (Sheffield: Sheffield Academic Press).

Gazzo, M., ed. (1986) *Towards European Union*, vol. 2. Brussels: Agence Europe.

Gaudet, M. et J. Amphoux (1968) 'La fusion des institutions des Communautés européennes, *Annuaire européen*, 16 (The Hague: Nijhoff, 1970), pp. 17–58.

George, S. (1990) *An Awkward Partner. Britain in the European Community* (New York: Oxford University Press).

Gerbet, P. (1983) *La Construction de l'Europe*. Paris: Imprimerie nationale.

Gerbet, P. (1987) *La naissance du Marché Commun*. Paris: Editions Complexe.

Gerbet, P. (2007) *La Construction de l'Europe*, 4th edn (Paris: Armand Colin).

Gerbet, P (2009) 'Traité de fusion des exécutifs communautaires' in P. Gerbet, G. Bossuat and T. Grosbois (eds) *Dictionnaire historique de l'Europe unie* (André Versaille éditeur).

Gillingham, J. (1991) *Coal, Steel, and the Rebirth of Europe, 1945–1955: The Germans and French from Ruhr Conflict to Economic Community* (Cambridge: Cambridge University Press).

Gillingham, J. (2003) *European Integration, 1950–2003* (St. Louis: University of Missouri).

Gormley, L. (1985) *Prohibiting Restrictions on Trade within the EEC: The Theory and Application of Articles 30–36 of the EEC Treaty* (Amsterdam/New York: North Holland).

Gowland, D., A. Turner and A. Wright (2010) *Britain and European Integration since 1945: On the sidelines* (New York: Routledge).

Grant, C. (1994) *Delors: Inside the House that Jacques Built* (London: Nicholas Brealey Publishing).

Gray, M. (2000) 'Negotiating EU Treaties: The Case for a New Approach' in Edward Best, Mark Gray and Alexander Stubb (eds) *Rethinking the European Union: IGC 2000 and Beyond* (Maastricht: European Institute of Public Administration).

Gray, M. (2002) 'The European Commission: Seeking the Highest Possible Realistic Line' in F. Laursen (ed.) *The Amsterdam Treaty. National Preference Formation, Interstate Bargaining and Outcome* (Odense: Odense University Press), 381–403.

Gray, M. and A. Stubb (2001) 'The Treaty of Nice: Negotiating a Poisoned Chalice?' *Journal of Common Market Studies*, 39(Annual Review): 5–23.

Green, A. W. (1969) 'Review Article: Mitrany Reread with the Help of Haas and Sewell', *Journal of Common Market Studies* 8(1), 50–70.

Greenwood, S. (1992) *Britain and European Cooperation since 1945* (Oxford: Blackwell).

Grieco, J. (1996) 'State Interests and Institutional Rule Trajectories: A Neorealist Interpretation of the Maastricht Treaty and European Economic and Monetary Union', *Security Studies*, 5, 261–306.

Griffiths, R. T. (1988) 'The Schuman Plan Negotiations: The Economic Clauses' in K. Schwabe (ed.) *Die Anfänge des Schuman Plans 1950/51 – The Beginnings of the Schuman Plan* (Baden-Baden: Nomos).

Griffiths, R. T. (1990) 'Die Benelux-Staaten und die Schumanplan-Verhandlungen' in L. Herbst, W. Bührer, and H. Sowade (eds) *Vom Marshallplan zur EWG. Die Eingliederung der Bundesrepublik Deutschland in die westliche Welt* (München: Oldenbourg).

Griffiths, R. T. (2000) *Europe's First Constitution: The European Political Community 1952–54* (London: Federal Trust).

Griller, S. and J. Ziller, eds (2008) *The Lisbon Treaty: EU Constitutionalism without a Constitutional Treaty?* (Vienna: Springer-Verlag).

Grosbois, T. (2009) 'L'approche par les homes: la 'generation Benelux' et la naissance de la CEE' in S. Devaux, R. Leboutte and P. Poirier eds, *Le traité de Rome: Histoires pluridisciplinaires*. Brussels: P.I.E. Peter Lang, pp. 45–60.

Grygiel, J. (2012) 'One Market, One Currency, One People? The Faulty Logic of Europe', *Foreign Policy Research Institute E-Notes* (January), http://www.fpri.org/enotes/2012/201201.grygiel.europe.html.

Gurland, R. (1974) *The Common Market: a common sense guide for Amsterdam* (New York: Paddington Press).

Haas, E. B. (1958) *The Uniting of Europe: Political, Social, and Economic Forces 1950–57* (Stanford, CA: Stanford University Press).

Haas, E. B. (1964) *Beyond the Nation-State; Functionalism and International Organization* (Stanford, CA: Stanford University Press).

Haas, E. B. (1967) 'The Uniting of Europe and the Uniting of Latin America', *Journal of Common Market Studies*, Vol. 5, pp. 315–43.

Hall, P. A. and R. C. R. Taylor (1996) 'Political Science and the Three New Institutionalisms', *Political Studies* Vol. 44, pp. 936–57.

Hall, B. and T. Barber (2010) 'Europe Agrees Rescue Package', *Financial Times*, May 10, http://www.ft.com/intl/cms/s/0/f96a6c14-5b48-11df-85a3-00144feab49a.html#axzz1mlmDTh00 (accessed 18 February 2012).

Hallstein, W. (1962) *United Europe: Challenge and Opportunity* (Cambridge, MA: Harvard University Press).

Harryvan, A. and J. van der Harst (2003) 'Swan Song or Cock Crow? The Netherlands and the Hague Conference of December 1969', *Journal of European Integration History*, Vol. 9, No. 2, pp. 27–40.

Halligan, A. (2003) 'The End of a Long and Bumpy Road?' *Convention Intelligence*, 16 June 2003 (Brussels: European Policy Centre).

Heater, D. (1992) *The Idea of European Unity* (New York: St. Martin's Press).

Heller, J. R. III. (1963–4) 'Agricultural Policy of the European Economic Community', *Harvard International Law Journal*. 45, 45–64.

Héritier, A. (1999) *Policy-Making and Diversity in Europe: Escaping Deadlock* (Cambridge: Cambridge University Press).

Herman, V. and M. Hagger, eds (1980) *The Legislation of Direct Elections to the European Parliament* (Westmead: Gower).

Herzog, P. E. (1966) 'The Procedure before the Court of Justice of the European Communities', *Washington Law Review*, 438–88.

Hiepel, C. (2003) 'In Search of the Greatest Common Denominator: Germany and the Hague Summit Conference 1969', *Journal of European Integration History*, Vol. 9, No. 2 (2003), pp. 63–82.

Hitchcock, W. I. (1997) 'France, the Western Alliance, and the Origins of the Schuman Plan, 1948–1950', *Diplomatic History*, 21(4), 603–30.

Hix, S. (2005) *The Political System of the European Union*. 2nd edn (Basingstoke: Palgrave Macmillan).

Hix, S., A. G. Noury and G. Roland (2007) *Democratic Politics in the European Parliament* (Cambridge: Cambridge University Press).

Hoepli, N. (1975) *The Common Market* (New York: H.W. Wilson).

Hoffmann, S. (1966) 'Obstinate or Obsolete? The Fate of the Nation-State and the Case of Western Europe', *Daedalus*, 95(3), 862–915.

Hoffmann, S. (1989) 'The European Community and 1992', *Foreign Affairs* 68/4.

Houben, P. H. J. M. (1965–6) 'The Merger of the Executives of the European Communities', *Common Market Law Review*, 3, pp. 37–89.

Howorth, J. (2007) *Security and Defence Policy in the European Union* (Basingstoke: Palgrave Macmillan).

Hughes, D. (2000) 'The Final Curtain on a French Farce' *Daily Mail*, 11 December.

Humphreys, Adam R. C. (2010) 'The Heuristic Application of Explanatory Theories in International Relations', *European Journal of International Relations*, Vol. 17, No. 2, pp. 257–77.

Hsia, S. E. and J. F. Lane Jr. (1964–5) 'The External Tariff on the European Economic Community: The Commission and Supranationalism', *Virginia Journal of International Law*, 211, 211–28.

Intergovernmental Conference on the Common Market and EURATOM (1957) *Treaty establishing the European Economic Community and Connected Documents* (Brussels: Secretariat of the Interim Committee for the Common Market and EURATOM).

Jackson, Patrick Thaddeus (2011) *The Conduct of Inquiry in International Relations – Philosophy of Science and its Implications for the Study of World Politics* (London: Routledge).

Johansson, K. M. and A. Svensson (2002) 'Sweden: Constrained but Constructive' in F. Laursen (ed.) *The Amsterdam Treaty: National Preference Formation, Interstate Bargaining and Outcome* (Odense: Odense University Press), 341–57.

Jonsson, H. and H. Hegeland (2003) 'Konventet bakom kulisserna – om arbets-metoden och förhandlingsspelat i Europeiska konventet', SIEPS Working Paper, 2003:2u.

Kaiser, W. (2001) 'Institutionelle Ordnung und Strategische Interessen. Die Christdemokraten und 'Europa' nach 1945' in W. Loth (ed.) *Das Europäische Projekt zu Beginn des 21: Jahrhundert* (Opladen: Leske + Budrich).

Kaiser, W. (2006) 'From State to Society? The Historiography of European Integration' in M. Cini and A. K. Bourne (eds) *Palgrave Advances in European Union Studies* (Basingstoke and New York: Palgrave Macmillan).

Kaiser, W. (2007) *Christian Democracy and the Origins of European Union* (Cambridge: Cambridge University Press).

Kaiser, W. and B. Leucht (2008) 'Informal Politics of Integration. Christian Democratic and Transatlantic Networks ion the Creation of ECSC Core Europe', *Journal of European Integration History*, 14(1), 35–49.

Kaiser, W., B. Leucht and J.-H. Meyer (eds) (2009) *The History of the European Union. Origins of a Trans- and Supranational Polity 1950–72* (New York: Routledge).

Kaiser, W. and J.-H. Meyer (2010) 'Non-State Actors in European Integration in the 1970s: Towards a Polity of Transnational Contestation', *Comparativ. Zeitschrift für Globalgeschichte und Vergleichende Gesellschaftsforschung*, Vol. 20, No. 4, pp. 7–24.

Karlsson, C. and A. C. Svensson (2006) 'Sweden: In the Shadow of Enlargement?' in F. Laursen (ed.) *The Treaty of Nice* (Leiden: Nijhoff).

Keohane, R. O. and S. Hoffmann (1991) 'Institutional Change in Europe in the 1980s' in Robert O. Keohane and Stanley Hoffmann (eds), *The New European Community: Decisionmaking and Institutional Change* (Boulder, CO: Westview Press), pp. 1–39.

Keesing's Report (1975) *The European Communities: Establishment and Growth* (New York: Charles Scribner's Sons).

Kerremans, B. (1998) 'The Problem of Capacity and Control in an Enlarged EU Council' in P. H. Laurant and M. Maresceau (eds) *The State of the European Union*, 4, pp. 87–109.

Kerremans, B. (2006) 'Belgium: More Catholic than the Pope?' in F. Laursen (ed.) *The Treaty of Nice* (Leiden: Nijhoff).

Knudsen, A.-C. L. (2009a) *Farmers on Welfare: The Making of Europe's Common Agricultural Policy* (Ithaca: Cornell University Press).

Knudsen, A.-C. L. (2009b) 'Delegation as a Political Process. The Case of the Inter-Institutional Debate over the Budget Treaty' in W. Kaiser, B. Leucht and M. Rasmussen (eds), *The History of the European Union: Origins of a Trans- and Supranational Polity, 1950–72* (New York: Routledge), pp. 167–88.

Knudsen, A.-C. L. (2005) 'The Politics of Financing the Community and the Fate of the First British Membership Application', *Journal of European Integration History*, Vol. 11, No. 2, pp. 11–30.

Küsters, H. J. (1987) 'The Treaties of Rome (1955–57)' in Roy Pryce (ed.) *The Dynamics of European Union* (London: Croom Helm), pp. 78–104.

Küsters, H.-J. (1988) 'Die Verhandlungen über das institutionelle System zur Gründung der Europäischen Gemeinschaft für Kohle und Stahl' in K. Schwabe (ed.) *Die Anfänge des Schuman-Plans 1950/51 – The Beginnings of the Schuman Plan* (Baden-Baden: Nomos).

Küsters, H.-J. (1989), 'The Origins of the EEC Treaty' in Enrico Serra (ed.) *The Relaunching of Europe and the Treaties of Rome* (Brussels: Bruylant), pp. 211–38.

Kutchner, H. (1977) Speech at the Swearing-In of the first Members of the Court of Auditors, 25 October 1977 (eca.europa.euportalplsportaldocs1133869.PDF, 27.5.2010).

Ladenburger, C. (2007) 'Fundamental Rights and Citizenship of the Union' in G. Amato, H. Bribosia and B. De Witte (eds) *Genèse et destinée de la Constitution européenne* (Brussels: Bruylant).

Laffan, B. (2003) 'Auditing and Accounting in the European Union', *Journal of European Public Policy*, Vol. 10, No. 5, pp. 762–77.

Laffan, B. (1999) 'Becoming a "Living Institution": The Evolution of the Court of Auditors', *Journal of Common Market Studies*, Vol. 37, No. 2, pp. 251–68.

Laffan, B. (1997) *The Finances of the European Union* (London: Macmillan).

Lamb, R. (1995) *The Macmillan Years, 1957–1963. The Emerging Truth* (London: John Murray).

Langendoen, M. and A. Pijpers (2002) 'The Netherlands: The Mixed Fruits of Pragmatism' in F. Laursen (ed.) *The Amsterdam Treaty: National Preference Formation, Interstate Bargaining and Outcome* (Odense: Odense University Press), 267–89.

Lappenküper, U. (1994) 'Der Schuman-Plan: Mühsamer Durchbruch zur deutsch-französischen Verständigung', *Vierteljahreshefte für Zeitgeschichte*, 42(3), 403–45.

Larsen, H. (2006) 'United Kingdom: New Approach and New Influence?' in F. Laursen (ed.) *The Treaty of Nice* (Leiden: Nijhoff).

Lasok, D. (1986) *The Professions and Services in the European Economic Community* (Deventer, the Netherlands: Kluwer Law and Taxation Publishers).

Lasok, D. and W. Cairns (1983) *The Customs Law of the European Economic Community* (Deventer, the Netherlands: Kluwer Law and Taxation Publishers).

Laursen, F. (1990) 'Explaining the EC's New Momentum' in F. Laursen (ed.) *EFTA and the EC: Implications of 1992*. Maastricht: European Institute of Public Administration, 1990, pp. 33–52.

Laursen, F. (1992) 'Explaining the Intergovernmental Conference on Political Union' in F. Laursen and S. Vanhoonacker (eds) *The Intergovernmental Conference on Political Union: Institutional Reforms, New Policies and the International Identity of the European Community* (Dordrecht: Martinus Nijhoff), pp. 229–48.

Laursen, F. (1994) 'The Not-So-Permissive Consensus: Thoughts on the Maastricht Treaty and the Future of European Integration' in F. Laursen and S. Vanhoonacker (eds) *The Ratification of the Maastricht Treaty: Issues, Debates and Future Implications* (Dordrecht: Martinus Nijhoff), pp. 295–317.

Laursen, F. (2001) 'EU Enlargement: Interests, Issues and the Need for Institutional Reform' in S. S. Andersen and K. A. Eliassen (eds) *Making Policy in Europe*. 2nd edn (London: Sage).

Laursen, F., ed. (2002a) *The Amsterdam Treaty: National Preference Formation, Interstate Bargaining and Outcome* (Odense: Odense University Press).

Laursen, F. (2002b) 'Institutions and Procedures: The Limited Reforms' in F. Laursen (ed.) *The Amsterdam Treaty: National Preference Formation, Interstate Bargaining and Outcome* (Odense: Odense University Press).

Laursen, F. (2003) 'Theoretical Perspectives on Comparative Regional Integration' in F. Laursen (ed.) *Comparative Regional Integration: Theoretical Perspectives* (Aldershot: Ashgate), pp. 3–28.

Laursen, F. (2005) 'The Amsterdam and Nice IGCs: From Output Failure to Institutional Choice' in A. Verdun and O. Croci (eds) *The European Union in the Wake of Eastern Enlargement: Institutional and Policy-Making Challenges* (Manchester: Manchester University Press), pp. 153–73.

Laursen, F. (2006a) 'The EU from Amsterdam via Nice to the Constitutional Treaty: Exploring and Explaining recent Treaty Reforms' in D. Webber and B. Fort (eds) *Regional Integration in Europe and East Asia: Convergence or Divergence?* (London: Routledge, 2006), pp. 131–49.

Laursen, F., ed. (2006b) *The Treaty of Nice: Actor Preferences, Bargaining and Institutional Choice* (Leiden: Nijhoff/Brill).

Laursen, F. (2006c) 'The Politics of the Constitutional Treaty: Elements of Four Analyses' in J. From and N. Sitter (eds) *Europe's Nascent State? Public Policy in the European Union* (Oslo: Gyldendal Akademisk), pp. 37–59.

Laursen, F., ed. (2008a) *The Rise and Fall of the Constitutional Treaty* (Leiden: Nijhoff/Brill).

Laursen, F. (2008b) 'Theory and Practice of Regional Integration', *Jean Monnet/ Robert Schuman Paper Series*. Vol. 8, No. 3 (February). http://aei.pitt.edu/8219/1/ LaursenLongSympos08RegIntegedi.pdf (accessed May 2012).

Laursen, F., ed. (2011) *The EU and Federalism: Polities and Policies Compared* (Farnham: Ashgate).

Laursen, F., ed. (2012a) *The EU's Treaty of Lisbon: Role of the Member States* (Brussels: P.I.E. Peter Lang).

Laursen, F., ed. (2012b) *The EU's Lisbon Treaty: Institutional Choices and Implementation* (Farnham: Ashgate, 2012).

Laursen, F. (2012) 'The Treaty of Maastricht' in E. Jones, A. Menon and S. Weatherill (eds) *Oxford Handbook of the European Union* (Oxford University Press), pp. 121–34.

Laursen, F. and S. Vanhoonacker, eds (1992) *The Intergovernmental Conference on Political Union* (Maastricht: European Institute of Public Administration, and Dordrecht: Martinus Nijhoff Publishers).

Laursen, F. and S. Vanhoonacker, eds (1994) *The Ratification of the Maastricht Treaty: Issues, Debates and Future Implications* (Dordrecht: Martinus Nijhoff Publishers).

Leigh, M. (1975) 'Linkage Politics: The French Referendum and the Paris Summit of 1972', *Journal of Common Market Studies*, Vol. 14, No. 2, pp. 157–70.

Lindberg, L. N. (1963) *The Political Dynamics of European Economic Integration* (Stanford: Stanford University Press).

Lindberg, L. N. and S. A. Scheingold (1970) *Europe's Would-Be Polity: Patterns of Change in the European Community* (Englewood Cliffs, NJ: Prentice-Hall, Inc.).

Lindner, J. (2006) *Conflict and Change in EU Budgetary Politics* (London and New York: Routledge).

Lipgens, W. (1982) *A History of European Integration 1945–47: The Formation of the European Unity Movement* (Oxford: Clarendon Press).

Lipgens, W. (1984) 'EVG und Politische Föderation', *Vierteljahreshefte für Zeitgeschichte*, 4, 637–88.

Louis, J. V. (1966) 'La fusion des institutions des Communautés européennes', *Revue du Marché Commun*, 97 (December), pp. 843–56.

Lowenfeld, A. F. (1963–4) 'How the European Economic Community is Organized', *Business Lawyer*, 126, 126–34.

Ludlow, P. (2001a) 'The European Council at Nice: Neither Triumph nor Disaster', *Background Paper*, CEPS International Advisory Council, 1–2 February.

Ludlow, P. (2001b) 'The Treaty of Nice: Neither Triumph nor Disaster', *ECSA Review*, 14(2) (Spring), 1–4.

Ludlow, P. (2002) *The Laeken Council* (Brussels: Eurocomment).

Ludlow, P. (2004) 'Brussels Breakdown', *Prospect*, Issue 95, February 2004. Downloaded from http://www.prospect-magazine.co.uk.

Ludlow, N. P. (2003) 'An Opportunity or a Threat: The European Commission and the Hague Council of December 1969', *Journal of European Integration History*, Vol. 9, No. 2, pp. 11–26.

Ludlow, N. P. (2006) *The European Community and the Crises of the 1960s: Negotiating the Gaullist Challenge* (London and New York: Routledge).

Luitwieler, S. and A. Pijpers (2006) 'The Netherlands: From Principles to Pragmatism' in F. Laursen (ed.) *The Treaty of Nice* (Leiden: Nijhoff).

Lumb, R. D. (1961) 'The Treaty of Rome and the European Economic Community', *University of Queensland Law Journal*, 297, 297–303.

Lundestad, G. (1998) *Empire by Integration: The United States and European Integration: 1945–1997* (Oxford: Oxford University Press).

Lynch, F. (1988) 'The Role of Jean Monnet in Setting up the European Coal and Steel Community' in K. Schwabe (ed.) *Die Anfänge des Schuman Plans 1950/51 – the Beginnings of the Schuman Plan* (Baden-Baden: Nomos).

McDonagh, B. (1998) *Original Sin in a Brave New World: An Account of the Negotiation of the Treaty of Amsterdam* (Dublin: Institute of European Affairs).

Magnette, P. (2003) *Contrôler l'Europe, Pouvoirs et responsabilités dans l'Union européenne* (Bruxelles: Editions de l'Université de Bruxelles).

Magnette, P. (2005) *What is the European Union?* (Basingstoke: Palgrave Macmillan).

Magnette, P. and K. Nicilaïdis (2004) 'The European Convention: Bargaining in the Shadow of Rhetoric', *West European Politics*, Vol. 27, No. 3, pp. 381–404.

Mahony, Honor (2012) 'Twenty Five EU Leaders Sign German-Model Fiscal Treaty', *EUobserver*, 2 March. http://euobserver.com/843/115460 (accessed 3 March 2012).

Majone, Giandomenico (1996) *Regulating Europe* (London: Routledge).

Mansholt, S. (1973) Speech at the Inauguration of a New Community, http://aei.pitt.edu/13914/1/S207.pdf (accessed 28 May 2010).

Marinho, M. (2002) 'Portugal: Preserving Equality and Solidarity among Member States' in F. Laursen (ed.) *The Amsterdam Treaty: National Preference Formation, Interstate Bargaining and Outcome* (Odense: Odense University Press), 291–310.

Marjolin, R. (1989) *Architect of European Union: Memoirs 1911–1986* (London: Weidenfeld and Nicolson).

Mashaw, J. L. (1965) 'Federal Issues in and about the Jurisdiction of the Court of Justice of the European Communities', *Tulane Law Review*, 21, 21–56.

Mathijsen, P. S. R. F. (1985) *A Guide to European Community Law* (London: Sweet and Maxwell).

Maurer, A. (2002) 'The European Parliament: Win-Sets of a Less Invited Guest' in F. Laursen (ed.) *The Amsterdam Treaty: National Preference Formation, Interstate Bargaining and Outcome* (Odense: Odense University Press), 405–50.

Maurer, A. (2003) 'Less Bargaining – More Deliberation: The Convention-method for Enhancing EU Democracy', *Internationale Politik und Gesellschaft*, 1: 167–90.

Mazzucelli, C. (1997) *France and Germany at Maastricht Politics and Negotiations to Create the European Union* (New York and London: Garland Publishing Inc.).

Mazucelli, C. (2003) 'Understanding the Dutch Presidency's Influence at Amsterdam: A Constructivist Analysis', European Union Studies Association 8th Biennial International Conference, Nashville.

Mazzucelli, C. (2008) 'Maastricht as Turning Point', Miami-Florida European Union.

Center of Excellence, *European Union Miami Analysis (EUMA) Papers Online*, Miami, http://www6.miami.edu/EUCenter/.

Mazzucelli, C., U. Guérot and A. Metz (2007) 'Cooperative Hegemon, Missing Engine or Improbable Core? Explaining French-German Influence in European Treaty Reform' in D. Beach and C. Mazzucelli (eds), *Leadership in the Big Bangs of European Integration* (Houndmills: Palgrave Macmillan), pp. 158–77.

Megret, J. (1965) 'La fusion des exécutifs des Communautés Européennes', *Annuaire Français de Droit International*, 11, p. 692–709.

Menon, Anand (2003) 'Britain and the Convention on the Future of Europe', *International Affairs*, Vol. 79, No. 5, pp. 963–78.

Milner, H. V. (1997) *Interests, Institutions, and Information: Domestic Politics and International Relations* (Princeton: Princeton University Press).

Milward, A. S. (1984) *The Reconstruction of Western Europe* (London: Routledge).

Milward, A. S. (1992) *The European Rescue of the Nation-State* (London: Routledge).

Mioche, P. (1988) 'La patronat de la sidérurgie francaise et le Plan Schuman en 1950–1952. Les Apparences d'un Combat et la Réalité d'une Mutation' in K. Schwabe (ed.) *Die Anfänge des Schuman Plans 1950/51 – the Beginnings of the Schuman Plan* (Baden-Baden: Nomos).

Mitrany, D. (1965) 'The Prospect of Integration: Federal or Functional', *Journal of Common Market Studies*, 4(2), 119–50.

Molegraaf, Johan H. (1999) 'Boeren in Brussel. Nederland en het Gemeen-schappelijk Europees Landbouwbeleid 1958–1971', unpublished dissertation, Utrecht: University of Utrecht, 1999.

Monnet, J. (1978) *Memoirs* (London: Collins; New York: Doubleday & Company Inc).

Moravcsik, A. (1991) 'Negotiating the Single European Act: National Interests and Conventional Statecraft in the European Community', *International Organization*, 45/1, pp. 19–56.

Moravcsik, A. (1993) 'Preferences and Power in the European Community: A Liberal Intergovernmentalist Approach', *Journal of Common Market Studies*, 31(4) (December), 473–524.

Moravcsik, A. (1998) *The Choice for Europe. Social Purpose and State Power from Messina to Maastricht* (Ithaca and London: Cornell University Press).

Moravcsik, A. (1999) 'A New Statecraft? Supranational Entrepreneurs and International Cooperation', *International Organization*, 53(2): 267–306.

Moravcsik, A. (2006) 'What Can we Learn from the Collapse of the European Constitutional Project?' *Politische Vierteljahresschrift*, Vol. 47, No. 2, pp. 219–41.

Moravcsik, A. (2007) 'The European Constitutional Settlement', *The State of the European Union. Vol. 8. Making History: European Integration and Institutional Change at Fifty* (Oxford: Oxford University Press), pp. 23–50.

Moravcsik, A. and K. Nicolaïdis (1999) 'Explaining the Treaty of Amsterdam: Interests, Influence, Institutions', *Journal of Common Market Studies*37, no. 1, 59–85.

Mourlon-Druol, E. (2010) 'The Emergence of a European Bloc? A Trans- and Supranational History of European Monetary Cooperation from the Failure of the Werner Plan to the Creation of the European Monetary System, 1974–1979', unpublished dissertation, Florence: European University Institute.

Mourlon-Druol, E. (2009) 'The Creation of the European Council at the December 1974 Paris Summit' in M. Rasmussen and A.-C. Knudsen (eds), *The Road to a United Europe: Interpretations of the Process of European Integration* (Brussels: Peter Lang), pp. 349–64.

Nelsen, B.F. and A. Stubb (2003) *The European Union: Readings on the Theory and Practice of European Integration* (Boulder: Lynne Rienner).

Neuhold, C. (2006) 'The European Parliament and the European Commission: You can't always get what you Want' in F. Laursen (ed.) *The Treaty of Nice* (Leiden: Nijhoff).

Nicolaides, P. (2000) 'The Feira European Council and the Process of Enlargement of the European Union', *Eipascope*, 2000/3.

Noack, P. (1985) 'EVG und Bonner Europapolitik' in H.-E. Volkmann and W. Schwengler (eds) *Die Europäische Verteidigungsgemeinschaft. Stand und Probleme der Forschung.* (Boppard: Harald Boldt).

Noel, É. (1966) *La fusion des Institutions et la fusion des Communauté Européennes* (Nancy: Publications du Centre Européen Universitaire, Collection des Conférences Européennes No. 1).

Norman, P. (2000) 'Leaders have Second Thoughts as Marathon Runs its Course' *Financial Times*, December 12.

Norman, P. (2003) *The Accidental Constitution: The Story of the European Convention* (Brussels: Eurocomment).

'Note présentée par la délégation française sur les questions à soumettre aux ministres des Affaires étrangères (19 septembre 1956)', http://www.cvce.eu/viewer/-/content/36c37ebf-be56-44c0-854a-6dd16b3da64a/fa4ad2fa-e055-4f71-ada5-87696ed5f1c7/fr (accessed 22 May 2012).

Office for Official Publications of the European Communities (1978) *Treaties Establishing the European Communities: Treaties Amending These Treaties: Single European Act: Resolutions, Declarations* (Luxembourg: Office for Official Publications of the European Communities).

Official Journal of the European Communities (1985) European Parliament Resolution on the outcome of the Milan European Council (9 July 1985) C 229, 9 September 1985.

Official Journal of the European Communities (1992) *The Treaty on European Union*, No. C 224/1 (Brussels: Council of the European Union).

Oliver, P. (1996) *Free Movement of Goods in the European Community: Under Articles 30 to 36 of the Rome Treaty* (London: Sweet and Maxwell).

Olsen, L. L. (2006) 'Enhanced Cooperation: Lowering the Restrictions – and Creating the Basis of a Hard Core?' in F. Laursen (ed.) *The Treaty of Nice* (Leiden: Nijhoff).

Parsons, C. (2002) 'Showing Ideas and Causes: The Origins of the European Union', *International Organization*, 56(1), 47–84.

Parsons, C. (2003) *A Certain Idea of Europe* (Ithaca and London: Cornell University Press).

Pastor-Castro, R. (2006) 'The Quai d'Orsay and the European Defence Community Crisis of 1954', *History*, 91(303), 386–400.

Patijn, S. (1970) *Landmarks in European Unity: 22 Texts on European Integration* (Leyden: A.W. Sijthoff).

Pedersen, T. (1998) *Germany, France and the Integration of Europe: A Realist Interpretation* (London: Pinter Publishers).

Pentland, C. (1973) *International Theory and European Integration* (London: Faber and Faber Limited).

Peterson, J. (1995) 'Decision-Making in the European Union: Towards a Framework for Analysis', *Journal of European Public Policy*. Vol. 2, No. 1, pp. 69–93.

Peterson, J. (2001) 'The Choice for EU Theorists: Establishing a Common Framework for Analysis', *European Journal of Political Research*, Vol. 39, pp. 289–318.

Peterson, J. and E. Bomberg (1999) *Decision-Making in the European Union* (New York: St. Martin's Press).

Petite, M. (1998) 'The Treaty of Amsterdam', *The Jean Monnet Working Papers*, no. 2 (New York: The Jean Monnet Centre for International and Regional Economic Law and Justice).

Phillips, L. (2010) '"Small, small, small" EU treaty change to deliver "quantum leap"', *EUobserver* (29 October) http://euobserver.com/18/31163 (accessed 15 March 2012).

Pierson, P. (1996) 'The Path to European Integration: A Historical Institutionalist Analysis', *Comparative Political Studies*, Vol. 29, no. 2, pp. 123–63.

Pierson, P. (2004) *Politics in Time: History, Institutions and Social Analysis* (Princeton: Princeton University Press).

Pine, M. (2007) *Harold Wilson and Europe: Pursuing Britain's Membership of the European Community* (London: Tauris Academic Studies).

Pineda Polo, C. and M. den Boer (2006) 'The Charter of Fundamental Rights: Novel Method on the Way to the Nice Treaty' in F. Laursen (ed.) *The Treaty of Nice* (Leiden: Nijhoff).

Piris, J. C. (2006) *The Constitution for Europe – A Legal Analysis* (Cambridge: Cambridge University Press).

Piris, J. C. (2010) *The Lisbon Treaty: A Legal and Political Analysis* (Cambridge: Cambridge University Press).

Pitman, P. M. (2000) 'Interested Circles: French Industry and the Rise and Fall of the European Defence Community, 1950–1954' in Michel Dumoulin (ed.) *The European Defence Community, Lessons for the Future?* (Brussels: P.I.E.-Peter Lang).

Pollack, M. A. (1997) 'Delegation, Agency, and Agenda Setting in the European Community', *International Organization*, 51(1), 99–134.

Pollack, M. A. (2003) *The Engines of European Integration. Delegation, Agency, and Agenda Setting in the EU* (Oxford: Oxford University Press).

'Procès-verbal de la conférence de Messine (1er au 3 juin 1955). http://www.cvce. eu/obj/minutes_messine_conference_june_1955-en-ceafc91b-3e9c-4296-97b1-1b808c2c4e3e (accessed 22 May 2012).

Putnam, R. D. (1988) 'Diplomacy and Domestic Politics: The Logic of Two-Level Games', *International Organization* 42(3) (Summer), 427–60.

Rafferty, N. (2000) 'Blair Claims Victory for UK after Deal is Finally Done at Tetchy Nice Summit' *Business a.m.* (Scotland), 12 December.

Rasmussen, M. (2009) 'Supranational Governance in the Making: Towards a European Political System' in W. Kaiser, B. Leucht and M. Rasmussen (eds), *The History of the European Union. Origins of a Trans- and Supranational Polity, 1950–72* (New York: Routledge), pp. 34–55.

Regulation 25, *Journal Officiel des Communautés Européennes*, 20 April 1962, Vol. 5, No. 30, pp. 991–3.

Reflection Group (1995) 'Reflection Group's Report. Messina, 2 June, Brussels, 5 December. Available at http://www.europarl.europa.eu/enlargement/cu/agreements/reflex2_en.htm (accessed January 2012)

Rittberger, B. (2001) 'Which Institutions for Post-War Europe? Explaining the Institutional Design of Europe's First Community', *Journal of European Public Policy*, 8 (5), 673–708.

Rittberger, B. (2003) 'The Creation and Empowerment of the European Parliament', *Journal of Common Market Studies*, Vol. 41, No. 2, pp. 203–25.

Rittberger, B. (2005) *Building Europe's Parliament: Democratic Representation beyond the Nation-State* (Oxford: Oxford University Press).

Rittberger B. (2006) '"No Integration without Representation!" European Integration, Parliamentary Democracy, and Two Forgotten Communities', *Journal of European Public Policy*, 13(8), 1211–29.

Rittberger, B. (2009) 'The Historical Origins of the EU's system of Representation', *Journal of European Public Policy*, 16(1), 43–61.

Rittberger, B. and F. Schimmelfennig (2007), 'Explaining the Constitutionalization of the European Union', *Journal of European Public Policy*, Vol. 13, No. 8 (December), 1148–67.

Rosato, S. (2011) *Europe United: Power Politics and the Making of the European Community* (Ithaca and London: Cornell University Press).

Roussellier, N. (2007) *L'Europe des traités: De Schuman à Delors* (Paris: CNRS Éditions).

Rosamond, B. (2000) *Theories of European Integration* (Basingstoke: Macmillan Press).

Rosengarten, U. (2008) *Die Genscher-Colombo-Initiative: Baustein für die Europäische Union* (Baden-Baden: Nomos).

Ross, G. (1995) *Jacques Delors and European Integration* (New York: Oxford University Press).

Roy, J. (2005) 'The Nature of the European Union' in P. Van Der Hoek (ed.) *Public Administration and Public Policy in the European Union* (New York: Taylor and Francis).

Roy, J. (2006) 'The European Union: an introduction' in J. Roy and A. Kanner (eds) *A Historical Dictionary of the European Union* (Blue Ridge Summit, PA: Scarecrow Press).

Roy, J. (2007) 'Inertia and Vertigo in Regional Integration' in J. Roy and R. Domínguez (eds) *After Vienna: Dimensions of the Relationship between the European Union and the Latin American-Caribbean Region* (Miami: European Union Center of Excellence/ Jean Monnet Chair).

Roy, J. (2008) 'Reflections on the Treaty of Rome' in J. Roy and R. Domínguez (eds) *Regional Integration Fifty Years after the Treaty of Roma. The EU, Asia, Africa and the Americas* (Miami: European Union Center/Jean Monnet Chair).

Roy, J. (2009) 'Lisbon Fado: Fate and Hope' in J. Roy and R. Domínguez (eds) *Lisbon Fado: The European Union under Reform* (Miami-Florida European Union Center/Jean Monnet Chair).

Ruane, K. (2000) *The Rise and Fall of the European Defence Community. Anglo-American Relations and the Crisis of European Defence, 1950–55* (Basingstoke: Macmillan).

Rynning, S. (2006) 'European Security and Defence Policy: Coming of Age?' in F. Laursen (ed.) *The Treaty of Nice* (Leiden: Nijhoff).

Sahm, U. (1951) *Der Schuman-Plan. Vertrag über die Gründung der Europäischen Gemeinschaft für Kohle und Stahl. Textausgabe des Vertrages sowie des Abkommens über die Übergangsbestimmungen und der Zusatzprotokolle* (Frankfurt/Main: Verlag Kommentator).

Salmon, T. and W. Nicoll (1997) *Building European Union: A Documentary History and Analysis* (Manchester: Manchester University Press).

Sandholtz, W. and A. S. Sweet, eds (1998) *European Integration and Supranational Governance* (Oxford: Oxford University Press).

Sandholtz, W. and J. Zysman (1989) '1992: Recasting the European Bargain', *World Politics*, 42/1, pp. 95–128.

Sarotte, M. (2010) 'Eurozone Crisis as Historical Legacy', *Foreign Affairs*, 29 September, 1–3 online, http://www.foreignaffairs.com/articles/66754/mary-elise-sarotte/eurozone -crisis-as-historical-legacy.

Sarotte, M. (2009) *1989 The Struggle to Create Post-Cold War Europe* (Princeton: Princeton University Press).

Sauga, M., Simons, S. and Wiegrefe, K. (2010) 'Was the Deutsche Mark Sacrificed for European Integration?' *Der Spiegel*, 30 September, http://www.spiegel.de/international/germany/0,1518,719940,00.html.

Sawer, G. and G. Doeker (1962) 'The European Economic Community as a Constitutional System', *Inter-American Law Review*, 217, 217–36.

Schäuble, W. and Lamers, K. (1994) 'Reflections on European Policy', document by the CDU/CSU Group in the German *Bundestag*, 1 September.

Scharpf, F. (1999) *Governing in Europe: Effective and Democratic?* (Oxford: Oxford University Press).

Schelling, T. C. (1960) *The Strategy of Conflict* (London: Oxford University Press).

Schimmelfennig, F. (2001) 'The Community Trap: Liberal Norms, Rhetorical Action, and the Eastern Enlargement of the European Union', *International Organization*, Vol. 55, No. 1, pp. 47–80.

Schimmelfennig, F. (2003) *The EU, NATO and the Integration of Europe: Rules and Rhetoric* (Cambridge: Cambridge University Press).

Schimmelfennig, F. and B. Rittberger (2006) 'Theories of European Integration: Assumptions and Hypotheses' in J. Richardson (ed.) *European Union. Power and Policy-Making* (Abingdon: Routledge).

Schmitter, P. C. (2000) *How Democratic the European Union ... and Why Bother?* (Lanham: Rowman & Littlefield Publishers).

Schmuck, O. (1987) 'The European Parliament's Draft Treaty Establishing the European Union (1979–84)' in R. Pryce (ed.) *The Dynamics of European Union* (London: Croom Helm), pp. 188–216.

Schout, A. and S. Vanhoonacker (2006a) 'France: Presidency Roles and National Interests' in F. Laursen (ed.) *The Treaty of Nice* (Leiden: Nijhoff).

Schout, A. and Vanhoonacker, S. (2006b) 'Evaluating Presidencies of the Council of the EU: Revisiting Nice', *Journal of Common Market Studies*, 44, no. 5, 1051–77.

Smith, B. P. G. (2002) *Constitution Building in the European Union: The Process of Treaty Reforms* (The Hague: Kluwer Law International).

SN 511/00: 'Meeting Document. Subject: Elements for an overall agreement', Nice, 9 December 2000. Kindly provided by the Danish Foreign Ministry.

SN 514/00: 'Mødedokument. Vedr.: Elementer til en samlet aftale', Nice, 9 December 2000. Kindly provided by the Danish Foreign Ministry.

SN 521/00: 'Konferencen mellem repræsentanterne for medlemsstaternes regeringer, Arbejdsdokument Vedr.: RK 2000 – Formandskabets endelige kompromisforslag', Nice, 10 December 2000. Kindly provided by the Danish Foreign Ministry.

SN 522/00: 'Protocol on the Enlargement of the European Union and Declaration on the Enlargement of the European Union to be included in the Final Act of the Conference (This Annex Cancels and Replaces pages 88-96 of CONFER 4816/00)', Nice, 10 December 2000. Kindly provided by the Danish Foreign Ministry.

SN 533/00: 'Treaty of Nice: Provisional text approved by the Intergovernmental Conference on Institutional Reform', Brussels, 12 December 2000. http://www.deltur.cec.eu.int/english/nicetreaty.pdf (accessed March 2010).

Snoy et d'Oppuers, J.-C. (1989) *Rebâtir l'Europe. Mémoires: Entretiens avec Jean-Claude Ricquier* (Paris–Louvain-la-Neuve: Éditions Duculot).

Spaak, Paul-Henri (1971) *The Continuing Battle: Memoirs of a European 1936–1966* (Boston: Little, Brown and Company).

Spierenburg, D. and R. Poidevin (1994) *The History of the High Authority of the European Coal and Steel Community: Supranationality in Operation* (London: Weidenfeld and Nicholson).

Stein, E. (1981) 'Lawyers, Judges and the Making of a Transnational Constitution', *American Journal of International Law*, Vol. 75, No. 1, pp. 1–27.

Stirk, P. M. R. (1996) *A History of European Integration since 1914* (New York: Pinter).

Stone Sweet, A. (2004) *The Judicial Construction of Europe* (Oxford: Oxford University Press).

Strasser, D. (1992) *The Finances of Europe: The Budgetary and Financial Law of the European Communities*. Luxembourg: Office for Official Publications of the European Communities, 7th edn.

Stubb, A. (1998) *Flexible Integration and the Amsterdam Treaty: Negotiating Differentiation in the 1996–7 IGC* (London: London School of Economics and Political Science).

Stubb, A. (2002) *Negotiating Flexibility in the European Union: Amsterdam, Nice and Beyond* (Houndsmills: Palgrave Macmillan).

Svensson, A.-C. (2000) In the Service of the European Union: The Role of the Presidency in Negotiating the Amsterdam Treaty 1995–97. *Acta Universitas Upsaliensis. Working Paper*, No 137 (Uppsala: Statsvetenskapliga föreningen).

Tallberg, J. (2006) *Leadership and Negotiation in the European Union* (Cambridge: Cambridge University Press).

Taylor, Simon (2011) 'Barroso Says Eurobonds will 'be seen as Natural', *European Voice*, 17 November. http://www.europeanvoice.com/article/imported/barroso-says-eurobonds-will-be-seen-as-natural-/72630.aspx (accessed 18 February 2012).

Thatcher, Margaret (1993) *The Downing Street Years* (New York: HarperCollins).

Thiemeyer, G. (1998) 'Supranationalität als Novum in der Geschichte der Internationalen Politik der Fünfziger Jahre', *Journal of European Integration History*, 4(2), 5–21.

Tonra, B. (2006) Ireland: A Tale of Two Referenda' in F. Laursen (ed.) *The Treaty of Nice* (Leiden: Nijhoff).

Tracy, Michael (1989) *Government and Agriculture in Western Europe 1880–1988* (New York: Harvester Wheatsheaf).

'Traité instituant un Conseil unique et une Commission unique des Communautés européennes', *Journal Officiel des Communautés Européennes*, No. 152 (13 juillet 1967), pp. 1–22.

'Treaty Establishing a Single Council and a Single Commission of the European Communities', *Journal of Common Market Studies*, Vol. vi, No. 1 (September 1967), pp. 60–87.

'Treaty amending certain budgetary provisions of the treaties establishing the European Communities and of the treaty establishing a Single Council and a Single Commission of the European Communities', *Journal Officiel des Communautés Européennes*, 2 January 1971, L/2-12 [1970-treaty].

'Treaty amending certain financial provisions of the Treaties establishing the European Communities and the Treaty establishing a single Council and a single Commission of the European Communities' in *Official Journal of the European Communities*, 31.12.1977,L 359 [1975-treaty].

Treaties establishing the European Communities (1987) (Luxembourg: Office for Official Publications of the European Communities).

'Treaty of Lisbon amending the Treaty on European Union and the Treaty establishing the European Community, signed at Lisbon, 13 December 2007', *Official Journal of the European Union*, 17 December 2010, No. C 306/01.

'Treaty establishing the European Stability Mechanism ...' 2 February 2012, http://www.european-council.europa.eu/media/582311/05-tesm2.en12.pdf (accessed 12 March 2012).

'Treaty on Stability, Coordination and Governance in the Economic and Monetary Union ...' 2 March 2012, http://european-council.europa.eu/media/639235/st00tscg26_en12.pdf (accessed 15 March 2012).

Tsakaloyannis, P. and S. Blavoukos (2006) 'Greece: Continuity and Change' in F. Laursen (ed.) *The Treaty of Nice* (Leiden: Nijhoff).

University of Pittsburgh Law Review (1964–5) 'European Economic Community: Treaty of Association with Certain African States' (1963), 971–1008.

Uri, P. (1991) *Penser pout l'action: Un fondateur de l'Europe* (Paris: Éditions Odile Jacob).

Van der Harst, J. (2007) 'Sicco Mansholt: Courage and Conviction' in Dumoulin (ed.), *The European Commission, 1958–1972: History and Memories* (Luxembourg: Office for Official Publications of the European Communities), pp. 165–80.

Van der Harst, J. (2003) 'The 1969 Hague Summit: A New Start for Europe?' *Journal of European Integration History*, Vol. 9, No. 2, pp. 5–10.

von der Heydte, F. A. and Wanke W. (1952) *Das Vertragswerk zur europäischen Verteidigungsgemeinschaft. Einführung, Erläuterungen, Kritik* (München: Walther de Bouché).

Vanhoonacker, S. (1997) 'CFSP from Maastricht to Amsterdam: Was it Worth the Journey?', *Eipascope*, No. 2, 6–8.

Vanhoonacker, S. (2012) 'The Treaty of Amsterdam' in E. Jones, A. Menon, S.Weatherill, *The Oxford Handbook of the European Union* (Oxford: Oxford University Press), pp. 135–48.

Vauchez, A. (2005) '*Les juristes et la construction d'un ordre politique européen*', Critique internationale, 26 (mars), http://www.ceri-sciencespo.com/cerifr/publica/critique/criti.htm (accessed February 2012).

Vauchez, A. and M. R. Madsen (2005) 'European Constitutionalism at the Craddle: Law and Lawyers in the Construction of a European Political Order (1920–1960)' in *Recht der Werkelikheid, Special Issue: Lawyers' Networks and European Integration*, April.

Vaulont, N. (1981) *The Customs Union of the European Economic Community* (Luxembourg: Office for Official Publications of the European Community).

Wall, S. (2008) *A Stranger in Europe* (Oxford: Oxford University Press), pp. 53–4.

Wallace, H. (1980) *Budgetary Politics and the Finances of the European Union* (London: Allen and Unwin).

Wallace, H., J. A. Caporaso, F. W. Scharpf and A. Moravcsik (1999) 'Review Section Symposium: The Choice for Europe: Social Purpose and State Power from Messina to Maastricht', *Journal of European Public Policy* 6:1 March 1999: 155–79.

Wallace, W. (1983) 'Less than a Federation, More than a Regime: the Community as a Political System' in H. Wallace, W. Wallace and C. Webb (eds) *Policy-Making in the European Community* (Chichester: John Wiley and Sons).

Walsh, A. E. (1972) *Into Europe: The Structure and Development of the Common Market* (London: Hutchinson).

Walt, S. M. (1985) 'Alliance Formation and the Balance of World Power', *International Security*, Vol. 9, No. 4, pp. 3–43.

Walt, S. M. (1988) 'Testing theories of alliance formation: the case of Southwest Asia', *International Organization*, Vol. 42, No. 2, pp. 275–316.

Waltz, Kenneth N. (1977) *Theory of International Politics* (New York: McGraw-Hill).

Watt, D. C. (1985) 'Die Konservative Regierung und die EVG 1951–1954' in H.-E. Volkmann and W. Schwengler (eds) *Die Europäische Verteidigungsgemeinschaft: Stand und Probleme der Forschung* (Boppard: Harald Boldt).

Weigall, D. and P. Stirk (1992) *The Origins and Development of the European Community* (Leicester, UK: Leicester University Press).

Weiler, J. H. H. (1997) 'The Reformation of European Constitutionalism', *Journal of Common Market Studies*, Vol. 35, No. 1 (March), 97–131.

Weiler, J. H. H. (1999) *The Constitution of Europe* (Cambridge: Cambridge University Press).

Weiser, G. J. (1962–3) 'Freedom of Competition in the European Economic Community: An Analysis of the Regulations Implementing the Antitrust Provisions', *Patent, Trademark & Copyright Journal of Research and Education* 20, 20–40.

Verhelst, S. (2011) *The Reform of European Economic Governance: Towards a Sustainable Monetary Union?* Egmont Paper 47 (Brussels: Royal Institute for International Relations).

Wester, R. (2002) 'The European Commission and European Political Union' in F. Laursen and S. Vanhoonacker (eds) *The Intergovernmental Conference on Political Union* (Maastricht: European Institute of Public Administration), pp. 205–14.

Whitlow, R. S. (1957–8) 'The European Economic Community', *Business Lawyer*, 813, 813–30.

Willis, F. Roy (1968) *France, Germany, and the New Europe 1945–1967* (London: Oxford University Press).

Willis, R. (1975) *European Integration* (New York: New Viewpoints).

Young, J. W. (1993) *Britain and European Unity, 1945–1992* (Basingstoke: Macmillan).

Zakaria, F. (1992) 'Realism and Domestic Politics: A Review Essay', *International Security*, Vol. 17, No. 1, pp. 177–98.

Ziller J. (2007) *Il nuovo Trattato europeo* (Bologna: Il Mulino); also published in French (2008): *Les nouveaux traités européens: Lisbonne et après* (Paris: Lexis-Nexis) and in Portuguese (2010): *O Tratado de Lisbona* (Lisbon: Leya).

Ziller, J. (2008) 'The Law and Politics of the Ratification of the Lisbon Treaty' in S. Griller and J. Ziller (eds) *The Lisbon Treaty – EU Constitutionalism without a Constitutional Treaty* (Vienna-New York: Springer).

Index

Note: Page numbers followed by "n" indicate notes.